Critical Studies in Native History
(continues Manitoba Studies in Native History)

Jarvis Brownlie, Series Editor

17 *Elder Brother and the Law of the People: Contemporary Kinship and Cowessess First Nation*, by Robert Alexander Innes

16 *Indigenous Women, Work, and History: 1940–1980*, by Mary Jane Logan McCallum

15 *Life Stages and Native Women: Memory, Teachings, and Story Medicine*, by Kim Anderson

Gerald Friesen, Series Editor

14 *"A Very Remarkable Sickness": Epidemics in the Petit Nord, 1670–1846*, by Paul Hackett

13 *Preserving the Sacred: Historical Perspectives on the Ojibwa Midewiwin*, by Michael Angel

12 *Muskekowuck Athinuwick: Original People of the Great Swampy Land*, by Victor P. Lytwyn

11 *"A National Crime": The Canadian Government and the Residential School System, 1879 to 1986*, by John S. Milloy

10 *Night Spirits: The Story of the Relocation of the Sayisi Dene*, by Ila Bussidor and Üstün Bilgen-Reinart

9 *Women of the First Nations: Power, Wisdom, and Strength*, edited by Christine Miller and Patricia Chuchryk, with Marie Smallface Marule, Brenda Manyfingers, and Cheryl Deering

8 *The Ojibwa of Western Canada, 1780 to 1870*, by Laura Peers

7 *Severing the Ties that Bind: Government Repression of Indigenous Religious Ceremonies on the Prairies*, by Katherine Pettipas

6 *Aboriginal Resource Use in Canada: Historical and Legal Aspects*, edited by Kerry Abel and Jean Friesen

5 *The Dakota of the Canadian Northwest: Lessons for Survival*, by Peter Douglas Elias

4 *The Plains Cree: Trade, Diplomacy and War, 1790 to 1870*, by John S. Milloy

3 *"The Orders of the Dreamed": George Nelson on Cree and Northern Ojibwa Religion and Myth, 1823*, by Jennifer S.H. Brown and Robert Brightman

2 *Indian-European Trade Relations in the Lower Saskatchewan River Region to 1840*, by Paul Thistle

1 *The New Peoples: Being and Becoming Metis in North America*, edited by Jacqueline Peterson and Jennifer S.H. Brown

INDIGENOUS WOMEN, WORK, AND HISTORY 1940 – 1980

Mary Jane Logan McCallum

UMP
University of Manitoba Press

Indigenous Women, Work, and History, 1940–1980

22 21 20 19 18 2 3 4 5 6

University of Manitoba Press
Winnipeg, Manitoba, Canada
Treaty 1 Territory
uofmpress.ca

Cataloguing data available from Library and Archives Canada
Critical studies in Native history ; ISSN 978-0-88755 ; 16
ISBN 978-0-88755-738-5 (PAPER)
ISBN 978-0-88755-430-8 (PDF)
ISBN 978-0-88755-432-2 (EPUB)

Cover design by David Drummond
Cover image courtesy Ruth Christie
Interior design by Karen Armstrong Graphic Design

Printed in Canada

The University of Manitoba Press acknowledges the financial support for its publication program provided by the Government of Canada through the Canada Book Fund, the Canada Council for the Arts, the Manitoba Department of Sport, Culture, and Heritage, the Manitoba Arts Council, and the Manitoba Book Publishing Tax Credit.

Funded by the Government of Canada | Canada

Contents

Acknowledgements

Over the past ten years, I have been privileged to devote much of my time to learning about the rich history of Indigenous women in Canada. I drew a lot of inspiration from stories of women's dynamic twentieth-century experiences, be they told to me in person, in books, or through the sometimes lucid but often messy, complicated and veiled archival record. The women whose lives I have studied worked with integrity in their given fields and strived to nurture the lives of their loved ones and advocate for their families and communities. They made, at times, what must have been difficult personal decisions while seeking out opportunities large and small to effect change in their own lives, their communities, and the world around them. Thinking through the significance of their work has been an honour.

This book is the result of many generous conversations, ideas, criticisms, acts of inspiration, and words of encouragement, and I am grateful for the time, work, and friendships that have gone into its making. Many thanks to the individuals who shared their knowledge in the research of this project, including Ann Callahan, Myrna Cruickshank, Eleanor Olsen, and Dorothy Stranger, and a special thanks to Ruth Christie, who took me canoeing around Loon Straits and, over many lunches, visits, and tours, has taught me more about the cultural, social, and political histories of Winnipeg, Selkirk, Lake Winnipeg and the second best river in the world, the Red. Thanks also to the Aboriginal Nurses Association of Canada, Faye Isbister-North Peigan, Rosella McKay, Carol Prince, Marilyn Sark, and Marilyn Tanner-Spence for their time in the history of nurses project. Thank you to those who made this research possible, Ryan Eyford, Mary Young, Leslie Spillett, and Judith Bartlett, and to Margaret Horn, then at the Aboriginal Nurses Association of Canada, and Debbie Dedam-Montour at the National Indian and Inuit Community Health Representatives Organization for their help and interest.

Parts of this book were at one time a thesis, and I would like to thank my thesis committee, Dr. Adele Perry, Dr. Robin Jarvis Brownlie, Dr. Joyce Chadya, and examiners, Dr. Karen Dubinsky and Dr. Kiera Ladner, for the privilege of your engagement. Thank you, too, to the University of Manitoba Press for supporting this book and its ideas. Glenn Bergen saw that this book made it through to completion, and I am especially thankful to him. Thank you to the peer reviewers of the manuscript, you have helped to make this a better book. A huge thank you to good friend and sharp editor, Jill McConkey. Jill has seen this work from essays written when we were both students at the University of Manitoba through to its final draft and spent many hours copyediting and advising. For those hours and the many more spent road-trippin', pant-hitchin', and playin' Cronk, thank you, friend.

Presenting my work to diverse intellectual communities has benefited it greatly. Taking part in the meetings of the Native American and Indigenous Studies Association was invaluable, as were the many "on-the-house" critiques, contributions, and conversations of an informal network of Indigenous historians from Ohsweken to Saskatoon to Auckland. Support from and engagement with the Aboriginal health research community in Manitoba and beyond, and especially the Manitoba First Nations Centre for Aboriginal Health Research (MFN-CAHR) and the Network Environment for Aboriginal Health Research (NEAHR), strengthened this work immensely. Also vital to developing arguments in this book was presenting them to various medical and medical history communities, including the Manitoba Association of the History of Nursing, the Aboriginal Nurses Association of Canada, and the Manitoba History of Medicine Society. At the University of Manitoba and the University of Winnipeg, a big thank you to staff, faculty, and friends in the history departments, including Carol Adam, Chris Dooley, Barry Ferguson, James Hanley, Esyllt Jones, Tom Nesmith, Angela Schippers, Eliakim Sibanda, Greg Smith, and Ravi Vaitheespara, for supporting this piece of work at different junctures and in different ways. Thank you also to the Universities of Manitoba and Winnipeg libraries staff, especially Janice Linton, for their unique research skills and assistance. I would also like to acknowledge University of Winnipeg students in my courses who have listened to the ideas in this book and provided thoughtful insights on them—thank you. I am grateful for input and development from earlier publications; the conclusion is based on an article in the *American Indian Quarterly* (2009), and Chapter 5 is drawn from research done in the writing of *Twice as Good: A History of Aboriginal Nurses* (2007).

For making the research and writing of this book possible, anushiik to the Munsee Delaware Nation for continued post-secondary support. The Social Sciences and Humanities Research Council of Canada generously funded the initial phases of research and writing through a doctoral fellowship, and the Canadian Institutes of Health Research, Institute for Aboriginal People's Health provided much needed end-of-doctorate support through a graduate award administered by the MFN-CAHR and the Manitoba NEAHR. My research was sustained by awards and bursaries including an Aboriginal Issues Press Scholarship, the Dr. Margaret Allemang Scholarship for the History of Nursing, a Dr. James Burns Award in History, a Raymond F. Currie Fellowship, a Drummond Fellowship, a J.G. Fletcher Graduate Research Award in Arts, a Duff Roblin University of Manitoba Graduate Fellowship, the J.S. Stewart Memorial Fund for Research in the Public Archives of Canada, and additional grants from the Universities of Winnipeg and Manitoba. These awards were sources of economic support at critical points and boosted me during the sometimes arduous task of research and writing. I was very fortunate to be named a NEAHR-New Investigator by MFN-CAHR, a position that allowed me to complete the research and writing for this book and establish a new research agenda. I am indebted to this wonderful centre and its staff and research affiliates, especially Cathy Cook, Linda Diffey, Joe Kaufert, and Dawn Stewart, for their knowledge and engagement.

Thank you to family and friends for support, interest, and empathy. My partner, Craig Tulloch, is the funniest person I know, and I love the bones of him. Thanks for making every day better. My mom, Judy, my dad, Graham, and my brother, Ian have each supported and influenced this project in different ways. They were the first to teach me the importance of knowing where I come from and where I am. My uncle Ray Hughes, who passed away while this book was in its final stage, was an important source of humour, wisdom, and intellect, and he always made me feel that what I was doing was interesting and important. My uncle Ray and aunt Evelyn were the first people with graduate degrees I ever knew, and aunt Evelyn continues to provide support and counsel in my education and in life generally. Over the past five years I have had the good fortune to come to know Tom, Gloria, and Bruce Tulloch. Driving up to Selkirk to visit on Sundays and holidays has become a wonderful part of my life. To friends Jenara Franklin, Denise Fuchs, Aroha Harris, Susan Hill, Karen Hunter, Jennifer Koole, Danielle Soucy, Krista Maxwell, Krista Walters and others, thanks for the conversation, food, road trips, and humour—and especially for always cheering me on. For their encouragement and advice at different junctures, thank you to educators Mr. (Calvin) Darby at Shanty Bay Public School, Dr. William Hanley at McMaster University, Dr. Ollivier Dyens at l'Université Sainte-Anne, and Dr. John Milloy at Trent University. A special thank you to my always thoughtful and inspiring supervisor, adviser, and mentor, Dr. Adele Perry. And for the motivation, anushiik to all of my inspiring relations, including the newest, Mamie.

Tables and Illustrations

INDIGENOUS WOMEN, WORK, AND HISTORY 1940 – 1980

Introduction

The 18 January 1958 edition of the "Real Manitobans" section of the *Winnipeg Free Press* was dedicated to Indigenous women workers. There was plenty to catch your eye in the full-page spread. The article opened with an excerpt from Henry Wadsworth Longfellow's *Hiawatha*:

> Ye who love a nation's legends
> Love the ballads of a people,
> That like voices from afar off
> Call to us to pause and listen—
> Listen to this Indian legend
> To this song of Hiawatha.

To the left, a drawing of a confident "Real Manitoban," hands on skirted hips, towers over the Golden Boy on top of the legislative building in downtown Winnipeg and the prairie and woods beyond. Around the text were four black-and-white photos of smartly dressed women learning stenography at the Manitoba Technical Institute, smiling from an office at the Tuberculosis Registry of the Manitoba Sanatorium Board, studying night school course notes on comptometry, and setting a wave for a customer in a beauty salon. "Indian Girls Pave the Way for Others," the article announced: "It's a song more than tinged with sadness—but a song not without hope—sung by Canada's native sons and daughters as they try to find their way in the strange and awesome reaches of the city. Each day brings more Indian girls from reservations and other rural points to establish themselves in Winnipeg and quite a number succeed—paving the way for others as they go."

Indian girls were, according to the article, "displaced persons in their own land...endeavouring to bridge the gap between generations ago when their proud race was left far behind, and present day conditions of our so called civilization. Just as our pioneer forbears fished and hunted and farmed, so runs the saga of their people up to the present day. They come to the city to catch up with education in modern institutions of learning...and to find employment that they may share in the fruits of Canada's growing prosperity."[1]

This description exemplifies the contemporary postwar obsession with "the Indian today."[2] At once racialized and inauthentic, ancient and displaced, backwards and forwards, marginalized and urban, such ambivalent images are typical when it comes to Native people, even in current historical scholarship. Ideas about modernity and the state frame Native people's labour and bring these images into focus. As workers, Native women "share" in the nation's prosperity alongside its other citizens. Working at typewriters, permanent waves, and business ledgers, the women portrayed modern skills and education in well-known locales in Winnipeg. By looking at the history of Native domestics, hairdressers, community health representatives, and nurses, I hope to illuminate how Aboriginal women's wage labour was shaped by the politics of modernity and the state. In so doing, I hope to also challenge common narratives of Aboriginal displacement in the twentieth century.

Labour

I came to the topic of Indigenous women's work history in a few ways. One was through my earlier research on the history of Girl Guides in Indian residential schools in Canada.[3] I found that Girl Guides continued the curricular objectives of the schools and the vision of the federal government to reform Indian girls by teaching them "proper" gender roles and preparing them for Canadian citizenship and integration. Ironically, at the same time, Girl Guides also espoused an image of the "authentic" Indian and used that image to teach non-Native girls the same lessons. While doing my research, I wondered about what happened to some of the students who were once Girl Guides. While there is much written about primary and secondary Indian education, there is relatively little about what happened to pupils once they graduated from or left federal Indian schools. This is not true of the contemporary records, which, I found, were quite preoccupied with the topic of employment and depicted it as a going national concern. What makes education a topic of Indian history but not labour?

Historical studies about Native people and wage work tend not to be closely connected to historical studies about education (although some studies of unemployment are). Nor have they been driven by a focus on trade unions, the labour movement, working-class culture, and "everyday-ness" the way other Canadian labour histories have. Instead, until recently, fur trade economics and a desire to locate and describe a response to capitalism in the collapse of the fur trade have been the context for the bulk of Aboriginal labour history. These works attempted to explain the long-term effects of trade on Aboriginal people, economies, cultures, and communities. The literature generally centred on a debate over whether Native cultures and communities "declined" or "persisted" after the fur trade period.[4] In many ways, decline, and the matter of its scheduling, was (and, sometimes still is) *the* question in Aboriginal history, and the only question asked about Aboriginal people by most historians in the Canadian field.

This question was first framed to understand materialist change: how did the transition to modern imperial economic systems account for the so-called cataclysmic decline, dependence, and ultimate irrelevance of Indian people to the Canadian economy? Later, it appeared in culturalist form: how did Indians, as active agents of ethnohistory, selectively participate in capitalist economies for reasons and in ways that supported their cultural communities as well as their local and regional economies?[5] To be sure, other frames have been used for analyzing Native labour history in ways that do not isolate Native people from broader historical questions, including health, voyageur culture, masculinity, exhibitions and performance, longshoring and the waterfront, and citizenship and enfranchisement.[6] But like the earlier work, there seems to be a particular geography to most studies of Indian labour history. A disproportionate amount of the work focuses on the west, British Columbia, and resource-based primary industrial labour.

Another striking feature of studies about Aboriginal people and work is that the vast majority are about and by men, further obscuring Indigenous women's work. The tendency to exclude an analysis of gender in Aboriginal history is an important oversight, not only because the term and the idea of "Indian" too often represent only Indian men, but also because when gender is not made visible, we risk reproducing a history in which women are absent. As Andrea Smith finds, "many scholars argue that men were disproportionately affected by colonization because the economic systems imposed on Native nations deprived men of their economic roles in the communities more so than women." Smith argues that narrowing the field of analysis to the economic realm can "minimize the histories of oppression of Native women."[7] Moreover, by ideologically separating Native women from economic systems, we inadvertently suggest either that they played no significant or public economic roles or that their exclusion from the economy was natural and not also part of the experience of colonization.

The scarcity of histories of Indigenous women's work, particularly in the post–fur trade era, has resulted in part from the erroneous middle-class assumption that Aboriginal men were the main or sole family breadwinners and that their work counted for more than that of women. As scholars such as Karen Flynn have shown, this ideology was rarely applicable to non-white people, for whom the labour of women was essential to survival.[8] Some recent work on Native women and labour also complicates this picture. For example, Carol Williams's analysis of seasonal labour and doorstep economies in late-nineteenth-century British Columbia and Tressa Berman's more contemporary study of kinship in the production and redistribution of goods, wage work, and informal economies in North Dakota have examined Native women's economic contributions to family survival as the central subject of historical inquiry.[9] Two scholars who study women and production, Kathy M'Closkey and Sherry Farrell Racette, have insisted on shifting the focus in this field from the products women make to women workers themselves. They find that one of the reasons we do not think about women's wage labour is because we think about women's production as object (rug, coat, basket, artifact) and as the subject of something else (tradition, beauty, art or craft, authenticity) rather than as evidence of women's labour.[10]

It is very rare for studies of Native women and work to look past the Second World War, and apart from the work of Colleen O'Neill on Navajo household economies and diverse, responsive economic strategies, which spans 1930 and 1970, few studies bridge the war on either side.[11] Non-Native women's work patterns have received more consistent attention to change over time in these years. The war itself has framed a field of women's work history that highlights patterns of movement towards full-time waged employment in munitions plants and elsewhere and then a retreat out of the workforce after the war, an analysis that has been recently re-examined.[12] However, "Rosie the Riveter" was not typical of women workers during the war, and most non-white women, Patty Leow argues in the U.S. context, took clerical, domestic, or telephone jobs, and their realities were "a far cry" from popular images of women's war work.[13]

Also perhaps somewhat misrepresented is the retreat to domesticity and away from paid labour after the war. The postwar years have been a period of interest for women's historians, with a recent focus being on post-structuralist analysis of the discourses used and formulated about gender, sexuality, family, and "normalcy."[14] To be sure, the Departments of Indian Affairs and National

Health and Welfare each endeavoured to "normalize" the Aboriginal public in the postwar period using tools such as practical health education, integrated labour programs, and vocational post-secondary programs. But while these trends did have an impact on the lives of many Aboriginal women in these years, the so-called retreat of Canadian women to the domestic sphere after the war may not translate.

Much of the scholarship on Canadian women and work has been useful in illuminating how gender inequality gets written onto the work that women do; however, Indigenous women's work history also departs from standard narratives of women's history in the twentieth century. Native women workers, like all women workers, were subject to common understandings about space which determined that the city—and thus also working in cities—was "bad" for women. Also, Native women worked in occupational fields such as domestic service that were racialized and gendered in a variety of ways. However, labour was also part of a colonial apparatus meant to, among other things, extinguish Aboriginal title and status. In regards to Aboriginal women, employment has been popularly paired with notions of cultural decline and integration. It has also been associated by Aboriginal women workers themselves with the social and cultural responsibilities of building Indigenous communities and as an important means of resisting the Canadian state.

We must be doubly aware when dealing with Indigenous women's history that we have been conditioned to think about Aboriginal women as private-sphere figures circumscribed not only by the home, but also by the reserve or community in which they lived.[15] This book is in many ways a history of public women, or women in the public. In the public, Native women suffered the worst moral and social regulation of the era, subjected to separate schooling, added surveillance, and special laws meant to contain and discipline them. In addition, Indigenous women faced on an everyday basis the intense denigrations of Canadian racism.[16]

For many scholars who have studied non-white women including Native women, a key question has been whether it was gender discrimination or racial discrimination that most affected them.[17] What is more important, gender or indigeneity, patriarchy or colonialism? In this book on women and work, racial and gender oppression is understood as interconnected because gender or womanliness is not exclusively white, nor indigeneity exclusively masculine.[18]

Modernity

While "labour," as an analytic tool used in this book, arises out of the study of economic history and merges in many ways with social and gender history, "modernity" as a tool of analysis comes from the cultural studies field. The study of modernity, in this context, is the study of the social and cultural impact of late-nineteenth to twentieth-century developments marked by an enthusiasm for material and technological progress, the expansion and organization of industrialism and capitalism, and the development of and faith in scientific laws and theories meant to explain the universe and human life in their entirety.[19] Certain assumptions about Indigenous people and Indigenous cultures have led many to assume that modernity developed quite apart from Indigenous people. In this book, I borrow largely from the work on modernity by Philip Deloria, Paige Raibmon, and Colleen O'Neill, each of whom asks some version of the question, "What if we take as a premise that modernity is not something that Indians by nature or by tradition are prohibited from partaking in and indeed creating?"

Philip Deloria explains how Indians were produced as "unexpected" in a modern setting, their authenticity drawn from their location outside of modernity in an unspecific primitive past. Located outside of modernity, Indians (as they were imagined by non-Indians) became a means to critique modern, urban, industrial America. The assumption that modern America existed so far away in time and space from the cultural context of "Indianness" meant that, set within this context, Indians were "unexpected." Deloria uses moments of unexpectedness to draw out a history of expectations that reveals the very profound problems with popular understandings of Indianness. In many ways, Native women workers styling hair in beauty parlours or moving through the ranks of the nursing profession exist as "unexpected labour"—revealing *not* their incapacity to be hairdressers or nurses, but the broader assumptions about Indianness that make Indian hairdressers and nurses seem so anomalous.[20] Deloria calls stories of unexpectedness "secret histories," suggesting the various ways that they have survived and are talked about in a modern context.

Paige Raibmon, in her book *Authentic Indians: Episodes of Encounter from the Late-Nineteenth-Century Northwest Coast*, teases out the definitions of Indian authenticity in relation to imperialism in one particular region. She argues that certain binaries defined Indianness on the West Coast: Indian versus white, traditional versus modern, primitive versus civilized. She also argues that "authentic" Indianness conformed with colonial legitimacy and ideas of white racial superiority, thus adding a clear dynamic of power to the study of modern Indianness.

In her work, Colleen O'Neil focuses on the binary of tradition and modernity in the postwar period. She argues that this dichotomy is a product of modernization theory, which is a "linear way of thinking about economic change that has shaped ideas about development as well as our understanding of dependency." At the core of modernization theory are older ideas about social evolution, "white man's burden," and progress that worked under the assumptions that the West provided the best model of living and that modernity for Indigenous people, unlike others, signified cultural deterioration and entailed conformity to white society. Using the example of post-colonial literature, O'Neill argues that "tradition" gains meaning in relation to the modern and that the two have been painted in a false dichotomy. While "traditional" has been a useful political strategy of resistance in Canada, we must be aware of how it is also used to discipline, manage, simplify, and reduce Aboriginal people's broad experiences of the world.[21]

In terms of Indigenous scholarly labour, anthropologist Audra Simpson calls this the "Ethnographic Trap": that Native people can only ever be, talk to, and engage with things certified authentically Indigenous. Andrea Smith argues that scholarship about Aboriginal people has focussed on how "cool, spiritual and interesting we are" as objects of inquiry rather than producers of scholarship. Pushing this further, within American Indian studies, Native studies, and Indigenous studies there is a tendency to limit the fields of analysis open to Indigenous scholars: "we can only talk to each other, and no one else on planet earth," argues Smith.[22] Likewise, "modernity" is too often used as simple shorthand for decline, loss, and colonialism—the subject of someone else's active past. When efforts are made to include Aboriginal people in the twentieth century, the method frequently used is to turn collective "victims" into individual contributors to Canadian culture and identity rather than to engage in theoretical analysis of change over Indian time.

Many Canadian historians seem profoundly uncomfortable with Aboriginal modernity, as evidenced by the chronologies and scholarship available to the student of Aboriginal history. Aboriginal history is heavily weighted on the eras of early contact and the fur trade. The language used by historians to discuss Indianness after the fur trade is indicative of this discomfort with change over time, as well as of the whiteness and indeed arrogance of the labour history field, where some scholars trade in dismissive terms like "irrelevant," "dependent," and "oblivion."[23] While the late-nineteenth and early-twentieth centuries have been of more interest to historians as of late, the newest work still stops at around 1940, leaving the study of the 1950s and the 1960s largely to sociological research. It is not entirely coincidental that Indian history itself is said to have arisen out of "relative obscurity" in the 1960s; according to the standard chronologies of Aboriginal history, this coincides with their emergence from a supposed "era of irrelevance."[24] The Native people in those histories are suspiciously similar, though, to the ones in the contact and fur trade years; that is, they are depicted as culturally incapable of withstanding change over time. With a brief reference to the White Paper, Indian political organizations, modern treaties, and land claims at the end of the average Aboriginal history course, the Indian timeline is basically complete.

The gap in our history that exists after the so-called closing of the frontier, the "disappearance" of the buffalo, the signing of the numbered treaties, the plotting of reserves, and the consolidation of the Indian Act (each usually described in similarly passive ways) makes it appear as if Native people retreated from "planet earth" only to appear again, angry and tardy, in 1969. The gap in our history is more often called "absence," and it is always easier for historians to find proof of absence than of presence when it comes to Native people and especially when it comes to Native women. We must be careful not to use absence as a method and a foundation of our work.

In critiquing the tendency to emphasize absence, I do not deny the very real history of marginalization and colonization of Aboriginal people in Canada. Likewise, in emphasizing the state and modernity, I do not advocate these as the only analytic tools for understanding the past. Nor am I suggesting, as others have, that a satisfactory "middle ground" between conventional understandings was ever reached. What I hope to do in this book is to show how marginalization and displacement could and did exist simultaneously with other experiences, and that a history of decline or persistence, coercion or autonomy, difference or accommodation cannot adequately represent our past. The idea that we are limited to "either/or" responses on the one hand or to conciliation on the other is foundational to the ways our history is written.

The State

The lack of material on modern Aboriginal labour history has resulted in part from a broader trend in Canadian history writing to dissociate Canadian history from its colonial past. Until recently, imperialism and Canadian nation building have been understood as two distinct projects, often distinguished by the world wars. However, for Indigenous people, the Canadian state functions in much the same way as empire, and when I talk about Canadian state operations with respect to Indigenous people, I am talking about twentieth-century forms of Canadian colonialism.

Writing on gender and empire has been useful particularly in contextualizing Canadian nursing and Aboriginal health in imperial medicine. Historians in this field have considered the ways in which non-Native nurses have participated in and benefitted professionally from colonialism, challenged the idea that imperialism is a male project only, looked at how outpost nursing was a transgressive space for non-Native nurses, and examined how notions of whiteness have influenced the development of the profession.[25] In Aboriginal health history, scholars have focussed on the regulatory aspects of colonial health policy and in so doing have portrayed a disciplined, medicalized, and ultimately passive Aboriginal patient population that peters out around 1960.[26] This work is a departure from earlier historical scholarship that concentrated on the impact of new diseases and medical models and on the work of missionaries, traders, nurses, and doctors to alleviate sickness in Indigenous communities. That scholarship failed to acknowledge the colonial context in which epidemics and non-Aboriginal healers prevailed, ignored or oppressed Native and Inuit concepts of health and healing, and cast Indigenous people in reactive, passive, and even dependent roles. The newer scholarship also provides a much-needed critique of current health sciences research in the Aboriginal health field, which still continues to produce Aboriginal health as a subject of racial determinism, deviance, and discipline.

To put Aboriginal women's labour into its imperial context does not mean to focus again on the history of non-Aboriginal people, but rather to examine how discourses of Native women's labour furthered the intentions and aims of imperial rule, including the dispossession, domination, and disempowerment of Indigenous people. It can also be a way of creating valuable new fields of inquiry that resist state-centred exceptionalism.

Two structures of state power are central to this book: the Department of Indian Affairs and the Department of National Health and Welfare; in particular, the branches of these two departments that deal with administering Indian health, Indian education, and Indian employment. The Canadian federal government assumed jurisdiction over Indian lands and Indian peoples in the British North America Act at Confederation. The state's operations in the field of health in particular were a matter of constitutional law, treaty obligation, compulsion, and custom. The Indian Health Service underwent a gradual transformation from ad hoc local aid to a more centralized structure within the Department of Indian Affairs around the turn of the century and in 1945 transferred to a branch of the (then new) Department of National

Health and Welfare (now Health Canada). The service continued to be called Indian Health Services (IHS) until 1962, when Indian Health Services merged with Northern Health Services and five other federal health programs to form the Medical Services Branch (MSB). In 2000, the MSB was renamed the First Nations and Inuit Health Branch (FNIHB). The name "Indian Health Service" will be used throughout the book when referring to the pre-1962 era (mostly in Chapters 1 and 2), and the name "Medical Services Branch" will be used for the post-1962 era (mostly in Chapters 3 and 4). Regardless of its changing title, Native people have consistently argued that these services are owed to them by the state through treaty and custom. Predictably, perhaps, both the IHS and the MSB maintained throughout the period that the state was not legally obligated to provide services to status Indian and Inuit people in Canada, but did so on a humanitarian and voluntary basis.

The second, and equally complicated, structure of state power Indigenous people in Canada have had to deal with is the Department of Indian Affairs (DIA). In operation since the mid-eighteenth century, an "Indian Department" had been administered by a number of entities, including the British military, the Crown Lands Department, the Secretary of State for Canada, and the Department of the Interior. From 1936 to 1950, Indian Affairs was governed through the federal Department of Mines and Resources, and in 1950 it was transferred to the Department of Citizenship and Immigration, where it remained until 1965. At this point, Indian Affairs fell under the Department of Northern Affairs and National Resources, which became the Department of Indian Affairs. Since 2011, the DIA has been calling itself "Aboriginal Affairs and Northern Development." The DIA is the federal department charged with implementing the Indian Act, which was a mid- to late-nineteenth-century consolidation of earlier colonial Indian policy and outlined how the Canadian government would manage its jurisdiction over Indian lands and Indian peoples. First, the Act legally defined "Indian" and required a registry of status Indians. It set out the terms of eligibility for treaty rights, participation in tribal government, and access to Indian land and resources. It also defined Indian women on different terms than men. By the Act, the definition of Indian extended to the wives and widows of Indian men; at the same time, any woman married to a man who was not a status Indian was no longer legally an Indian by the Act. In losing Indian status, Aboriginal women who married non-Indians were forced to cut all ties to the band and renounce Indian status and rights. As such, by law, Native women who "married out" were legally excluded from their own communities. So were any children from this marriage.[27]

The Act also defined "reserve," outlined a set of regulations that applied to Indians and to reserves, and stipulated how Indian land could be surrendered, how Indian funds would be managed, and how First Nations would be officially governed (the chief and council system). It also described the process of enfranchisement, the method of becoming Canadian citizens by relinquishing rights to land and legal status as Indians. Enfranchisement was the legal embodiment of the department's philosophy of management: it aimed to revoke all Indigenous claims on the state by making Indigenous people legally indistinguishable within it. In organizing these duties, the DIA had a number of different branches dealing with, for example, education, welfare, and lands management of Indians everywhere in Canada. In the early to mid-twentieth century, the department's education operations spilled into the field of vocational training and employment, which is the focus of this book.

The emphasis on the state in this book is not meant to challenge the argument several historians have made that the postwar period was one in which centralized federal power was devolved significantly to the provinces, a movement that is troublesome for many Aboriginal people, whose primary relationship is with the federal Crown. While the goal was ultimately to devolve power to the provinces, Indian Affairs and Health Canada remain federal departments charged with responsibilities to deliver education and health services to Indigenous people in Canada. For the most part, employment measures were by the 1970s handled by the provinces; however, the provinces often engaged in cost-sharing agreements whereby Indian funds would be funnelled through programs built and managed by and for non-Aboriginal people. In the period under study, however, it remains that the federal government did desire to manage the employment of Aboriginal populations; it did undertake the responsibility of counting, regulating, and defining Aboriginal populations; and it did play an important role in Aboriginal women's labour.

In part, this book seeks to clarify that role where possible. Many of the stories herein start in federal Indian schools, and I demonstrate the clear function that Indian Affairs played not only in the training, but also the recruitment, contracting, disciplining, and regulation of Native labour. Principals, Indian agents, and teachers were critical figures in the process by which Aboriginal nurses, for example, accessed post-secondary education. Apart from formal education, health services for status Indians and Inuit were administered federally as well and, indeed, several programs for labour placement in this and other fields were conceived of and controlled at the federal level.

Methodology

How does a historian begin to write a twentieth-century history of Aboriginal women and work? First, not all Indigenous women are represented in this book. While geographically and culturally my interests spanned Manitoba (where I live) and Ontario (where I am from), I almost immediately moved outwards, through the connections of professional organizations, federal labour programs, and the mobility of Aboriginal women workers themselves. There was no single set of records I could refer to when researching the history of Native women and work, so I went to a number of places and consulted a range of different kinds of sources. Practically, the research ended up focussing on women who are Registered Indians (but its findings are not limited to this group) in continental southern, English-speaking Canada. With the exception of the community health representatives, most of the women I talk about were younger adults. Most were funded or placed by Indian Affairs and declared themselves of Indian ancestry. This study is therefore dependent upon a colonial system of identification that aimed to integrate, segregate, and penalize Aboriginal people, and I call attention to the fact that many Aboriginal women for various reasons and in various ways eluded, avoided, and/or resisted this system.

The book has taken on the form of four case studies, each of which follows a particular occupation or field of work and highlights the interaction of the key interrelated frames of labour, modernity, and the state while offering a critique of the condition of Aboriginal history in Canada. Each of the case studies considers different employment training and placement programs of varying duration and geographies and seeks to describe the ways in which the state involved itself in Aboriginal women's lives. These programs serve different functions in the chapters, sometimes only as points of reference for other stories about Aboriginal women and work. The case studies are set roughly chronologically.

My research began with what is now Chapter 4, on Aboriginal nurses, and in many ways this work influenced the directions that the book took thereafter. While a background in the history of Indian education was an inspiration for the research, an interest in Aboriginal health and federal health policy in the postwar period was the real starting point. In this research, I grew frustrated with how the Indian Health Service was written as heroic and expansionist without reflection on how it relied on equally simplistic images of Aboriginal people as isolated and sickly dependants. That inspired me to study the labour of Aboriginal people who worked in a significant number of paid health care positions both inside and outside of the Medical Services Branch. The case study on Aboriginal nurses examines over thirty years of Aboriginal nursing history through themes developed by the Registered Nurses of Canadian Indian Ancestry (RNCIA, now the Aboriginal Nurses Association of Canada or ANAC), namely, Native people's involvement in public health issues, employment in the Medical Services Branch, and post-secondary education. The chapter takes as a starting point three goals of the organization, to improve Aboriginal health, Aboriginal representation in the nursing profession, and nursing education, and works backwards to contextualize these goals in a longer past.

The sources and methods I use in the nursing case study closely overlap. Initially inspired to study the history of nurses using RG 29 (Health Canada) files, my interest in these records waned due to the restrictions put in place by Access to Information and Privacy laws. I gathered what I could from the records I could gain access to, wrote an essay on Aboriginal nurses in the Medical Services Branch, and shared it with the ANAC. In response, I was asked to write a more substantial document on the history of Aboriginal nurses for the organization. That work involved researching nursing records at its headquarters in Ottawa (which included newsletters, conference programs, and published materials) and a group of ANAC records at the national archives (a collection of documents that includes a survey of Aboriginal nurses undertaken in the early 1980s, membership applications, and minutes of meetings). All of these records were collected, organized, and managed by the ANAC. The research also involved conducting seven interviews with Native nurses connected to the organization and developing a history of Aboriginal nurses in Canada in the twentieth century. This project, including the research that went into it, will be referred to in this book as *Twice as Good: A History of Aboriginal Nurses*. In doing this project, I was able to get invaluable feedback from leading Aboriginal nurses throughout the country. I was also able to provide the organization with a working database of Aboriginal nurses I had assembled in my research to add to their records.

My approach to the study of Aboriginal women's history in the mid-twentieth century is to use both interviews as well as written records. Oral history is often considered by disciplinary historians as the reverse of the written record: either false and subjectively adulterated hearsay, or the only method of documenting "true" experience and conducting "responsible" research.[28] Likewise, the use of oral history has been a central subject of methodological debates about the nature of our work as historians: is our job to locate truth about the past or is it to examine how our past is understood in the ways we can and cannot speak about it? Each side of these debates creates its opposite, and yet in reality many practising historians in Canada rely on any kind of evidence they can reasonably both access and assess. For this book, interviews and archival research were not isolated but interrelated: those whom I interviewed were named in and had themselves created written records, and I often read records like the RG 10 (Indian Affairs) files housed at Library and Archives Canada as well as contemporary current affairs periodicals with individuals and interview questions in mind. Of these periodicals, the *Indian News* was especially useful. The *Indian News* was a news publication issued by the DIA between 1954 and 1982 to First Nations people and communities. Most of its contents tended to focus on community and economic development, education, and governmental policy changes; while its main goal appeared to be managing a positive image of Indian Affairs, the periodical provides coverage of important aspects of First Nations social history, albeit from a federal point of view.

I also consulted life histories and oral history collected by others in the course of my research. These histories focussed on individuals and their life experiences and ranged from an interview by the Department of National Defence, to published academic work, to Aboriginal journalism, to general collections of profiles of Aboriginal people meant for a broad Aboriginal and Canadian audience. These works, as well as the interviews I conducted, helped me to gain a broader understanding of the lived lives of Aboriginal women in the twentieth century. They were extraordinarily useful for providing historical context as well as guidance as to what questions are important to ask of the history of Aboriginal women. They also familiarized me with certain narratives meant to organize, explain, and teach about Aboriginal women's experiences of post-secondary education and work.

Importantly, in mere numbers, registered nurses were a minority among Aboriginal people working in health care, and especially among those who worked at hospitals. There were far more nurse's aides, ward aides, hospital workers, and interpreters, about whom records are harder to find. Broadening the scope of the study seemed to make sense. Knowing that I would be crossing a lot of boundaries that distinguish accredited nurses historically and professionally from domestic service, I found it impossible to discuss nursing without including those who worked in non-licensed roles. This is why I eventually turned to the topic of Native women and domestic labour.

In Chapter 1, I begin with a discussion of the connection between federal Indian education policy, girls' curriculum, and girls' employment, particularly in residential schools and Indian hospitals. Much of this is based on secondary literature on the Indian residential school system, RG 10 (Indian Affairs) records, and Native women's life writing and literature about schools, girlhood, and the process of becoming conscious about Indian identity. In the second part of this chapter, I deal with a program run in the early to mid-1940s by the DIA to place Aboriginal students from three schools in northern Ontario as domestics in Ottawa. Several themes significant to Native women's working history arose in this set of records, including family involvement in the decision to work; clothing and transportation; working conditions; the homes; ward status and wage labour; and sexuality, reputation, and regulation in an off-reserve setting.

The sensitive nature of some of the material in the RG 10 archives was surprising, especially considering that the Access laws had prevented me from seeing what was in fact mundane material in the RG 29 (Health Canada) records. When writing, I therefore used some discretion when it came to names and some of the details in these records. At all times while researching the history of Aboriginal women and work, I was aware of recent debates in my field about ethics, including the censorship of unethical primary source material, ownership and ultimate applications of the research, and control over rights to consult and utilize material. I was aware, for example, of how access restrictions can support status-quo history and how guidelines for ethical academic research are constructed with primarily non-Indigenous academic researchers in mind. This produces results that can in practice flatten or even prohibit more complex research questions and limit the types and range of research questions. Finding DIA records saturated with paternalism and patronizing language, and primarily motivated by a need to discipline and control First Nations people, I looked to many different secondary sources for help in interpreting this material.

While reviewing the RG 10 records pertaining to domestic work, I kept coming across references to the Indian Placement and Relocation Program. In Chapter 2, I focus on this program, which was run by the DIA from 1957 onwards. In the first part of the chapter I show how the program was built upon the aims of the Canadian state to permanently integrate Aboriginal people by urban relocation and employment. The second part deals with one particular profession the program encouraged, hairdressing. Using work on race and the beauty industry in the United States, I draw out some of the complexities surrounding beauty, authenticity, nationalism, and modern, urban wage labour particular to Native people in Canada.

In many ways, the Placement and Relocation program was about structure: administration, operations, wages, housing, transportation; but it did not exist apart from colonial discourse on integration and ideas about the Indian at work, the Indian and the city, and the Indian woman. That discourse is made by the material circumstances of colonialism—the theft of resources and land—but also by the cultural impositions of imperialism. Structural management involved discourses of conquest, racial superiority, and discipline.

The records on the Placement and Relocation program mostly consist of labour surveys, studies, case files, and Indian Affairs' favourite, forms. These forms can only really provide a limited number of details, and only within a starkly employment-for-integration-focussed structure of a colonial institution. In another section of the archives, there were also files of Indian Affairs and Health Canada photographs dealing with vocational training and placement; many of these pertained to the Indian Placement and Relocation Program as well as the Community Health Representatives (CHR) program I describe in Chapter 3. Indian Affairs and Health Canada photos show change over time and illustrate contemporary ideals about labour, health, and education. As starkly different as the glossy 8x10s of pretty, uniformed, and smiling white nurses were from the little squares of nervous-looking, small-moustached, white-man bureaucrats before them, the vocational training photograph also provided me with yet another point of entry into the topic.

Here I found a picture of my mother, who had trained as a teacher in London, Ontario, and taught at the day school in Munsee, Ontario, in the 1960s. She was in her early twenties, wearing a mini-skirt and a mod hairdo, with a trademark wad of tissue in her pocket. The clock read 2:30, and with a spelling list on the blackboard and chalk stains up and down her side, she looked like Indigenous methodology was not likely foremost on her mind. But it sure was on mine. There she was, among photographs of licensed practical nurses and electricians and stenographers and community health workers, the black-and-whites of those odd, postwar departmental employment and training programs that I was trying to write about. What did it mean that in that context my mom was supposed to be embodying Indian policies of self-sufficiency and integration, which, in other readings, also stood for assimilation and loss? When I asked my mom about the picture, what she recalled was a conversation she had had with a fellow student in teachers' college who asked her, "Why on earth would you want to work on a reserve?" Also, she asked me, a graduate student at the time, if I was not perhaps in a labour placement program myself!

Outside of historical monographs and auto/biography, literature on Indigenous labour exists in thick books by sociologists or thin, bulleted studies by consultants for the federal government. Therefore, photography, television, radio, film, comics, and novels were all important sources in studying Indian labour, not only because they often provide important humanized and personalized historical insight on an otherwise state-centred record of the twentieth century, but also because they often allude to a range of varied meanings of labour and sometimes even a strikingly different perspective on the federal government. For example, when examining some photographs related to the Community Health Representatives, I found that the director of the program, Ethel Martens, had carefully named each individual in each photograph, often creating what seemed like personal scrapbooks that ultimately ended up in the Indian Health Services records at the national archives. These photographs stand quite apart from the majority of photographs that are often unnamed, and if labelled at all are captioned in a way that directs the viewer to interpret the photo as evidence of the department's success in its integration policy.

I became interested in the CHR program while studying nurses. This program intrigued me because it was designed to be supervised by MSB nurses. It also intrigued me because it was so different from other formal training programs. Not only did the CHR program grow out of efforts in community development, it was also heavily influenced by international health research on Indigenous people and the particularities of the local context of the Medical Services Branch. The program was characteristic of how the federal government viewed Indian health, education, and labour in reserve settings.

What struck me most from reading federal materials about this program was not just the racialized labour hierarchy (white professionals, Indian paraprofessionals) but how patriarchy was institutionalized in the program. In this chapter I use a feminist approach to analyze the early history of the CHR program. This approach asserts that ideas about the nature of womanliness and manliness have made for inequalities in labour that subordinate women in patriarchal societies. Taking up Indigenous feminists' call for "feminism without apology,"[29] I am speaking to those in Indigenous history who continue to view feminist approaches as not authentically Indigenous and therefore essentially worthless. "Such a position," Jennifer Nez Denetdale argues, "fails to name the colonial space in which…women find themselves and the way in which a history of colonization has wreaked havoc in their lives while they also struggle to reclaim their lives, culture and history."[30]

When I originally wrote about the CHR program, I was interested in the content of federal health education for Aboriginal people. I found out about lots of things I did not know about before, including the Clean-Up Campaign on reserves in the 1960s; that health was seen as merely a matter of "attitude"; that the National Film Board and Indian Health Services both unashamedly advertised for and promoted the Milk Foundation, the Canadian Dental Association, and the Canada Food Guide, not to mention the Hudson's Bay Company store. I learned how to work "with" and not "for" an MSB nurse and an Indian agent; how to freehand a steamy pork chop; and simple steps for motivating Indian communities and bridging the race and class gap between Indians and health professionals. I wrote a paper on the early history of the CHR program and shared it with Debbie Dedam-Montour, Executive Director of the National Indian and Inuit Community Health Representatives Organization, who graciously read it and provided corrections, feedback, and direction. This paper became an introduction to the CHR chapter, which then explores in more detail the role that gender played in the selection, training, and supervision of Community Health Representatives.

There are a few lacunae in this book: I do not, for example, deal with teachers, doctors, lawyers, and social workers. Originally, the book grew out of an interest in Indian health, and so I was most firmly grounded in that literature and oriented best to contribute to it. Also, I do not trace a creation or recreation of a twentieth-century Aboriginal middle class in this book. I deal with some issues of labour and professionalization, which could be seen as part of middle-class formation, but that is not my primary concern here.

The four case studies that follow are not meant to limit or to complete a history of Aboriginal women in Canada. Instead, they are meant to challenge historians and others to think about twentieth-century Aboriginal women's history in new ways and open new avenues for further scholarship in these and other ways Aboriginal women worked and lived. This book will show that Native women's twentieth-century wage labour was shaped in part by the workings of state power in the fields of health, education and labour. It will also insist that Native women were not "displaced" by modernity, but rather laboured in modern Native ways from the 1940s to the 1970s.

CHAPTER ONE

Sweeping the Nation:
Indigenous Women and Domestic Labour in Mid-Twentieth-Century Canada

Figure 1.1. Cartoon from The Forgotten People, *Summer 1972. Used with permission of Denise Rudniki.*

In a 1972 issue of *The Forgotten People*—the national newspaper of the Native Council of Canada (now the Congress of Aboriginal Peoples)—a comic strip depicts Digger, a long-haired, bell-bottom-clad Indian with a feather in his hair, encountering a Red Power poster featuring a clenched fist and the message: "The Indians are sweeping this country!!!" In the next frame, you see him scribbling away on the wall beside the sign so that by the third frame, beside "The Indians are sweeping this country!!!" it reads, "That's the only job they can get!"[1] Like many comics, its wit lies in its ability to hint at many concepts in a sketch and few words. It speaks to a range of issues at the forefront of Indigenous resistance movements in the twentieth century, including limited access to education, discrimination in the workplace, and state policies that severely limited career options. Indigenous people, especially women, had reason to be cynical of their prospects for employment in mid-twentieth-century Canada. As Digger's graffiti suggests, one of the few jobs readily available to them was domestic labour.

The Department of Indian Affairs' industrial and boarding schools, with their labour-based curriculum, were training grounds for domestics. At the same time, Indian agents and school staff were engaged in the placement of Native domestic labour, matching youth on reserves and students in residential schools with jobs. In addition to training, recruiting, and contracting domestic labour, the DIA was also involved in its supervision and regulation through correspondence with domestics and employers. By examining the domestic training Indigenous youth were subject to in residential schools, as well as an experimental domestics placement program operating in Ottawa from the early to mid-1940s, this chapter shows that the DIA guaranteed that domestic labour was, indeed, one of the only jobs Native women could get.

Indigenous Women and Household Labour

Historical scholarship has acknowledged two main forms of Indigenous women's domestic labour. The first is the celebrated domestic work of Indigenous women who oriented the disoriented in Indigenous territory, especially during the fur trade in the eighteenth and early nineteenth centuries and in the "Canadian North" in the twentieth. Women's work in the fur trade has not always been acknowledged by historians. In fact, it has been part of the historical interpretation of the fur trade only since the early 1980s, thanks to the groundbreaking work of historians like Jennifer Brown and Sylvia Van Kirk. Their work, and that of others since, has shown that Indigenous women's labour was crucial to the trade. Women's activities included the provision of food, including pemmican, fish, rice, maple sugar, berries, and small game; women also made clothing, moccasins, and snowshoes; cleaned and dressed furs; made canoes and paddled them; and acted as guides, interpreters, and diplomats in trade. Relationships with Indigenous women—formalized by Indigenous custom—were sometimes the only way traders could access female labour, secure trading ties, and communicate in the customs and languages of Indigenous people. Considering the myriad tasks performed by wives in the domestic sphere, including child rearing, it is clear that "custom of the country marriages" were the fundamental social relationship through which fur trading societies developed in North America. Joan Sangster and Myra Rutherdale show that such work did not cease in the twentieth century: Indigenous women were essential guides, helpers, companions, and translators for white women who worked in the North as missionaries and nurses.[2] Native people will sometimes point to this type of work as the unacknowledged but essential labour of helping strangers to adapt to their territory.

Sometimes this early domestic labour is cast as part of a cultural and spiritual conversion to Christianity, especially in Jesuit and Church of England historical accounts. While an earlier emphasis on cultural and religious assimilation or conversion (i.e., the success or failure of the mission) put conflict and loss at the centre of many historical accounts, newer work focuses on the impact of cross-cultural encounters on the status of Indigenous women, notions of women's respectability, and Indigenous women's connections to female reform work through their contributions to church organizations, preaching and evangelizing, and household labour.[3]

Unfortunately, in much of the literature about Indigenous women's history, Indigenous women's labour often appears as static "women's roles," and women themselves feature as remote economic figures with neither a social nor a political historical context.[4] In fact, what is sometimes called "traditional" Indigenous women's domestic work in the fur trade and mission contexts contrasts significantly with the ways in which domestic labour is perceived in the modern era. At this point, Indigenous women's "traditional" domestic work becomes pathologized and the assimilation of Indigenous women to Euro-Canadian standards became a priority. In this era, domestic labour and the home were targets of colonial policy; it was in the home where cultural norms were to be reformed, produced, and reproduced. Scholars such as Paige Raibmon, Victoria Haskins, Jane Simonsen, and others have shown how domestic assimilation was indelibly linked to colonization and white settlement. Indigenous homes were imagined as the locus of backward and pathological Indigenous cultures, and as such were targets of sexual, moral, and social regulation that implicated white women as activists, workers, and employers. Likewise, schemes to reproduce model European homes for Indigenous inhabitants sought to reconfigure the social relations of Indigenous families, like residential schools policy did. The notion that European-style homes and domestic skills in Indigenous settings were valuable tools for cultural assimilation continued to dominate perspectives on Indigenous women's labour through the twentieth century.[5]

This chapter focuses on two modern forms of domestic labour that were prominent in the twentieth century. The first is Native women's work at federally run, segregated Indian schools and hospitals and the homes of the non-local and mostly itinerant workforce of church and government officials. This waged work was made invisible as expected, as essential, and as a natural transition from manual training in school. It is important to look at this labour in this era because it is so obviously related to troubled Indigenous economies resulting from the colonization of homelands and coercive federal Indian policies. Ideally closely supervised, housekeeping work at residential schools and in the homes of government and church staff was thought to be especially beneficial for Indian girls. It was seen as a continuation of educational objectives to instill work ethic and discipline and to provide practical experience of modern, Canadian gender roles, and the idealized domestic sphere.

The second form of Native women's domestic labour occurred in private homes, hotels, and tourist resorts, non-Indian hospitals, and homes for the elderly. This work was obtained either through the state (most often the DIA) or by Indigenous women themselves. While some historians have assumed that it was relatively rare, in fact, this form of domestic labour was quite common. Perhaps its everyday place within Indigenous social history has made it appear somewhat unremarkable. This form of waged labour could, for some workers, be distanced somewhat from church and state surveillance; however, the state managed to maintain a considerable investment in recruiting, contracting, and disciplining this labour force. This was especially clear when domestics contravened or outright rejected idealized norms. Both of these forms of Indigenous modern domestic labour here have an important place in our histories. Economically, women's, like men's, waged labour was often part of a multi-faceted economic strategy that included hunting, trapping, gardening, the sale of handicrafts, and other cottage industries. For many, it was a means of escaping or alleviating the pressures upon exhausted family economies.[6] Young women's help at home was often counted on by multigenerational families, and it was when family resources were strained that wage work as a housekeeper, farm labourer, waitress, secretary, or department store clerk, for example, was sought.

Interestingly, women's own histories suggest that they did not necessarily identify closely with a history of domestic service. For example, trying to get women in my own family to talk about domestic work in detail was extraordinarily difficult. It seemed to them that my interest in the history of domestic service was misplaced, and that there were far more important subjects I should be examining. Moreover, stories about Native women and domestic work are often told in relation to family responsibilities, other forms of work or activism, family violence, poverty, scarcity, and welfare (or a lack of it), rather than in terms of the history of wage labour. For example, a significant number of the women elders interviewed as part of a Sandy Bay, Manitoba, history project mentioned cleaning houses, hotels, and hospitals both "in town" and "around the reserve" as part of a longer list of jobs that included babysitting, digging Seneca root, working at fisheries, hoeing sugar beets, haying, threshing, stoking and other farm labour, cutting wood, picking berries, waitressing, working as a cook, and selling eggs, weasel, and smoked fish.[7] Domestic work was also associated with "hard times," particularly for those who started working very young because their families could not afford to support them. Lilly Harris was one of the Tobique women who organized in the mid-1970s to challenge discriminatory Indian Act legislation that was harmful to living conditions for women and children. She recalls finding domestic work in the 1930s in the U.S. by word of mouth, starting at the age of fourteen. When she was younger, she had picked berries and fiddleheads, and after working as a domestic, she got a job hand-sewing moccasins (which, she recalls, was considered a man's job, but during the war they hired women to do it). Another Tobique woman, Ida Paul, also had to start working at the age of fourteen. She went to work for an older woman who made baskets on the reserve, cleaning house and washing floors and clothes.[8]

Domestic work was often associated with a social, travelling stage of life. It was often first pursued in young adulthood, and was, for many, their first paid job. Domestic work could widen women's social circle, and work could be readily obtained by them in areas both far and near. As it was highly in demand, domestic work also involved a certain degree of choice and was widely taken as both a stop-gap measure and a short-term stepping stone to other kinds of work. Thus, domestic work could be, depending on your point of view, evidence of the economic, social, and physical impacts of imperialism and colonial policy on Indigenous women; manifestation of the efforts of Native women in one generation to hold it together for the next; or an entirely ordinary thing for women to do. It could also be all these things at once. Indigenous women's histories of domestic work amount to an important body of knowledge about the Indigenous twentieth century.

Closer examination of Indigenous women's domestic labour in federal institutions and private establishments can also broaden our understanding of the ways that domestic labour has been gendered, racialized, and colonized in Canada. While early feminist Canadian labour history helped to situate domestic work as feminized working class labour,[9] newer studies on immigration and migration have shown how women's household labour was also imbued with notions about race, colonization, and nation-building.

Studies of immigration policies and programs can illuminate how the labour of domestic servants, and the Canadian labour market more generally, was influenced by racial hierarchies and the priorities of white settlement.[10] For example, Adele Perry's and Lisa Chilton's work on imperialism and domestics adds to our understanding of how white women's domestic labour was put to the service of imperialism and settlement. Chilton's focus is on the British societies that managed female migration from Britain to Canada and Australia and the women who ran them, the "agents of empire." These women attempted to control, indeed "improve," the types of women who were settling in the colonies and make migration safer and more respectable.[11] Perry demonstrates that domestic servants from Britain were encouraged to immigrate to British Columbia in the nineteenth century. She argues that they were seen as a social panacea to "myriad gendered and racialized dilemmas" in colonial B.C. They would be a stabilizing presence for white men otherwise perceived to be part of a footloose, rough, homosocial backwoods culture, compelling them to normative standards of hetero-masculinity, respectability, and permanent settlement. Additionally, immigration of white women domestics was meant to tackle the widespread problem, as imperial advocates saw it, of mixed-race marriages. As symbols of imperial authority, immigration programs for domestics privileged ordinary working white women as they defined the boundary between races. As her work aptly demonstrates, the processes of dispossession and settlement were not discrete, but mutually dependent and deeply entwined.[12]

Anti-racist feminist scholarship on citizenship and non-white immigrant women domestic workers has shown that the workforce was not always straightforwardly permanent.[13] In uncovering the uncertainties associated with non-white domestics' citizenship, such work has been helpful in drawing out similar uncertainties around Native women's labour status as wards of the state. Canadian citizenship was, in many ways, seen as something that protected the labour of "real" Canadians, compelled the labour of non-Canadians, and rewarded the labour of "new" ones. While the history of domestic workers is also almost always depicted as a story about women coming from elsewhere, in fact, as many as 36 to 57 percent of Aboriginal women participated in the domestic service labour market between 1920 and 1940. For Indigenous people until the 1960s, enfranchising meant a loss of Indian status, treaty rights, and band membership. Single and widowed women could and did apply for enfranchisement (married women would have been subject to their husbands' status), a process that involved applying to the federal government and, if successful, receiving a per capita share in the band funds, which, depending on the band, could be considerable. Enfranchising also required that enfranchisees cut all ties to the band, revoke band membership, forfeit annual treaty annuities and rights, and give up access to community resources and services. This option was chosen at considerable risk by Indigenous women. However, as a study by Robin Jarvis Brownlie shows, for Anishinabe and Mohawk women in southern Ontario, enfranchisement was an economic decision, and to many, an attractive one. Brownlie finds that between 1920 and 1940, one-quarter of the enfranchisement applications came from women, and of the twenty-eight women in Brownlie's study, at least sixteen were employed as domestic servants.[14]

Historians of African-American and Latin-American domestic workers have shown how in a domestic's workplace—the home—relations of race, class, and gender are all played out.[15] This is true also for Native women domestics. It is unfortunate that this scholarship has developed so completely separately from the literature on making Native space. Agnes Calliste points out in her studies of migration schemes for Black domestics how economic demand, political concerns, and prevailing ideologies worked together to restrict Black immigrants in the early twentieth century. Despite a strong, continuing demand for domestic service, fuelled in part by factors such as the expansion of wartime industries and the migration of women to cities, the continuing low status of domestic labour meant that anyone with other opportunities would not be attracted to do it. With a diminishing supply of British domestics, Black domestics were seen as a cheap, intelligent, industrious, and devoted alternative. Their "moral character" was the ideological clincher for restrictive policies. Morality was a defining feature of racialized women's domestic labour, whether white British, Black Carribbean, or Indigenous.[16]

The regulation of domestics' migration and placement has been a central source of information for historians of women and labour. But I have found that white women's feminist organizations, maternal or otherwise, played an inconsistent and highly localized role in the placement of Native women in domestic service in colonial institutions as well as in private homes and businesses. More central to domestic labour issues were Native women themselves, Indian Affairs officials (mostly men), and individual white women who drew their income from their own or their husbands' work in political or government careers.[17] Once a branch of the Department of Mines and Resources, Indian Affairs moved to the Department of Citizenship and Immigration in 1950, suggesting the surveillance at once of the labour and resources of both immigrants and Indigenous people, more frequently called Canadians "New" and "Original" in postwar citizen-focussed nationalist jargon.[18] While this might suggest similar schemes for domestic work, there were no distinct government policies that aimed to place Indigenous women only in domestic labour, as there were for immigrants. However, it is clear that a key directive of federal schooling for girls was domestic service work. Principals and Indian

Agents working for the Department of Indian Affairs heavily influenced the options available to female students when they completed school, distinguishing between those "suited" to domestic work in urban or rural[19] areas, as well as those who were not suited to work in domestic service at all. With Indian Affairs' surveillance of workers' bank accounts, private or "off-work" time, relatives, and in many cases their relations with employers, as well as other social services including the Indian Health Service, the Children's Aid Society, and the police, domestic work often involved long-term and profound involvement of the state in the lives of Indigenous women and their children. The price of failing at a domestic post, however, was never as high for Native women as for immigrants. Neither the threat of deportation nor the promise of citizenship was an effective incentive for Native women to work as domestics under poor conditions. However, lacking qualifications, with an education compromised by federal Indian school curricula, alternative options for employment were few. Moreover, most public and professional schools were effectively closed to Indian students until well after the 1940s, and so further training and certification was denied to those women who wanted or needed to work.

Indigenous Domestic Labour in Indian Schools and Hospitals

Education, in schools devised and controlled by non-Native people, had always been a factor of the civilizing mission in Canada. A main goal of federally controlled Indian education has been to reorient Native children away from community, family, and culture towards the state and Canadian status quo citizenship. In the late nineteenth century, a particularly oppressive system of Indian residential schools developed through the joint cooperation of the Department of Indian Affairs and the Christian missionary churches in Canada. The Indian Act gave the Minister of Indian Affairs discretionary powers to establish, maintain, and operate schools and to compel school attendance for Indian children between the ages of six and sixteen (and sometimes much older). By 1948, there were seventy-two schools across Canada, and 60 percent of the Indian school population were in federal schools.[20] Especially by the 1940s, but also much earlier than that, the schools were the subject of numerous complaints of psychological and physical abuse.[21]

From the 1880s until well after 1951, manual labour and academic study were mandated to share equal space in the curriculum of Indian residential schools. This was also called the "half-day" system. Manual labour education was strictly divided along gender lines, reflecting broader ideologies in Canadian society in which "suitable tasks" were supposedly innate according

Figure 1.2. Students doing the school laundry at Brandon Indian Industrial School, Manitoba.
Library and Archives Canada, National Film Board of Canada, Still Photography Division, R1196-14-7-E.

to gender. Outdoor work was reserved for men, whereas women were confined to the indoor domestic sphere.[22] Thus, girls' education in residential schools included mending, sewing, sweeping, cooking, cleaning, washing and ironing, dairying, canning, gardening, hygiene, and home nursing.

Domestic science became a fundamental element of girls' education throughout North America in the late nineteenth and early twentieth centuries. At the time, it was felt that this kind of education would provide the necessary skills to succeed as a woman. However, this training had even more specific functions in the philosophy and direction of Indian education. First, it was supposed to prepare young Indian women to be "civilized" mothers and wives who would extend the influence of their residential school education to their own homes. Second, Indian residential schools were fully dependent upon the manual labour of Indian students, and so domestic training was often simply a thin veneer to induce the student labour that was needed to run the institutions. Third, domestic training, it was felt, would best prepare Indian girls for what was assumed to be their lot in life: to enter the labour

Figure 1.3. Students washing dishes at Portage la Prairie Indian Residential School, Manitoba.
Library and Archives Canada, Winnipeg Tribune, PA-185879.

market and socio-economic order as domestic servants when they left school.[23]

At the very basic level, domestic training in the schools was unwaged (and unfree) student labour. The institutions themselves, often attached to farms and gardens, were meant to be lessons in self-sufficiency, and their operation depended on student labour, rather than sound staffing, budgeting, and planning.[24] In light of the deplorable conditions at many of the schools, the

Figure 1.4. Two ex-students of All Hollows Indian Residential School, British Columbia, in domestic service.
Library and Archives Canada, Department of Indian Affairs, C-056774.

lesson must have been a hollow one indeed. The schools failed to comply with health regulations in design, hygiene, heating, ventilation, wiring, sewage, and dietary provisions and were in a state of decay that had well-documented effects on the health of the students. Moreover, the emphasis on labour at the schools contributed directly to their abysmal failure as academic institutions; the majority of students did not complete an elementary education.[25] Arguably, Native children's labour was one of the central reasons for forcing school attendance until the age of sixteen, even though most of the schools were only elementary.[26]

On the other side of this labour training was significant local demand for the labour of Native people. Older students engaged in more formal waged labour at colonial institutions, including residential schools, hospitals, nursing stations, mission stations, and the private homes of missionaries, teachers, principals, nurses, and doctors. First Nations author Jane Willis talks about this type of work in her 1973 memoir *Geniesh: An Indian Girlhood.* One day at the St. Philip's Anglican Residential School (in Fort George, Quebec) in the 1950s, Reverend Montgomery, the principal of the school, approached her and her friend: "You girls will be graduating from this school in June," he said. "I called you in here to discuss your future.... Legally you're supposed to stay in school until you're sixteen. So what I had in mind was for both of you to live and work here at the school. Violet, you could work in the kitchen, and, who knows, maybe someday you could work yourself up to assistant cook. Janie, we could put you in the laundry, and maybe someday you'd be in charge. But since you cannot legally quit school for another two years, you'll have to continue with your lessons.... That way you can earn money while you're learning. We'll start you off at five dollars a week." For Janie, it was a "tempting offer, but high school was more tempting." While she waited until arrangements were made for her to attend a public high school, she focussed on schoolwork, working part-time as a babysitter for the Montgomerys.[27]

Formal and informal programs of apprenticeship like the one described by Willis placed students in domestic service not only at the schools themselves, but also in the homes of people who lived near the schools. Historian J.R. Miller argues that for the female students this was "merely a continuation of their employment as domestic workers in the schools, or in some cases as the private maids and helpers of principals' wives." To the DIA, the advantages of apprenticeship included "acquiring increased proficiency in the English language...[and] the habits and ways of thought pertaining to the whites. Moreover, it kept young women isolated from their own people at an age when marriage was a possibility." Miller also points out the department's ambiguous views of apprenticeship—it raised the problem of unsupervised after-school time and spending money.[28] This issue would also bother the department when it came to Indigenous women doing work after they left the schools.

Student employment in the private homes of principals and other school employees would often lead to their placement as domestic servants once they left the schools. Director of Indian Affairs H.M. Jones explained in

1955 that "the older girls" at the residential schools "take turns working in the principal's residence and in the homes of other school employees." He boasted that "as a direct result of this training, a number of girls have been successfully placed in non-Indian homes as domestics."[29] It appears that the domestic labour of students was indeed assumed to be part and parcel of the privileges owed to principals and their wives. In *Geniesh*, Jane Willis describes working as a "full-time maid" six days a week for the wife of the principal during a summer visit home from Shingwauk, where she had started attending high school. She describes in great detail her workday, which started when the children awoke at 7:30 a.m. and went until late at night, when she was expected to be on call for babysitting without notice and without extra pay. Her work included feeding, washing, and dressing the children and taking them out for a walk, putting them down for a nap, or sending them out to play while she dusted, swept, mopped, laundered, ironed, polished silver, washed windows, and washed dishes. All the while, Mrs. Montgomery napped, sipped tea, wrote letters, rested, watched her, or complained "Oh dear! We have so much work to do today." Janie writes, "[I had] the feeling that the Montgomerys thought they owned me just because they paid me five dollars a week." After four weeks, she had had enough and one day refused to go to work. The Reverend went straight to her house and yelled, "Who do you think you are anyway?... Do you think you're any better than the other Indians just because you've had a few years of high school? Well, you aren't." Turning to Janie's mother, he yelled, "That's gratitude for you! I offer her a job and what does she do? She thinks she's too good for it. I've heard of ungrateful people before, but she beats all." Then, he turned to Janie. "A lot of girls on this island would be thrilled to have your job," he continued. "If this is an example of what a higher education does for you, then I'm all for keeping Indians ignorant."[30] Even when employers had "good" intentions with regards to employing Native domestics, depending on the employer and the availability of other options for female employment, domestic service could become highly exploitative.

Indian hospitals, clinics, and nursing stations—and the doctors and nurses who ran them—also depended on the domestic labour of Indigenous women and men. In fact, the early Indian Health Service relied almost entirely on part-time, unpaid, or poorly paid female domestic labour. Very few full-time doctors or nurses were employed by Indian Health Services before the 1950s, and those who were worked mostly at Indian hospitals. Outside of those institutions, there were travelling nurses by the 1920s; however, they were few and far between. Field matrons and dispensers, a largely unpaid group of female workers, were appointed where the population was seen as too small to warrant full-time medical personnel. Field matrons were to provide instruction and advice in personal and household hygiene and, like dispensers, provide drugs, dressings, and simple remedies. The on-the-ground health care workforce of the Indian Health Service was for many years an ad hoc network of local, voluntary, philanthropic, and unqualified white women supplementing the trained services of non-local white nurses, all of whom required the support of Indigenous labour to do their jobs.

Maids and handymen for nurses were often paid out of nurses' own salaries, in kind, or in Hudson's Bay Company credit. For example, in 1925 at Oxford House and God's Lake in Manitoba, the doctor suggested that a girl be stationed at each of the reserves "as companion and interpreter" for the nurses. "I should place the nurses' salaries at $1500 per year," he recorded, "with an allowance for freight and $200 for the Indian girl, a total of perhaps $2000 for each nurse."[31] Religious hospitals operated along the same lines. For example, the laundry workforce at Dynevor Hospital near Selkirk, Manitoba, was "as a rule" all Native by the 1920s. All Saints' Hospital in Aklavik, Northwest Territories, in 1931 was run by the Church of England and employed "three grad nurses, one house matron, a native ward-maid and an outside handyman."[32] In the suggestions of all health professionals from the earliest service, it is clear that there was a perceived role for female Aboriginal health care providers in First Nations communities. That role was assistant, helper, and housekeeper.

When Indian Health Services modernized in the postwar era, the terms "ward aide," "nurse's aide," and "hospital maid" began to replace the more generalized terms "housemaid and "housekeeper" that were used previously. Aides and maids served as messengers, carried and collected trays, made beds, cleaned rooms, and cared for and visited with patients. In her youth, Ann Callahan, a Cree elder from Peepeekisis Nation, Saskatchewan, worked as a nurse's aide at the Fort Qu'Appelle Sanatorium before entering nursing school at the Winnipeg General Hospital in the 1950s. She explains that this work also involved taking patients for walks and visiting with them.[33] Eleanor Olson, an elder from Peguis, Manitoba, worked as a ward aide at the Norway House hospital on weekends while she was in school. It was this work that first sparked her interest in becoming a nurse. She remembers following and watching the other nurses working and asking them lots of questions about how to become a nurse. She later studied to be a licensed practical nurse at St. Boniface Hospital in Winnipeg and worked at Fisher River Hospital, Hodgson Hospital, and as a community health nurse in Peguis, Manitoba.[34]

Because of the specialized nature of ward aide and nurse's aide training, on the one hand, and limited access to levels of education necessary for entering specialized programs on the other, there was a debate between Indian Health Services and Indian Affairs over which federal department was responsible for training this workforce. Staff at Indian hospitals would sometimes devise "modified" programs whereby hospital maids would advance to ward aides or nurse's aides after a period of training.[35] These courses taught cleanliness, punctuality, efficiency, and discipline, as well as bed-making, room-cleaning, preparation of foods and trays, and patient care. One such uncertified nurse's aide training program was offered by hospital staff in the Northwest Territories in the 1940s.[36] This program grew out of informal training practices in the area and engaged mission hospitals at Fort Smith, Aklavik, Fort Simpson, and the Resolution Indian Residential School. Laurie Meijer Drees finds in her research on Aborginal nurse training programs that this program aimed to teach students "elements of dietry [sic] and plain cooking," and how to "take temperatures, do simple dressings, make up dressings, give enemas, properly make beds and give sponge or bed baths." Moreover, students "should also understand the use of simple cathartics and have some knowledge of the proper use of simple remedies which are used in every home, such as the application of mustard, the use of pneumonia jackets and they should also be taught the elements of hygiene with particular regard to preventing the spread of tuberculosis in the home and out at camps."[37] While the training provided in this program was much like practical nurse and nurse assistant training, it was organized specifically for Aboriginal women. Training reflected some of the presumptions about Aboriginal people that characterized Indian policy at the time; namely, that close supervision, discipline, assimilation, and reform were necessary elements of education. Additionally, as uncertified programs, their graduates had severely limited options for employment and no occupational and job mobility. Meijer Drees argues that this early program "characterized by lack of solid federal support, low expectations, and a piecemeal approach, could be viewed as the pattern for things to come in the field of Aboriginal nurse training until the 1970s."[38]

By the 1950s, the Department of Indian Affairs had become concerned that the staff of Indian hospitals should include Indian labour. In response to a memorandum regarding "Training Farm Labourers and Domestic Workers," Superintendent of Education R.F. Davey noted that the "Indian Health Services have also been most helpful in giving training on the job at most of their hospitals."[39] Around the same time, P.E. Moore, director of

Indian Health Services, affirmed his department's policy to employ Indian labour: "wherever possible, Indians are given the preference," although, he explained further, "occasionally...a nurse who is a newcomer to the district will hire a non-Indian maid or housekeeper during the time she is becoming acquainted with Indians of the community in which she serves." The tendency to hire non-Native domestics for nurses at the Montagnais Innu community of Point Bleue, Quebec (now Mashteuiatsh), in the mid-1950s brought to light antagonisms over Indian education and employment between Indian Health Services and Indian Affairs. While Indian Affairs wanted all federal services to give preference to Native labour, Indian Health Services seemed reluctant to follow through, which, it was felt, reflected poorly on the DIA. DIA Regional Supervisor Jules D'Astous stated: "It serves little purpose to have meetings with Indians, encourage them to get better education, tell them that we are badly in need of nurses, nurse's aides, school teachers, etc., when in practice we find that they cannot even qualify for housekeeping duties."[40]

Residential schools created a significant pool from which to draw institutional labour, and it is worthwhile to think about the state's role in developing its own workforce. In his investigation of southern Alberta's sugar beet industry, Ron Laliberte argues that the DIA's involvement in recruiting an Indian agricultural workforce from northern reserves in Alberta and Saskatchewan relieved that industry's labour shortage. It created a working class of Aboriginal people that prevented the profound destabilization of labour and education practices.[41] Laliberte's work gives warrant to further investigation into the employment practices of both the Department of Indian Affairs and Health Canada, especially as these workforces have historically been so dissatisfied. The removal of children from their homes for school gave the state a particular advantage in terms of a pool of labour to draw upon, even more so when the students were orphans or from impoverished families and communities that could not readily support them. Additionally, since the federal government recruited Indigenous people only for more menial, lower-paid positions, they had no real incentive to improve the standards of Indian education. Indeed, since the substandard education provided at Indian schools severely limited graduates' options for further education or better jobs, the government could be seen to be more invested in maintaining low standards.

For many Native women who worked in various capacities at hospitals and nursing stations throughout the country, this work was often arranged through their school principals and teachers. For example, elders at Sandy Bay, Manitoba, remember that some of the girls were taken after they finished school to work at St. Boniface Hospital in Winnipeg. One elder worked in the annex as a nurse's aide and also in the kitchen with two of her friends. She recalls that "when some of the girls finished school, the Father came and got us to work for the farmers in Lavinia. … Other girls were also taken to St. Boniface to go and work. I worked in the annex as a Nurse's Aide, I emptied bed pans and made beds every morning. I also worked in the kitchen." Another elder remembers being taken to St. Boniface by the priest to work at the sanatorium when she left school at the age of eighteen.[42]

By the 1960s, Indian Affairs sought to develop a more modern "on-the-job training" program at residential schools. In 1961, H.M. Jones, director of Indian Affairs, reported that a recent survey indicated that there were "approximately 300 Indian employees at residential schools of a total staff of approximately 1200. However, most of these employees are engaged as unskilled labourers." These statistics inspired a program of on-the-job training in residential schools "designed primarily to prepare Indians for employment in the schools." Training, including "supervision, cooking, stationary engineering and maintenance," would be offered to trainees, who, housed in regular staff quarters or other facilities, were paid a salary of about $125 per month out of "educational funds." The length of training was commensurate with skill level but, it was suggested, was not to exceed the regular school year. After this time, "every effort" was to be made by headquarters "in negotiations with the religious denominations responsible for the operation of the Government-owned Indian Residential Schools to accept such trainees for full-time employment when they have received the necessary qualifications." Regional placement and education officers would be responsible for ensuring that "provincial requirements are met to obtain proper qualifications and rates of pay."[43]

In Manitoba, six schools participated in this program in 1961: Assiniboia, Mackay, Birtle, Brandon, Fort Alexander, and Portage la Prairie. Assiniboia was chosen because it was accessible to the Manitoba Technical Institute and vocational schools that provided low-cost, non-credit courses for adults. MacKay, the largest residential school in the region, employed "competent engineers…and experienced caretakers" who could provide on-the-job instruction for maintenance workers. Birtle, the only school still operating a farm, could provide training in grading, packaging, and storing meat, dairy and poultry products, and vegetables. Brandon was chosen because it could provide on-the-job training for cooks and cook's assistants. Fort Alexander was chosen because, located on a large reserve, it could select trainees locally, and Portage la Prairie because it had the necessary staff to train supervisors.[44]

A progress report of the trainees in this program counted one kitchen and laundry helper who trained for four months and then, after a brief visit home, went on to Grace Hospital in Winnipeg to train as a nurse's aide, and two full-time laundry, dining room, and cook staff who had undergone training for ten months.[45]

The "on-the-job training" program formalized the Department's vision of moving students into paid domestic labour. Moreover, providing a direct route to a job, the program also suited its goals to fill its ranks with Indigenous labour. While the program offered perhaps a few more job options to Indigenous graduates of residential schools, and promised to meet provincial standards of qualifications and pay, employment continued to be menial, reflecting the government's continued investment in low standards of education. It is significant too that the program was created just as residential school education itself was falling out of favour and residential schools across the country were closing their doors.

For various reasons—including the disgusting physical state of the schools, a new vision of educating parents alongside children, and a belief that integrated schooling would accelerate the assimilative process—by the mid-twentieth century, the Department of Indian Affairs and its resistant partners, the churches, had already begun closing residential schools. They were replaced with reserve-based day schools or integrated provincial schools. The existing boarding schools became a "supplementary service" for those who could not commute by bus to federal day schools or provincial schools, and they were resorted to only after "all other avenues, such as foster homes, day school attendance and improved housing [had] been explored."[46]

Residential schools also turned into hostels for Native high-school students who came from areas where no secondary school existed. When hostels reached capacity, students were placed in private homes while they attended integrated high schools. This boarding program was an economical alternative to building schools on reserves and in sparsely populated areas, and by 1969 there were 4,000 students boarding in private homes compared to 7,704 students in residential schools.[47] One example of this situation was Shingwauk school in Sault Ste. Marie, Ontario, which, through an agreement made in the mid-1950s with Sault Ste. Marie schools, became a hostel for students from Sioux Lookout and Moose Fort. When it reached capacity, Native students were placed in private homes locally or transferred to homes in North Bay, where they continued high school.

Janie Willis was one of these students, and the experience she recounts in *Geniesh* is instructive of the ways in which Indian education dovetailed with domestic labour to create possibilities for student labour even as residential schools were in the process of closing. Struggling with the very unsatisfactory residential arrangements at Shingwauk and threatening to drop out, Janie was presented with another option: to go to a public high school and be boarded in a private home. She agreed, because she desperately wanted to leave, and moved to North Bay. She writes that, intuitively, after arriving at her new lodging, "I sensed that my new life with the stern-faced old woman before me was going to be no improvement over the last ten and a half years.... Gray hair in pincurls, wrinkles dripping with face cream, massive body wrapped in a boldly flowered robe, upper lip curled disdainfully, she stood glowering at me.... My 'new mother', Mrs. Fulton, was in her sixties...I learned very quickly that she had taken me in for purely selfish reasons. She wanted a live-in maid. Before the second week was out, she had me doing everything but the cooking and changing her bed."[48]

It is significant that even in a period of integration, domestic labour remained a key element and goal of Indian education for girls. The rejection of the 1969 White Paper, an explicit expression of Canada's policy of termination by integration, highlighted the injustice of that policy with regard to Indian rights and federal responsibilities. Meanwhile, the live-in student-domestic situation reveals two other elements of the overarching integration philosophy. First, integration was not simply a matter of race, but would always also follow along class lines and would only work if it served Canadian citizens and the Canadian nation state. Second, Indian policy for integration was no longer considered the exclusive business of Indian Affairs and the missionary churches, but of all Canadians.

It is difficult to reconcile this history with existing published work on Indigenous women's history in Canada. While trying to carve a space for their own history, women's historians in the 1980s wrote onto Native women's history that same absence that they themselves felt unreasonable. Labour historians have done the same thing. The historical literature on domestic service has shifted from a focus on women's work, to the organized involvement of the women's movement, to studies of the imbricated relations of class, gender, and race, to migration and citizenship. Native domestics, however, have rarely been acknowledged in these discussions, or if so, only in circular references to other published works which also provided little information on Indigenous women's domestic labour history.

To be fair, relying on studies of Native labour would have yielded very little information about Native women. Up to the 1980s, social scientists were interested in Indian agricultural, logging, mining, hunting, and fishing work pursued primarily by men, and they rarely included information about the wages, working conditions, and employment patterns of Native women. Moving towards studies of reforms in Indian education, welfare, and community development, the newer focus on the need for professional training for self-determination has yet again left out a large part of the working population and kept men at the centre of inquiry.

We are told by Canadian labour historians and Canadian women's historians, for example, that Native women were not recruited on a large scale for domestic service, as if that was the end of the story.[49] However, the presumption that domestic servants always originally came from somewhere else has obscured a long history of Indigenous women's significant involvement in that labour force. Their participation highlights some important connections between gender, colonialism, racism, and waged labour in the broader Canadian experience and also brings to the fore some distinct experiences of Indigenous women's oppression at the hands of the Canadian state. The DIA played a central role in both recruiting and compelling Native women's labour; it also dealt in advertising, administering, contracting, and regulating Indian labour for domestic service. Moreover, at a structural level, it is important to study Native women's wage labour in domestic service because it was so highly in demand. This is a particularly unclear side of the labour equation in the historical literature on domestic service. By the early 1940s, reports of Indian agents across Canada highlighted "requests" for Indian women's labour both "locally" and from "outsiders," and in many cases they reported that the demand far exceeded the number capable of undertaking the work. Agents recorded that "Indian girls" had an excellent reputation as workers and were working for sympathetic employers for "good" wages—at File Hills Indian Agency in Fort Qu'Appelle Saskatchewan, for example, for around twenty-five dollars per month with board.[50] The demand for domestic labour was so high, in fact, that some agents felt they should regulate Native women's participation. These reports demonstrate a widespread demand for Indian labour, full participation in domestic wage labour by Native women, and the DIA's interest in their success in this form of work on a permanent basis.

Figure 1.5. Several consecutive residential school students were placed as domestics at "The Manor House," home of Senator Cairine Wilson, in Rockcliffe Park, Ottawa, Ontario, during the Ottawa Experiment.
Library and Archives Canada, Cairine Wilson, C-008414.

The Ottawa Experiment

In 1943, a residential school principal wrote to Mr. Morris at the Department of Indian Affairs, responding to a request for five girls to be placed in domestic work in Ottawa:

> I have persuaded three young ladies to go. I told them that I would write to you and that I was sure you had positions for them. They are Indian girls of course.... They are of excellent moral character and quite trust-worthy. Their reputations are of the best. And I feel that it will certainly be for their best interests if they can work for a time in some good homes. They all went to the 8th Grade in school—speak English quite well, and are in good health. They would prefer Catholic homes if possible.... Do you think you could place them? It would, I am sure, be for the welfare of our Indian charges. They would prefer private homes to work in.[51]

R.A. Hoey, superintendent of welfare and training at the DIA, agreed to arrange for the purchase of clothing so that the "girls" (who were sisters) could be "made presentable" and enclosed three transportation warrants for rail travel to Ottawa, where they were to report to the Indian Affairs office on arrival. He added, "it is our intention to have them medically examined. This is purely routine. The girls need not worry about it. The Department will make all the necessary arrangements. It might be well for you to inform them of our intention so that they will understand." The sisters were placed in three homes close together in the wealthy Ottawa borough of Rockcliffe.[52]

These three young women from the Spanish residential school became part of what the DIA called an "experiment" in the placement of Native women in domestic labour in Ottawa. The Ottawa Experiment was an ad hoc domestic labour placement program developed by the Welfare Division of the DIA in conjunction with residential school principals and Indian agents in Ontario. Run in the early 1940s, the program sought to place older students (ideally graduates) of the schools in domestic service jobs in Ottawa, serving both the demand for domestic labour and an ideological vision which saw young Indigenous women as ideally "suited" to, and as benefiting greatly from, domestic service. The Ottawa Experiment was perhaps the first attempt by the DIA at an organized domestic labour placement program, one of the few (along with nurse's aides programs) that targeted women, and likely one of the first that involved the transportation of women workers.

The program seems to have been initiated by R.A. Hoey and Mr. Morris, and run in connection with the Spanish, Shingwauk, and Chapleau residential schools, each located north of the Great Lakes (all approximately 600 kilometres from Ottawa), and Mount Elgin school in southwestern Ontario. The schools were all manual training institutions with an enrolment of mostly (but not always) local children and orphans from elsewhere in the province. Several agents, perhaps most notably C. R. Johnson, Indian Agent at Manitowaning, Ontario, were also involved, through their connection to First Nations and schools within the Indian agency.[53] At Indian Affairs headquarters, Hoey and Morris inquired among agents and principals regarding students who were about to be discharged from the schools. They also maintained waiting lists of potential employers, kept in touch with employers, and made decisions in problem cases.[54] Agents and principals interviewed and evaluated potential candidates, made travel arrangements, spent allocated funds for transportation and clothing, and, in many cases, cooperated with Hoey in dealing with problems. Ideally, domestics would be placed in homes for a period of at least six months, and, it was hoped, much longer.

A memorandum from 31 January 1943 explained, "We have succeeded during the last year in securing positions for a number of girl graduates of the Mount Elgin, Chapleau, and Spanish Residential Schools. There appears to be an acute shortage of domestic help in a number of larger centres throughout the Dominion and this shortage is very much in evidence in Ottawa. These girl graduates have been placed in a number of better class homes and are rendering satisfactory service. A number of these girls have also been placed at Ottawa General Hospital. At the present time, these girls are brought in from the residential schools and placed in the General Hospital by way of trial. Later, when they express a desire to go into domestic work, positions are found for them. Of the 12 or more girls already brought in, only one has abandoned her work."[55]

The experience and qualifications of domestics in the program varied, as did their means and motivations for joining it. Sometimes students requested placement. Some already had experience working for wages in the residential schools and Indian hospitals. They had various levels of education and a few had grade eight, but all had limited access to higher education. Most were between the ages of fifteen and twenty-two, but a few were in their late twenties and thirties. Importantly, they all shared a common experience of institutionalized federal Indian schooling, English language skills, and good health. This was the generation of Indians so heralded by Indian residential schools as those who could communicate in both worlds and who would "raise their people."

The Department of Indian Affairs had a certain way of inscribing manual labour onto the bodies of domestics: they were "strong," "stocky," and prepared for the types of heavy physical labour that their employers could or would not do. Descriptions of their physical health were sometimes separately guaranteed by a medical exam or an X-ray.[56] Candidates for the program were also distinguished intellectually and by their work ethic and habits. It was ultimately the department's decision whether and where a domestic could work, and it identified "types" suited to urban employment, favouring local employment for those who needed "more supervision."[57]

Unfortunately, the only substantial information I could find about the Ottawa Experiment comes from a block of Indian Affairs records that includes only headquarters correspondence, little of which was by the employers or the domestics themselves.[58] By my best estimate, the records hold around seventy cases of requests and placement attempts, for which there exist varying levels of detail on fifty. Still, these records can relate a little information about the ways the department engaged with the domestic labour of Native women in these years and help draw out some of the broad themes about this type of work: family involvement; clothing and transportation; working conditions; ward status and wage labour; and sexuality, reputation, and regulation.

Before accepting a domestic into the program, the DIA, through agents or principals, usually consulted the candidate's family members, who often objected on the grounds that she was needed at home to care for relatives, that her absence would cause hardship to the family, or that she had better educational or work opportunities elsewhere.[59] This reminds us that Native women engaged in wage labour not simply as individuals, but as members of families and communities. If the department decided that "the parents of these girls are not responsible and will not provide a good home for them," then agents and principals followed through by encouraging "suitable" candidates to accept domestic employment against the wishes of parents or without their permission.[60] In letters, the department called these justifications "family reasons," a phrase which covered a range of material, cultural, and gendered connotations. In some cases, students did not have homes to return to; in others, the department disapproved of the students' parents and/or disparaged that reserve life could be damaging to young graduates. In at least two situations, there was recognition that the department had been too hasty in their decision and that the girls should have stayed with their families.[61] Religion also played an important role in placement—preferably, Catholic domestics were to be placed in Catholic homes and Protestant domestics in Protestant homes.

Grants or loans to cover transportation and clothing costs were standard in Indian labour programs in these years, and they were part of the Ottawa Experiment, too. Clothing and transportation funds were provided on the condition that the domestic agreed to work for a minimum of six months.[62] Domestics, armed with letters of identification, came by rail to Ottawa and either were met at the station by officers from Indian Affairs or reported to the Traveller's Aid desk. Taxis were sometimes arranged to take the domestics to the homes where they would be working.[63] At no time were the domestics met at the station by their employers. Perhaps this afforded the department a clear intermediary and regulatory role in the process and underscored the domestics' utmost responsibility to the state.

Clothing allowances were approved so that the domestics would appear "presentable." Domestic servants represented the department and its schools, and so the investment in clothing was in no way altruistic or philanthropic. For many of the domestics, though, the extra money for clothing may have been an incentive; for some it would have been a relief from dreary school uniforms. Even so, clothing allowances were very basic. Clothing funds in one case allowed only for the purchase of a coat, and in another just a pair of RCAF (Royal Canadian Air Force) shoes. In another case a candidate was rejected because it was suspected that she had agreed to the program only because the department would "supply her with a full new outfit of clothing" and that she would "only stay a couple of weeks and might spoil the chances of some other Indian girl wishing to go to Ottawa to work at some later date."[64] It was also made clear that only status-registered Indians would have transportation and clothing covered. One domestic, who was the daughter of an enfranchised Indian, was informed that she would have to reimburse the department for any expenses related to her placement, in that case, the cost of transportation.[65]

Until the Second World War, domestic service was the single most important source of employment for women. Because it was still considered "naturally" women's work, it was also considered unskilled and held low status. As with the working conditions of many domestics, the wages, hours of work, and responsibilities of Aboriginal domestics in this program varied. According to Hoey, wages were to start at twenty dollars per month and increase according to qualifications and ability. He noted that several girls earned thirty-five dollars per month, with room and board. In only one instance was a domestic offered more than thirty-five dollars (she was offered thirty-eight dollars per month, including three meals per day, from which fifteen dollars would account for a room somewhere in the neighbourhood), and this was to lure her away from a more lucrative job at a tourist resort. In another case, a domestic took a five-dollar pay cut from her domestic job in a residential school to work at a private home in Ottawa. Her new employer agreed to raise her salary only if she proved "qualified" in her new position.[66]

Native women working as domestics in the Ottawa program earned significantly less than did non-Native domestics and women working in other sectors. The average weekly wage in manufacturing for women in 1943 was $19.33, and in some war industries, including aircraft manufacturing and shipbuilding, wages could be as high as $31.81 per week.[67] Wage comparisons for domestic service, with its low status, unfixed hours, and live-in situations can be difficult, especially as these conditions could vary. For example, one employer, Principal Blanchard of the Mackay Institution for Protestant Deaf Mutes, requested of Indian Affairs "three girls to act as waitresses, one in the staff dining room and two in the children's dining room. Their duties would be to keep the rooms clean, set tables, serve food, clear tables and use dishwashing machine." He also requested a "girl with some knowledge of cooking to assist our regular cook and take over her duties on her days off; and a girl to clean vegetables and general help in the kitchen." Their living conditions would be "separate bedrooms, one half day a week off and some time off on Sundays, in addition to a rest period of about two hours each afternoon." For this they would earn $30–$35 per month, plus room and board.[68]

Some effort was made by the Department of Labour to elevate domestic service during the Second World War. Recognizing that there was still a high demand for domestic labour, and that women were moving out of domestic service because higher wages were paid in industry, the Department of Labour classified some domestic servants[69] as providing an "essential service" to the country and argued for the legislation of improved conditions for workers. A departmental memo noted that ads for domestic help in the *Globe and Mail* offered salaries of $30–$50 per month in 1942.[70] It is interesting that no connections between federal involvement in organizing domestic labour during the war in its National Selective Service and the Ottawa Experiment could be found. This helps to make clear that the Indian Affairs department did lowball Indian labour in the Ottawa Experiment. This is especially significant in light of the years of domestic training and experience Indian girls in the Ottawa Experiment would have amassed while at residential schools, where they would have worked at domestic chores at least three to four hours per day for several years.

Vacations were no small matter for the program, since the domestics had relocated for work. The case of two domestics who went to Ottawa together and were refused a trip home illustrates the department's philosophical and administrative vision of Indian labour. Each had been in Ottawa for a full year, and their return home for a vacation was anticipated by their principal, the students at their school, and their families. A vacation would, the principal argued, not only benefit the domestics, but also give "new prospects" a good "impression in regard to post-graduate employment in Ottawa." At first Morris and Hoey concurred with him and the domestics who wanted to return home for a break, consenting that their absence made "Ottawa less attractive to the bigger girls and will prejudice them against going there."[71] However, they ultimately conceded to the employers' objections.

One domestic had worked at the Ottawa General Hospital, but had shifted to private domestic work for eight or ten months before returning to the hospital. (Her hospital work was not as well-paid as work at private homes, but might have afforded more freedoms.) Because she had not been working steadily at the hospital, she could not obtain leave with pay. In her

Figure 1.6. The Dining Room of the Manor House, Rockcliffe, home of Senator Cairine Wilson and workplace of several consecutive residential schools students placed as part of the Ottawa Experiment.
Library and Archives Canada, Cairine Wilson, PA-209036.

case, the department argued, "We feel that if the Indian girls cooperate with the people with whom they are working when the time comes that there are many other girls looking for domestic work the services of the Indian girls will not be dispensed with and the white girls given the preference. It is our hope that they will establish themselves in a permanent way as domestics."[72] The other, who had been working for Senator Cairine Wilson, had advised the DIA in April that she wanted to go home in June. But when Mrs. Wilson was contacted, the senator stated that she had made arrangements for the whole family and staff to go to her St. Andrews estate in New Brunswick for July and August, and it was her practice to not give holidays to the staff until they returned to the city. She thought that if her Indian domestic were permitted to go home, it would create a precedent of privilege and entitlement among other members of her staff.

Needless to say, the department's decision caused dissatisfaction for friends and family back home, from whose point of view the girls deserved a visit home. Appeasing the demands of employers, however, outweighed the desires of both the department to encourage more participation in the program and the workers themselves to visit home. This is somewhat ironic, as the department knew it could not supply enough labour to meet the demand, nor could it even anticipate this ever happening. But once the department was "constantly receiving requests to obtain Indian girls to work as domestics in homes in Ottawa,"[73] it felt obliged to satisfy them, above all else. In doing so, the department attempted to fill requests partway through the school year, denied vacations and requests for transfers, and sided with the employer when questions about working conditions and wages arose. Their obligation became all the more urgent when a domestic left or threatened to leave a home, or refused to go to one, as was quite frequently the case. One Indian agent practically begged the reluctant mother of one student to allow her to go, promising special arrangements for night school and assuring her of her daughter's "kindest treatment" and "good supervision."[74] These efforts are revealing of the artificial labour market the department attempted to control and of its efforts to remove labour power from the hands of Native women and put it directly into the hands of their employers. In a way, the department viewed employers as their clients and domestics as the "product" they manufactured.

The Department of Indian Affairs' Ottawa Experiment was in many ways very different from schemes to place Indigenous domestic labour in the U.S. and in Australia. In those contexts, Indigenous domestic labour placement was largely the work of women and women's organizations, who saw their work in terms of "saving" Indigenous women, not just from their own background, but also from "predatory" white men. But while the Ottawa employers themselves may have subscribed to similar ideals, they did not run the program, or, it seems, have any real influence in the program's creation, initiation and operation. Instead, apart from influencing decisions over their own existing employees, it appears that they fully relied on the DIA—all non-Native men except for the female principal of the girls' school in Spanish, Ontario—to do the recruitment and placement work. The employers may have been club women with a particular drive to "assist" Indians, or religious women hoping to continue the missionary and assimilatory goals of the residential schools, but they acted as an extension of departmental control and discipline in an off-reserve setting. Hiring an Indian domestic was likely thought of as a modern, safe, and appropriate (and profitable) way to appear publicly engaged with the "Indian Problem."

So who were those "responsible women" who ordered up domestics from the Department of Indian Affairs, and where were their "desirable homes"? While it is important to recognize that the public lives of employers were facilitated by Indigenous and other women's domestic labour, they were also, if only temporarily, important figures in the lives of the women they employed. They, too, have a place in this history, and it is worthwhile considering how they came to participate in it.

The Ottawa Experiment seems to have had connections to high-ranking government officials and elite Liberal circles, including senators. Senator Cairine Wilson and Mrs. Dorothy (A.C.) Hardy stand out. Wilson, the first woman named to Canada's senate, was involved with the Victoria Order of Nurses, the YWCA, the Salvation Army, and later in the 1940s was on the Senate Committee of Immigration and Labour. She had eight children and would have been in her late fifties when she became involved in the program. Wilson lived in Rockcliffe and was likely connected to another employer, Mrs. G.E. Ethel Fauquier, also of Rockcliffe, through the Elmwood School, a private girls' school popularly attended by the daughters of Ottawa's elite. Both Fauquier and Wilson hired a string of Native domestics in 1943 and 1944 to work in their homes, and another was hired to work at the Elmwood School. The wooded village of Rockcliffe is one of the wealthiest neighbourhoods in Ottawa and is located on the south bank of the Ottawa River, northeast of downtown Ottawa. Its large houses and wide lots have long attracted Ottawa notables, including ambassadors to Canada.

Dorothy Hardy, wife of Senator Arthur C. Hardy and daughter of Senator George Taylor Fulford, also wrote to the department looking for maids. After requesting to switch domestics with a Mrs. Messer of Rockcliffe, she asked, "If you could send two to Mrs. Elmer Johnston and two to the Brockville Shelter, I think they would be very glad of good maids and there would be the companionship for them."[75] Hardy's father had run a home for elderly women in Brockville (the Fulford Home for Ladies), and she and her husband had bought the Brockville Home in 1934. They may have continued to run the home. Hardy would have been in her early sixties when she sought domestic help from the DIA.

At least two federal government employees acquired maids. Mrs. W.J. McCarthy, supervisor of the secretarial staff of the National Selective Service's mobilization section, wanted a domestic for her mother. Mrs. Camsell, the wife of Dr. Camsell, geologist and deputy minister of the Department of Mines and Resources (which was responsible for Indian Affairs at the time) as well as namesake of the Charles Camsell Indian Hospital in Edmonton, employed several maids through the program. Mrs C.B. Petrie, Mrs. Boggart, Mrs. S. Palef, Mrs. E.A. Evans, Mrs. A.F. (or F.F.) Rogers, Mrs. Wilgress, and Mrs. F.A. Heney each employed one or more domestics between 1943 and 1944, but there is no record of their or their employees' experiences. It appears that in many cases employment did not span longer than a few months. There were few details about why the terms of employment were so brief (whether this was driven by employers or employees), however, in many cases it may have been due to the nature of the work itself; because working conditions could be undesirable and because there was no shortage of jobs, those who were unhappy in their positions had a good chance of finding something else.

Hospital domestic staff, too, were obtained through the program. Sister St. Jacob, superintendent of the Ottawa General Hospital, requested that the department supply ten "girls" of fifteen years of age or older to work at that hospital. Originally, four students were approved to be discharged from the Spanish Residential School; however, the parents of two objected.[76] Other hospitals were altogether unsuccessful in obtaining domestic labour from the program because of insufficient supply.[77] At the same time, Native domestics were hired to work at the Roxborough Apartments, built in 1910 for prestigious people with ties to the government. It appears, then, that the DIA had a preference to supply private homes and facilities. Employers in the program were, for the most part, well-to-do white women whose careers and families connected them to the government of Canada. For the most part, they were part of an elite, or at least upper-middle-class, sector in Ottawa, and their lives and experiences would have differed drastically from the lived realities of the domestics they hired. With the exception of perhaps Mrs. Camsell and Senator Wilson, they would likely have had little to no familiarity with their background. If they did have knowledge or opinions about Native people, they did not express them in their correspondence. Rather, at least on the surface, it appeared that to the employers, "Indian girls" were merely to fill a role in their households that could be filled by any other "girl." Alternatively, the Ottawa Experiment may have been a nepotistic network of cronies who wanted access to cheap maids.

The majority of the domestics in the Ottawa Experiment came from four residential schools. The Spanish Girls School in Spanish, Ontario, and St. John's Indian Residential School in Chapleau, Ontario, sent perhaps the most. Shingwauk Indian residential school in Sault St. Marie also participated in the Experiment, and Mount Elgin Residential School sent perhaps the fewest domestics to Ottawa.

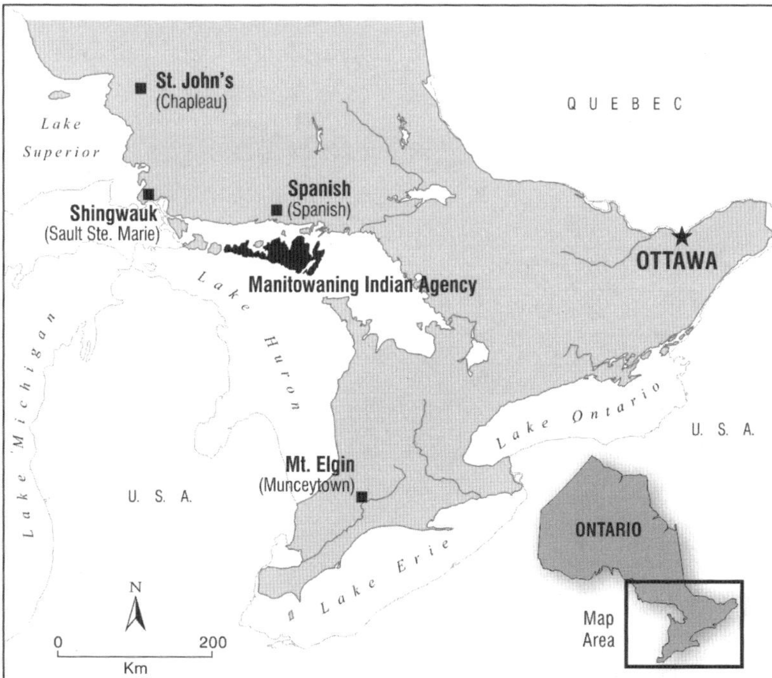

School and Denomination	Dates of Operation	Domestics' Home Communities
Spanish Girls' School (Roman Catholic)	1916-1958	Garden River First Nation Golden Lake (Algonquins of Pikwàkanagàn) First Nation Cutler, Serpent River First Nation Caughnawaga (Kahnwá:ke) St. Regis (Akwesasne)
Shingwauk Indian Residential School (Anglican)	1935-1971	Walpole Island (Bkejwanong First Nation)
St. John's Indian Residential School (Anglican)	1907-1948	Cree First Nation of Waswanapi Mattagami First Nation Brunswick House First Nation Missanabie Cree First Nation
Mount Elgin Indian Residential School (Methodist, United Church)	1867-1946	Cape Croker (Chippewas of Nawash Unceded First Nation)
Manitowaning Indian Agency		West Bay (M'Chigeeng) First Nation Sucker Creek (Aundeck Omni Kaning) First Nation Sheguiandah First Nation Manitoulin Island Unceded Band (Wikwemikong Unceded First Nation)

The Ottawa Experiment. The map identifies schools and home communities of some of the students who were placed as domestics in Ottawa.

These four schools held some commonalities. By the late 1930s, it appears that Chapleau was a place where students who were "hard to handle" were sent from Mount Elgin. Runaways from the schools—most noticeably Chapleau—were a constant problem. Moreover, by the 1940s many of the students at these schools, like many other residential schools, were from broken and disrupted homes. Some staff at the schools were abusive, and as institutions the schools relied too heavily on student labour. Several complaints by parents and First Nations band councils tell of the constant issues of poor provisioning for the students, inadequate and spoiled food, acts of cruelty, severe beatings and physical abuse, a lack of medical care, and inadequate clothing. Such conditions were known to the department. John Milloy recounts Hoey's visit to Mount Elgin in 1942, stating that he found there "the most 'dilapidated structure that [he had] ever inspected.' Parts of it were 'literally alive with cockroaches,' and the 'odours…throughout the buildings were so offensive' that he 'could scarcely endure them.' He was certain that 'if this [were] not a government-operated institution…it would be closed by the municipal health authorities.'"[78] Assessments of the schools in the 1940s included one by Dr. P.E. Moore, the department's director of Indian Health Services, who initiated a study of Chapleau, Spanish, and Mount Elgin in 1944–45 by the Nutritional Services section of the Red Cross. This study found low standards of food preparation and unpalatable meals, unsanitary facilities, and flies and cockroaches everywhere at Chapleau. At both Chapleau and Spanish, the inspection revealed that the students' diet was sorely lacking in vitamin A and ascorbic acid, and that at Spanish older students were consuming far fewer calories than needed.[79] Indeed, due to the shocking conditions contributing to the poor health of the students, including dilapidated, unsafe buildings, both Mount Elgin and Chapleau were closed in 1948. The domestics involved in the Ottawa Experiment attended school in a very dark era within a dark history—at a time when already pitiful funds for education were being diverted elsewhere and just prior to the point when the department shifted its education policy and began to close residential schools in favour of integrated schooling.

While their diet and physical surroundings may have improved greatly, the domestics would have faced relations of power in the homes of elite Ottawa women similar to what they encountered at the schools. One of the few letters in the files written by one of the domestics outlined the unsatisfactory conditions she worked in at the home of Dr. and Mrs. Petrie:

> Mr. Morris really I don't like to go back to work...cause [she's] cross at me one minute, the next minute she's nice. The oldest

> girl is very naughty. She used to slap my face. I don't feel like as if it's my home there. I'd love to work another place where a person can always be nice to me also the children. Many times I use to cry. So Mr. Morris I will love to work another place where there is only one child I love children alright but not when they tell me to shut up or tells me to come back home.

The response from the department to this request for a transfer was to suggest that she somehow owed it to the employer to stay, and Morris argued that continuing on at this place was the best option by stressing the benefits of staying:

> They have been very kind to you in that they provided you with holidays with pay.... My idea is that if you continue working and endeavour to bank some of your money, together with your separation allowance, when the war is over you will have a nice bank account which will enable you and your husband to set yourselves up properly keeping house and perhaps have a small farm.... It looks like a real opportunity for you to save money and plan for your future happiness.[80]

This correspondence reminds us that Native domestics critically observed non-Native families. At the same time, they faced assertions of authority and licence associated with whiteness and class, even by children.

It is clear that Native domestics in many cases got what they had bargained for. They likely went to Ottawa for social reasons, to be with and make friends in the city. In many cases they just wanted to see the city itself, escape the purview of the schools, and make some spending money. When disappointed, most did not last very long in the same place. Participation in the program was initially done on a temporary basis only and most women returned home or found work elsewhere. It is important to remember that they had other options. Mid-war, work in munitions plants was available and, in the field of domestic work, tourist resorts provided work that was by all accounts a lot more fun. The department favoured domestic work in private homes over both of these other options; in the first case because "as soon as the war is over most munition [sic] workers will be out of jobs, whereas, the girls who are doing satisfactory domestic work will be retained";[81] and in the second because resorts were mainly seasonal and did not provide "proper supervision." These justifications suggest that, in the department's view, relocated domestic labour was to be a permanent occupation for Native women. This was not the reality, however. One Indian agent's efforts to lure two young women away from a tourist resort job to work in Ottawa for less money failed miserably, even when he tried to involve the parents.[82] In another case, one of the domestics had found housework in a hospital and preferred to go there, as she knew two other of the hospital's employees.[83] In eastern Canada, where work was plentiful and more remunerative nearer to home or on the American side, the department had to frequently decline requests for "Indian girls."[84]

As the popularity of transnational labour for Native people attests, Native wage work is not simply "Canadian" labour. It was however regulated by the state through Indian Act law, a layer of legislation that separated Native labour, as immigration law separated that of other non-Canadians in Canada. In the 1940s, for example, Native people were still commonly thought of as wards of the state. Wards, like minors without guardians, were subject to the "parental" authority of the state—a category under which, theoretically, all status Indians and Inuit fell until 1961. The Indian Affairs department worked effectively as attentive middlemen in labour arrangements between employers and wards (which included the parents of the employees as well as employees themselves). The double-edged sword of departmental supervision was that while the domestics made several claims on them in terms of transportation, clothing, holidays, and placement with friends and family members, so too did their employers, who felt obliged to alert the department of any dissatisfaction.

Can wards work for wages? Ward status was not a full and complete status through which Indian labour was uniformly defined, but rather only a clarification in certain cases where "free will" was questioned. For example, in a late 1950s' INCO labour dispute with the International Hod Carriers, the department was questioned as to whether Indians, as wards of the state, were exempt from mandatory union membership or whether they worked under "free will" and could therefore be subject to union law.[85] Unlike recruitment of immigrant domestic work, which relied on debt, contracts, and "citizenship" as incentives to work, Native workers could come and go as circumstances allowed. The department's ambivalence towards domestic work rested on this capacity and its suggestion of liminal participation in the workforce, partial acceptance of work ethic, and the freedom to spend time as and with whom they wished. In the domestics program, the word "ward" arose only in moments of uncertainty: to authorize (not compel) work without parental permission and to take steps to discipline Native women workers in an off-reserve setting.

The state treated all Indian labour as principally ward status. However, in the program, the domestics were not always status Indians, many were nearing or over the age of majority, and most of them had parents or guardians who were active in family decision-making. These three determinants also helped to define what "ward" meant in practice. One domestic who was just under the age of twenty-one questioned this status after her father and aunt forced her to return from working at a sanatorium in the United States. Not sure of her rights, she asked the Indian agent, who in turn asked the department, if she was free to leave home to accept employment. The branch decided that "under the circumstances there would not appear to be any justification in having this girl return from remunerative employment. It is quite true that she may be of service at her grandmother's home...but it must be remembered that she has reached a stage in life where she will have to have some training along definite lines to assist her later on. It is very doubtful if she can obtain such training under home conditions as they appear to exist." He suggested that she "agree to contribute a certain amount weekly towards the upkeep of the home table in lieu of her father agreeing that she go off the reserve to receive employment."[86] In this case, the category "ward" was not used to compel her to work against her will, and it allowed her agency, at least to do what she, not her father, wanted. Significantly, the department did feel within its rights to suggest how she should spend her wages.

I did not find any evidence of blatant coercion to work, such as the instances of withholding rations and welfare among some Native farm workers in the 1960s; however, this knowledge may well be only accessed from those who experienced this history first hand.[87] It appears that ward labour status was defined most commonly by the associated responsibilities of the department. The department managed bank accounts and annuities, for example, as one of its responsibilities to its wards, and this is especially evident for those domestics who incurred debt while in Ottawa. One sixteen-year-old student, whose father had enlisted in the army, was first matched with Mrs. F.A. Heney at her "very lovely home" on Richmond Road in the summer of 1943. There is a gap in the correspondence until March 1944, when it is clear that she had transferred at least once and had most recently been working at the Elmwood School in Rockcliffe, but had left that position in February. While at Elmwood, she had incurred a telephone bill amounting to $18.60 for two calls to Timmins, and the school requested that the department collect on it. The request went through Hoey to the agent, who involved the RCMP in trying to locate her. In the meantime, the agent decided to "not pay her any treaty money." Along with a signed statement authorizing the

Indian Affairs branch to apply her annuity towards the debt until the account was paid in full, she sent a letter arguing, "As you know I haven't had my treaty money for the last three years, so that's twelve ($12) dollars I have already payed and I still owe you six dollars and sixty ($6.60)." In this case, the department appears to have stopped annuity payments to the domestic when she started working, perhaps because she worked off-reserve. Yet these very annuities were the source of cash to repay debts incurred off-reserve. Her reasoning was rejected, and C. Roberts, of the Welfare Division, agreed to have the full amount paid directly from her savings account. D.J. Allan, superintendent of reserves and trusts, paid $8.53 by emptying the account and agreed that her 1945 annuity could be forwarded, but he notified the agent that allocating treaty money was not the desired course of action, and if the Elmwood school wished to collect the balance owing, they would have to do it themselves.[88] In at least two other cases, the department helped themselves to domestics' savings and trust accounts, once to pay off a debt incurred while working at the Ottawa Civic Hospital[89] and once to pay fees associated with hospital confinement.[90]

To qualify for Indian education funds and health services, an "Indian" (as opposed to modern) "mode of life" was the official requirement. For the young women in this program, however, lifestyle did not much affect their ability to escape the surveillance and discipline of Indian Affairs, and their status as both wards and workers makes this clear. Certainly moving to Ottawa did not mean that the domestics had escaped the purview of the department. The department intervened freely in their funds as well as their off-work time, even as they worked in modern homes in Ottawa. There was no doubt in anyone's minds that despite their modern lifestyle, they were still subject to the state as Indians.

The term "ward" was not consistently used in departmental correspondence about the program; however, the terms "Indian girl," "Indian maid," and the even more jarring term "Indian maiden" were, suggesting the extent to which the work of domestic service had particular meanings when Indian women did it. Historian Mary Kinnear argues that the term "girl" was shorthand for the contemporary assumption that paid working women would be both young and single.[91] To be expected to work hard for wages at the age of fourteen, for example, was not unusual. Domestic labour did, however, correspond with a stage of life for many—one that is significant for a number of reasons. Often this was a time of life when women went travelling with friends, crossing borders of all types. And it was a time of life when the written and unwritten rules of racism and social class came to be understood and, in many cases, most profoundly and publicly resisted. This is why "supervision" is the most predominant theme in the departmental records about women of this era.

"Indian maiden" and "Indian maid" also evince the discourses of popular literature and culture, that fantasy of the Indian princess whose beauty was often connected to notions of docility and deference. "Maid" and "maiden" associated Indian woman with the home—a space that represents gendered morality, uplift, and assimilation; they incorporated Native women into the nation by defining their domestic work as the fuel for evolutionary progress.[92] Indian maids and Indian maidens were also box-office hits; as the "femme fatales" of forties films, they personified fantasies of exotic female sexual power irresistible to white men, inherited and passed down through Indian blood.[93] In the department's written records, "Indian maids" stood for a less racy but no less compulsive desire to supervise, discipline, dominate, and rescue Native domestics.

The cases involving two seventeen-year-olds, Doris and Kitty, who refused to submit to the department illuminate some of the ways the department supervised and disciplined Native domestics and reveal how vulnerability could turn into incorrigibility from the point of view of the department. For Native women in particular, the department wanted to take steps to enforce discipline and conformity. As has been shown, it was heavily invested in the image of Indian girls as domestic workers and in encouraging their employment by upper-middle-class and elite white women. Doris went from being recommended as a "good type of girl" by Principal Strapp at the Mount Elgin residential school, to being accused of being "restless and not amenable to discipline" and possibly "mentally unbalanced or definitely sub-normal" in a matter of four months and three placements, including Mrs. Camsell's home. Signs of her "mental unbalance" included neglecting to take her "ration book" with her when she left for Ottawa, losing her (Indian?) registration card, and failing to turn in an application for another, which she had been told to "carry...with her all the time." Kitty had come from the Chapleau Indian Residential School. After being "tried as a domestic in Ottawa and found wanting," she was "returned" to Chapleau for "a year of solid domestic training."

The initial disciplinary action in such cases was to haul the domestics into the office for a "sound talking to" and then send them back to work for an additional "trial." The next step was to send the girls home or back to school to work or to have them render service as a domestic in a rural home for "solid domestic training" and "extra supervision." Once found to be "improved in manners, outlook and ability," "competent to go to work," and showing "no sign of Tuberculosis," Kitty was sent back to Ottawa to work for Mrs. Heney, of 145 Richmond Road. She was supplied with "whatever clothing she needs" to be paid out of her "funds on deposit in Savings Account and War Savings Certificates." However, by January 1944, reports began that she had again "not been conducting herself in a proper manner." According to R.A. Hoey, she had become "unmanageable—staying out very late." At this point, she was called back to the office for questioning and given one last chance—an "additional" six-week trial, along with weekly reports on her.

Department discipline did not work in either case. Kitty avoided going to the office when called and lied to officers once she was caught. When the department discovered that she had been staying at a hotel, "apparently in a room with some man," she was deemed "incorrigible" and sent to the Salvation Army Rescue Home while Hoey and Indian Agent F. Matters contemplated what punishment was in order: returning her home to her family (which is what she wanted); placing her "in the care of some responsible Indian family who would report her actions...monthly"; sending her back to the residential school; or incarcerating her in a detention home. Matters argued that "six months in a detention home, where she would get lots of hard work and little or no reward, would be the best cure for her." Knowing her record, he could not recommend a new placement as it "would not be fair to the other Indian girls who are good, [and] as she apparently has no intention at present of trying to go straight, to place her with any other family would mean we would have to keep her, this also is not necessary or should not be necessary, as she is capable of working for herself." Moreover, her mother had passed away, her father was "unreliable," and his "second wife is not much better than he, however he may have more influence over her than anyone else, but I am afraid that she will go wrong there also." Matters ultimately left it to Hoey, recommending the detention home for six months and then back to the residential school or to her home, where, he said, "if she is going to go wrong, let her go wrong with her own people responsible." He added, "if she were left here [in Ottawa] then I know that [her father] would feel that the department or myself were responsible if anything untoward happened to her."

Doris refused the opportunity to take work as a domestic near her reserve. When she was found to be "out every night with men and living at a very undesirable home," her Indian agent sought advice from the department on whether she should be placed in a correctional institution "before she gets into serious trouble." Hoey attached a copy of Chapter 384, The Female

Refuges Act, Section 15, Subsection B, in the Revised Statutes of Ontario, to his response. Because "[she] is a ward of the Indian Affairs Branch," he argued, "we are responsible for her good behaviour. If she is leading a dissolute and idle life then she can be committed with the approval of the local magistrate to the Merser Reformatory in Toronto. Any costs in connection with her transportation and maintenance at this institution will be paid by this Branch."[94] Knowing the contemporary connotation of those words "dissolute and idle life" as a public rejection of chastity, childbirth outside of marriage, and the sale of sex, this squarely aligned the department with contemporary Canadian sexual regulation of women.[95] Under the Female Refuges Act, punishment did not require proof that a crime had been committed, but only information from any source about behaviour that suggested promiscuity, illegitimacy, or venereal disease. For Native women, the time of day during which they associated with men (i.e., after work) and their use of cars and telephones were all interpreted as degrees of incorrigibility. These were also modern, urban activities; in other contexts they were called "leisure" or "amusement."[96]

For Indigenous women, their leisure time was an escape from the dreary, low-paid nature of the work, and many found company with friends. A particular concern of the department was unsupervised heterosocial leisure activity in the evenings. As with non-Native women in urban areas, concern about women's newfound leisure time associated time spent with male friends, with "downfall." In some cases, domestics in the program became pregnant. I was unable to follow up on these cases due to the scarcity of records; however, Margaret Jacobs's analysis of a domestic placement program for Native women run in the San Francisco Bay Area in the 1920s and 1930s provides important insight. She found that 25 percent of the women in the program became pregnant out of wedlock while working as domestics. Maternity and wage work were seen as incompatible, and these women were pressured to give up their children and remain working as domestics, even while most white single and married mothers at this time were pressured to do the opposite. Moreover, Jacobs points to the fact that schools had trained Native women only for jobs so low-paid that they were unable to afford to keep children without great hardship. The U.S. Bureau of Indian Affairs had created for Native women an "irresolvable and untenable" situation, Jacobs finds: "On the one hand, they had been removed from their homes to attend boarding schools ostensibly to be trained in domestic skills and prepared to keep a home and mother children in a white, middle-class way. Yet in the BIA's efforts to make Indians less dependent on government assistance, they were also expected to work for wages and participate in the labour market, often far from their home communities and sources of support."[97] She finds that the roots of widespread practices of adoption and removal, as well as sterilization programs for American Indian women in the postwar period, can be traced to this era, the placement of Aboriginal women in domestic service, and the pressure on workers to give up their children.

Marriage, which on the surface appears to resolve many of these concerns, was also heavily regulated. In historical literature, marriage regulation is most often discussed in terms of gender discrimination in section 12(1)b of the Indian Act. New work by Sarah Carter has shown how important imposing a distinct form of monogamous marriage encoded with explicit gender roles and defined as indissoluble, sanctioned, and regulated by colonial law and Christian ethics was to nation building in Canada.[98] It is not surprising, therefore, that the DIA was highly interested in evaluating potential marriage partners, and sometimes intervened in engagements it disapproved of by removing women to work as domestics. The records pertaining to the Ottawa Experiment reveal two marriages that were investigated. The first was Minnie, a twenty-one-year-old graduate of Shingwauk who had worked as a housekeeper in Sault Ste. Marie and most recently at Chapleau, Ontario. According to Matters, she was "very intelligent, good living and a good worker," but since taking a domestic post at Chapleau, "had got acquainted with a chap, white man, who is a bad character...past any reformation." Matters was worried that Minnie was "under the delusion that she had reformed him and was going to marry him," so he endeavoured to "open her eyes to his way of living" and expected to have him sent to jail for a second offence of "supplying liquor to Indians." He inquired about the possibility of sending her to Ottawa to work as a domestic. As it turned out, "Mrs. G.E. Fauquier, Manor Road, Rockcliffe," was "very anxious to have" her, and Hoey was happy to make the arrangements. Also, he congratulated the agent on his handling of this case: "the officers here feel that she should be very grateful to you for taking the interest to advise her and to guard against marrying this white man, which would only mean disappointment and hardship for her for the rest of her life."[99]

In the nineteenth century, programs promoting the immigration of poor white women as domestics envisioned a particular role for them in the settlement process; they were supposed to tame working-class white men and encourage them to settle down in white marital homes and have white legitimate children. Here, we see something completely different: domestic service placement was used to sever relationships between Native women and white men. This separation was not an outright recognition of paternalist racial violence associated with colonialism, as it was elsewhere. Rather, Joan Sangster argues, "the ideological outcome of a century of colonial efforts to 'tame' native women's sexuality was the heightened 'sexualization' of all aspects of their lives, making them the inevitable target of legal and social regulation by the twentieth century."[100] Under the supervision of Ottawa homeowners, with a highly controlled work environment that encroached on free time, these Native women would ideally be kept away from any men at all.

In another case, the department investigated the intended marriage of Helen, a twenty-six-year-old of "excellent moral character" who worked in Ottawa as a domestic through the placement program, to Jack, a Native private in the Royal Canadian Army Service Corps at Borden, Ontario. Before the wedding, Jack's commanding officer contacted Morris for a character reference for Helen. In turn, Morris decided that he would obtain information regarding Jack's character and family. It turned out that Jack had a police record, had been incarcerated twice, fined twice, and had a suspended sentence for several offences, including theft and driving without a chauffeur's license. Hoey wrote to Helen's former principal and told him of the record, urging that "every effort [be] made to persuade her to give up any thought of marrying him." Hoey repeated the advice of a local mayor that if Helen "is a good Indian girl, under no circumstances should she marry [Jack]." He also asked the commanding officer not to approve the marriage at least until the fiancé had "over a period of time, prove[d] that he has mended his ways and that he intends to settle down." The local priest had contacted Helen's parents and requested the department send her home because they were quite distraught. Not wanting to "disrupt" Helen's work arrangement with the Petries, who objected to her leave, Hoey as usual sided with the employer and refused; he agreed, however, to send her home two weeks later. In the meantime, Jack's commanding officer advised the department that he had been "paraded before his Company Commander and states that...Helen is fully aware of his past police record and is quite willing to marry him in spite of the same." Also, he stated that "a year had passed since he had been found guilty of an offence, and that he has learned the error of his ways and intends to keep out of trouble in the future."[101] Indeed, in spite of the fact that the young women in the program had moved away from the closely regulated contexts of residential schools and reserves, bureaucratic interference in their personal lives continued.

Documentation of the "Ottawa Experiment" abruptly ceases after little more than two years into its operation, leaving readers with only fragmented stories told from one perspective. I have yet to find any other reference to this program, which suggests its marginal and temporary role in the lives of most of the participants as well as the employers. Yet the program can tell us much about gendered Indian policy and wage labour history in the early twentieth century. While most Native women entered into employment outside of federal surveillance like the program described here, and despite the apparent failure of this formal endeavour to place Native women as domestics, debate, interest, and programming initiatives on Native women's labour continued in the years after the war.

Conclusion

Requests to the DIA for domestics continued well past 1945 and into the 1960s as did efforts of the DIA to train and place First Nations domestics, many similar to the Ottawa Experiment. G.H. Gooderham, regional supervisor of Indian agencies, reported in August 1952 on an "employment plan for young Indian women coming to Calgary and Edmonton." He reported that there "had been only one recent instance where the Department is paying the bill for accommodation. In the other cases the girls have been placed the same day they com [sic] to town, or they have been in a position to pay their own expenses." He noted that the "Social Worker has encouraged them to do this as far as it seems reasonably possible. Nine girls were placed in employment within a period of three months, five of whom were placed through the [National] Employment Service and four through direct contact between the employer and this office." Gooderham also noted that the Camsell Hospital had been cooperating in employment placement. Still "three other girls" had asked for placement but were "discouraged from coming to town" because of a "previous poor work record" and a "tendency to promiscuity." "It is felt," he argued, "that an urban environment would be worse still for them." He also noted a few others who had come to cities to find employment on their own but had not made contact with the office or the social worker. He observed that "Domestic placements have proven successful usually, to the point even that they have led to enquiries from other prospective employers. The girls have been especially successful in caring for little children," a factor that "made their services quite valuable to the mothers." Interestingly, while the DIA had tried to find openings for ward aides and kitchen help in hospitals, they had had no success, but when the girls tried on their own, they were successful.[102] It is possible that hospitals and other employers preferred to avoid bureaucratic interference from the DIA; or that those successfully hired without DIA assistance were not identified as Indian.

A similar scheme in the mid-1960s involved a Mrs. Otter and A.J. Karch, who operated a domestic placement agency in Calgary.[103] Working on a part-time basis for the DIA, Mrs. Victoria Otter was "to maintain liaison with the placement candidates that are presently working and established in Calgary...[and] to provide emergency assistance in Calgary other than cash, for candidates that find employment through their own efforts, but require limited assistance in order to become established. It is not anticipated that many individuals will require this assistance."[104] In 1964, "54 Indian girls from southern Alberta were placed in Calgary homes as domestics, babysitters and housekeepers." Women were placed into service for a period ranging from a few days to over a year, and it was reported that "[i]n some cases the girls have gone on to other jobs or training possibilities, but have remained to board with the family." It was observed that "Domestic work for many girls is a useful 'first step' to the broader experience of living and working in today's changing society. Non-Indian families and neighbours develop a deeper appreciation, and understanding of Indian young people; the girls, in turn, obtain first-hand living and working experience with a family which will prove invaluable in years to come."[105]

In Saskatchewan in 1960–1, the Indian and Metis Service Council wished to meet with regional supervisors to discuss the possibility of training "suitable selected Indian girls as housekeepers" in Prince Albert for placement in training-on-the-job contracts funded on a fifty-fifty basis by the DIA or possibly as a co-op type of placement with half-time work for a "personal allowance," and part-time formal vocational instruction. This particular program was designed to operate closely with appointed members of the Indian and Metis Service Council and the Business and Professional Women's Association of Prince Albert, which was interested in sponsoring on-the-job training. As a result of a general disappointment in this area of job placement on the part of the DIA, already noted in 1960 on a national level, there was some lack of enthusiasm on the part of the Saskatchewan regional supervisor of Indian Affairs, N.J. McLeod. In a letter about the proposal, he outlined the reasons for the limited success of domestic employment placement among Aboriginal women. First, he said, there were the limited income, low social status, and uncertain working conditions that made the work particularly unattractive. He wrote, "in most cases girls have entered this work because of lack of education and work skills required for more remunerative employment, rather than by choice. In many cases they see it as a ready resource for short-term employment, or as a stepping stone to some other type of work." Second, there had to date been some home economics education provided in the schools; however, no job-focussed training program existed. Third, he also noted that there was "limited assessment of the home situation by the N.E.S. [National Employment Service] or [the] Branch prior to placement as in most cases the requests for domestics have been received by N.E.S. by telephone." The regional supervisor's opinion was typical in that it did not reject domestic placement altogether, instead stressing the many "positives" of domestic work—namely, its general accessibility to those with minimal education, its service as an "introduction to the non-Indian community" and the "opportunity" it afforded to "learn something of running a home off the reserve." Moreover, he stated, this serves "as a preparation for marriage; and ... a measure of supervision, providing the employer is capable and prepared to offer this." He was ultimately in favour of this program as he saw the Indian and Metis Service Council playing "a vital role ... [by providing] supervision and counseling" and the program was set to operate under "as much local control and guidance as possible."[106]

The DIA also demonstrated continued interested in developing the training aspect of domestic job placement, especially as it moved out of residential school education. Day schools were often equipped with equipment for domestic training and a continued emphasis was placed on domestic education in Indian education curricula for girls. The DIA also developed ad hoc training programs outside of schools. For example, the regional supervisory to the District of Mackenzie reported on a twelve-month domestic training-on-the-job program of the Department of Northern Affairs in 1961. That program trained a total of sixteen girls (nine Indian, four Eskimo, and two non-Indian), five of whom completed the program. In the scheme, "The trainee received $25.00 per month for the first six months and the employer received $50.00 per month for the same period, paid by the Department of Northern Affairs." The failure of this program was attributed to insufficient selection of trainees and employers, no supervision during the training, no syllabus for training (leading to "excessive amounts of routine housework and drudgery"), lack of interest on the part of both trainee and employer, "the pull of home/family," and lack of social contacts. "Under the best of circumstances," one official wrote, "domestic training and employment seems to interest only a small percentage of girls." He continues, "However, the educational value and experience acquired should have some weight. Girls with domestic experience usually gravitate to related work, which has more appeal i.e. in restaurants and institutions, etc. as waitresses, maids and kitchen help."[107]

Overseeing the relocation and labour of those seeking work through a program or on their own fell within the duties of the department's social workers by the 1950s. New to the department in the postwar years, social workers were especially responsible not only for encouraging work placement but for ensuring that Native people spent their leisure time in responsible ways, away from "danger spots."[108] There were fewer than ten social workers for the entire country, so their surveillance was fairly targeted and dependent upon their connections with local religious and civic organizations. Nurses, too, through Indian Health Services, continued to be active in projects involving the placement of Indian domestics in hospitals, nursing stations, and clinics.

By the late 1950s, the placement officer joined the social worker in the state's broad efforts of surveillance and regulation of Native labour. Indian Affairs placement officers worked with the NES to place Aboriginal women in domestic service positions in private homes, homes of chronically ill people, nursing homes, and hospitals. Placements as domestics in this new program were very common, even though they were seen as "casual" placements, as opposed to permanent positions involving vocational training and relocation, which was the program's original vision. It is this formal Placement and Relocation Program to which we now turn.

CHAPTER TWO

The Permanent Solution:
The Placement and Relocation Program, Hairdressers, and Beauty Culture

"Well adjusted and suited for her position," "neat and very presentable," "eager to learn and become self-supporting," "employer pleased," "very satisfactory"[1]—these are some of the comments in the "social" and "vocational" adjustment section of the case file of a hairdresser in the Indian Placement and Relocation Program.[2] Begun in 1957 and run by the Department of Indian Affairs, this program embodied the contemporary conviction that permanent employment would facilitate Indian integration into—and thus also equality within—Canadian society. The Placement and Relocation Program was not exclusively for women, or for hairdressers; rather, program officers counselled young Indigenous adults into a range of different types of work. Hairdressers, however, provide a fascinating and illuminating lens through which to understand how gender was implicated in Indian policy in the mid-twentieth century. In this context, hairdressers were celebrated as symbols of successful assimilation and, it was hoped, permanent relocation off-reserve. While it was not a lucrative occupation for most women, a career in hairdressing did offer significant opportunities for independence and mobility. Additionally, hairdressers were an integral part of an expanding, modern, urban beauty culture, and thus also actively shaped, reflected, and even resisted images of women in the era. In this chapter, I use hairdressing as a way to talk about labour and the politics of the state on the one hand and modern Indigenous beauty culture on the other. In particular, I focus on efforts to regulate women's labour in federal Indian policy-making and also raise themes of class, entrepreneurship, identity, and beauty culture in the Indian postwar years.

The evidence for this chapter is drawn largely from the records of the Department of Indian Affairs. The department and its officers kept placement files and compiled information about the Placement and Relocation Program, including lists of students taking vocational training, inventories of Indian labour, and program evaluations. But these sources did not analyze specific post-secondary education programs or gender-specific experiences; different placement officers logged different kinds of details about placement candidates, despite their standardized forms; and they provide only basic details about a candidate at one point in time. Together with other placement records, personal recollections, and audio-visual and print media from the era, however, these sources provide a glimpse into a common but relatively hidden experience of Indigenous women in twentieth-century Canada.

The Indian Placement and Relocation Program

Initiating the Program

Unlike the Ottawa Experiment and other, earlier placement programs implemented in a local, more ad hoc manner, the Indian Placement and Relocation Program was the first organized national labour program and it sought to place First Nations people in permanent positions in urban areas. Until then, Indian Affairs had provided some employment assistance, but only to those who lived on reserves and continued a traditional "Indian mode of living." Furthermore, that assistance focussed on short-term, seasonal employment such as agricultural and domestic work, reserve roadwork and construction and resource-based labour, and a few federal service positions. As we saw with the department's efforts to train and place ward and nurse's aides and domestics, the objectives of employment assistance were to feed First Nations labour into Indian Affairs' infrastructure at the lowest levels, reinforce federal Indian services, and manage periodic and seasonal unemployment. Some of the larger-scale, project-based, and seasonal employment projects included sugar-beet farming, radar line construction, labour associated with surveying, clearing bush roads and sites for mining operations, firefighting, railway right-of-way maintenance and bridge repair, commercial fishing operations, iron-ore processing, berry and potato harvesting, logging, mining, canning, and hops and tobacco picking. Placement was mostly done locally by Indian agents and regional supervisors, but it was also managed by Indian Health Services, missionary, and school staff; it was not, however, part of their official responsibilities and depended on the initiative of local staff and available opportunities in the area.[3] The Indian Placement and Relocation Program was thus indicative of a more substantial interest on the part of Indian Affairs in a more formal program of First Nations training and employment.[4]

While the Placement and Relocation Program was the first official program of the Department of Indian Affairs to encourage urban employment, it operated in similar ways and with similar objectives and underlying ideologies as contemporary urban relocation schemes in other white settler colonial contexts globally. For example, in the United States, a large Relocation Services Program initiated by the Bureau of Indian Affairs (BIA) in 1952 undertook four major kinds of activities: relocation to selected urban communities, adult vocational training, on-the-job training, and job placement.[5] By 1960, this program had provided services to an estimated 32,000 people, and material about the program was requested by and referred to by Canadian placement specialists. In Australia, the Aborigines Welfare Board in the 1960s targeted "worthy" Aboriginal families for relocation to urban areas, hoping that selected families would serve as models for others. The relocation of Māori became official New Zealand state policy in the 1960s, although movement to cities had already begun. The state encouraged rural families to relocate with urban accommodation, employment, and other general assistance. Such programs demonstrate the desire for highly regulated state-sponsored systems that could contain the movement of Indigenous populations and manage Indigenous labour to suit the demands of the modern nation state.

In Canada, the early Indian Placement and Relocation Program was influenced by the existing National Employment Service (NES) and was carefully shaped in such a way as to not encroach upon its activities.[6] The NES had been initiated in the context of an increased federal interest in organizing a comprehensive plan to address a perceived crisis in manpower during the Second World War; it replaced a federally managed employment service set up in 1919. The scope and powers of the NES were derived from the Wartime Registration Program, part of the War Measures Act, which made mandatory registration a condition of access to unemployment relief. Resistance to registration came from many parties, including First Nations labour. In 1941, the NES became affiliated with the Unemployment Insurance Commission and until 1966 (when it moved to the Department of Citizenship and Immigration, later Manpower and Immigration) was governed under the same branch of the Department of Labour. The goal of the service was to match unemployed workers with unfilled job vacancies via employment centres. According to Canadian historian Jennifer Stephen, the

NES channelled Canadian workers "through a complex process of personnel assessment, training, and deployment to areas where they were needed most: staffing the machinery of war, and then rebuilding for the peace."[7] By 1942, the NES directed special efforts to attracting women into war industries; it was reshaped after the war to usher them out of employment or into highly specialized—often also highly feminized—employment sectors.

The NES never fully committed to serving Indigenous labour. When the Indian Placement and Relocation Program was created as an independent program of Indian Affairs, it used the "Special Services" Branch of the NES. This branch administered groups not then served by mainstream NES programs—including young adults, disabled people, and women—through the work of "Special Placement Officers."[8] First Nations workers in the Indian Placement and Relocation Program would be referred to the NES by its own placement officers only if the special placement officer indicated that there was a reasonable prospect of employment within two weeks of the candidate's first reporting to their office. All other Indigenous people who approached the NES were served on the same basis as other applicants in similar categories. This system was not regarded as effective for Aboriginal clients. For example, Mr. Frank Howard of the Skeena riding of British Columbia documented his concerns about the NES in the House of Commons in 1959. In his view, it did not seem

> to operate too effectively when it comes to attempting to provide employment for Native Indian people. The attitude of some of the officials—I would not say a great number of them—in the N.E.S. offices that I have spoken of appear to look upon the Indian as being outside their jurisdiction and they do not give the Indian the consideration that should be given to that person in seeking employment. … I do not think the fullest possible consideration is being given by the N.E.S. officials in attempting to find employment for native Indian people.[9]

So, while the DIA was careful that its Placement and Relocation Program did not encroach on the services of the NES, the NES did not necessarily see its services as extending to First Nations anyway. Howard suggested that this was not a "matter of conscious discrimination," but rather of "our whole attitude toward Indians in that they may not even come to the N.E.S. offices as much as would non-Indian persons." In part, the Placement and Relocation Program was needed because the NES did not apply itself to Indigenous clients.

In discussions about the Placement and Relocation Program prior to its initiation, it was linked to placement operations for immigrants, or "New Canadians," suggesting that histories of the management of Indigenous and immigrant labour by the state intersected in important ways in the postwar era. While there was marked competition between immigrant and Indian labour, especially for preference in larger construction and agricultural labour contracts, placement operations were linked. In 1950, the federal government combined its management of immigration and Indian Affairs under a new federal department, the Department of Citizenship and Immigration.[10] Prior to the Indian Placement and Relocation Program, a separate service provided by the Canadian Immigration Branch of Citizenship and Immigration was established to deal with distinct issues arising for immigrants to Canada. At the time, the Immigration Branch employed officers responsible for placing immigrants in "suitable employment," maintaining relations with employers and social agencies, and compiling an index of employment opportunities.[11] Indian Affairs Branch staff met with Immigration Branch staff to discuss their experience with placement services and to ask for assistance to develop its placement program.[12] This may have strongly influenced the nature of the early program. For example, it appears that the earliest Indian Placement and Relocation forms were very similar to those used in the Immigration Branch. Moreover, pamphlets such as *Basic Information on Canada* by the Immigration Branch were made available to and ultimately distributed by officers of the Indian placement program.[13] In a study of the early Placement and Relocation Program, Delaware masters in social work student and Indian Affairs employee Carl Latham noted that "almost all of the organizations with which [Indian] placement candidates were employed hired immigrants."[14] The overlap led some to question whether Indians actually had sufficiently different needs from those of new immigrants to necessitate the establishment of a distinct service, warning that this could act as a barrier to Indian integration.[15]

Finally, the Placement and Relocation Program took its cue in many ways from rehabilitation programs connected with tuberculosis sanatoria.[16] Linked to a postwar interest in people living with disabilities as a potential source of manpower, rehabilitation joined case finding,[17] isolation, rest, surgery, and chemotherapy as accepted treatments for tuberculosis. Some of the larger hospitals under the jurisdiction of the Indian Health Services branch of the Department of National Health and Welfare offered rehabilitation programs to young, single adults. As part of these programs, recovered patients could, with adequate rest periods, continue or commence vocational programs

Figure 2.1. John Tanche (here with wife Denise) undertook barber training while at the Charles Camsell Hospital in Edmonton, Alberta. Rehabilitation programs at TB hospitals influenced the development of the Placement and Rehabilitation Program. Library and Archives Canada, E011052427.

like watch repair, upholstery, carpentry and cabinet-making, barbering, and commercial courses for men, and Practical Nurse and Nurse Assistant, stenography, and hairdressing courses for women. The programs also provided vocational and social counselling and, in some cases, placement services.

A 1961 article in the *Indian News* about a couple from the Mackenzie River district in the Northwest Territories who participated in the rehabilitation program at Charles Camsell Indian Hospital in Edmonton, Alberta, is revealing of the gendered and racialized aspects of living and working in mid-twentieth-century urban Canada. After his bout with TB, John Tanche trained as a barber at Camsell. He initially found a position with an Edmonton barber, and then rented his own shop after only six months. His wife, Denise—who had been disenfranchised as a status Indian when her mother married a non-Indian but regained status when she married John—helped with the shop, the bookkeeping, and the banking while also doing some of the barbering on the side.[18] Records from the Camsell program show that women's programming focussed on homemaking skills, including budgeting and banking, however, these skills may also have been taught in the men's program.

Rehabilitation programs at Indian tuberculosis hospitals like Camsell indicate the federal government's increased interest in Indigenous employment, and the economic success of such programs justified the funding of later programming. For example, the Sanatorium Board of Manitoba conducted a study in the early 1960s that tracked rehabilitants' employment rates and paid income tax to show how Indian rehabilitation, normally framed as philanthropy, was a sound investment.[19] The rehabilitation programs also gave the federal government some experience in modern urban Indian labour management; approximately 125 young people had been placed in employment and training through the Charles Camsell Rehabilitation Program by the time the Indian Placement and Relocation Program was launched.[20] Rehabilitation programs are also rhetorically linked to the Placement and Relocation program by their shared enthusiasm for "self-sufficiency," emphasis on "social adjustment" and "transition," and insistence on the need for special assistance and surveillance of Indian rehabilitants, who, it was presumed, could not cope in urban settings.

Indeed, the Indian Placement and Relocation Program was shaped and initiated in a context of racialized employment programming, from similar colonial policies elsewhere targeted at Indigenous people, to the nature of Canada's National Employment Services and the distinct services seeking to place immigrants in "suitable" jobs. The Placement and Relocation Program was initiated to address government concerns about employment issues and Aboriginal people specifically, and so examining program materials can help to explain the federal view of Indian labour in the postwar years—a view that has, in an enduring way, informed Indian policy as well as the historical narratives of Aboriginal people in the modern era.

Framing the Program

There did not appear to be a single cohesive and longstanding vision for the Indian Placement and Relocation Program, perhaps in part because it drew from and was rooted in such various employment schemes and different government departments. However, it was framed by three oft-repeated, circular, and interconnected narratives about Indigenous modernity. One narrative was about failing "traditional" Indian economies in the face of industrial capitalism and the imposition this made on Canadian taxpayers. Another held that for Indigenous people, equality in Canadian society would follow full-time permanent employment. Finally, the Indian Placement and

Relocation Program was framed by a narrative that Indigenous people had vastly improved levels of education and training and were thus "prepared" for employment and equality.

The placement program was almost always introduced by way of a romantic and nostalgic gesture to an unspecific yet vaguely ethnographic and unambiguously masculine past unreached by modern life, a time when Indians were happy and healthy, rode horses, knew forests and streams, practised traditions, made crafts, were proficient hunters, and presided over small populations with lots of land. This mystery history is then interrupted by the jarring modern racket of airplanes, bulldozers, and cars.[21] The associated economic argument was that the Indian needed to be awoken from outdated economies that were too concentrated on hunting, trapping, fishing, and farming. In the view of the federal government, these economies afforded only "declining opportunities for employment" and were "incapable of expansion," "subject to fluctuations in the economy," and "intermittent in nature."[22] The state's role was to help people transition to an industrial economy so that they would not be left behind, not only materially in terms of living conditions, but also in terms of human progress and evolution. Compounding this issue was the concern that the population of Indigenous people was "no longer vanishing," but instead was growing faster than "traditional means of livelihood" were ever capable of sustaining.[23] To the federal government, a declining economy and an expanding population signalled only one possible outcome—poverty, dependence and burden.

To the Department of Indian Affairs, Canadian wealth and Indigenous poverty were distinct and developed independently. Thus, while the wealth Canada has derived from its appropriation of Indigenous lands and resources far exceeds the wealth it derives from taxation, Indian policy has consistently responded to the premise that First Nations are an unfair "burden" upon Canadian taxpayers. This has justified minimal funding and lower standards of services to Indigenous people than to other Canadians. When it was introduced by a Conservative federal government, the Indian Placement and Relocation Program came with the promise that funding would be small and well-managed and also a sound fiscal investment. Funds for the Placement and Relocation Program were approved by the treasury board and funnelled through the program to individual placement officers in cities across Canada who then processed DIA loans to candidates under closely monitored conditions.[24] Such spending was justified, Superintendent General of Indian Affairs J.W. Pickersgill explained in a 1956 issue of the *Indian News*, "unless [Canadians] are prepared to let these Indians become mere pensioners of the

Government."[25] A placement officer in northern Ontario explained in the early 1960s that each Indian cost Canadian taxpayers $240 annually over and above the benefits available to all people of Canada. Therefore, he argued, it was "economically sound to help [Indians] into regular employment and to become independent." In his estimate, the cost of establishing Native people in permanent employment averaged from $125 or $500 for families.[26] One program publication reported that "the costs of establishing young people under the Placement Program are not great.... As against this expenditure, the annual income of the 100 or more established here since 1959 is over $250,000, and the revenue paid to the Government in income tax following establishment totals over $50,000. It is obvious from these figures that the program pays for itself, and contributes significantly to the gross national product."[27] But, of course, the program did not actually "pay for itself" in income tax, rather, the Placement and Relocation Program was bought and paid for by Indians themselves. Candidates were just as often not funded, and when they were, it was by loans that were to be repaid in full. A study of thirty candidates placed in Toronto between 1957 and 1961 found that nearly half of the respondents relocated without any financial assistance from Indian Affairs (using their personal savings or support from their immediate family), and that standard loans amounted to between $40 and $50, "or enough to pay for two weeks room and board and other incidental expenses."[28]

It is significant that while the department recognized that the economies of many reserves could not sustain First Nations people adequately,[29] its response was not to re-examine treaties or redistribute national wealth, but to resettle some First Nations in urban centres. Closely associated with this, but very rarely explicitly stated, was the goal to close reserves and ultimately terminate Aboriginal title. Historian Donald Fixico has shown that in the United States urban relocation was a key instrument of federal termination policy. Because the relocation process involved freeing tribal groups from federal trust restrictions, vacated Indian territories could readily be sold on the free market.[30] In Canada, the Placement and Relocation Program was rhetorically connected to the department's long-term policy of enfranchisement—which was Canada's version of termination policy. According to the Indian Act, in order to become voting Canadian citizens, Indians had to renounce status and band membership and land and in return draw a per capita share of band funds and property. While the policy of enfranchisement was nominally voluntary for all men and only single women, clauses in the Indian Act allowed for the involuntarily enfranchisement of individuals when Indian Affairs determined it was in their best interest and of First

Nations women who married enfranchised, non-status, or non-Indian men. With the exception of clauses involuntarily enfranchising First Nations women, which lasted until 1985, enfranchisement policy was in place until 1960, when First Nations people could first vote in federal elections without sacrificing their legal status as Indians. Until this time, in the rhetoric of the program, permanent employment placement was directly associated with enfranchisement. In the words of Pickersgill, the Placement and Relocation Program would help Indians "prepare themselves for enfranchisement so that, when they are enfranchised and on their own, they will be able to hold their own on reasonably equal terms with other Canadians.[31] It is significant that Placement and Relocation Program application forms included space for questions about the future use of and probable income from applicants' on-reserve property and personal effects. This section of the form was explained by the chief of the Welfare Division in 1958; while the placement officer was to record the value of property held, "there is no thought that he should influence the candidate toward the sale of personal property on the reserve…if the man's livelihood has been dependent on these resources. Their sale should only follow establishment in the new location."[32] This popular contemporary language is indicative of both the goals of enfranchisement and faith in the open market ("our economy") to make those goals a reality. One author looking at a similar labour program in the U.S. concluded that, ironically, such programs expanded rather than eliminated federal services to Indians, bringing the state into the fields of public housing, adult education programs, and urban Indian centres, each of which contributed in part to the growth of self-determination movements.[33] This is also true of the Canadian context, in spite of a spate of illogical, mean-spirited, and sometimes esoteric policies that aimed to curtail services for some First Nations people. For example, candidates were informed that they were able to access rights and services as Indians only until they were employed. Thereafter, they would be officially ineligible for federal services, and any claims on the state would be void. A 1963 policy, for instance, outlined that Indian and Northern Health Services would provide dental care for those cases "where the facial appearance of the candidate is a critical factor in placement"; those training in the specific fields of mechanics, plumbing, and welding were ineligible, and those who had already been placed were to be referred to private dentists whose services would be repaid by the individual.[34] In spite of highly specific policies about services, there remained fundamental confusion about basic issues such as the payment of provincial sales tax on expenditures related to relocating off-reserve. Chief of the Economic Development Division, R.F.

Battle, confirmed in 1961 that "the individual is responsible to pay provincial sales tax on articles purchased, particularly as he is a resident of the non-Indian community."[35] However, some Treaty First Nations people insisted that no matter where they purchased and used goods they should remain exempt from being taxed.

Nothing in the Indian Act compelled individuals to participate in the Placement and Relocation Program, and voluntary participation was one of the program's three general principles. Yet survey materials of the program show that most candidates were approached by Indian agents and program officers, some of whom were quite persistent in their efforts.[36] One candidate recalled, "I did not want to leave the reserve but they would not leave me alone so I agreed to come to Toronto," and another stated that the "Placement Officer talked to my parents three or four times before I met him."[37] At the same time, many more did desire increased mobility and the opportunity to access education and employment, "see the world," and "get away." For this reason, the program was also "selective," meaning that it was not meant for all or even the majority of Native people. Its third guideline, however, that it was "comprehensive," suggests that for those who did participate, the program was meant to be permanent in all ways. A proposed full program of testing, funding, and vocational training followed by supervision of job performance and counselling in budgeting, deportment, punctuality, and healthy recreational activities indicated the department's commitment to success.[38] John Borrow's essay on physical and philosophical mobility helps to contextualize these principles in terms of broader regimes of the nation-state. He argues that mobility—specifically, being too mobile or not mobile enough—has been used to undermine Indigenous peoples' rights. In this case, the program clearly saw relocation as far more than simply physical movement through space, something Indigenous people have always done—it was paired with the permanent severing of people from lands and communities.[39]

The program thus identified the "problem" in failing economies and growing populations, and the "burden" this would cause to taxpayers, and located a solution in the full integration of First Nations into the Canadian economy, population, and tax base. This solution would also, it was argued, allow First Nations to pursue an equal standing with others in Canada, which was measured mostly in terms of a vaguely defined "standard of living." Those who wrote about the program argued that improved basic education had already enabled many First Nations students to advance to academic and vocational post-secondary institutions. Desegregation of schools was seen to have had a central role in this shift. While it was indeed an important indicator of changing attitudes among many Canadians, desegregation was not part of a movement to address widespread racism and inequality in Canadian schools, cities, and workplaces at the time. Instead, to the department, desegregation of schooling in the postwar years was evidence that First Nations could, given the opportunity, fit in with non–First Nations and that they were prepared to "compete" with non-Indians.[40] The argument followed that equality for Native people would and could only result from (and not precede) education and full-time employment. According to the Superintendent General, "useful and gainful employment" as well as "incentive to work regularly and continuously when work is available"[41] would improve the overall standard of living of Indians. But not just any kind of work would bring about this end result. Examples of full-time jobs that "suited" Indians included: motor and diesel mechanic, clerical and stenographic work, appliance repair, barbering and hairdressing, accountancy, building trades, machine shop, drafting, welding, radio operator, nursing assistant, electrical technicians, carpentry, cabinet work, welder, store clerk, utility man, labourer, industrial plastics, and warehouse man.[42] These occupations demanded training in modern technical skills and were highly specialized. At the same time, they did not require a university education and were not well remunerated.

The idea was that, through permanent full-time employment, Indians would take a place in a labouring citizenry and serve the state, the city, and industry. The goal was not exactly to create a working-class culture (not of its own making), but rather to integrate a class of working Indians into an idealized working-class culture of the department's imagination.[43] In this vision of the program, Native peoples' place within cities was as wage workers only, benefiting others who lived in cities by social, cultural, and economic conversion to a capitalist, industrial, modern society—or, in the department's terms, "adjusting" to the "new" world around them. To those running the program, successful permanent placement meant assimilation and invisibility in the urban community. The discourse on employment in this program was one of "bridging" two worlds, of taking one's "rightful place" "side-by-side" with non-Indians in a world that was defined as non-Indian. In his book *"Enough to Keep Them Alive": Indian Social Welfare in Canada, 1873–1965*, Hugh Shewell shows that this approach conveniently disengages with the history of Indian-European encounter and the process by which Western liberal capitalism and ideology became hegemonic in North America.[44] Likewise, the vision framing the Placement and Relocation Program was that full appreciation of the open, free market coupled with the adoption of a work ethic thought to be foreign to Indian people would lead to equality for Aboriginal people in Canada.[45] In the literature about the Placement and Relocation Program, references to Indian workers presumed they were all men. Women workers were discussed as a distinct group—as the exceptional or special cases. And, in reality, women had labour opportunities that *were* distinct. For example, in the late 1950s and 1960s, it was expected that women had a more temporary attachment to the labour force than men because of the demands of marriage and children. Moreover, because of widespread discrimination in the workplace, women were paid less and had fewer opportunities for advancement than did men. Nonetheless, the program had vocational placements, including clerical work and hairdressing, that were exclusively for women, and so it is frustrating that placement officers and others involved with this program for the most part avoided these realities and failed to address them in a meaningful way. This suggests the extent to which the program was invested and imbedded in the dominant patriarchal culture.

The Placement and Relocation Program was seen to be a sound investment, with its plan to relocate and enfranchise First Nations people, thus reducing government funding for reserves and adding to the Canadian tax base. In addition, employment training and placement was seen to provide necessary skills for Indigenous people to integrate into the Canadian citizenry. In its economic and social goals, the Placement and Relocation Program focussed on the working First Nations male citizen as a "good investment" for the future. Why were women not similarly targeted? Perhaps this was because First Nations women's social and economic position was inherently linked to men's; it was also easier to enfranchise women in other ways, such as through marriage to non-Indian and non-status men. In addition, in a number of different ways that will become clear, the department viewed and treated First Nations women differently than they did men; women were more closely monitored and judged on the one hand and yet received far less support on the other.

The Program at Work

The Placement and Relocation Program records are, in one respect, a window into federal Indian employment policy as it was implemented at the local level and seen through the eyes of a federal civil servant: the placement officer. The deadline for applications for the job of Placement Officer[46] for the DIA was 13 September 1956. According to the job posting, candidates for the position were to be university graduates (preferably with social science training[47]), experienced in placement work (including the preparation and interpretation of case files), and knowledgeable of apprenticeship systems, vocational programs, and social service work. They were to have "initiative; good judgment; satisfactory physical condition," and they also had to be personable and suited to the work. Officers were paid an annual salary of between $5,280 and $6,000 and were hired according to the "Order of Merit subject to Veterans' Preference," which gave priority to civil service applicants who had served in the military.[48] Initially, four officers were hired: Mr. John Rayson (Winnipeg), Mr. J.J. Fransen (southern Ontario), Mr. J.D. Addison (British Columbia), and Mr. R.N. Sutherland (Alberta), and they worked out of downtown offices in Toronto, Winnipeg, Vancouver, and Edmonton. There were placement officers in eight other regions across the country by 1960, and there were seventeen in 1964, with three additional appointments expected.[49]

Placement officers were the front-line workers for the program, and their job was to recruit and select candidates, determine the type and extent of assistance required, develop employment opportunities, and collect data on job vacancies, vocational programs, and housing. They were responsible to a range of other DIA officers, including regional placement supervisors, the superintendent of welfare, and the superintendent general, and also liaised with other federal, provincial, and municipal authorities, private agencies, trade unions, educational and training facilities, landladies, community organizations, and, of course, employers. Victoria Haskins's recent scholarship on the U.S. Bureau of Indian Affairs' "outing matrons," who placed Indigenous women in domestic labour, is an important reminder that in many ways, placement work involved monitoring and containing the presence of Indigenous people and patrolling and negotiating cross-cultural relationships. As agents of state surveillance and control, placement officers were involved in organizing and administering national policy in such a way as to produce a society "in which the various unruly individuals and affiliations were reconstituted as distinct and hierarchically organized groups who each knew their 'place' in relation to each other and to/within the nation state."[50] Such work upheld a racial hierarchy that separated First Nations from non–First Nations people while shaping interaction in such a way as to facilitate the DIA's policy of integration.

Placement officers differed substantially from the outing matrons and other employment agents of the earlier twentieth century in that they were all men, and all members of a distinctly "modern" profession—the employment counsellor. Vocational and employment counselling as a profession had grown substantially by the late 1950s, nurtured by wartime and postwar government-sponsored mobilization and demobilization efforts, some service development by social agencies such as the YW/YMCA, increased support for vocational education (and a baby-boom population set to take advantage of it), and, of course, the growth and professionalization of the fields of social work and psychology, especially "applied psychology."[51] Placement work initially involved "matching" workers with jobs, but by the late 1950s, increasing consideration was given also to workers' preference, motivation, and individual assessment by a counsellor. For officers of the Placement and Relocation Program, this work was largely pre-empted by a prevailing ethnographic discourse that presumed Indians had no motivation to work at all. According to popular views, Indians were not inclined to work regularly and continuously and "cannot see much sense in going on working to earn extra money after their ordinary needs and wants have been met"[52] (an ethic which inevitably led them to poverty and dependence on the federal government). In addition, Indians lacked an understanding of "basic conventions" such as "the need for promptness and regular attendance."[53] Indeed, Indians presented a distinct placement problem—by nature, they were unplaceable. Thus placement officers' work involved the careful selection of individuals who appeared not to have these characteristics and counselling First Nations people to become particular kinds of citizens who suited the perceived economic, social, and cultural imperatives of Canada's urban labour market and social sphere—happy, grateful workers who were self-supporting and planned for the future.

In addition to selecting and preparing Indians for employment, the placement officer's other major role was the positive representation of Indian labour to prospective employers and others. They needed to instil in urban employers and others a desire to hire and accept Indigenous people. Placement officers saw their work as helping Indians and employers to "understand" one another and overcome their overwhelming differences. They had their work cut out for them. A 1960s study of urban Native labour found that "Indian labour is often considered unacceptable by employers on the grounds of irresponsibility and lack of dependability." Moreover, it found that "in the literature to interpret the situation of Indians to the general public the following expressions appear: unreliability which is reflected in lateness and absenteeism; carelessness in the use of property and in personal appearance; lack of job skills and work habits; a low threshold to tolerate routine and frustration; lack of drive, initiative and imagination; laziness; arrogance; unpredictability; indolence; inertia; sullenness; dully; apathy; unresponsiveness; improvidence; dirty; and, abuse of alcohol."[54] Importantly, prejudice was acknowledged, but only in that it created even more trouble for cities. "Too many have tried and found it difficult," one federal booklet suggested, "due to their differences and to prejudice against them on the part of employers, to find suitable employment. Unfortunately there has been a general lack of interest in the Indians on the part of the better class of community residents, with the result that Indians have often found that only in slum areas were they accepted for companionship and living accommodation, and the type of employment offered to them was most unattractive."[55] In response to this dilemma, the placement program meant to "provide for a more orderly movement to urban centres," so that the Indians concerned "are equipped to obtain employment and meet the problems of modern day living."[56] "The move from reserve to city presents problems," argued the department, "particularly because these young people are also moving from one culture to another."[57] Much effort was put into bridging the so-called "unstructured reserve" and the "demanding environment of the world of work."[58] Volumes were written about how to facilitate the all-important task of "social adjustment," including appropriate accommodation, activities, and supervision. Significantly, all adjustments needing to be made were to be made by Aboriginal people. Changing the perceptions of employers, landladies, and others was held out occasionally as an ideal; however, their prejudices were much less commonly identified because similar perceptions were embedded in department policy and program initiatives.

Candidates for the program were not to be relocated unless early placement was likely, and so there was a "very careful" screening process.[59] Officially, only those candidates who had an academic standing of grade eight were to be accepted, however, applicants with less education were also accepted. Candidates were ideally single, over the age of sixteen, and preferably recent graduates. Consideration was given to "young couples with small families but only when the likelihood of adjustment [was] good."[60] The ideal applicant for the Indian Placement and Relocation Program was a single man (without dependants was assumed), but many families and many single women, some with children, were placed as well. Gender was not a declared factor in the screening process; however, there were two or three times as many men as women in the program, a trend that was especially noticeable in northern areas.[61] The program favoured candidates from southern parts of the provinces, where it was assumed that "the higher educational levels, and vocational competency and longer period of association with non-Indian communities"[62] made them more suitable for permanent work. Candidates from other areas were welcome to apply, but it was assumed that they would require additional "academic upgrading and social orientation followed by vocational courses or on-the-job training to prepare them for employment."[63]

Candidates for the program came to the attention of placement officers via individual requests for assistance from First Nations people themselves and referrals from Indian agency staff and the staff of educational institutions in which Native people were enrolled.[64] Applicants had to be in good health and provide evidence of it with a recent medical examination and, if possible, a chest X-ray. Additionally, it was an official condition that the family and band council of the applicant were in favour of the candidate's relocation (although it did not occur to some applicants to consult, especially with band councils). Where possible, the applicant was to provide an employment history to ascertain the likelihood of securing employment in an urban centre. Applicants also had to detail "attitudes, interests, reasons for entering the city and personality factors which may influence adjustment to the city."[65] Above all, successful candidates possessed "the following; the necessary motivation, the ability to grasp what is required on the job and in the community, work skills or the potential to develop these, and the stability necessary to cope with the pressures and anxieties involved in working and living in the new environment."[66]

Narrative and statistical data about candidates can be found in case files maintained by placement officers. Contents of the case files include a number of forms addressing questions about the individual candidates, their background, and their experience of urban placement. The original IA 3-121, or the Placement Information Record, was the main form used by placement officers, and it reads somewhat like a mix between a resumé, a medical file, a loan application, and a school report card. It included sections for information about the applicant's name, band, band number, and address; date of birth, sex, height, and weight; and marital status, religion, and next of kin. Other sections of the form asked if the applicant was willing to leave the reserve for permanent employment and for a list of dependants prepared or not prepared to leave the reserve with the applicant. In another section, placement officers were to outline the number of years the candidate had completed at school, their command of English and French, the type of school they had attended (Indian day school, public school, Indian residential school, or other), any vocational school or special training he or she had obtained, and what training, if any, would be suitable for the candidate. Yet another section outlined their hobbies, leisure time activities, and involvement in organizations. The last section covered the placement candidate's employment history over the previous twelve months, including the nature of the work, approximate earnings, reasons for wishing to leave, and names and addresses of references. These forms were sometimes accompanied by a Superintendent's Report of the Placement Information Record, which assessed the applicant based on knowledge of the individual and personal interviews. This form included space for an assessment of family and band support for relocation, previous experience living away from the reserve, social problems that could have bearing on the placement, and "other social problems." Another section assessed the applicant's personality, habits, and character and their ability to adjust satisfactorily to a new environment. Space was also provided to evaluate the candidate's physical condition, plan for relocation, and expectations.

We can qualify the IA 3-121 forms as "case files," defined as "records generated by political, social, legal, and other institutions entrusted with the task of categorizing and assessing certain populations, usually for the purpose of supervising, treating, punishing, servicing, and/or reforming individuals or groups deemed in some way deviants or victims."[67] While the files are indicative of ways the Indian Affairs department measured the potential of candidates for the program, there are limits to the amount and type of information one can glean from them. This is because forms were mostly left blank. We are left to assume either that much of the decision-making was done according to the placement officer's sense of an individual applicant or that these questions did not really matter once an individual had chosen to take part in the program. Much more detail appears in evaluative notes regarding "social adjustment" after relocation and in formal correspondence between placement officers, regional supervisors, and Indian Affairs headquarters about "problem cases." These are filled with comments like "although... exceptionally neat, clean and presentable...proved unsatisfactory"; "needs some encouragement," "could speak well... [but] not too anxious to work and care for her child," "could be lonely," and "will only be a source of trouble if located in Winnipeg."[68] Other comments, such as "recently invited a girlfriend for a weekend to the parental home at Deseronto" and "does not reveal any Indian facial features and prefers not to associate with other Indians in the city," reflect an awareness of at least some of the ways that racism and race affected the experience of candidates and suggest that the Placement and Relocation Program was not simply about employment, but also about efforts to track and study the social aspects of urban migration.

A substantial bulk of placement files were IA 8-30 forms (Reports of Monthly Expenditure) and accounts of funds borrowed and repaid. The practice was to "estimate carefully with the candidate the costs of re-location, and to provide assistance which may be necessary to supplement the candidate's best efforts on his own behalf. Accurate records of all costs are kept and presented to the candidate following placement and initial adjustment. The placement officer then worked out with the candidate a reasonable arrangement for repayment in keeping with the individual's circumstances."[69] The records suggest that payroll deduction was not used at any point, but officers were encouraged to visit candidates on the days that they were issued paycheques. The emphasis on planning suggests that candidates and placement officers collaborated to create a plan and that there were clear and identified guidelines for loans and repayment when in fact this was not the case. It is evident from the correspondence that candidates did not know for sure how much or how little they would be able to borrow. Assistance to candidates initially covered transportation, accommodation, a subsistence allowance pending the receipt of wages, an allowance for clothing and uniforms, and funding for tuition and supplies.[70] One year into the program, however, the Indian Affairs Branch requested to allow loans for furniture and household effects so that placement candidates would not have to seek furnished accommodation in less desirable sections of town to avoid high rent.[71] The program was based on a loose policy of minimal loans for "basic items...essential to establishing a family in suitable housing." Furnishings were bought through Eaton's, where the department had a 10 percent discount. In some cases where families relocated, the program also facilitated the purchase of a house. Loans were drawn up based on placement records. The placement officer also developed an expenditure, repayment, and counselling plan based on the wages of the placement candidate.[72] In the Placement and Relocation Program, lien notes stated that until assistance was repaid, all "chattels"[73] belonged to Her Majesty the Queen in right of Canada and, if funds were misused, could be expropriated by the department, its officers, agents, or employees.[74] It was to be stressed to Eaton's, though, that purchases were made by the individual and not guaranteed by the department, and in at least one instance the whole purchasing and repayment plan involved not only the family and the placement officer but also the store manager.[75] Coinciding with this ambivalent shift towards increased access to relocation funds while the department aimed to decrease federal activities in the department more generally, the IA 3-121 form included a new section on "Property and Personal Effects" owned by the applicant. This section covered financial obligations to the department, the band, and "other," and listed assets available to establish the applicant from their own resources or those of the family, the band, and "other." It outlined the cost of relocation. The form also included sections on whether the individual was "genuinely interested in finding employment," any prior experience living away from the reserve, and any social or other problems. It asked for a general appraisal of the individual and/or family with detailed information about ability, personality, habits, and character. However, it appears that the department was, at least unofficially, not all that interested in the full repayment of loans. Placement officers recognized that successful candidates were paid very little and that this made repayment impractical and unrealistic.

In spite of the large pile of awkward, patronizing, and disturbing records, the Indian Placement and Relocation Program was not a highly centralized program with uniform policy initiatives, and, while recorded in standardized (but mostly blank) forms, the program took shape differently in different regions. In some areas, on-the-job training was particularly popular. In Edmonton and London, placement services were contracted out to municipal family service bureaus, which carried out counselling services to placement candidates, provided placement financial aid, and assisted with "urban social adjustment."[76] In Saskatchewan, the program rapidly became as much about accessing urban housing as it was about employment.[77] The Placement and Relocation Program is given virtually no currency in either Aboriginal or labour history, perhaps because its influence was relatively brief and highly individualized, and also perhaps because it was a special program related to the much larger National Employment Service, catered to a relatively small and specific workforce, was available to status Indians only, and was superseded by several larger federal and provincial employment initiatives in the late 1960s and 1970s.[78] At the same time, it appears that the program meant very little to the candidates themselves. A 1964 survey of 30 of the 191 Indians assisted in the placement program found that only half of those surveyed were contacted by the placement officer after they had secured employment, suggesting that, for many, the officer was relatively unimportant in their longer working lives. From his research on the program, Latham notes that several of the placement candidates he interviewed in the late 1950s were actually unaware that they were in the Indian Placement and Relocation Program. "It would seem that the name conveys little meaning to participants," Latham suggested, and participants "selected what was of interest to them, that is, how the program could help them."[79]

And indeed, despite all of the records the placement program left behind, the department's annual reports show that relatively few people were actually placed. In Manitoba in 1959, after a year of the program, thirty-one people had been accepted for placement; thirteen were placed and working, nine were in training, and nine had "failed to develop."[80] By 1961, a total of 627 young people had been brought into the program throughout Canada.[81] The main reason for the low numbers, according to the department, was that "the emphasis in this program continues to be placed on careful selection rather than on large numbers of placements."[82] The department argued that it was better for the program to operate "on the basis of quality rather than to undertake relocation of large numbers."[83] Until the late 1960s, these numbers remained low nationwide (there were 591 active placement candidates in urban centres in all of Canada in 1965[84]) despite the increasing numbers of Aboriginal people moving to the cities. By January 1958, for example, there were more Native people living in Winnipeg than on any single reserve in Manitoba.[85] We can assume that most people managed to avoid placement officers and their crews and found jobs on their own, through family and community connections, or directly through the NES. Reports, such as this one in the *Globe and Mail*, that the "teenage Indian no longer comes to Toronto on speculation hoping to find a job. He comes as part of a group to start a carefully planned program of study and job training"[86] were highly exaggerated. However small it was, the program was characteristic of the contemporary labour operations of the Welfare and Training and Economic Development branches of Indian Affairs. It also reflected the department's understanding of Indian labour and its interests in managing and directing the movement of Indigenous people in the postwar era. After all, urban migration involved assessing Indians for their "preparedness" for relocation, providing information that would motivate them to relocate, and developing a range of community services for them when they arrived.[87] The program also provides some insight into the contemporary discourses on Indians and cities in Canada, and more particularly on Aboriginal women, and urban, modern labour.

Imagery and Representations of Indigenous Urban Labour

It is worthwhile thinking about the ways in which cities and modern urban labour were seen to influence Indian experience in the twentieth century. In Canadian popular culture, an award-winning 1966 episode of the CBC drama series *Wojeck*, entitled "The Last Man in the World," featured an Indian placement program and the effects of its relocation efforts. The episode focussed on the experiences of Joe Smith, a Cree man played by Ojibwe actor and broadcaster Johnny Yesno, who arrived in Toronto from Moosonee. When Joe goes to the National Employment Service, he is sent to a "Special Counsellor" of the "Indian Urbanization Program," even though, as he says, "I just want a job." The counsellor explains, "What we're trying to do, Mr. Smith, in this Indian urbanization, is consolidate two cultures, yours and ours. Now, to establish you firmly in the framework of the integrated society, we're going to have to give you a series of tests."[88] He continues, "now, in the first test, Mr. Smith, all we will determine is how fast your brain responds to neural stimuli. Now, on the board, there is this plaque with a series of holes in it. Now, there are pegs to fit into these holes: square peg in a square hole, round peg in a round hole." Joe asks, "What happens if I put a round peg in a square hole?" To which the counsellor responds, "Well, it just wouldn't fit, would it, Mr. Smith?" Joe then leaves the office—without a job.[89] This is the initial phase in a downward trajectory, recounted in part two of the program, which includes being refused liquor at a bar by a white waiter ("go down the street" / "you're in the wrong place"), being stopped by police for being in an alley, getting hit by a car while crossing the street ("go back to the reservation!"), getting offered whiskey by his white girlfriend, who later dumps him, getting arrested in a barroom brawl ("chief, your squaws are pretty good"), and finally committing suicide in a jail by hanging himself with a belt. The belt, both real and metaphorical, is what prompts coroner Wojeck's investigation.

The episode is similar to films of the era depicting urban relocation that were produced by the Department of Citizenship and Immigration and the National Film Board (NFB).[90] Joe's experience of urban life was what mainstream society generally painted as the struggle faced by Aboriginal men when confronting modernity, and for a while this was popular content for Canadian educational films. While his story dealt to a limited extent with urban spatial geographies of race, gender, sexuality, and class, it did so mostly from the point of view of non-Native waiters, girlfriends, placement officers, police, and coroners. The *Wojeck* episode stands apart from the (also often gloomy) NFB films in that the protagonist actually confronts, but does not successfully overcome, urban racial prejudice. At the same time, the episode reproduces a common representation of cities as innately "bad" for Indians.

Gender definitely influenced the experience and image of Native people in urban areas, and the *Wojeck* episode would have told a much different story, or perhaps none at all, if Joe had been a woman. In the last twenty years, several historians have investigated how ideas about femininity, race, social class, sexuality, and respectability have been constructed in the historical context of industrializing cities.[91] Social historians studying urbanization have examined how urban narratives reflect relations of power including heteropatriarchy, capitalism, and racism. They have also studied various forms of informal and formal moral and legal regulation that limited women's behaviours, activities, and ways of living and defined myriad transgressions for which they could expect real consequences. In the restrictive, punative geographies of postwar white settler cities in the Canadian context,[92] the regulation of women sharpened as did notions that women did not belong. For First Nations women, a key concept was that the Canadian city, due to its "sophistication," was foreign and frightening to Canadian Indians, who were naturally used to "protective" and "quiet" reserves and thus required special attention and assistance. Narratives of Indigenous people tended to focus on appropriate living arrangements and leisure activities not unlike urban narratives of turn-of-the-century white women, and they likewise affirm gender, race, and class segregation and hierarchies.

Less than half as many women as men were placed in the Indian Placement and Relocation program.[93] Yet two distinct popular narratives about Native women in cities emerged and have shaped our understanding of Native women's urban history. The first depicted Native women as particularly vulnerable to disreputable influences and "little...prepared for the city and how quick others are to take advantage of them."[94] In this narrative, Native women's mere presence in urban areas would inevitably lead to their demise if they were not constantly scrutinized and helped. The second narrative is perhaps less familiar to readers today; it depicted urban Native women workers as attractive, successful, feminine citizens who integrated economically, politically, and socially into the modern urban Canadian landscape and were a credit to their Indian race. In this narrative, the women's distinctive Native attributes positively accented mainstream white Canadian society.

The narrative of Native female decline was characterized by three leading concerns: living arrangements, leisure activities, and loneliness, and these concerns can tell us about the on-the-ground operations of the placement and relocation program. In determining living arrangements, placement officers relied on the services of landladies and kept lists of women who were willing to accept First Nations tenants in their houses; some landladies accommodated more than one candidate at a time, and some housed successive candidates. In one instance, placement officer J.J. Fransen arranged for four Toronto hairdressing placement candidates to live at the same two east Toronto addresses, Mrs. Barnet's at 120 Galt Avenue and Mrs. Moran's at 24 Bellhaven Road. He also made boarding arrangements for other hairdressing candidates in west Toronto and Forest Hill. Racism was a subtle but pervasive feature in the lives of Native women who relocated with the program—despite placement officers' efforts to smooth the transition. For example, the two female candidates who responded to questions about landladies in a 1961 study of the placement program in southern Ontario by the department felt that they were treated the same as non-Indians; however, in

Figure 2.2. Many women who moved to the city for school and work lived in boarding houses with landladies. This photo depicts Winnifred Ashkewe (Chippewa of Nawash) who worked as a typist for the National Employment Service in Toronto, her landlady Mrs. Sweeny, and Patricia Contin (Parry Sound Agency) and Freda Nicholas (Tobique), who were taking hairdressing courses, in Toronto, c. 1961..
Library and Archives Canada, E011052461.

the two and a half years they had been in the placement program, one had moved five times and the other had moved three times.

While the department tellingly insisted that placement candidates were "free, of course, to move at any time," it was preferred that all arrangements were made through the program prior to their arrival in cities.[95] According to *The Transition*, a contemporary film about the placement program, this crucial service "spared [candidates] the ordeal of knocking on a door and being met with a stony face and that look which says 'oh you're Indian. Sorry, we have no room.'"[96] But the responsibility for living arrangements also furnished placement staff with a wide field for the intimate surveillance and regulation of Indian women's social lives, free time, and mobility. For their part, landladies' primary incentive for taking in boarders would have been the income they could draw from renters, and many arrangements required some form of labour, in addition to rent, as remuneration. For women renters, this was usually domestic work. Boarding arrangements with the Placement and Relocation Program had an added incentive for landladies: rental agreements were overseen by federal officers of the Department of Indian Affairs, and when confronted with problems, landladies did not hesitate to contact placement officers, who made themselves available for discussions about candidates' "adjustment." For example, Mrs. Uno of 50 Balsam Avenue, Toronto, reported that her boarders were "involved with men friends in their apartment" and "receiving telephone calls throughout the night from all sorts of men asking for 'girls.'"[97] This situation subsequently escalated into a full-blown crisis involving counsellors, social workers, psychiatrists, and the young women's parents; yet at no point were the officers interested in the candidates' job placement or work.

In the narrative of decline, vulnerability shifted to culpability, and this is because narratives of decline rarely seek to understand what makes Aboriginal women unsafe—male domination and white racism. This is not to say that department staff and others were unaware of the social and racial segregation Native women experienced in cities and the discrimination First Nations people faced when looking for housing. Indeed, staff feared that this, in addition to low wages, might lead them to live in "undesirable" quarters and socialize with "undesirable" people. In light of the overall goal of integration, concentrations of First Nations workers in cities were a concern, and First Nations women were encouraged to stay at regular student and worker residences, not only because they charged reasonable board rates and provided a modicum of supervision, but also because they offered "social contacts and living experiences with non-Indian girls."[98]

Concerns over living arrangements for young, unmarried working women converged with needs to house outpatients, the recently paroled, and students furthering their education. In cities across Canada, branches of several organizations, including the YWCA, the Sanatorium Board, the Salvation Army, and Roman Catholic, Presbyterian, and United Churches operated boarding homes for young people. But at the same time there was a shortage of satisfactory accommodations that accepted Native women. Speaking to the Women's Missionary Society of the United Church, Mrs. Oddson, a social worker for the department, noted that "the Dept. of Indian Affairs does not encourage girls to come to Winnipeg to work because there is no place for them to stay. They are not accepted in the better districts." Miss Oddson felt that if the girls lived in a home under church auspices, they might be more readily accepted.[99] Due to low wages, many placement candidates could not afford to return home for visits, and so comfortable accommodations were paramount. One solution was to establish Indian-run boarding homes. The Indian-Métis Reception Lodge at 367 Selkirk Avenue, Winnipeg, opened in 1962 and was managed by Stanley and Dorothy McKay of Fisher River. The McKays had been assisted by the Placement and Relocation Program in 1959; Dorothy worked for the Indian and Métis Referral Centre, and Stanley was placed with Scott-Bathgate, a food products company. Perhaps not surprisingly, bitter protests were brought to the city from neighbouring residents, who charged that the boarding house would "degrade the area."[100]

Despite the range of background experiences of First Nations women in Canadian cities, there was a persistent discourse that suggests an inherent unfamiliarity with cities and everyone who lived in them. While homesickness was a reality for many, this discourse on the complete isolation and ignorance of First Nations women was not in effect accurate. A 1962 case in which three business school graduates moved to Toronto in search of work before making arrangements with the Toronto placement office illustrates how the assumption of ignorance led the department to micro-manage female urban migration. The most serious issue in this case was that the First Nations women had moved to Toronto without prior notice from the placement officer of "their own" region to the Southern Ontario staff and had sought placement assistance. While the Regional Supervisor of Indian Agencies Mr. Bonnah made it clear that the young people were "free, of course, to move at any time," he scolded their local staff for not having persuaded them to wait until the "employment situation" had been "assessed... and the point cleared as to whether or not services can be made available by placement specialists... on the basis of prior consultation and referral."[101] The failure to consult was a serious problem—but only in how it related to the presumed "destitution of [the] girls and their ignorance of city life" and the "vicissitudes of life in *such a big city* as Toronto" [emphasis in original]. In response, the Maritime Regional Supervisor wrote the only really fiery letter I found in the files (most of the correspondence was irksomely indifferent): "In reviewing the incident I cannot help but think that my [colleagues?]... pressed the panic button a trifle early," he wrote. "These girls on their own wanted to go to Toronto with Indian friends...[and] the presence of [three] friends drew them there.... These girls were told by our Superintendent and our Placement Officer to seek advice and guidance from the Regional office only if in need, on the same basis as one would seek out an Embassy Office if in trouble in a foreign country. The fact that the girls tried to find employment on their own ought to have been sufficient evidence to Toronto

Regional Office that they were not referred to them by us." Moreover, he explained, one of the girls had been born, raised, and educated in two different Canadian cities, while the other had spent a number of years in a large American metropolis. In short, he argued, "I don't feel that the Big City of Toronto will throw them completely."[102] The women involved in this case would not have been unique: there is evidence that at least one-third of the candidates in the program studied here were familiar with each other in one way or another, and many came from reserves located close to urban areas.

Yet in an era of segregation and racism, places where Indians were welcome became important points of urban Indian geographies. These places commonly did not adhere to the norms of middle-class respectability. Thus, as with living arrangements, the records of the placement program contain as much or more information about the leisure activities of candidates than about their actual job placements. Candidates, it was believed, needed to "make friends" with people who were "wise in the ways of the world" yet who were also genuinely concerned about their welfare. Indeed, newcomers relied on Indigenous people who already were established in urban centres for assistance, and in some areas department staff asked for help from volunteer groups such as church and women's organizations, including the Catholic Women's League, business and professional women's clubs, local Councils of Women, and the YM-YWCA. Indigenous people often used such contacts to initiate and support their own organizations and activities that in turn informed newcomers. YMCAs, Indian clubs, and friendship centres organized dances, sports, and other social activities. In addition to functioning as meeting places, they also acted as information and referral centres. In her work on the North American Indian Club of Toronto, Heather Howard-Bobiwash examines women's experiences in the history of Toronto Native community-building. She argues that the experiences of women are far more complex than have previously been understood and that a focus on "social problems" and Native peoples' "failure to assimilate" has obscured the diversity and complexity of the socioeconomic lives of Native people in cities. She points to some women who were "members of an emergent Native middle class" and who used class mobility to support Native community organization and to participate in Native image-making.[103] In photographs, it is clear that these were also places for respectable Indians to meet and engage in socially approved activities and relationships. Considering the narrow confines in which First Nations men and women could go out in public without being harassed, it is perhaps not surprising that the history of

Indian friendship centres forms such a central part of the existing literature on urban Indian history.

The department never seemed concerned about First Nations women socializing with First Nations men. Rather they were preoccupied with the so-called "foreign element"—white and perhaps immigrant men—and Native women's susceptibility to being taken advantage of by them.[104] Such fears were again concentrated on those in very specific socioeconomic circumstances, often extreme poverty and social dislocation. Familiar late-nineteenth-century fears of "white slavery" and early-twentieth-century fears of "promiscuity" (including mixed- race relationships) rang forward through the mid-twentieth century. So too did the accompanying desire for moral and social regulation. Likewise, the telephone, the alleyway, the curfew, and the car were similar signals of some sort of perilous situation involving an interracial relationship. In a rare discussion about women's participation in the Placement and Relocation Program, Carl Latham suggested that they should perhaps be excluded from the program because of their "temporary attachment to the labour force" as well as "social factors other than employment."[105] He found that there was "a higher percentage of Indian women [who] are marrying non-Indians than Indian men marrying non-Indian women," and concluded that "[o]ne of the unintended consequences of the Indian Placement Program could be to aggravate this trend and the resultant social implications."[106] He was vague on what those implications were; he did not refer directly to the fact that First Nations women (and not First Nations men) married to non-Indians lost Indian status and the children of these relationship could not inherit it; however, this may have been his concern. This loss of status meant that First Nations women who entered these relationships would be denied access to services, as would their children, making them in a very real way vulnerable in the non-Native world of the city. One cannot help but consider that this kind of discourse played favourably into the hands of those who wished to have more control over the lives of First Nations people. By depicting Native women as "naïve," officials, and even mainstream organizations, could ignore the serious lack of services for Native women in cities, and racialized violence against First Nations women—especially everyday forms of it—could be normalized as self-induced or even inevitable.

There is little if any documentation of those who did not graduate from the program, those who dropped out, those who changed course, or those who quit or were fired. From the records, we are not able to know the specific circumstances that informed those diverging experiences. In a way, we always know more about stories of success, and these stories constitute a strikingly different narrative that dominated media coverage of working Native women. This version was a celebratory tale of courageous, patient women who were coming to the fore, and the proof was that they were earning their own living: "She is a Labour Representative" (for the "hello girls" of the Bell Telephone Company in Montreal); "She is a Bank Cashier" (at the Royal Bank branch office in Sturgeon Falls); "She Has Her Own Business" (operating a restaurant on Walpole Island), "She is a stenographer with the Territorial Government"; "[She] is an efficient and well-liked supermarket cashier."[107] These Native women were in demand and being "accepted" everywhere. Labour featured somewhat more centrally in this narrative than it did in the narrative of decline; yet whereas the "vulnerable" women's narrative focussed on the social sphere, so too did that of the successful women. There were three commonly repeated characteristics of successful urban Native women: their success in graduating and obtaining work; their broad popularity; and their physical attractiveness.

The narrative of success in some ways represents a departure from common non-Native stereotypes of Native women. To early explorers and traders, First Nations women undertook hard physical labour and held significant sexual and economic freedoms, which, seen through European eyes, were unfeminine and immoral. In spite of efforts of the state to remake Indigenous women into "helpful, industrious and health conscious rural housewi[ves]," and to involve itself in every aspect of women's lives, by the 1920s, common stereotypes of First Nations women depicted them as idle and slovenly, lacking domestic and housekeeping skills. These images also, importantly, depicted First Nations women as responsible for poor conditions of reserves in the era.[108] Just as these images reflected, as Pamela White argues, a state policy aimed to restructure and transform the domestic economies of reserves in ways that suited goals for "progress" through white settlement and Indian assimilation and civilization, so too did images of postwar First Nations women reflect a desired shift at that time to the broad integration of First Nations people into Canadian society. In such media as the *Indian News*, First Nations women were depicted as attractive, feminine, competent and hardworking, and also devoted to the advancement of their own people.

In some ways this narrative was managed by the department itself in its constant promotion of Indian labour in print, audio, and visual media. This work involved both managing negative press (about the department and First Nations) and generating positive press. According to Norman Riddiough, an information officer with the Department of Citizenship and

Immigration, who spoke to placement officers in the late 1950s, there was a general lack of knowledge and understanding about Indians among the population, but public relations, or disseminating information about Indians on a broad national scale, was helping to create a "more enlightened attitude towards the Indians." Indian Affairs had a crucial role to play in this work, as Riddiough reminded his audience: "every act performed by you is an act of public relations."[109]

The narrative of success is reflected in a multitude of Department of Indian Affairs and media photographs of the era. These photographs tend to represent moments in time that the department was proud of, and in which the department could celebrate the success of Indians and promote its role in that success. In these black-and-white photographs, Native women are crisply dressed with impeccable hair and are smiling from under nurses' caps, over typewriters, or behind notebooks and pens. Some analyses of such images have argued that they promote an image of a singularly assimilated woman. Whereas they do represent a departure from earlier images of Native women's work, this interpretation assumes that there is one single vision of Native womanhood and thus a limited number of ways Indigenous women can express themselves as "authentic" Native women. Success is also a lived expression of Native experience, and so it is important to look at the narrative that frames it. In these images, First Nations women are consistently passing courses, beginning new careers, and being awarded for their scholastic and vocational achievements. These photographs document a collective history of Indigenous achievement, intelligence, and hard work. And, yet, like any other one-dimensional image, they add little depth to the stories of lived lives.

The images are telling, however, of the narrow and restrictive range of socially approved ways of being a First Nations woman living and working in the city. This is perhaps most obvious in scholarship photos; these images have a fairly consistent ratio of four men to one woman, reflecting the department's assumption that Native women mostly just were not suited to education and a modern career, mirroring typical contemporary gender discrimination and reflecting the work force in general at the time. However, it should be noted that urban migration patterns show that in fact more women than men migrated to cities. By 1960, about 15 percent of Aboriginal people had moved to urban areas, with this population increasing every year. In 1966, 16.5 percent of status women lived off-reserve while only 15.4 percent of status men did; this difference was to become more pronounced over time.[110] The photographs also reflected the idea that cities could be "good" for some select Native women who embraced the opportunities they afforded to integrate with the broader Canadian citizenry. This emphasis on cities reveals a shift in the geographical target of the department's goal of termination. In the nineteenth century, the segregated reserve was envisioned as an ideal space for the civilization process to take place; by the mid-twentieth century, it was cities. With its focus on integration, the "positive" narrative of urban Native women seems also to suggest that cities could actually "de-racinate" or "de-Indigenize" Native women.

While loneliness was a characteristic of the urban working woman in decline, broad social popularity was one of the key characteristics of successful Native women. Such popularity suggested that racism and prejudice, rarely acknowledged in the contemporary sources, were not obstacles, and it also underscored the feasibility of the policy of Indian integration. The popularity of successful Native women actually referred to their ability to appeal to and "get along" with respectable white women and white men. For example, commenting on the Placement and Relocation Program for the *Globe and Mail,* Superintendent of Education for the Indian Affairs Branch Howard Rodine explained, "[d]iscrimination against the Indians [in the placement program]...has not been a problem.... In fact evidence of any kind of segregation has been remote.... Indian girls, some of whom are strikingly pretty, are very popular with white boys. There has been no trouble arising from social life between the two groups."[111] References to Native women's attractiveness constitute a common aspect of the narrative of urban success. Their youth was probably the single most common reference about their appearance, and women's ages were commonly cited.

Narratives that contain Native urban experience have not disappeared—if anything, the dichotomous narratives of vulnerability and success have become even more widespread and pronounced. Yet because they are historically constructed, the ways vulnerability and success are defined have changed considerably over time. In the postwar era, the two common narratives indicate that Native women's labour was never simply or even primarily about work, but rather about how the women adapted to the modern, presumably "foreign" city with the help of the state. Together, they also demonstrate that many Canadians saw the mid-twentieth century as a moment of possibility for women, for Native people, and for the nation. While neither narrative can really claim to represent anything except social anxieties, in the end, they exceed and cancel out each other. The complex reality of Native women's experiences could never adequately be contained in simple dichotomous narratives. Both narratives of "success" and "decline" masked the realities that Aboriginal women seeking education and work in Canadian cities faced.

The Placement and Relocation Program, with its emphasis on integration and assimilation, inherently rejected the cultural, social, and economic priorities of many Indigenous women. Moreover, Indigenous women had few opportunities, at least until the 1960s, to play a role in the production of representations of themselves. Arguably, one of these opportunities was to engage in the expanding postwar beauty industry. Its emphasis on beauty and visibility, its highly specialized training in an expanding and stylish industry, and its numerous job opportunities made hairdressing an attractive option for a considerable number of Indigenous women who moved to cities for education and employment at this time.

Hairdressing and Indigenous Women's Urban Labour

After business college programs leading to stenographic, clerking, and secretarial work, the most popular option for women in the Placement and Relocation Program was hairdressing school. This mirrors Canada-wide trends; for women under the age of forty-five in Canada in the 1960s "Stenographers, Typists and Clerk-Typists" was the top choice of occupation, followed closely by "Clerical Occupations" and "Barbers, Hairdressers, Manicurists."[112] With a standardized and regulated education system feeding into an expanding market, it is perhaps not surprising that so many working women in Canada chose the hairdressing trade. Moreover, by the postwar era, hairdressing became a predominantly female consumer industry, and, unlike most professions that were still closed to women, hairdressing was an occupation dominated by women.

Across Canada, hairdressing schools were abundant and included the nationwide Marvel School, as well as provincial technical colleges such as the Manitoba Technical Institute and local, privately owned beauty schools. Schools were located in downtown areas of cities and towns and offered programming year-round, often with options for both day and evening classes and programs commencing at regular intervals, even as often as twice a week. For example, Marvel's regular advertisement in the *Globe and Mail* encouraged women to "Join Canada's Leading School. Be A Hairdresser. Great Opportunity. Learn Hairdressing. Pleasant, dignified profession, good wages: thousands [of] successful Marvel graduates. America's greatest system: illustrated catalogue free. Day and evening classes. Write or call Marvel Hairdressing School, 358 Bloor St. West, Toronto. Ontario Branches, Hamilton and Ottawa."[113] Compared to other post-secondary options, hairdressing school involved a relatively small commitment. The hairdressing profession was regulated provincially in an apprenticeship system, which involved two parts. The first was formal, practical training at an accredited institution, which covered shampooing, cutting, styling, chemical treatments, scalp treatments, hairpieces, and in some places also other esthetic services. This course of training could last between six and twelve months. The second part of the system entailed a period of apprenticeship as an "improver," usually equal to the time spent in formal training. At the end of this stage, students took an exam that qualified them to work as a hairdresser.[114]

The DIA supported hairdresser training because the course of study required a relatively small financial outlay. It cost approximately $400 per student for training, including tuition and tools of the trade. Additionally, the educational requirements suited most candidates in the Placement and Relocation Program: while most training programs required grade 10 and preferably higher, many schools were flexible on this account.[115] Placement and Relocation Program candidates had between grade 8 and grade 11, with an average being between grade 8 and grade 9. Placement funds, when they were granted to hairdressing school students, followed a pattern of covering room and board and incidentals for two months. In Toronto, the rate for room and board was $65 per month and for incidentals $15 per month. After obtaining certification, hairdressers often found positions immediately, with the help of a placement officer or on their own.

Louise McGillvary's story of placement was recounted in the *Indian News*. Six years after she left Prince Albert Residential School as a student (where she also worked), Louise's mother told her to get advice from the Indian agent regarding her interest in hairdressing. He in turn made the arrangements for her to enter a hairdressing course at the Manitoba Technical Institute in 1957. At the end of her eight-month hairdressing course, she was interviewed by a placement officer. The officer told her about an opening at Dema's Beauty Parlour in Portage la Prairie that had come through the National Employment Service. The placement officer went with Louise to Portage la Prairie, where she was interviewed by the NES. Then she went to Dema's Beauty Parlour to meet the proprietor, where she was hired.[116] Louise was also placed in a "good home for board and room" with an "elderly couple who are taking an interest."[117] She worked at Dema's for nine months, and then was released because the owner was reducing staff and moving the shop to her home because of ill health. After a brief visit home for a week, she returned to the Portage NES, where she was referred to another employer and hired. "I have been able to acquire very suitable lodgings in a boarding home," she is quoted, "and my reception here also has been most kindly. I am very happy living and working in Portage." Like many hairdressers, Louise hoped to one day open her own beauty salon.[118]

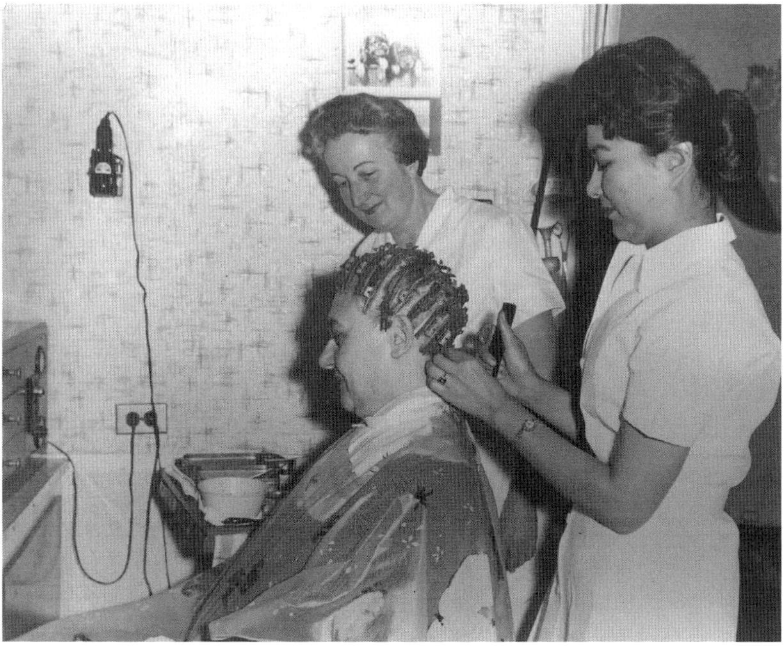

Figure 2.3. Hairdressing was one of the more popular choices of vocation in the Placement and Relocation Program. This photo is of Louise McGillvray (of The Pas), while she was learning to be a hairdresser in Portage La Prairie.
Library and Archives Canada, E011052437

Stories like this one are in some ways characteristic of the emphasis in the *Indian News* on "new" sectors of employment, formal education, and urban integration.[119] While the ideology of integration shaped the Indian placement program and would have had a very real impact on the lives of women in the program, it coexisted with the personal pursuit of employment. In their examination of the history of the hairdressing profession in New Zealand, Barbara Brookes and Catherine Smith show how the trade could be genuinely attractive to so many women. They argue that unlike in other feminized occupations, deskilling was not evident in women's hairdressing; rather, the profession became more technical and innovative over the course of the twentieth century. "This is a profession," they argue, "that demanded incredible technological feats—turning straight hair to curls and brown hair to blonde." It took technical, and, in the language of the day, "scientific" proficiency and demanded practical and theoretical knowledge of trade machinery and chemicals. The enthusiastic adoption of technology by women's hairdressers (predominantly women, but also some men) and the simultaneous stagnation of the barbering trade led to the dominance of women as consumers and practitioners within the industry. The extravagant beehive of the 1960s was a symbol of the technology and experimentation in women's hairdressing, and Brookes and Smith argue that "hairdressers and their technologies were essential collaborators in these stylistic changes."[120]

For many years, the hairdressing salon and the hairdressers who worked there were overlooked as subjects of historical investigation, and this is still true of the Canadian literature. Perhaps this is a result of historians' inattention to the activities of women and working people before the 1970s. As well, it was common among second-wave feminist scholars to dismiss the beauty industry for subjugating women. Over the last decade, however, several historians, including Kathy Peiss, Julie Willett, Julia Kirk Blackwelder, and Tiffany M. Gill, have sought to explore this history and to complicate its analysis by examining how the industry was a means for women's resistance and empowerment. Some of the most compelling aspects of this literature deal with African-American women in the trade and the impact of racial segregation on the beauty industry. While segregation in training and work in many ways put African-Americans at a disadvantage, it also ironically bolstered African American entrepreneurship and economic and occupational independence by creating an exclusive customer base. Moreover, beauty parlours were creative sites of political discussion in the twentieth century, and beauticians themselves played important roles in civil rights activism in the United States. Finally, this literature shows how the African-American beauty industry contributed significantly to the formation of modern, Black, female identities.[121] Thus, for African-American women, the beauty industry was not frivolous, irrelevant, or oppressive—it was vital to community formation and stimulated social, political, and economic change.

In Canada, the hairdressing school business was not formally segregated. However, an informal yet very common practice of racial segregation in the service industry prevailed throughout the postwar years. A demand for product lines, hairstyles, and skilled labour meant that Black Canadian-born and Caribbean hairdressers could forge a space for themselves in the larger beauty industry in Canada, especially in large urban centres like Toronto. Like the Black Canadian and Caribbean nurses examined by Karen Flynn in *Moving Beyond Borders*, hairdressers, too, experienced racism and exclusion; some migrated to find work, and some took part in the larger community-building efforts.[122]

First Nations labour history follows some similar patterns: racism and exclusion; exploitation within an industrial capitalist economy that did not serve them well; and pressure from the federal government to assimilate. But are there other ways to think about First Nations women's labour? Any argument for resistance or agency among hairdressers in the Placement and Relocation Program must be understood within the context of colonial regulation and the imposition of a patriarchal social order by the DIA, churches, and social service agencies. The vision for Canada at the time was that Aboriginal people would eventually disappear as Aboriginal. Moreover, as Philip Deloria points out in his work on Native Americans and modernity, society did not associate Native women with consumption, modernity, beauty, technology, labour,[123] or, as others have argued, even womanhood for that matter.[124] Thus, hairdressers do challenge the core of our ideas about Aboriginal people in postwar Canada generally and First Nations women in particular. As such, histories of hairdressing and the beauty industry writ large can tell us much about urban Indian class formation, Indian entrepreneurship, and expressions of Indian politics in the contemporary beauty culture.

Wages and Integration

The American literature on race and the beauty industry helps to elucidate the very distinct historical context for the rise of Indigenous women in the field of hairdressing. First, in the 1950s and 1960s in Canada, hairdressing schools were never officially segregated by race as they were in the U.S. For example, a photograph of the 1961 graduating class at Olga's Beauty Salon in Penticton, BC, featured three Okanagan women, Rose Marie Baptiste, Pauline Gregoire, and Patsy Eli. According to the *Indian News*, Pauline "set the standard" for the rest of the class.[125] Author Maria Campbell's 1960s' hairdressing course in Edmonton included "a Black girl, a Japanese [girl] and a Blackfoot woman" as well as herself, a Métis. She recalls, "the majority of the students were young, white, poor, and uneducated women from farms and small towns."[126] To the DIA, it was such integration that justified financial and philosophical support for Aboriginal women's salon training. Their ability to "fare well" in non-segregated vocational classrooms proved the policy was feasible and working, and the DIA viewed experiences of segregation in education, housing, and social life as impediments to this process. Indeed, the department commonly emphasized integration in its photo captions, pointing out "non-Indian" clients and students working alongside Indian students.

For Aboriginal women, race was not a barrier to training in hairdressing, nor did skin colour determine if one could obtain a job, although it could determine where one could obtain a job.[127] Of the women who trained as hairdressers in Winnipeg as part of the Placement and Relocation Program, a significant number were placed in salons in middle-class neighbourhoods like River Heights, including the Magic Mirror Beauty Salon, Bloomquist's River Heights Salon, Hilde's Beauty Salon, the American House of Beauty, Charmette Beauty Salon, and Virginia's Beauty Clinic.[128] This could indicate a pattern of integration by residence similar in some ways to Auckland, New Zealand's scheme of relocating Māori families amongst middle-class urban whites in order to speed up and encourage successful assimilation. It could also show those salons that were most accepting of First Nations workers. More likely, as it was placement officers who contacted salons, this pattern may simply reflect salon owners who took part in the Indian Placement and Relocation Program or the salons initially contacted by the placement officer.

Apart from Indian ancestry, hairdressers in the Placement and Relocation Program predominantly shared the other social and cultural categories of experience, age, and marital status. There is evidence that some older and married women took up hairdressing careers; however, most of the women entering training were between the ages of seventeen and twenty-two, and most were single. Like other occupations dominated by young, single women, hairdressing was a relatively low-paid job. For example, a placement candidate who was a hairdresser in Winnipeg in 1961 earned $40 per week,[129] or approximately $1,920 per year. It seems that the women in the placement program were paid the same or less than the Canadian average for the trade. The 1961 census statistics for earnings of women barbers, hairdressers, and manicurists do not distinguish full-time from part-time work. The largest wage category for this group, at 39.8 percent of the workers, was making more than $2,000 annually.[130] While such figures make hairdressers' wages appear straightforward, in fact the pay structures at salons were usually more complicated. There are four main models of compensation in the hairdressing profession: owners of shops "rent" chairs to hairdressers who are paid directly by clients; owners of shops pay a "straight salary" to workers; workers earn a "straight commission" based on a percentage of the revenue from their clients; or workers earn a combination of a minimum "salary plus a commission" when the revenue from their clients reaches a specific level. Commonly, in the mid-twentieth century, hairdressers worked for a "wage plus commission." Commission could be paid once annually, which could require a hairdresser to stay with one salon for an entire year to see full wages.

Many women in the Placement and Relocation Program changed jobs frequently, and thus within this wage structure they experienced a distinct disadvantage. It was and is common to tip hairdressers, an aspect of income that is difficult to measure and was impossible for workers to predict. In the mid-1960s, Manitoba Hairdressing Association president Bruno Dudar estimated that 60 percent of Manitoba hairdressing establishments refused to allow tipping. "It's demeaning," he stated, as "We consider hairdressing a profession." However, a survey of Winnipeg salons done by the *Free Press* contradicted Dudar's estimate, revealing that many managements did not interfere in tipping customs. Regardless, Dudar explained, wages "vary greatly" between $65 and $150 per week, and his preference was to simply ensure decent wages for hairdressers; a "good operator," he estimated, should earn $100.00 per week.[131] In a 1958 survey of placement candidates in Toronto, the hairdresser, age seventeen, was the second to youngest of the group. She had spent two-and-a-half years in the program, had changed employers three times, and had lived at five boarding homes. She had been hired through the NES, initially earning $35 dollars per week, and at the time of the survey, she earned $40 per week. Her wage tied with apprentice metal mechanic for the lowest earnings among those surveyed.[132] Even accounting for the rise in wages in general between the late 1950s and mid-1960s, her salary would have been low; want ads for hairdressers in the *Winnipeg Free Press* in 1957 promised $45 or $50 per week plus commission.

Remuneration was an important aspect of the program, especially as it was one of the main incentives for placement candidates entering the program, although it was rarely discussed in depth. It is difficult to get a sense of the average placement candidate, especially when it comes to the average woman who participated in the program. Nonetheless, studies of the program suggest some basic information about their wages and education. Carl Latham's 1958 study of the program observed that candidates should have been far better remunerated, especially as placement candidates included some of the "best qualified Indian youth." Latham found that women in the Indian Placement and Relocation Program were not only more educated than their male counterparts, they were also more educated than the average Canadian woman. Of the six women included in the study, all had some high-school education, four had grade 12, and one had grade 13.[133] All had been educated in Indian day schools and non-Indian secondary schools. In spite of this, they were paid very low wages, with no one (male or female) in the program earning more than $50 per week and most earning around $35 per week.[134] This wage amounted to almost $7 per week *less* than the average of wage-earning women in manufacturing in 1958 ($19 less than salaried women in manufacturing). There were no statistics for average wage earnings of office workers in factories in 1958, but the wages of women in the Placement and Relocation Program survey amounted to $15.80 less for the year 1957 and $19.44 less for the year 1959.[135] Only one of the twelve candidates was in a union job, and all other placements were in small businesses, in offices, and in government jobs where there were no unions.

A 1961 survey of twelve of the more than 200 placement candidates in southern Ontario who had entered the program in Toronto in the previous four years records the wages of ten candidates. In this survey, the placement officer "purposely avoided the inclusion of Indian girls that married and returned home to live with their husbands who never had been to Toronto,"[136] and gender was not recorded, making it difficult to identify the nine men and three women included in the study. Based on gendered occupations and pronouns used in the analysis, we can draw some conclusions, however. Weekly salaries for the women in the program ranged from between $40 for the hairdressers (it is unknown if tips were accounted for) and $61 for the Clerk III. It is significant that one of the three women counted in this study had moved to Cleveland for work; First Nations commonly observed that remuneration was poorer in Canada compared to what they could make in the U.S.

Another 1961 study of thirty candidates during the first four years of the program in Toronto found that women were still more educated than men but by a smaller margin.[137] This study also found that average weekly earnings were approximately $10 less than the average weekly earnings quoted by the Dominion Bureau of Statistics. It was suggested that this was due to the "limited number of years that respondents have been on the labour market or the kind of occupation they have gone into."[138] However, this does not seem to correspond with the records. In a sample of placement files of hairdressers, more than half referred to previous work experience prior to placement. Of these, one had worked at a restaurant, one at a residential school, one in farm labour, and another at different salons on the weekends. Four had worked as domestics, and, of these, three had worked at the same rate of pay—$15 per week. As the same placement officer filed all three cases, this suggests the possibility that the officer was recruiting and setting the wage for domestic work outside the placement program. Moreover, it suggests that this placement officer had a policy of his own to place female applicants as domestics first before accepting them as placement candidates, perhaps with the goal of testing their abilities or building up their savings before their move to the city.

According to Maria Campbell, the allure and excitement of hairdressing school, particularly for "a young woman from the bush," did not quite measure up to the promise of "great jobs and great pay." Hairdressers, she explains, were all "exploited women, but they thought they were better because they were into beauty." After only a brief time working as a hairdresser, Campbell took a waitressing job, finding it more lucrative and enjoyable.[139] Other women also left hairdressing to work as stenographers, clerks, waitresses, and at factories and other businesses where work was more lucrative. Details of employment placement following training are hard to find; however, of twelve candidates whose information is accessible, only six were placed in hair salons. Four of the candidates quit the program: one completed the course but decided before placement that she would rather be a department store clerk or telephone operator. Another quit or was fired after several placements, which she explained was because of the low earnings. Another hairdresser was placed at several different salons but only ever temporarily. The last dropped out of the program after two different placements, the second one lasting just three weeks. Candidates gave several different reasons for leaving a placement: low earnings, unsatisfying work, temporary positions, salon closed or went out of business, failed course, discharged/released, or returned home. It is also very possible that racism or patronizing attitudes from clients, co-workers, or employers came into play in decisions to quit. It is significant that of the many women who were trained and celebrated by the department, I could find information for only one who set up shop on her own and become a salon owner: Olive Lafond, of the Muskeg Lake Band, set up her business in Blaine Lake, Saskatchewan, after working in a few different salons. But most of the women who were placed through the program were certainly not in a position to own shops. And the placement program itself was designed to create workers, not owners; wages barely covered living expenses and the program did not address larger issues of First Nations people's lack of access to capital. Thus "integration" for First Nations women was to follow a fairly prescribed pattern, one that is not all that distinct from earlier patterns in First Nations education or, ironically, patterns of African-American segregation; it would steer them predominantly towards the lower rungs of Canadian society.

Entrepreneurship and Loans

A limited access to capital, in addition to low wages, goes a long way to accounting for the fact that very few Native women started up their own salons. Unlike the experience of African-American women in the U.S., or even in

Canada,[140] Native entrepreneurship did not develop as a significant element of the beauty industry. But, like African-Americans and many postwar immigrants in the U.S. and Canada, Aboriginal entrepreneurs faced debilitating discrimination when applying for loans to set up family-owned businesses. The distinct skills and techniques associated with African-American women's hairdressing is one way this unique history is framed. Yet First Nations people also have distinct traditions and customs related to hair care, hairstyling, and haircutting; while no distinct market developed for hair products, there is one for First Nations hair accessories. Two circumstances set Native hairdressers apart. First, Aboriginal women did not have personal or community resources or First Nations lending opportunities to rely on, and families or communities could offer little in the way of previous experience and capital to share. Second, the success of entrepreneurs of colour, like Viola Desmond's family, described in Constance Backhouse's book *Colour-Coded*, relied upon a Black clientele barred by bigoted barbers and beauticians.[141] There did not exist enough of a popular demand for Native urban hairdressing expertise and therefore a Native-oriented market did not develop. While integration did not mean that First Nations women were necessarily always welcomed at all hair salons as clients, First Nations hairdressers could not rely on a Native clientele that was fully dependent on Native expertise. Moreover, even if it existed, a solely Native clientele could not sustain a Native business in the same way.

First Nations people were disqualified from most kinds of bank loans because they could not use their land or property as collateral. By the Indian Act, both reserve land and reserve property belonged to the band collectively and was controlled by the Department of Indian Affairs in the name of the Crown, as opposed to privately by individuals. The policy of integration through citizenship promised freedom from these restrictions—while it also entailed the loss of Indian status and the dissolution of federally recognized Indian territories. Many of those who needed the capital and had no other choice resorted to voluntary enfranchisement as a means to access cash. Enfranchisement had been a mainstay of Indian policy since 1857, and it allowed First Nation men and *unmarried* First Nations women to access their proportionate share of band funds and land (in addition to Canadian citizenship) in exchange for Indian status and band membership. Enfranchisement was in fact the only way First Nations could gain access to their portion of their community's assets. Robin Jarvis Brownlie's analysis of women and enfranchisement in inter-war Ontario shows that "virtually all the applicants [for enfranchisement] had moved off the reserves, some of them as children, to take advantage of work opportunities that were not available if they remained there." Moreover, fully one-quarter of the enfranchisement applications from the two Indian agencies studied (Parry Sound and Manitowaning, Ontario) between 1920 and 1940 were from women and 100 percent of these applications were successful, a higher success rate than applications by men.[142]

Hairdressers who did own shops had to either use their own resources to buy the necessary equipment or negotiate with the Department of Indian Affairs for loans, a process that required the department's involvement in their business ventures. The experience of Linda Maloney, who trained as a hairdresser in the early 1960s, illustrates the difficulties First Nations women entrepreneurs faced in the era. After working at various beauty salons in Nova Scotia, she opened her first business with money she had earned herself. However, to expand, she needed more. She approached banks in Truro, but said, "When they find you are an Indian, forget it." She then approached a finance company. Here, she could only get the loan, she said, "if I would pay off a loan owed by another Indian whom I did not even know." She did this, and kept building. When she decided to move again, wanting a more fashionable salon, she "tried to borrow money from the Bank of Montreal," but found "they would not hear of it because I was an Indian." The Department of Indian Affairs had to agree to guarantee her loan under the Economic Development Fund, and only with this assurance did she get her loan from the CIBC.[143] Those Aboriginal people who wished to be entrepreneurs had to work with Indian Affairs to guarantee loans, requiring departmental involvement in and approval of their business ventures.

Demobilization programs for ex-servicewomen presented another avenue into the trade. After the war, two Aboriginal servicewomen, Edith Gordon and Mary Ann Mirasty, took up the army's offer of hairdressing courses when they were discharged. Their experiences were recorded by Grace Poulin in her book *Invisible Women: WWII Aboriginal Servicewomen in Canada*. Gordon would have preferred to go into civilian policing, but that job was not open to women at the time. She also turned down the army's alternative, to work at Kingston Penitentiary as a guard. Mirasty took up the offer for a hairdressing course, but after working for a while, she decided to do clerical upgrading to get a good government job instead. Unused to working with men, she went into the salon business with Gordon, who had been in the same company. Mirasty continued on her own until retirement after Gordon left in 1969. She recalled that she "didn't see any Indian people in Ottawa for years and years."[144]

While owning an urban business was a slim possibility, this did not mean there was no demand for Native hairdressing skills, and a number of women set up reserve-based shops. The 1961 departmental survey of placement candidates found that five of the participants were uncertain if they would return to the reserve, two replied decisively "no," one wanted to return after retirement, and two were optimistic of eventually establishing small businesses there.[145] Thus it was not uncommon for placement candidates to plan to return to the reserve later on, either during their working lives or after retirement. In addition, as vocational education funding expanded, many First Nations women from southern reserves did not have to leave reserves for hairdressing school. The department was aware of the potential hairdressing as a business had for reserve economic development, releasing a fifty-six-page book on "Establishing Beauty Salons and Barber Shops on Indian Reservations" in 1975. Many on-reserve shops were run out of people's own homes, as was the case for Mrs. Julian of the Milbrook Reserve near Truro, Nova Scotia, who had trained at the Trans-Canada Beauty Industries School in Moncton, New Brunswick. Mrs. Julian was twenty-eight years old and widowed, and, although she received some financial help towards her fees, she had paid for her own board and lodging while in Moncton. She "bought the necessary equipment from her own resources" for her successful beauty salon.[146] Mrs. Peter Skye and Mrs. Gilbert Thomas and her daughter Eva started up beauty salons at Six Nations in the late 1960s. Skye, who set up a "small modern beauty salon" in Oshweken, had trained in Brantford. The Thomases started a "small but convenient" hairdressing shop at the back of their house, reporting that "although the situation was tough at the beginning...there is [now] enough money to pay the bills."[147]

Racial discrimination and segregation in hairdressing education and the beauty industry shaped contours of an African American hairdressing business history that was dominated by African American women. This history did not unfold in the same way for First Nations women in Canada. The way in which First Nations and "Indianized" hair accessories, such as feathers, headbands, and leather, shell, beaded, or woven clips and attachments, were appropriated by mass culture is one indication of how First Nations entrepreneurship was precluded by a market dominated by non–First Nations people. The policy of integration did not offer First Nations women economic equality, but rather limited space within a larger service industry dominated and controlled by non–First Nations people. But while economic limitations were restrictive in terms of entrepreneurship, innovations in and popularization of First Nations style was not so easily constrained, and indeed flourished even in this highly regulated era.

The Indian Politics of Beauty and Style

Why was hairdressing a popular option for Aboriginal women when it was so poorly paid? Hairdressing courses were short, relatively inexpensive, and held a promise of work upon completion. This work may have afforded an opportunity for independence to those who had few other options. For those with a genuine interest in shaping and creating images and popular representations of women, hairdressing would have had unique appeal. Working as a hairdresser not only inherently resisted contemporary imposed and popular images of Indian women, it was also was a means to create, practise, and popularize alternative representations. Hairdressing also flaunted the choice people had in fashioning their appearance, which becomes especially noteworthy when contrasted to histories of enforced bodily conformity, especially in residential schools. Agnes Grant writes that the cutting of Indigenous children's hair was an expression of cultural and colonial domination, and the imposition of uniformity was another strict measure of the discipline of the schools. For Indigenous people, consciously making a choice about one's appearance was also a political act. The literature on African-American beauty culture links hairdressing as a trade to questions of how notions about beauty and style influenced politicized racial and national identities. It remains to be seen if and how First Nations urban labour, hairdressing, and beauty culture more generally are linked to the flourishing of new forms of modern Indian styles in the postwar period, particularly in the 1960s and 1970s.

Scholarship on Aboriginal women has demonstrated that the construction of simplistic, binary "Princess"/"Squaw" images was characteristic of the gendered nature of the colonization process.[148] These constructions spoke more of the desires and anxieties of non-Natives, and yet they had a very real impact on the lives of women. This imagery does not, however, tell the whole story. Women's own concepts of beauty stood as important community and personal standards for both belonging and leadership. Those who study images have tended to distinguish "good" from "bad," "realistic" or "unrealistic" depictions, but it can be more instructive to evaluate the context in which the images were used. Images of women could, for example, demonstrate integration and "progress" to some; cultural survival, nationalism, identity, and experience to others; and assimilation, colonialism, genocide, and propaganda for termination programs to others still. Wendy Kozol and others argue that it is in this "ambivalence," or in the slippery space of interpretation, where enormous possibilities lie for forcing a reckoning of colonialist narratives and the experience of colonialism, resistance, and belonging.[149] Hair—and the labour behind it, hairdressing—were undoubtedly a part of the larger style-making processes going on in the 1960s and 1970s; yet, it was rarely the focus of attention. Stepping back, however, Indian Princess contests, which were run annually at stampedes, exhibitions, and fairs, became popular especially in the 1960s and 1970s and were important sites for the making and reproducing of Indigenous style and beauty including hairdressing. Some of the contests include: the "Carnival Queen" and "Fur Queen" competitions of the Northern Manitoba Trappers Festival,[150] the Miss Manitoba Indian Princess pageant,[151] the Miss Totem Princess Beauty Contest, run at the All-Indian Buckskin Gloves Boxing Tournament in Vancouver,[152] and the Miss Indian Princess of Canada pageant. Many women participated in multiple contests. Angeline Monkman, for example, then a typist at a city insurance office, was named Fur Queen at The Pas Trappers Festival and went on to be named Miss Manitoba Indian Princess by the Indian and Métis Friendship Centre, later representing the centre in a national contest at Garden River, Ontario.[153] Aboriginal women also participated in non-Native beauty contests. In 1961, Marvel student Madeline Murdock, from Fisher River, was selected as the school's representative in the annual Miss Manitoba beauty contest held at the Red River Exhibition, and Diane Smith of Six Nations won Miss Ontario in the same year.[154] There was even a Miss Indian Affairs contest, part of the annual Queen of the Year competition sponsored by the Ottawa Civil Service Recreational Association. The Miss Indian Affairs title came with a trophy and a cash prize of $200 for the queen and $50 each for runners-up.

How do we begin to think about beauty and style as aspects of Indigenous politics? Looking for the larger cultural impact and meaning behind beauty contests, feminists have argued that beauty contests, like Indian Princess contests, were shallow and superficial and glorified mainstream representations of beauty that failed to reflect the lived realities of women. Jennifer Nez Denetdale reminds us of how images and contests of Indian beauty operated within gendered and colonial structures of power, many of which were disciplinary rather than liberating, and imposed rather than "traditional." Indeed, as per the contest rules, the year Janet Morris was crowned, Miss Indian Affairs contest winners were paraded before judges and audiences and then came out one at a time to be rated by judges. Marks were assigned for "Head" (hair should be well groomed, suitably styled for office wear, and face should be attractive and suitably made-up); "Figure" (should be well proportioned for the contestant's height); "Dress" (suitable for office wear); "Poise" (should have erect posture and be outwardly at ease); and "General impression" (overall impression of appearance and conduct). For that contest, it was stated that "we are looking for the girl who is most typical of the Government

Figure 2.4. First Nations women competed successfully in mainstream beauty contests as well. Here Diane Smith (Six Nations) is presented a trophy for being Miss Dominion of Canada by the previous year's winner, Edna MacVicar of Hamilton, 1961. Library and Archives Canada, E011052446.

girl—attractive, suitably and becomingly dressed, well-groomed from head to toe—a girl whom you might meet any day in any office. Office dress will definitely be worn."[155]

In their book *Seeing Red: A History of Natives in Canadian Newspapers* Mark Cronlund Anderson and Carmen L. Robertson argue that Canadian news stories related to Indian Princesses "satisfied human interest with little expectation for 'hard news.'" More seriously, they argue that these stories "served the purpose of commodifying Aboriginal women, in the best case, as shallow, empty, vapid and non-threatening." They concede that the reality was much more complicated, especially as the events were taken seriously and offered "positive opportunities for numerous Indigenous women."[156] Yet Indian Princess contests evoked a sense that Indian women's beauty was derived from two contexts—being trapped in a romanticized and conciliatory past or being integrated in a modern, non–Indigenous present. If Canadian media missed some of the larger political contexts of the Princess contests, it does not mean that they did not have a politics at all. Significantly, especially in an era of increased political attention from the mainstream, Indigenous cultural concepts of beauty, academic achievement, and political activism at community, provincial, and national levels were framed within Indian beauty culture as projected in Indian Princess contests. Indian Princess Canada 1967 was judged not simply "on beauty alone," one newspaper reported. "Their attitude in public, what they have done for Indian people, their achievements, speaking ability, deportment, poise, talents and education are just a few points taken into consideration by the judges."[157] Additional qualifiers for the 1969 competition included "character, education, Indianness which includes both language and dress, general grooming and poise, especially when speaking to a group of people."[158] At the 1970 Miss Manitoba Indian Princess contest ("open to girls 18 to 25 years of age" and "of Indian descent") "contestants were to have two native costumes, and must be able to give a three-to-five-minute speech on any subject relating to Indian history or to the present circumstances of the Indian people." That knowledge relating to "Indian History" be deemed an aspect of the contest is in some ways significant, as the telling of historical—or contemporary—lives of Indian people has never been an unpolitical task. Their clothing—contemporary and historical—made reference to this past, and became embodied and performed on them as they competed. For example, Dolores Nanie (Maniotu Rapids Reserve), was crowned Manitoba Indian Princess, 1967 wearing a floor length "heirloom buckskin with beaded cape" that had belonged to Mary Louise Defender and was made in the 1870s.[159] What effect does this have? While it may be perhaps read as "romantic" to non-Native audiences, contestants were creating a First Nations style that is embedded in a long history of presence and importance of Indigenous women's work.

A spectacle as any other, the Indian Princess contest can also be read as representation and imagery, and as such for whether or not the contests projected a novel and useful political expression for First Nations women, or were just another attempt to sanitize the lived realities of First Nations people in Canada. Like Myra Rutherdale and J.R. Miller argue in their exploration of the Indian Pavilion at Expo '67, Indian Princess contests were, in a way, in a "transitional phase" in the history of First Nations representation, attempting to balance "the theme of Indians 'joining the mainstream' with assertions of First Nations' pride, grievance, and entitlement." Significantly, the Expo also featured Indian "Hostesses" chosen from a nation-wide competition open to women between the ages of eighteen and twenty-five. Those selected—a mix of office workers/technicians, clerks/receptionists, students, and one accountant—were given training in makeup, posture, grooming, and walking, and were to be able to speak both English and French. Like Indian Princesses, the thirteen hostesses were to embody both modern and traditional imagery, but, Rutherdale and Miller conclude, projected an overall "pacific and non-confrontational" message that had a "short-lived impact" on its non-Indigenous audiences.[160]

The women who participated in such contests lived lives that could not so easily be dismissed. Margaret Brant, a "Modern Mohawk miss" of Tyendinaga Reserve who completed grade 12 at Belleville Collegiate with a four-year commercial course, was chosen Miss Indian Affairs for 1960. She was secretary-treasurer of the Indian Association of Ottawa, then newly formed. The association had "36 members and meets twice monthly for social evenings and dances. Non-Indians usually are invited." She was also a member of the Ontario Department of Highways bowling league in Ottawa and played the guitar for recreation.[161] When stenographer Miss Janet Morris, an eighteen-year-old artist and graduate of the C.B. Business College from Eskasoni, Nova Scotia, won Miss Indian Affairs 1965, she was featured in the *Indian News*. The article's title, "This Time She Really Is...Really Is Indian!"[162] reminds us of the relatively few Indigenous women working in the federal service at the time—even in the Indian Affairs department. In a 1966 issue of the *Micmac News* (a newspaper published out of Sydney, Nova Scotia), she contributed an article entitled "Living in Ottawa." In this article, Janet Morris explained how she had "taken advantage of my youth and education for off-reserve employment to improve my culture as an Indian." She also wrote that "the people in Ottawa are very friendly and discrimination is not an existing factor." She shared a furnished apartment with two "French girls," one of whom also worked at Indian Affairs. She enjoyed living on her own and returning home for visits. She concluded the article with her hopes for the future: "I am proud of the fact that I am Indian and I hope to see the educated Indian youth of Nova Scotia step out on their own to build careers worthy of recognition, and to build up their culture as Indian and Canadian citizens."[163]

Another First Nations woman, Kahn Tineta Horn, dubbed "Mohawk Princess," was a fashion model, actress, and Mary Kay cosmetic saleswoman (and Department of Indian Affairs employee). She combined beauty with assertiveness to become one of the most famous Aboriginal activists of the 1960s. She advocated for Indian control of land and resources, a return to traditional ways, and was involved in protests from the Jay Treaty to Oka and beyond.[164] Crowned Indian Princess Canada in August of 1963, Horn had her title withdrawn under a cloud of controversy less than a year later, by the National Indian Council, which sponsored the contest. According to the *Winnipeg Free Press*, "some council members thought Miss Horn, a Montreal model, was projecting her own point of view as council policy. She is known as an outspoken advocate of Indian rights."[165] Jeanette Corbière was chosen Indian Princess of Canada in 1965. Around this time, she worked at the Native Canadian Centre of Toronto as a social, court and youth worker and, like several other Indian Princesses, had spent time with the Company of Young Canadians, travelling across the country working with Native communities. Six years later, Corbière began a significant court challenge to the discriminatory section 12(1) b of the Indian Act. The figure of the Indian princess was thus more than a simple, one- or two-dimensional depiction of Indian women. In the records of the speeches of Indian princesses, it is clear that they did not shy away from volatile topics such as racism, Native-non-Native relations, the war in Vietnam, welfare, and Indian policy.

As Patrizia Gentile argues in her work on postwar beauty contests, the spectre of contests like "Miss Indian" should not be cast merely as a ridiculous stereotype, but rather considered carefully in the ways they posited new definitions of gender, sexuality, and labour practices that reflected changing cultural, political, and social needs.[166] Images of Indigenous womanhood that announced appeal, deportment, and urban middle-class status challenged racist notions that they were unattractive beasts of burden.[167] Moreover, Indian Princess contests posed serious questions to the powerful narrative that associated urban living with cultural loss. As opposed to the literature on women and sexual danger in cities, the literature on Native people and cities has endeavoured almost exclusively to recount the "realities" of urban Native people from a singular point of view. One "reality" dominates: "cultural loss" in the face of modernity. Even the best of this literature, which pays close attention to the important material circumstances of urban living (both in the cities and in terms of Indigenous sovereignty and land) and deals with associated issues of poverty, dislocation, and unemployment, relies on class and culture as a co-dependent program of loss.

In spite of this challenge, it is important to consider how images and contests of Indian Princesses are, at the same time, "hidden in the discourse surrounding Indian nations and nationalisms."[168] In her study of Navajo Indian Princess contests, Denetdale finds that the contests grew in an "atmosphere where Navajo leaders were extolling Navajo progress within the Western meaning of progress,"[169] including Western styles of Indian political organization. These systems, she and others have shown, resulted in a loss of Native women's traditional rights, including land use, property and livestock, and primary care of children; they secluded women in the domestic realm with little political and economic power, and subsequently wrote them out of leadership positions in tribal governments.[170] Princess contests, Denetdale argues, in many ways celebrated this marginal position as "traditional," or at the very least did little to contest its legitimacy: they presented a certain type of idealized Indian woman who was connected to both mainstream, modern, progressive society and a past continuum of culture and tradition. I would add to this that those photographs that remain from Indian Princess contests exist in files wholly separate from the many others that depict the "nimble fingers" of Native women doing people's hair,[171] thus seeming to celebrate the "natural" beauty while ignoring the labour behind it.

In 1970, the Manitoba Indian Brotherhood (MIB) sponsored an all-Indian pilot course at the Academy of Modelling and Self-Improvement on Portage Avenue. The class of six travelled to Toronto to model traditional and contemporary Indian clothing at the Canadian National Exhibition in a fashion show sponsored by the Indian Hall of Fame Committee. Three of the models worked for Indian political organizations (the MIB, the National Indian Brotherhood, and the Manitoba Métis Federation), and they all worked as secretaries, clerks, or receptionists.[172] At the time, three also held other beauty titles. Linda Lafreniere, a secretary at MIB, was also Miss Folklorama; Valerie Klyne, a secretary at the Manitoba Métis Federation office, was also 1969 Manitoba Indian Princess; and Pauline Wood, receptionist at the Manitoba Rehabilitation Hospital, was 1970 Manitoba Indian Princess.

Why would an Indian political organization sponsor a modelling class? Jo-Anne Fiske and others argue that, in many ways, women are symbolic representations of the nation.[173] While this may sound like a powerful cultural role, Denetdale points out that the Indian Princess presents a combination of ideal Indigenous womanhood and imposed notions of ideal Euro-American, middle-class womanhood, including purity, chastity, morality, virtue, and domesticity. Her body was a "site of surveillance" subject to strict moral and social regulation.[174] Contest rules eliminated women who were over twenty-four years of age, had ever been married or pregnant, consumed alcohol or tobacco, or cohabited with a man as a couple. Along with this surveillance of age, sexuality, and behaviour came questions about race and heritage, reminding us of how Indian Princess contests also espoused concepts of authenticity of colonial origin based on blood, physical appearance, and the state-imposed systems that regulated them. This analysis of Indian Princess contests holds true also outside of the Navajo nation. It is interesting that Indian Princess contest rules correspond not only to rules for other beauty pageants, but also to the narratives about Indian women in cities.

On a very important level, beauty is about visibility. Native people have used this concept to present images that quite often resist those imposed on them. Shelley Niro, a Mohawk artist from Six Nations, confronts the validity of visual and written images created by Euro-Canadians of Aboriginal people in her work. She said of her *Mohawks in Beehives* series that she gathered her three sisters and said "let's get rid of our kids and just have a fun day of it, let's go downtown [Brantford] and have lunch and be really loud and obnoxious.... I think that in a way, we were taking control." They put on make-up, did up their hair, and "invaded the city as an act of personal empowerment." She has another portrait of her mother under a hairdryer in the kitchen entitled "The Iroquois Is a Very Highly Developed Matriarchal Society."[175] "People have a stereotypical idea of what Native women are all about," she states. "We're portrayed in the movies as cardboard cut-outs and when you try to present a different image, people are disappointed. I want to blow that out."

Conclusion

The Placement and Relocation Program continued to grow, and as of January 1968 there were thirty-four employment and relocation counsellors and fifty vocational counsellors in seven administrative regions[176] who worked with the NES under new federal department of Manpower and Immigration (created in 1966 and now Human Resources and Skills Development Canada), provincial programs, and interested community organizations. While it never played a huge role in terms of numbers, the program held its place into at least the mid-1970s,[177] with the NES and Indian Affairs cooperating to assist a "carefully selected group of young Indians who wish to seek employment in urban centres" and to "insure that the Indian work force is provided with adequate opportunities for employment through the utilization of Canadian Manpower Centre programs."[178] Indian Affairs saw its role in this objective as complementing and enriching the services that Manpower provided,[179] so the department never fully committed to the business of recruitment, liaison, and placement of Indian labour.

The Placement and Relocation Program was in many ways characteristic of postwar Indian education and employment policy. The Placement and Relocation Program never indicated a commitment to a treaty right to education; it focussed on basic programs and service employment and did not encourage advanced education. It was designed only for a narrow slice of the Indian population who were formally educated and whom the department deemed "fit" for further training and relocation. The program was designed to "assist"—and thus, like other Indian policy, never saw education as a right, but as an arm of welfare assistance and a necessary step to full-time employment and, ultimately, integration. It is clear from formal Indian political organizations that efforts in the field of job placement were unsatisfactory. Significantly, the Task Force on Manpower for Native People, an interdepartmental committee struck in the mid-1970s, did make some minimal consideration of Native women's employment needs and experiences, outlining the ineffectiveness of existing manpower programs for Native women and acknowledging that Native women faced both racial and gender discrimination when looking for employment. Leah Cohen, who wrote the section on women, interviewed Native women who worked and lived in Ottawa in order to provide some background on this particular situation. Her findings are striking. She writes, "those women who attended schools of religious persuasion were enlisted as cooks and chars in maintaining the institutions. As a result, what limited education they received was both sporadic and insubstantial." She also observed that while it was "commonly believed that there are good jobs in the cities...[m]ost Native women experience an overall lowering of status [when they leave reserves for cities]. The occupations available are of marginal status and usually dead-ended.... The history of Manpower Programs as they relate to Native Women would suggest that they usually equip them with the most rudimentary skills. Furthermore, jobs often are not available when they graduate. Beyond upgrading, the courses available to Native women include secretarial skills, hairdressing, cooking and nursing assistant."[180]

Yet, in other ways, the Placement and Relocation Program cannot fit simply into one analysis and reflects many positive developments of the era as well, including the department's support for "upgrading" and financial assistance for post-secondary education. For example, by at least 1961, the department had committed funding—at least in theory—to every Indian child who "shows satisfactory progress—and requires financial assistance" for tuition fees, maintenance, books, transportation, and board (according "to the merit of the students and the financial circumstances of the families"[181]). Through the 1960s, the department put more emphasis on education and funding grants for economic development. For example, in 1963, the treasury board approved a significant "Education Assistance Program" for adult education that included tuition, books and supplies, transportation from place of residence to school and return, and room and board, personal allowance, and clothing—the nucleus of what has become the Post-Secondary Student Support Program. This program came to be articulated significantly by First Nations in Indian Control of Indian Education, and ultimately has now been fully reappropriated as a right, an expression of the treaty relationship, and a key First Nations historical experience in Canada.

In this chapter, I have attempted to outline some of the key features of the Placement and Relocation Program run by Indian Affairs in the mid-twentieth century. This program was in many ways similar to models of "rehabilitating" TB patients who were delivered to sanatoria in the post-war period. It is also similar to contemporary initiatives meant to relocate Indigenous people to urban areas in the United States and other white settler colonies. The program was part of a vision of integration that saw full-time labour as not only solving Indian unemployment, but also pulling First Nations out of ahistorical obscurity, poverty, and marginality to integrated and invisible equality through a careful process of vocational training and permanent employment played out by officers and candidates and written onto forms. The special period of "social adjustment" that was presumed necessary to this process allowed the department and its agents unfettered access into the social lives of Indian workers. Native women could not access just "any" kind of full-time urban employment. In the program, hairdressing courses were particularly popular, in part because the training was relatively brief and inexpensive and the job prospects were promising, but also because many First Nations women were drawn to the trade.

The Indian Affairs department associated relocation, training, and placement in the urban beauty industry with permanent social integration for Aboriginal women. They were, in the words of the department, among the "thousands of young Indian men and women who were torn between life tucked away on a reserve and life as a more fully contributing member of the Canadian community."[182] But it is clear that the story is far more complicated.

Moreover, the analysis of Aboriginal women's participation in a wage economy as some sort of clash with mainstream society and urban life is equally simplistic. Native hairdressers had to negotiate myriad expectations about cities and Indians, modernity, and tradition and even beauty and politics. The city was not the terminus of culture and tradition, nor was "tradition" a singularly liberating and decolonizing space for Aboriginal women. Likewise, beauty culture was informed by and informed Indian politics, and thus also an important site of Indigenous social and cultural history. Historian Philip Deloria asks us to rethink those "dichotomies built around crude notions of difference and assimilation, white and Indian, primitive and advanced" in order to discover the "complex lineaments of personal and cultural identity."[183] Aboriginal hairdressers force us to do just that.

While the Placement and Relocation Program supported training, education, and placement off-reserve, the federal government was involved in job placement in First Nations communities as well. Alongside the increasing number of First Nations women taking secretarial and stenographic training, others accessed a limited number of positions in the Indian Affairs department and Health Canada as well as band administrations. This was not the first generation of women working in such positions; rather, they joined earlier generations of First Nations women who worked for the government on the reserve.[184] However, by the 1960s, government positions had also begun to change, especially with respect to the roles and goals of First Nations labour. In the next chapter we will explore the advent and early history of one of these positions—the community health worker—in light of the historical context of early philosophies and programs of community development in Canada.

CHAPTER THREE

An Early Labour History of Community Health Representatives, 1960–1970

In 1962, the Medical Services Branch (MSB) of the Department of National Health and Welfare was formed by merging Indian Health Services with Northern Health Services and five other federal health programs. The MSB, today known as First Nations and Inuit Health Branch (FNIHB), was mandated to provide health services that fell outside of provincial health care jurisdictions, and its original focus was on public health priorities, delivered on-reserve.[1] This development was accompanied by a new federal mandate to promote Indigenous health workers—embodied in the Community Health Representatives program. This program drew from federal experience in the Placement and Relocation Program, ward and nurse's aide training and placement, and a broadening of federal involvement in on-reserve work placement.

A community health representative (CHR) is a public health educator who promotes well-being and access to services by applying specific skills in a community's language and culture. Titles for this kind of work included "Community Health Workers" and "Health Aides"[2]; however, I will be using "Community Health Representative," as it is the term that is used by the National Indian and Inuit Community Health Representatives Organization. CHRs were envisioned as liaisons between First Nations and Inuit communities and the non-local health professionals employed by the MSB. Officially, CHRs' original duties were to encourage fellow community members to use federal Indian health programs, to distribute official health education materials, and to explain the local culture and health needs to field nurses and other staff. Within this job, specific tasks were allocated according to gender. Women were to focus on maternal and child care and "health habits," while men were to focus on buildings and sanitation, including home improvements, water supply, garbage disposal, privies, and wells. With this gendered division of CHR labour, which was explained as "cultural," came different qualifications, duties, and wages.

Since 1970, most CHRs have been women, and so the CHR program's history touches on many aspects of twentieth-century Indigenous women's work, including federal labour programs and Indian education. It also has a distinct historical context as a community development labour plan to train and employ Indigenous people for distinct civil service positions within a particularly hierarchical and obstinate branch of the federal government. However, there is a silence around the gendered and colonizing aspects of CHR work in scholarly studies about it. There is in fact little historical analysis of the CHR program at all,[3] perhaps because of a lack of attention to Indigenous labour history and postwar Indigenous history. The dearth of scholarship on CHRs is even more noteworthy, however, in the field of medical history, where a recent expansion of interest in Aboriginal health history has resulted in the critical analysis of medical services in First Nations and Inuit communities, albeit with an exclusive focus on health "professionals," most notably doctors and nurses.[4] Moreover, Indigenous health care is often fashioned as a subject of community health science, a field that has historically tended to frame health care as provided by non-Indigenous people and Indigenous people as having low education and skill levels and an inability to access higher-end (and "relevant") health human resources positions. Such an approach not only ignores the myriad ways communities deal with health issues, it also fails to acknowledge racism and sexism in the systems, ideologies, and circumstances that influenced program development.

Background

According to Julia Adams, a CHR in Gitwinksihlkw Village, BC, a "CHR is very much the bridge between the health professionals and the community. We wanted to make sure that the new health professionals working in our communities have some cultural orientation to get to know the people. Our CHR program is linked to nursing and the CHRs assisted in implementing a cultural component into the CHR program. Speaking the Nisga'a language helps me to understand the needs of the elders."[5] These elements of the work—linking health professionals to communities, a connection to nursing work, and cultural and language skills—have remained fundamental elements of CHR work since its inception. As it unfolded as a federal labour force development initiative, these elements became part of a health professional training and labour program that involved a curriculum of health care training with practical and theoretical components, similar to a nurse's aide course. After completing this training, candidates entered the workforce on a probationary basis, which, if successful, became a full-time position as a CHR with the MSB. In this position, CHRs focussed on public health education and programming, reserve sanitation, visiting band members, and patient follow-up.

Three major factors stimulated the Community Health Representatives program. First, organized international efforts in the emerging field of community development influenced the founding principle of the CHR program that locally trained Indigenous people, employed by the state, would inspire communities to engage in projects to raise their own standard of living to that of the so-called developed world. By the 1960s, the United Nations had defined community development as "the process by which the efforts of the people themselves are united with those of Government authority to improve the economic, social and cultural conditions of communities, to integrate the communities into the life of the nations and to enable them to contribute fully to the national progress."[6] Community development as formulated in the CHR program was indeed about modernizing and improving Indigenous communities and integrating them with the nation so that all could work together for progress and share equally in its profits. Individuals engaged in CHR positions were to assist communities in "coping" with modernity or, as one proponent awkwardly put it, "to smoothen the jump into the 20th century."[7]

For Indigenous people in Canada, community development was enacted in policy by the federal government, the second key factor in the CHR program. Ethel Martens, an individual active in the international development scene, translated these ideas into a program that suited the needs of the MSB. Almost as a rule, the MSB workforce was non-local and transitory, and so it was thought that CHRs could bridge the "culture gap" between medical staff and First Nations and Inuit communities.[8] This gap was also one of economic and social class.[9] In addition, the CHR program was the culmination of the MSB's activities and efforts to involve First Nations and Inuit people in health care services delivered to them. Ironically, the CHR program remained characteristic of the postwar federal approach to Indigenous health, labour, and education programs in that it involved minimal financial commitment and no consultation with Indigenous communities until the final implementation stages.[10] Moreover, its ultimate goals were Indian integration and the transfer of responsibility for services from the federal government to provinces.[11] The CHR program was also a response to a fairly long-standing dispute between the federal departments of Indian Affairs and Health and Welfare over which department was responsible for educating a much-needed Indigenous health care workforce. In this case, Health and Welfare developed a three-part training program, for which Indian Affairs agreed to pay education and transportation expenses. This commitment reflected the department's (unofficial) post-secondary funding policy and practices in the Placement and Relocation Program.

Like the Placement and Relocation Program, the CHR program was justified with a well-worn argument about welfare and productivity. "Canada cannot afford to ignore the potential of the Indians to contribute to Canada's economy," Martens wrote. "Many are existing on welfare. It is sound economics to train as many as possible for productive jobs."[12] While there were serious problems of unemployment, the suggestion seems to be that First Nations people—especially those who would work as CHRs—were unskilled and unproductive, when in fact the opposite was true. For example, among the first group of seven CHRs, four were or had been involved in band governments, two of the men as chiefs and two of the women as councillors.[13] Two had served four years in the army, and three had technical, nurse's aide, and orderly training.[14] Other skills and experience CHRs brought to the job included farm and agricultural work, guiding, trapping, fishing, cooking, raising children, working with the Indian and Métis Friendship Centre, leadership courses, working as a community development officer, lay delegate for the United Church of Canada, and vocational training and employment as a ward aide. In addition, CHR positions were not always as promising as Martens's lofty goals suggested. After training and a period of probation, male CHRs, under the direction of a "committee," and female CHRs, under the direction of a public health nurse, were to be hired on civil service contracts with Health and Welfare. The contracts were originally supposed to be permanent, but in the end most were offered on a one-year renewable basis. Moreover, the CHR job was conceived as a dead-end and precarious position low on the Indian Health Services hierarchy and was ultimately created with the intention of being phased out to provincial services. Thought to be a "temporary expedient to solve a temporary problem," it was suggested that the resulting "disposal problem" of CHRs ("most of them...too old or inadequately educated for any other professional training") be dealt with by "turning them into social workers." By 1964, the program was slated to be "phased out" over a five-year period.[15]

While the program was inspired by international efforts and geared to suit infrastructure and objectives of the Canadian state, it is important to recognize what was taking place in postwar Indigenous communities. Greater access to education and employment opportunities, more control over the planning and implementation of health programs, and the overall improvement of the health status of their people were issues at the fore of 1960s Indian politics. But communities also had a long history of engaging in health care both inside and outside of federal health services. "In the days before there was a CHR program," Christine McKay, of Kahkewistahaw First Nation, Saskatchewan, states, "I think most communities had one or two members who informally fulfilled the same kind of role. My mother was that person in Kahkewistahaw. My mother was a midwife and was always available to help people with whatever their health or other problems were. She was available to support mothers in childbirth, assist in times of grief and loss, teach young families traditional parenting ways, and did it all with seemingly boundless love and energy. My mother was an inspiration to me and I have tried to model my role as CHR after her example."[16] At the same time, CHR work addressed health concerns arising from the effects and conditions of colonization, including dislocation, poverty, and inadequate housing. Indeed, the program addressed some of the most pressing public health issues on reserves—infant mortality, malnutrition, and sanitation, as well as immunization and X-ray programs to eradicate diseases like tuberculosis.

As we will see in Chapter 4, the CHR program came on the heels of a noteworthy expansion in the number of Aboriginal women training as registered nurses, licensed practical nurses, and registered nurse assistants in the 1950s. Most of these women moved to urban centres for training and found jobs serving urban communities, so the creation of locally trained health care providers on reserves appealed to many communities. Such labour was greatly in demand by the MSB, and CHR training expanded alongside other initiatives to train nurse's aides and sanitation aides, to set up health committees on reserves, and to teach health education and social leadership in Indian folkschools, health and sanitation workshops, Indian adult health education programs, St. John Ambulance home nursing courses, and other programs.[17]

The work of CHRs required their ready acceptance by their communities and by the MSB as both health professionals and community ambassadors. It was "hybrid" work, requiring them to be Indigenous, "grass-roots," and community-sensitive on the one hand; and, on the other, to be responsible to the directives of federal Indian policy and services. Yet CHR work was not universally respected by either the MSB or the communities. Fluency in Indigenous languages and recognized local leadership, while requisite for the job, carried no real status in the workplace; cross-cultural communication would not become a recognized skill until later on in the 1980s, when curricular shifts in nursing education indicated an interest in providing cross-cultural training to non-Indigenous nurses.[18] Moreover, as government workers, CHRs faced distrust and alienation from their communities, and program evaluators noted that the program was understood as just another government initiative in which the community had little say.[19] In their own monthly reports, CHRs stated that they were often thought of as agents of the state, confused with social workers, welfare workers, and Parks Canada and Ministry of Natural Resources staff.[20] They were indeed asked to help with fishing and mining prospector licensing and to act as interpreters for Indian Affairs, the RCMP, and others.[21]

Unlike other federal labour programs for Indians like the Placement and Relocation Program, which saw employment and assimilation into the dominant Canadian society tied neatly together, the CHR program endeavoured to train an Indigenous labour force that would be "true to its people." The "self-help" model at the heart of the CHR program was itself formulated on the principles of "indigenization," a technique used to govern Indigenous people and make them into productive citizens.[22] Program materials suggest that productivity was indeed a key objective of the program, as it produced myriad reports, surveys, notes, memoranda, and evaluations, each of which focussed on the success or failure of the program's goals to make the Medical Services Branch more efficient through the training and employement of Indigenous staff. To push this analysis one step further, we must also see if and how patriarchy worked in this indigenization process.

The MSB invited communities to participate in the CHR program by first explaining the program to nursing staff and Indian agents, who in turn would promote the program among chiefs and councils.[23] It was proposed that by 1962–63 there would be forty-six CHRs, and it was estimated that 170 would be employed by the end of a five-year period.[24] During the first year of the program, 1961–62, eleven CHRs were trained in Norway House, Manitoba, and placed in their own communities; within a decade, several other full and "refresher" CHR courses were undertaken, most of them north and west of Norway House.[25] By 1967, seventy-three CHRs had been trained and sixty-three of them were working with the Medical Services Branch.[26] In 1969, the goal was to hire one full-time CHR for every 500 people and one part-time for every 100 to 500 people. The MSB attributed the success of the program to three key aspects: "careful selection, adequate training, and the right kind of supervision."[27] Indeed, there is more material about these three aspects of the program than any other. The emphasis on selection, training and supervision reveals the very narrow vision the government had for the CHR workforce, in terms of who could work as a CHR, the extent and quality of CHR training, and the limited roles CHRs would have within the MSB hierarchy of health care labour and service.

Selection

The selection of candidates for training was the first step in the MSB's hiring procedure for CHRs. This process began by calling for applications from respected individuals who had a "desire to serve their own people"[28] and a "lifetime knowledge of his community."[29] Indian agents or other community authorities directly asked or invited individuals to train as a CHR. Julia Adams recalls that "one of my uncles who was on the band council at the time and the local priest approached me asking if I wanted to attend a CHR training that Health Canada was offering."[30] Next, chiefs and band councils compiled a list of finalists from among the applicants to submit to an MSB-appointed committee, initially the Regional Planning Committee (of Indian Health Services), which would make the final selection.[31] Criteria for selection were fairly consistent during the early phase of the program. The 1965 committee prioritized: "natural leadership ability; acceptance by band and Council; good all round health; maturity; language—being able to speak both English and the native language; educational standing."[32] While they appear to be generally inclusive, these qualifications were clearly meant to attract skilled and respected leaders to the position of CHR. Beyond this, the MSB applied further criteria meant to shape the workforce to suit its vision.

It is noteworthy that academic qualifications and technical training, which in other contexts have served to limit pools of candidates and justify a preference for hiring white and hiring men, were not highly ranked as qualifications for the job of CHR. Indeed, formal education followed in the selection criteria behind leadership and maturity, and "his or her ability to lead and to work with people."[33] It is difficult to describe exactly how one achieves this recognition; however, in an interview about the CHR program, Peguis, Manitoba CHR Dorothy Stranger explained a bit about her life before being a CHR, helping to clarify the kind of experience the MSB valued for this position. She was educated and literate; however, it was her experience growing up with her father's aunt (whom Dorothy thought of as a grandmother) that, she felt, prepared her to work as a CHR. Dorothy's great-aunt taught her how to work, how to cook, and traditional practices. She also took Dorothy out to church and band meetings with her. "That's how I got started, I guess," Dorothy recalls. Participating in public meetings "grew into me." "When I got married I still kept going to meetings.... Then I got on the council. That was the start."[34]

Although leadership was a priority, CHR job ads, application forms, and terms of reference all required specific skills, including not only the ability to speak the local language, but also the ability to speak, read, and write basic English in order to communicate with MSB staff and to file reports. "We were supposed to be talking all Indian language, but we didn't,"[35] recalled Dorothy. Yet an inability to speak English disqualified some other applicants from training. When asked about potential Inuit CHR candidates for a 1963 training session, O.J. Rath, the Medical Services superintendent for the central region, complained, "Unfortunately we did not find any. Northern Affairs Adult Education Officers had very successfully combed the villages for likely students for their several projects and left no English speaking available Eskimo."[36] In addition to language criteria, application forms called for details on formal education (including reasons for leaving school), occupational experience, income, and participation in community clubs and programs. The reverse side of the form, filled out by federal personnel, contained sections on "personality estimate" and "mental ability and attitude."[37]

A candidate's "maturity" was a consistent qualification, and it is worthwhile exploring what this term signified. In its use of the term "maturity," the MSB applied patriarchial and heteronormative values that at least officially restricted young and single men and all but older, married women from becoming CHRs. In addition to written subjective evaluation by the selection committee, the MSB was quite specific about what "maturity" meant in terms of age, dependants (in the case of women only), and marital status. The program stipulated minimum age requirements of twenty-five for men and thirty-five to forty for women.[38] Age qualifications were specified because, according to the branch, "the type of person wanted is the person who is influential in forming public opinion. This generally excludes the very young and inexperienced."[39] This logic was also explained as being sensitive to a "'respect due to age' attitude" among communities and a stereotype of youth as "irresponsible and 'roustabout.'"[40]

The separate age requirement for women, it was said, was for "practical" reasons. It was meant to discourage candidates with children below school age, a secondary qualifier of "maturity" and one that applied to female CHRs only. These regulations were written into the selection process on the grounds that the formal training program involved a substantial amount of time away from the community and the nature of CHR employment was full-time. It was noted several times that for all candidates, "long absences from home" caused problems of loneliness for families, worry over their welfare "etc.," and restlessness to return to their communities.[41] One 1965 pamphlet explained that in addition to transportation and allowance for board and lodgings, Indian and Northern Affairs provided "any support required by the family of a breadwinner away from home."[42] When she was asked to pursue CHR training in Norway House in 1961–2, Dorothy Stranger recalls, "They said, 'we'll find a babysitter' and my mother would babysit too sometimes, you know, like take charge? And I went."[43] Here is how Freda Augustine of Elispogtog First Nation in New Brunswick recalls the beginning of her twenty-seven-year career as a CHR:

> At about that time when my children started school, Medical Services came into our community. They spoke about new training programs and showed film clips about different ways that we can help improve the community. I thought to myself, "This is the type of work I want to do." In 1969, I left home and my family for six weeks to go to CHR training in Saskatchewan, thousands of miles away. Home sickness was a heavy burden on me but I prevailed. I completed my training, came back home and jumped right into my responsibilities, my dream to make my community a better and healthier community to live in.[44]

Table 1 (below) shows the average age of candidates upon entering training, revealing a shift towards the acceptance of younger applicants in the program's later years.

Table 1. Average Age at Time of Training, by Province/Region, 1961–1969 and 1969–1972.

Before 1969			After 1969	
Region	Average Age	Age Range	Average Age	Age Range
Montreal	n/a	n/a	37	29–50
Quebec	n/a	n/a	26	24–35
Ontario	41	29–60	33	24–55
Manitoba	39	29–55	33	24–55
Saskatchewan	38	24–55	34	24–60
Alberta	40	29–55	30	24–40
Pacific	37	29–65	37	29–50
North	33	29–65	24	24–45

Source: Adapted from Health and Welfare Canada, Task Force on Community Health Auxiliaries, *128.*

Marital status was also used as an indicator of maturity: married CHR candidates were preferred.[45] The MSB did not explain why marital status was important to the job, but likely this reflected contemporary values of the dominant Canadian society, which equated marriage with being safe, normal, and reliable.[46] (It is worth noting that the same requirement also applied to elected female chiefs in the same era.[47]) Married CHRs were also less likely to encounter "sexual jealousy" or other instances of mistrust or animosity during CHR training sessions or when working in a community, especially when doing home visits. In his 1964 report, sociologist Dr. Abramson explained,

> It is very difficult for a male worker to talk to the women of the reserve without arousing a great deal of suspicion and jealousy from their husbands, especially if they are away a great deal of the year. Similarly, the women workers find it difficult to talk to the men about improvements in the home, about digging garbage pits or about building privies, yet the man must be approached about these matters, even if through their wives, since such matters are thought of as men's responsibility. It seems that the women workers have had less difficulty with sexual jealousy than the men, but one would suspect that younger women would have more problems with it than the present workers.[48]

The question of marital status arose several times over the course of the first ten years of the program, particularly in instances where candidates met all other criteria. The need for a CHR in the area where the candidate lived was weighed against the candidate's status as single or common-law, and it appears that need prevailed as a deciding factor.

Thus, unlike the Placement and Relocation Program and other federal economic development programs targeted particularly at (although not exclusively used by) the young and the single, the CHR program in this era favoured older and married workers. It seems almost a reversal of the contemporary mainstream logic to target middle-aged married women with children for employment training and placement, particularly when, in Canadian society at large, it was still expected that women in public positions would quit upon marriage or at least once they had children. In reality, it serves as a reminder of how that trope is limited to the experience of white, middle-class women.

This unique characteristic of the program is especially clear when contrasted with nurses, the MSB's largest sector of employees, who were nearly all young, unmarried, and without dependants, as suited the ideals of femininity and sexuality in the field of nursing. Mobile, single, and independent, these women were the attractive face of the modern and expanding system of federal health care. Indeed, details about nurses' youth, eye colour, hair colour, stature, and attire invariably accompanied descriptions about their work; their physicality seemed to be enhanced by the "dirty" and rugged backdrop of their labour.[49] Behind the wheel of jeeps and station wagons, they flaunted a relationship with motor vehicles that flew in the face of what was considered normal for Canadian women. In the manly MSB uniform, reminiscent of a militarized Canadian womanhood, they showcased their sacrificial, non-traditional yet feminized work as heroic because it suited national interests,[50] and they expensively and attractively performed the work of the nation. Ironically, their primary task as public health nurses was to teach women how to be settled, married, and dependent—those lessons that informed the pamphlets, films, and felt boards of the time.[51] A temporary transgression from the confines of gender norms, MSB nursing really only reflected, rather than contradicted, the postwar feminine ideal.[52]

At the same time, the single status of MSB nurses was a source of some controversy in the branch, particularly in discussions of "fraternization" between white women and Indigenous men. One Aboriginal nurse, Jennie Neilson, working in Bermuda in the 1950s, recalls a nursing supervisor telling all the Canadian nurses, "You're in the top drawer of society and that's where you want to be at. Don't go out with Portuguese and Black men."The head nurse also told them that "just like in Canada they wouldn't go out with an Indian on a reserve, they shouldn't go out with men of other races in Bermuda."[53] The assumption was, of course, that MSB nurses were non-Aboriginal. To regulate interracial relations, MSB nurses usually lived in physically segregated, government-subsidized accommodations[54] not open to First Nations members of the community. Whereas "white weddings"[55] between non-Native people in Indigenous communities were made legitimate through widespread public celebration, mixed marriages between white nurses and Indian men were not so publicly celebrated.[56] Such marriages were normalized, however, in a popular romance genre that nonetheless limited the forms of expression these relationships could take, focussing on how a particular chemistry of patriarchy, labour, identity, anthropology, and postwar "integration" worked to create happy Canadianness.

One example of this was a double marriage between two white women to "Eskimo" men in the late 1950s. "Fraternization between whites and Eskimos, despite government anxieties, sometimes has a happy ending," began one article. One of these young women, Grace Margaret Pinder, of Goderich, Ontario, was a registered nurse at the Moose Factory hospital, where she met her husband Elijah Menarik, who worked as an orderly in the same hospital. "The nurses lived on the third floor of the Moose Factory Hospital and the orderlies on the second," the article explained. "In view of the close quarters and what Mrs. Menarik describes as a "grave boy shortage," fraternization was inevitable. While Mrs. Menarik's description can be located in a heterosexual nursing culture dominated by women, it also could insinuate that it was access to white men that was in shortage. However, "her decision to marry an Eskimo" was not how her "pre-marriage problems" were explained, rather they were attributed to their "differences in education" (Elijah was "raised at an Anglican mission and given a grade-school education") and the fact that "he is an orderly and she is a nurse and the officers shouldn't mix with the troops." Of their wedding, at a Presbyterian church in Toronto, she said that "the minister was only interested in whether my husband could support a wife." When the article was published, they were living in a "middle-class housing project in residential Manor Park," where "she gets along with her neighbours extremely well," and her husband was "hitting the books at night school to improve his English and mathematics" while working for the Department of Northern Affairs and National Resources. They looked "forward to a return to the wonderful freedom of the north" and planned to be transferred to Frobisher Bay, where "Mr. Menarik probably will supervise a rehabilitation centre with a staff of whites working for him." As if to reassure readers of his legitimacy in this position, the article explains that he was brought up in an Anglican mission: "The only thing Eskimo about him is his parentage."[57]

This case reflects that intermarriage was popularly perceived as a rarity, and it is noteworthy that any exceptions to unwritten health department policies were brought within acceptable norms. In the initial CHR program, however, there were no discussions of the exceptional single woman at all; rather the emphasis was only on women who were already married. The meanings the MSB associated with unmarried white nurses were simply not associated with unmarried Indigenous women. And any discussion of female CHRs and sexuality was confined to concerns about "sexual jealousy," and the close relationship of CHRs to fellow members of their communities presenting problems of trust and confidence in public health work.

In explaining his preference for selecting married women to attend a similar program to train Indigenous health workers in the Yukon in the late 1950s, Zone Director MacKinnon stated that although "training will involve child care and increased costs, the wastage resulting from teaching single girls that do not return to their homes will be greater." Here, MacKinnon was likely referring to a trend in Indian postwar education that resulted in longer-term relocations for training and employment. He would also be sensitive to (but not necessarily irritated by) the fact that the heightened gender discrimination written into the revised 1951 Indian Act meant that if Indian women married anyone from outside their community, they would lose community membership altogether and in fact not be permitted to return to their homes. He went on: "The young married adult men will be the next most effective group, particularly if given other education in health and training in building trades. The selection of a married couple for training is the best solution because the family unit would have clear objectives and the ability to carry them out."[58] In addition to "husband and wife" teams, "son and mother teams"[59] were also recommended, suggesting the underlying emphasis on family relations and gendered division of labour in the MSB.

That men and women should be trained as CHRs in equal numbers and hired on in communities in pairs was often argued. Male-female pairs of CHRs would divide labour by gender and thus increase the spread of community health teachings while lightening the workload of each CHR and maintaining societal gender norms. Additionally, seasonal employment justified employment in gendered pairs. If men were working off-reserve, single CHRs had to either forgo visits to them or travel great distances and be absent from the rest of the community. It was suggested by a Northwest

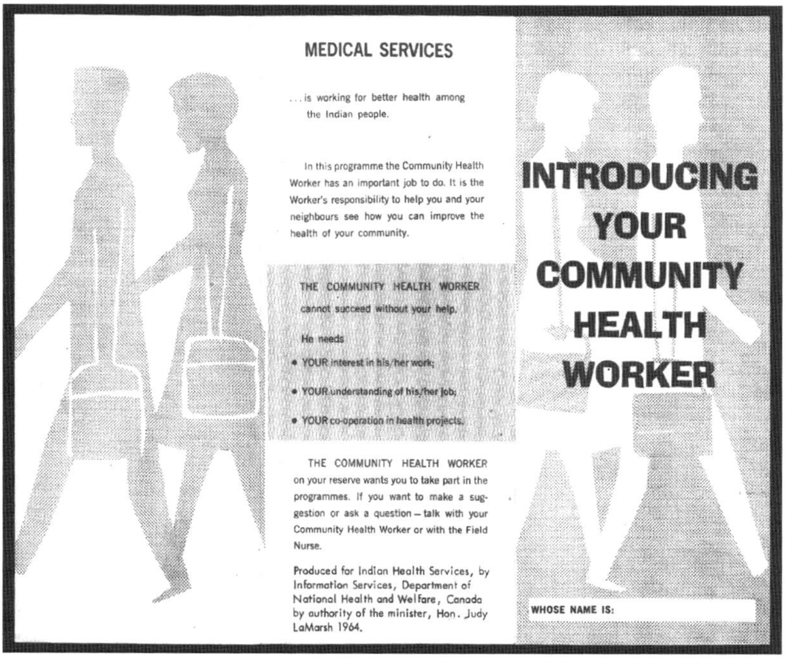

Figure 3.1. Indian Health Services, Department of National Health and Welfare Pamphlet that introduced the Community Health Worker (CHR) program to community members. Library and Archives Canada, E01098433.

Territories planning committee in 1966 that men could work in "outlying areas" and women in "more settled ones."[61]

For the first CHR training session in Norway House in 1961-2, seven men and four women were selected, with two other men who trained separately as dental assistants. None were married to each other or were related as sons and daughters. Each came from a different community and eventually worked separately at different communities. This pattern would ultimately prevail. The recommendation of "pairs" of CHRs was rejected by southern Manitoba zone superintendent J.G. Nicholas, who argued that "their main function is health education at which workers can set their own pace. Results will therefore depend, not on the number of workers, but on how well they can 'get through.'"[62] In another response to the Northwest Territories study, it was explained that while male and female health workers may be an "ideal solution" to sexual jealousies, "there is a limit as to the amount of health education we can push down people's throats and two workers in a relatively small area would soon saturate the community with health education and may even create antagonisms to health promotion in general."[63] In practice, whereas there was a recognition that women workers would contribute more to family health and men more to "community organization on solving problems,"[64] the MSB refused to fund two CHRs per community, and many individual CHRs in fact worked for more than one community.

While Ethel Martens's original plan was to train both women and men, she was not explicit about either gender parity or gendered pairs. For example, Martens recommended only male candidates for the second CHR training program in the Foothills region at Cambridge Bay in 1963, although not without criticism.[65] The planning committee was upset by her decision because the "big problems in the North" were seen to be "in the field of child and maternal health—care of children—nutrition, etc."[66] Indeed, the advantages of hiring female CHRs were readily acknowledged; they knew how to tend to the sick and injured, and were skilled in obstetrics and infant care.[67] But, Martens argued (without referring to the added stipulations about age and dependent children on female candidates only), recruiting women was more difficult than recruiting men.[68] Five Inuit people (two women and three men) and one First Nations man were at the fifth training program, held in Fort Churchill in 1967. Martens recorded that this group "had the smallest number of trainees than any previous course and their average [age] of 30 made them the youngest class to date."[69] Their educational background and command of English varied, but Martens was silent with regard to both marital status and number of dependants. The two sessions at Cambridge Bay and Fort Churchill seem to have been as close as Martens got to her original vision for the program, since she most frequently referred to them.

In an earlier incarnation of the CHR program, the eastern regional superintendent argued that "if they chose to select a woman...this may have advantages—the women are always at home if children are sick and need attention and always on hand for camp accidents while men may be away, also... women [have] always taken an active part in obstetrics and infant care."[70] The prioritization of public health concerns in which women held expertise is noteworthy, especially in CHR labour, which was essentially divided by gender. While men CHRs outnumbered women until the late 1960s, usually by about a third, by 1973 the majority of CHRs on staff were women and this predominance remains today.[71] Table 2 is based on incomplete and sometimes contradictory numbers culled from a variety of sources about the CHR courses, but it provides a sense of the changes in CHR selection over a period of about ten years. For example, despite goals to hire only older, married women, six of the twenty women in the 1970 program were unmarried (listed as "Miss"). Class photographs of CHR courses also reflect this shift towards including younger, single women.

Table 2. CHR Training Programs, 1961–1971.

Session and Date	Men	Women	Women "Miss"	Women "Mrs"	Total
Norway House 1961–2 (Full)	7	4	0	4	11*
Cambridge Bay 1963 (Full)	8	0	0	0	8
Norway House 1963 (Refresher)	5	0	0	0	5
Fort Qu'Appelle 1964 (Refresher)	5	2	0	2	7
Fort Qu'Appelle 1964 (Full)	15	10	0	10	25 **
Hobbema 1965 (Full)	15	10	n/a	n/a	25***
Inuvik 1965 (Refresher)	n/a	n/a	n/a	n/a	n/a
Norway House 1967 (Refresher)	n/a	n/a	n/a	n/a	n/a
Fort Churchill 1967–8 (Full)	4	2	n/a	n/a	6
Coqualeetza 1968	n/a	n/a	n/a	n/a	21
Miller Bay B.C. 1970	n/a	n/a	n/a	n/a	7
Fort Qu'Appelle 1970	11	20	6	14	31****
Brandon 1970 (Refresher)	8	6	0	6	14
Moose Factory 1971 (Full)	17	21	5	16	38*****
Saskatoon 1972 (Full)	n/a	n/a	n/a	n/a	55

**The 1961 Norway House course included an additional two male dental assistant students; the total counted in 1973 was ten.*
*** The 1964 Fort Qu'Appelle course included an additional three dental assistant students, two women (both "Miss) and one man; the total counted in 1973 was twenty-four.*
**** Based on class photo; another source records a total of twenty-six in the class.*
***** The number is also recorded as 27 and 32.*
****** The number is also recorded as 29.*

Sources: LAC, RG 29, vol. 2706, file 804-4-2, pt. 2, "Community Health Worker Training Program for Cambridge Bay, NWT"; RG 29, vol. 2706, file 804-4-2 pt. 3, "Reports Given at Refresher Course—Community Health Worker Training programme—Fort Qu'Appelle, Saskatchewan week of June 15, 1964," "Community Health Workers Refresher Course," "General Comments—Community Health Worker Training Programme," and news release, "Self Help Programme for Indians," 21 April 1964; RG 29, vol. 2705, file 804-4-2, pt 1, Community Health Representatives Training, August 1956 to December 1961; RG 29, vol. 2707, file 804-4-2, pt. 1 7B, "CHW Course—Fort Qu'Appelle, Sask"; LAC, Health and Welfare Canada Medical Services Branch Photographs Accession 1983-120, Box 05135, "Group portrait of Hobbema Aboriginal Community Health Worker Program," December 1965; RG 29, vol. 2702, file 804-2-1, Native Education and Training, June 1944–May 1964, letter to Director, Information Services Division, from P.E. Moore, 1 May 1964; Health and Welfare Canada, *Task Force on Community Health Auxiliaries*; and Dedam-Montour et al., *Voices of Community Health Representatives*.

After 1970, the number of students in CHR training courses increased dramatically.[72] Yet despite the growing numbers of participants, by 1973 only 67 percent of those trained were working as CHRs. Significantly, 47.9 percent of the men and 81.9 percent of the women who were trained got jobs as CHRs. On staff overall, there were ninety-nine women and forty-five men,[73] and while there was less of a discrepancy in Ontario and Manitoba, the Pacific region had twenty-two women and three men working as CHRs in 1973. What precipitated the shift towards training and hiring women, especially when CHR work encompassed both "traditionally male" and "traditionally female" work?

On a practical level, the federal government began to take responsibility for problems of water supply and waste management in First Nations and Inuit communities, which raised the question about whether male CHRs were still needed in certain areas.[74] It may also have been that more women than men applied in the first place, or that more women were approached to apply. This process of feminization was not confined to CHR work; it was also experienced in public health and health care professions more broadly.

What is clear is that for CHRs and feminized workforces in general—especially ones that are also racialized—gender discrimination was embedded in selection criteria and, as we shall see, job placement, and most notably remuneration.

Training

What did the training program look like for community health representatives in the 1960s? The most obvious and practical difference between the CHR program and other contemporary federal training and employment opportunities for First Nations and Inuit people was that CHR education and employment was set, controlled, and supervised by Health Canada personnel, not Indian Affairs or post-secondary institutions in conjunction with labour or professional organizations. It was also entirely non-transferable outside of the MSB. Because the CHR training program was created by Health Canada for Indigenous people, it reflected how the MSB perceived Indigenous people as students and as workers.

There were three basic components planned for CHR training. The first was an orientation running from six to eight weeks and supervised by field nurses. It involved surveying reserves for "facts" and "attitudes" about health conditions and learning about the work of teachers, the RCMP, missionaries, and government workers.[75] The second component was a period of formal classwork that lasted between six weeks and three months and took place in

Figure 3.2. Community Health Worker programs required long-distance travel and periods away from families and communities. Here Ethel Martens (health educator), Sammy Anderson, J. Courchene, Dorothy Stranger, E. Ettawakappow (students), and M. O'Flaherty gather at the end of the CHR Program on 9 April 1962. Library and Archives Canada, E011052428.

a local school, hospital, or community hall. Dorothy Stranger recalled that her training was led by Ethel Martens, who was "a world health educator and she was with a nurse and I think they called him an engineer, a sanitarian.... It was good, we had just three of them and...how they worked it they would, like, one day they would ask the RCMP to come over and talk to us, we could ask questions if we wanted. They'd ask the nurse to come. And a doctor. Teachers. Just everybody in the community. Maybe some old women. That's how they trained us."[76] Originally, the training embraced a small group approach, but over time the classes became larger, partly because it was more cost-effective and partly because of the increasing demand to fill CHR positions on relatively short notice.[77] The third component of the training program was a one-year probation period of supervised on-the-job apprenticeship in the CHR's own community. The idea was for novice CHRs to develop working relationships with local health teams and gain the confidence and support of the community. In 1970, the formal classwork

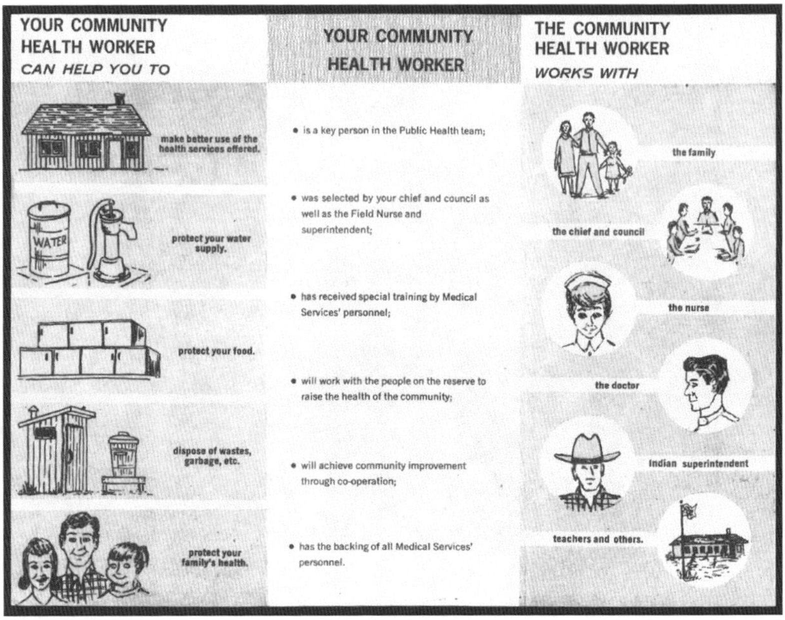

Figure 3.3. Indian Health Services, Department of National Health and Welfare Pamphlet.
Library and Archives Canada, E010984336.

was undertaken in two courses, eight and four weeks respectively in length, separated by a six-month apprenticeship. Periodic refresher courses were to provide ongoing training for CHRs.

CHR training was funded by the Department of Indian Affairs according to the ad hoc formula used to fund students attending vocational schools, colleges, and universities (transportation,[78] books and equipment, and a "monthly allowance" or wage, from which room and board were paid). Candidates each earned $100 per month during the orientation and classwork period,[79] and from which they paid approximately $70 for their room and board.[80] In at least one CHR course, Ethel Martens deposited everyone's cheques into one account at a local bank, out of which board, coffee, and recreation fees were paid. Then, each had access to an equal portion of whatever was left in the account.

The classroom work covered a range of public health topics including germ theory, nutrition, garbage and human waste disposal, drainage, springs, wells and safe drinking water, insect control, communicable diseases, dental hygiene, the hazards of smoking, alcohol, and drugs, fire safety, recreation, sanitation, and housekeeping. Training also covered first aid, sometimes in a St. John Ambulance course, anatomy, and care of a variety of different types of patients.[81] Instruction in "family health" from prenatal care to old age was integral to the course and included care of mother and baby, identifying and assisting neglected children, and educating the public about healthy family relationships. There were also discussions on social health topics, including racial prejudice and cross-cultural relations. The education was not simply theoretical, but also practical and technical, as students learned and practised different types of teaching methods and aids, including audio-visual aids like films and filmstrips, models, flip charts, felt boards, posters, and pamphlets,[82] to foster CHR communication, problem solving, team-work, and "community action."[83] The training program held in Cambridge Bay, Northwest Territories, for example, explored topics such as "water pollution," "introduction to excreta disposal systems," "how disease travels," "general sanitation, housing, lighting, ventilation," and "skin diseases and their control." It also explored teaching methods in a panel entitled "Teaching in the community—how people learn, barriers to learning."[84] Microscopes were set up, and the students observed microbes that contaminate food and water and cause epidemics.[85] The group took field trips to find and discuss "problems," attended inspections of kitchens and bathhouses, discussed food preparation and handling, and learned how to organize clean-up campaigns. A white rat experiment was conducted to learn about nutrition, and budgeting was taught by a trip to the Hudson's Bay Company store to price food.[86] Topics for training sessions centred on nine main areas: housekeeping/renovating, germ theory/common illnesses/diseases/skin conditions, child and maternal health, fire/accident prevention, food/nutrition, waste/water management, pest control, dental health, and first aid.[87] Significantly, in a 1973 survey, CHRs were asked if they had received sufficient training; 28 percent of respondents replied "yes"; 68 percent replied "no" and the rest had no response.[88] This may suggest that in spite of the wide range of CHR training and its intense nature, it remained inadequate in relation to the expectations of CHRs once they were working.

Gender segregation was written into the content of CHR training. The class was divided into men's and women's groups for up to two weeks of the formal coursework. In these groups, women attended discussions of "public health nursing subjects" taught by a nurse; men received training by a sanitarian in practical sanitation, safe water disposal, and housing and home improvements. While both men and women took a St. John Ambulance

Figure 3.4. World health educator Ethel Martens and teaching aids. Library and Archives Canada, E011052432.

course in first aid, women also took a home nursing course. During their on-the-job training, women were to focus on maternal and child care and "health habits" under the local nurse's supervision, while men were to solve "sanitary problems" (garbage disposal, constructing privies and wells) and reported to a local health committee comprised of local band and federal government authorities.[89]

At least one individual voiced criticism that the content remained too fixed on this gendered binary. In the 1970 course at Fort Qu'Appelle, Saskatchewan (in which twenty of the thirty-one students were women), MSB sanitarian F. Cayer noted that CHRs were "oriented toward working with nurses and health educators," and so "on graduating [they] will not appreciate the importance of calling on sanitarians for any problems." It was also pointed out that women in the program were excluded from meetings held with sanitarians. These meetings would have dealt with issues of waste management, possibly pest control, and water testing, chlorination, barrels, sampling, and wells.

Figure 3.5. The CHR program involved a wide range of public health education including diet, nutrition and homemaking; here CHR students in the 1964 Fort Qu'Appelle program shop at a grocery store in Qu'Appelle, Saskatchewan. Library and Archives Canada, E011052298.

Cayer also complained that people were "often treated as children during training."[90] This was a common approach of the MSB to First Nations health eductaion. Paule McNicoll, Frank Tester, and Peter Kulchyski characterize one of the popular contemporary health education books for the north, *The Book of Wisdom for Eskimo*, as an expression of modern Canadian colonialism in part because of the book's extremely patronizing and paternalistic content and style, its lessons in "self-reliance," and its racist content.[91] Similar themes can be found in the content of CHR training, which, while extending teaching roles to Indigenous people, still embraced a colonizing curriculum and infantilizing methods of instruction. The program used contemporary literature produced by Health Canada that was purposefully regulatory and simplistic and uncritically bolstered diet and health information packaged by the Milk Foundation, the Canadian Dental Association, and the Canada Food Guide that was as impractical as it was imperial for many of the Indigenous communities served by CHRs in these years. Most of it directly targeted women. Ethel Martens was also a fan of films, filmstrips, and animated short films, integrating at least one or two per day into the training schedule and often showing certain films repeatedly. The films were mostly

Figure 3.6. In the CHR program, women were to focus on child and maternal health while men were to focus on buildings and sanitation, including home improvements, water supply, garbage disposal, wells, and, as this photo of students in the 1964 Fort Qu'Appelle, Saskatchewan program illustrates, privies.
Library and Archives Canada, E011052451.

produced by the National Film Board, Crawley Films, or Health Canada, but some were Disney shorts from the 1940s and 1950s, all of which promoted Cold War North American politics of domestic containment, security, and heteroracist patriarchal nationalism ("Defense against Invasion," "Water: Friend or Enemy," "Planning for Good Eating," "Food for Freddie"). Such films depicted heterosexual nuclear families headed by male breadwinners and dealt with a range of topics from germs and good nutrition to adolescence and child safety. In all ways, they reflected the norms federal agencies wanted to impose on First Nations and Inuit communities.

These messages would not have been new to postwar Indigenous communities, but enacted in the imbalanced framework of CHR training, most notably characterized in wage scales, they seemed all the more problematic. There is a substantial amount of archival material surrounding the appropriate remuneration of CHR work. Debates over salaries for CHRs were inflected by the original vision of a voluntary labour force[92] and based on standards used by Indian Affairs in funding training. Ultimately, CHRs' wages were determined based both on gender and in relation to others working for Health Canada.

In the postwar period, Indian Health Services (IHS) saw itself as a long-serving Canadian charity rather than a shared and reciprocal institution embedded in the history of land and resource appropriation. The community development philosophy of self-help attached quite well to the IHS, bolstered also by postwar anthropological and sociological understandings of the havoc modernity (or "civilization") and dependency were wreaking in Indian communities. According to these ideas, Indigenous health workers would function, in the words of P.E. Moore, head of IHS, "on a part-time basis free-of-charge from a spirit of service to their communities." Part-time voluntary work would create a necessary "transitional step" to the industrial world of wage work while alleviating hostility for "culturally foreign elements" (like wages). Bands would thus gain a "valuable" lesson in self-sufficiency and escape a pattern of aggressive dependency.[93] H.M. Jones, welfare superintendent of Indian Affairs, though not always a voice of reason, pointed out that it would in fact be difficult to persuade Indians to volunteer their labour at work for which civil servants were paid. Furthermore, he argued, administrative control would be maintained by the department and its staff, limiting the extent to which Indian groups could be free to choose and act upon their own priorities, which were, in effect, the basic principles of community development.[94]

Since they were not perceived as integral to the program's ideals, salary issues were thus one of the most underdeveloped aspects of the program at its outset. Positions were kept outside of civil service regulations for both temporary and permanent employees until 1963, when a standard wage scale for part of the country was finally set by the Treasury Board. In one job description, the salary section was left blank, with the following statement: "Necessary adjustments will be made for the prevailing rate in each area. Environmental allowance will be paid where applicable."[95] Elements of the voluntary ideals remained in the program; for example, CHRs were not paid for overtime work.[96] According to one job description, the CHR's job was "full time" or "approximately 8 hours" daily, and the "nurse as a general rule, should know at all times where to locate the community health worker during regular working hours." Sometimes, however, it was necessary for CHRs to "work in the evening or on weekends," which was to "be considered as part of the week's work."[97]

During the first two phases of training, salaries were equal between men and women; however, upon entering the probationary period of apprenticeship, salaries differed markedly, and this was mandated from the start. "Women will be paid $150 monthly and men $175 monthly for one year," explained the initial job ad in 1961.[98] The Treasury Board affirmed this difference in its approval of wages for the "Graduate Nurses, Ward Aides and Hospital Attendants" regulations. Wage rates for health aides were broken down into three classifications (grades 1, 2, and 3) and two categories: health aide (health education) and health aide (sanitation and dental). Monthly wages differed by $50 between each grade of health aide (education) and health aide (sanitation), positions which were divided by gender.[99] In 1965, the differences were confirmed in progression, again in an ad for community health workers. Salaries for women and salaries for men were listed separately, with men paid $50 per month more than women.

Table 3. CHR Salaries by Gender, 1965.

	First Six Months	Second Six Months	Second year
Women	$185	$195	$205
Men	$235	$245	$255

Sources: LAC, RG 29, vol. 2704, file 804-4-1, pt. 1, "Medical Services Department of National Health and Welfare Requires Community Health Workers (Male and Female)," c. May 1965.

CHR wages were set relative not just to each other but also to other MSB staff. For example, it was decided that a male CHR should make at least as much as a janitor,[100] but less than a certified nurse assistant.[101] The greatest concern was that if a male CHR earned as much as a public health nurse there would then be no incentive for nurses. One health official commented, "A married community health worker will in most instances find himself in a better financial position than the nurse in charge under whose jurisdiction he works. We will only add discontent and confusion if this is allowed to continue." Another stated, "these aides are getting as much salary as our nurses and this is likely to engender the attitude, 'why the devil should I neglect my own work to help you when you are paid the same salary.'"[102] Along the same lines, a committee agreed that the salary scale for women be "below that of certified nursing assistant" (unless the person had certified nurse's training, and then adjustments could be made). No official salary was worked out for men by that committee, but it was suggested that basic salaries be the same as for women, with allowances for dependants.[103] Wage issues compounded with ideological differences and workload grievances to cause major dissatisfaction among rank and file Indian Health Service nurses and

CHRs. When the issue came up in a review of the program, one response was that revision of salary was not a priority, "particularly when a L.P.N., better educated and better trained, and carrying greater responsibility, only receives $210 (max) and has to pay board and lodging and income tax."[104] Indeed, one woman who was interested in participating in the CHR program was a certified nursing assistant. She indicated that the pay would be less than she received as a community health nurse assistant.[105] And many CHRs recall performing many of the services that the nurse would normally do, especially in communities where there was no permanent nurse or nursing station and visits from nurses were infrequent, such as Manito Sipi Cree Nation in Manitoba, where Jemima Ross was a CHR. She recalls, "I used to do a lot of the nurse's work, which included visiting elders, visiting whoever was sick or helping elders who needed help around the house. I would even do that with the doctors. We would go out and see elders and I would help them out by doing interpretation. We didn't have any cars, trucks or snowmobiles so I used to do my home visits by walking all over the community."[106]

Salaries for graduates were the topic of discussion between one Indian Affairs official and a missionary in the Foothills region in the early 1960s. The missionary argued that $175 per month was "not in keeping with the going rate for the Northwest Territories and that if candidates with leadership qualities were attracted, they would be lured away by more remunerative jobs later." He noted that that was only half the pay received by a janitor. Both wanted clarification of whether workers would be given an "isolated post allowance,"[107] which was indeed implemented when the Treasury Board approved the wage rates for graduate nurses, ward aides, and hospital attendants of the Department of Health and Welfare.[108] In their 1964 evaluation, Edward J. Abramson, Robert Arnold, and Gerald Piper proposed ways to develop and improve the Community Health Worker Program, one of which was to revise the pay scale for health workers. "A number of people suggested that the present salary is inadequate remuneration for the duties and responsibilities of the workers," they recorded. While no health worker discussed wages with any of them, they found that workers felt that as "the current pay is considered too low, a tendency exists for the health worker's job to be looked upon as another example of white exploitation."[109] It was said that the CHR salaries "are based on local prevailing rates and range, according to location, experience and any special responsibilities from $260 to $310 a month,"[110] more than the rates actually posted elsewhere by the Medical Services Branch.

Inequity in pay results when prevailing attitudes and assumptions about work traditionally associated with and/or performed mostly by women depress the value of wages paid for that work. It is often systemic in occupationally segregated and gender-based work. Pay inequity in CHR work was not formally addressed as such until two complaints to the Human Rights Commission near the end of the twentieth century. The first, filed 9 September, 1981, was brought forward by the Public Service Alliance of Canada on behalf of CHRs employed by the Medical Services Branch. This complaint was heard as part of a larger case alleging that the Treasury Board had discriminated in the employee classification and wages in the female-dominated "Hospital Services" (HS) group compared to employees in the male-dominated "General Services" (GS) group on the basis of sex, contrary to sections 7, 10, and 11 of the Human Rights Act. At the 1987 hearings that followed, the groups came to an agreement and a Consent Order was created: the Treasury Board was to revive classifications in General Services Standards and equalize wages in the "Hospital Services" and "General Services" groups at comparable classification standards. However, there was concern that there was continued gender discrimination in the effect of the new classification standards, and this led to tribunal hearings in 1989 and 1990. It was found that the classification level given to CHRs employed by the Department of Health and Welfare on reserves was under-evaluated, that there was a differential between the HS and GS classifications, and that systemic discrimination was the main, if not the only, element leading to the lower valuation of CHRs' work. One of the potential sites for this was CHR training. In the tribunal's decision they argued that:

> The under-evaluation of the specific vocational training factor in the face of a training manual calling for wide-ranging knowledge of health care practices may reflect the assumption that women, because of their traditional role as providers of routine health care in the home, particularly in rural communities, acquire much of this knowledge without special training. We wonder whether, if the job were regarded as a typically male role, it would still be the view that all this familiarity with health care practices is so readily acquired.[111]

The tribunal also took into consideration the "factor of environment," arguing that undervaluation reflected an assumption that "conditions encountered in making home visits or in carrying out routine screening or treatment procedures in a health care centre are not disagreeable." Continuing, they found that in fact these "are conditions which are commonly perceived as normal for women in their traditional roles as homemakers and care providers."[112] The claimant won this case, proving that CHRs had been wrongfully classified and should be further compensated. Any CHRs employed by the MSB between 9 September 1980 and 26 July 1987 were compensated "the difference between the equalization payments received pursuant to the Consent Order and the payments that would have been paid under the Consent Order if the Community Health Representative had been rated at a GS-5 level instead of a GS-4 level."[113]

These orders did not apply to CHRs who worked for First Nations entities (band CHRs). In this case, CHRs working for bands were being treated differently from CHRs who worked as public servants. As a result, the then-director of the National Indian and Inuit Community Health Representatives Organization (NIICHRO), the national professional organization of CHRs in Canada, filed a complaint with the Canadian Human Rights Commission (CHRC) on 9 December, 1992 on the basis that the former settlement was discriminatory. The CHRC found grounds for the complaint, and on this basis the government offered a settlement ($0-$5000 based on years of service). When that offer was rejected as too low, the CHRC advised that the case bypass the tribunal stage and proceed to federal court. The federal court refused to hear the case, and the complaint went back to the tribunal stage. Mediation was the next step, and the CHRs were awarded $45.7 million in a wage parity settlement in June 2000. This was the first time an Aboriginal group was awarded a settlement and had that settlement managed by an Aboriginal organization, NIICHRO. Before the settlement trust closed in 2008, 1,652 CHRs were compensated.

In the 1960s, women earned twenty-five to fifty dollars per month less than men. The undervaluation of CHR work continued from that time forward, and the only direct explanation I found for this pattern came from Ethel Martens, who argued that wage differentials by gender were "in keeping with the cultural pattern of Indian people."[114] Wages of CHRs were in fact relative to standard wages already established in the MSB and in keeping with "the cultural patterns" of the mid-twentieth-century Canadian civil service.

CHR Responsibilities and MSB Authority

The CHR program record reveals very little information about the work undertaken by CHRs in the first ten years. Rather, documents in the archive emphasize how they and their work would be supervised. It might be surprising that a new labour program in the field of community health did not record more on the actual work of the CHRs. Yet the philosophy of community development in health (which is self-help) ran counter to the mentality of IHS (which was "you work for us, we decide for you"). Therefore the original philosophy of the program did not function well in the context of the IHS, which throughout maintained its power, priorities, work culture, and administrative structures.

While they were integral to the work of IHS, CHRs were added near the bottom of a rigid gendered and racialized hierarchy of labour organized through a strict and centralized system of administration. Yet, remarkably, from Ethel Martens to the secretaries, cooks, and housekeepers[115] who worked for her, the CHR program was run by women. This could also help to explain why it was undervalued in the first place, as it was subject to yet another level of gender discrimination at IHS. Ethel Martens, who founded and directed the CHR program, supervised the MSB nursing staff working with the program, and trained and oversaw the employment of CHRs and local support staff, provides an excellent lens through which to view gender, race, hierarchy, and supervision in the 1960s IHS.

The distinctiveness of the CHR program in Canada was, in large measure, due to her influence. Martens was born in The Pas, Manitoba, in 1916 and taught school in northern Manitoba. During the Second World War, she worked as an accountant for the Canadian government, and while she was working in Ottawa, she was introduced to the Baha'i faith. After the war, she went to Australia and England (likely to teach), and then returned to start a BA in economics and international affairs at the University of Manitoba, becoming Baha'i in 1953 and earning the degree in 1954. She then worked as a health educator with the Province of Manitoba and obtained a master's degree in public health from Berkeley in 1957. Martens was hired by the Department of Health and Welfare in 1958 as the first health educator for the MSB, and she worked in this capacity until the mid-1970s. Meanwhile, she worked closely with other Baha'i in "Indian teaching work,"[116] first as a primary care consultant to the Baha'i international community, and then, after she retired in the late 1970s, establishing the Baha'i International Health Agency. She advised the Privy Council on health and women's issues from 1970 to 1972 and earned a PhD in social preventative medicine from the University of Saskatchewan in 1973. During her lifetime, Martens worked with the Canadian International Development Agency, USAID, and the World Health Organization, as well as Health Canada. She was named to the Order of Canada in 1998 for her international and national work in the field of culturally sensitive public health.

In her position with the Department of Health and Welfare, Martens would have been among a small number of Canadian women who earned more than the average Canadian man. Her job was an upper-level civil service position in a department where she would have been one of the only women, apart from nurses. Also, she would have been one of the most educated. In her book *Pick One Intelligent Girl*, historian Jennifer Stephen explores the massive mobilization and then demobilization of "womanpower" during and after the Second World War, including in the civil service, and describes some of the psychological, economic, and managerial techniques used in those projects between 1939 and 1947.[117] Ten years after Stephen's study ends, Martens became one of a markedly growing number of white women in career civil service positions at Indian Affairs and Health Canada. What did women bring to the civil service in the 1960s? Following Stephen's argument, the simultaneous modernization and professionalization of three areas administered by the federal government—rescue/social work, education/teaching, and nursing/public health—also corresponded with their feminization. Martens's job was, in effect, a combination of all three fields. These three fields opened opportunities for some white Canadian women, still considered inferior to white men but nonetheless superior to non-white men and women. Within the federal government they secured and expanded their roles noticeably in departments dealing with Indians. It is significant, for example, that in 1958, our first (and until the 1990s only) female head of Indian Affairs (which fell under Citizenship and Immigration at the time), Ellen Fairclough, also became the first female cabinet minister. But Fairclough's women's rights platform, which included equal pay for equal work, apparently did not extend to Indian people. It is important to recognize the power and authority both of and over racialized and feminized work in the 1960s.

Ethel Martens was probably originally more invested in the burgeoning field of international development than she was in IHS or education; however, the CHR program was an opportunity to marry these three professional interests. In 1960, she undertook a three-month World Health Organization travelling fellowship to study health projects among Indigenous peoples that aimed to "help" the Indian to "adjust" to "his environment" in the southwestern United States, Mexico, Guatemala, and Peru.[118] This work identified sanitation as one of the "primary problems with which all the developing areas of the world are faced." Back in Canada, she found similar conditions in Indigenous communities, where, she argued, standards of "housing, living conditions and health habits" were well below the average level of other Canadian communities and were reflected in high infant mortality rates. She argued that this resulted in "some lack of social acceptance of Indians and Eskimos by other Canadians."[119]

Martens's practical response to these issues was to work through the federal departments of Health and Welfare and Indian Affairs. Like others, she believed that a particular history of dependency had caused the deplorable living conditions on reserves and in northern communities. She, however, identified the roots of this dependency—the attitudes and approaches of the federal government towards Indians. She conceived the CHR program as a means to resist the top-down ideology of the Medical Services Branch and, in her words, the "paternalism" of the Department of Indian Affairs.[120] In her view, "participation by the native people in solving their own health problems is an effective means towards solution of such problems." She continued,

> because there are insufficient numbers of professional health personnel to cover all Eskimo and Indian communities, because there is need for trained native persons to help bridge the cultural gap between professional health personnel from one culture working with those from another culture, and because often there is greater acceptance of a member of one's own ethnic group rather than a member of an "outside" ethnic group when changes are promoted, it is planned that native health workers will be trained as Nurses' Aides and Sanitation Aides to be employed in Eskimo and Indian communities according to need. A few Dental Aides will be employed to assist Dentists.[121]

In explaining the program to others, Martens outlined the position of the community health worker:

> 1) The Community Health Workers must start out slowly and let people accept them in their role.
> 2) They are to work with the people of the community and not for them.
> 3) They are not sanitary inspectors but teachers of basic sanitation practices.
> 4) They do not tell or order people to do anything.
> 5) As their job is one of persuasion and not dictation—it will take a long time before the results will show (a slow, steady, solid program is better than a dictated one).

6) The Community Health Worker is directly responsible to the nurse but has his own program which should be planned with the help of the nurse (and the sanitarian when he is in the area.)[122]

Is there a gender politics to Martens's self-help plan? Yes, but it was so integrated into the philosophy of the program and the work of CHRs as to be commonplace to Martens. When Martens spoke of the "paternalism" of Indian Affairs, it was a genderless paternalism, but when she spoke of racism, her examples referred to Indian men's attempts to obtain employment. Though she likely would have been aware of equal pay for equal work legislation adopted in the late 1950s by most of the provinces and by the federal government,[123] she incorporated unequal pay and unequal work into the salary schedules and job descriptions of the new CHR program targeted at both men and women. In her program material, she included six pages of suggestions for men and just two pages for women (see Table 4). The differences are remarkable.

Table 4. Program Suggestions for Community Health Workers.

Programme Suggestions for Community Health Workers	**Suggested Programme for Community Health Workers (Women)**
Visit with the nurse to plan hours of work, office space, places where you will keep material and equipment.	Report to the nurse and talk about getting settled, a place for material, a desk, etc.
Start thinking about what clinics there are and when you might teach those who are waiting.	Talk about the training programme..., show daily programmes, share knowledge of teaching material brought back from the course.
Make sure your own place is in order, you may need to arrange with the nurse for some time to do this.	Take time to settle personal problems at home.
Go over map of the community and re-read the survey you did...you may want to put more on the map.	Interpret work (as they see it) to the nurse, doctors and other Medical Services Personnel.
Talk to Chief...about your work. Remind him about the Steering Committee.	Talk to Chief—solicit invitations to a meeting with Chief and councilors. Set up files for material. Plan month's work with nurse—teaching in pre-natal clinics, well baby clinics and home visits with nurse and on own. Work out monthly calendar, etc. Write monthly report. Meet with Steering committee.... Get invitations to talk to all groups.
... Talk with everyone... Try to meet with Pow-Wow or Rain Dance Committees.... Make home visits to some of the older people.... Have meetings with the Chief and Council.... Ask permission to invite non-Indians to come to the meeting.	

Source: Adapted from LAC, RG 29, vol. 2704, file 804-4-1, pt. 1, "Programme Suggestions for Community Health Workers" and "Suggested Programme for Community Health Workers (Women)."

The irony in this list of "suggested directions" to be undertaken is not missed. They are directions to give directions to people, when the CHRs were supposed to be working under their own initiative and avoid telling people what to do. The men's outline, as the headline reveals, did not actually specify gender and thus suggests that, in Martens's view, CHR work was innately and naturally men's work. Its suggestions, organized by month, included: "see the Indian Affairs Superintendent when he is on the Reserve. Arrange to spend some time with him to talk about your course and about the things you think need to be done"; "talk about fall clean-up campaign with people on the reserve, storekeepers, nurses, missionaries, R.C.M.P., Forestry"; "write to Zone for materials"; verify that "road equipment is working"; "If IAB are planning new wells, find out from them as much as you can and offer your suggestions about location and construction"; and "check school grounds for safety problems." It is possible that Martens assumed that First Nations and Inuit women (and not men) knew what work needed doing and therefore did not need specific instruction; however, Martens uses noticeably different language for men than for women. Men plan, build, and work in the public; women report, talk, and consult, or ask for invitations to consult.[124] This did not adequately reflect the approach taken by Freda Augustine, of Elispogtog First Nation, New Brunswick, who attended the 1969 CHR training program in Saskatchewan.

> One of my first responsibilities as a CHR was to conduct a community health survey. At the time everyone was getting sick, especially the babies. I wanted to know why so many children were sick and what was causing this. I went into the community to get to know people and their home conditions, the sanitation and safety. The survey allowed me to have a better understanding of the health condition of the community members and also the type of services that they needed. I reviewed the survey with the chief. I told him that we need a truck to haul the garbage out to proper dump sites and to give everybody garbage cans so people can properly discard their garbage. We also needed to provide more outhouses; most houses did not have indoor toilets. The chief and the band members all supported me and they did what they had to do. In my first three years of being a CHR I had accomplished every goal I had set out. Our community was looking so nice and healthy. That was my greatest experience and challenge and success and I called it "my highest degree of my world prosperity."[125]

Martens was as silent about class as she was about race and gender. "Help the people help themselves, don't tell them what to do"[126] was one of her favourite sayings. Based on a general self-help model, the idea was that Indigenous people would engage as "partners not passive recipients, in what is being done to help them become healthier."[127] It remains an irritatingly circular argument that addressed neither the colonial order (for which Martens worked) nor patriarchy (which she wrote into her CHR program). In the sources it is clear that at the time, Martens was a very popular instructor. Dorothy Stranger recalls, "Ethel Martens, boy I remember she was really strict, but a real nice person. She'd stand up there and she'd tell us things. I guess that's how professors work, I don't know. They just talk? And then she would ask us to write something or talk about something. I liked it, it was good."[128] While Martens preferred to see CHRs as the active agents in her program, rather than herself, it is clear that in practice their work functioned within a larger structure, which limited the authority and prospects of CHRs.

The CHR program was constructed to revolve around MSB nurses. The central region (Manitoba) was chosen to pilot the program, in part because its branch administration and staff were considered the most cooperative.[129] By this, it was intended that the program required the full cooperation of sympathetic field nurses. Originally, CHRs were to be hired only in communities where there was a full-time nurse and nurses could play a significant role in the selection and dismissal of CHRs.[130] Even when CHRs were hired in communities without nurses, nurses continued to be the constituents most frequently consulted about the program. During their orientation and probation periods, as well as after they were hired, CHRs worked under the supervision of the nurse, were directly responsible to her, and planned their program with her "help."[131] Nurses read (and sometimes wrote) CHR monthly reports and provided reports of their own on "their" CHRs.[132] While earlier monthly reports were anecdotal, made by both the nurse and the CHRs themselves, CHR monthly reports became standardized over time. The forms asked CHRs to describe the major aspects of their work (home visits, meetings, and public health projects), to quantify the use of teaching aids and films, to explain what advice was asked for by community members and what advice was given, and to outline plans for CHR work over the next month. Nurses were to fill out another standard form that verified and challenged these CHR reports, and there were also personal appraisal reports to be filled out by the nurse regarding the evaluation of the functioning of the CHR, providing an additional mode of supervision. It is therefore worthwhile to examine the work of CHRs and nurses in relation to each other. It is important to remember, too, that in some places by the 1970s there were many other people working in the health field, including health educators, environmental health officers and community health nurses, home care nurses, and home care workers; in the 1960s, all of this work was done by the CHR and the nurse.

One of the largest workforces of non-Native people in Indigenous communities, and by far the largest within IHS, nurses played a central role in the MSB. Nursing was not only central in a practical sense to the operation of IHS, it was also fundamental to IHS ideology and mythology. The picture of kindly female benevolence, authoritative medicine, and social and moral regulation, the nurse was the subject of a variety of films, statues, biographies, newspaper features, and even a sub-genre of non-fiction. MSB nurses claimed both professional expertise and heroic stature by virtually running the fringe of a modern medical system for Indians. In their work and by their example, they were depicted as making history by bringing modernity to First Nations and Inuit communities across Canada.

The nurse was an integral part of the modern medical system, composed of five regions subdivided into several more zones. Each region and zone had its own administrative team, the nucleus of which was a nursing supervisor trained in public health nursing who also acted as a consultant to the hospital nursing directors in her area. The beneficiaries of a golden age of expansion of health services in the 1950s,[133] professional MSB nurses worked in Indian hospitals, nursing stations, and health centres across the country. Hired centrally, usually in Ottawa or other cities in the south, nurses in this system were not encouraged to integrate themselves into the communities in which they worked. Their gendered influence lay in their objective "expertise" in Indian health and their distance in class and racial terms from the communities they served. They claimed this expertise in part through a professionalization process that had occurred earlier in the century and in part from their status as white women in Indigeous communities.

MSB nurses, like all professionals (including historians), were as a rule very protective of their particular expertise. It would be fair to say that the CHR program was generally and sometimes vehemently a source of anger and frustration to them. Not consulted before the program was implemented, having a supervisory role added to their already full work schedules, and, as a well-defined, empirically trained link in the hierarchy of health services, not entirely on board with how one could be trained and employed in the field of "self-help," MSB nurses were very clear about the subordinate position CHRs should have, not only in wage but also in status. As one nurse stated, the "nurse in charge is given the leading role and the top responsibility in his or her area," and she further warned that the zone and the region should "be on guard against inflating the value of the work of the CHW [CHR] in relation to that of the PHN [Public Health Nurse]."[134]

The CHR program added to a long list of nurses' grievances, including unsatisfactory working conditions, shortages, and problems with communication and overwork, which led to a long-standing and problematic high rate of turnover. For example, in 1959, thirteen field nurses left their posts in the Norway House and The Pas zones alone; in 1961, seventeen more staff members left those same zones.[135] The CHR program was envisioned in part to alleviate these problems. In their day-to-day labour, CHRs were meant to take on part of the workload of the MSB nurse, particularly her work in public health education. This was work that MSB nurses found very little time to do themselves. Moreover, most branch nurses did not have specific public health training (even though they were called public health nurses).[136] As one booklet on the CHR program explained, "the public health nurse, especially in outlying areas, has such a wide range of demands on her time and energy that frequently she feels discouraged, especially when she experiences disappointing results in some area of her work, and/or where the excessive demands themselves serve to discourage an attempt to solve problems."[137] In other versions, CHRs were to supplement or facilitate MSB nurse work. A survey in 1965 of nurses working with CHRs produced illuminating reflections on the work of the CHRs in relation to nurses. Mostly they saw CHR work as (language) interpretation, home visiting,[138] organizing clinics and clean-up campaigns, acting as a liaison, or continuing a program of public health "whilst [the nurse is] away from the reserve." One explained, "The Community health worker is most useful as an extension of the nurse's arm." Another opined, "The nurse working together with a good community health worker is like a hunter going out after game in a strange area accompanied by a good guide. Although the guide is the employee of the hunter, getting the game is 90% due to the guide."[139] This aspect of the program continued to haunt it, as nurses tended to define community health representatives as their "assistants" rather than working for the community.[140]

The duties of CHRs were in a very real way determined by how they fit with what was regarded as "professional work," including that of social workers, nurses, and sometimes sanitarians. For example, a report on the program made two recommendations regarding training: first, that mosquito control be included in the training, and second, that sex education ("sex hygiene"), particularly for "young newlyweds and youngsters reaching puberty," also be included in CHR training in order to deal with "the problems that result from illegitimacy and common-law marriages."[141] One response to these recommendations was that mosquito control was "somewhat too technical" and that sex education was "in the main, better left to nurses."[142] Another response to the suggestion that CHRs be trained to deal with "family problems" was that they "should not get deeply involved in family problems since this is not the function of the health aide [CHR]. If the health aide [CHR] becomes involved in family problems, he may be embroiled in family situations and his effectiveness as a health educator would be greatly diminished."[143] The report further recommended that CHRs be taught how to administer vaccines and other parenteral (by-injection) drugs. Opposition to this was justified because "health aides [CHRs] do not have the necessary background" and "wherever there are health aides [CHRs], there are nurses and there is no need for the health aides [CHRs] to be involved in the administration of vaccines and other drugs." In handwriting, someone added that "it depends on the intelligence of the CHW," and indeed, the situation varied depending not only on the CHR but also on the nurse.[144] It appears for the most part that in the context of immunization and X-ray clinics, technical medical procedures were to be undertaken by nurses while CHRs were to help bring people to the clinic and record their visit information.

In July 1965, the director of the Medical Services Branch wrote to all regional superintendents to report on the findings of a Committee on Community Health Workers. The role of the committee was in part to review a "situation" that had unfolded in the Northwest Territories. A dispute had caused the resignation of some workers and generated complaints against others. While details of the case were restricted, what was recorded and remains accessible reveals many of the issues CHRs faced with regard to their job descriptions. Like most labour disputes involving CHRs, this one was fashioned as personal, or a "conflict of personality" between nurses and the CHRs, rather than as a real labour issue. Yet at the same time it was felt that the "role of the CHW in a community was not always fully understood by some Nurses and Administrators in the north, who tended to regard them as technical assistants or sanitary labourers acting under their orders, nor by some white residents." The MSB director charged that "difficulties had arisen because some white leaders with the best of intentions tended to dominate and thus to frustrate local native initiative." He noted that the steering committee "seemed to act more as a directing committee rather than as supportive." He also noted that further misunderstanding resulted because a few of the workers had difficulty with the English language. It was suggested that in future there needed to be a fuller interpretation of the role of the Community Health Representative "as a teacher and stimulator to community action" to supervising professional staff and community residents. Furthermore, it was agreed that the roles of the steering committee and supervising personnel also needed to be clarified. Especially in smaller communities in the north where professional services were sporadic, the committee suggested that Community Health Workers should be enabled to undertake more responsibilities, "for example, female Workers doing more practical home care and male Workers organizing and operating community hygienic projects."[145]

When the program was first envisioned, male CHRs were to report to a sanitarian (when he was in the area)[146] rather than to the nurse. Because there were only a few sanitarians working for the Medical Services Branch in the 1960s, Martens must have envisioned male CHRs working more independently than women. Almost immediately, however, she suggested that steering committees act in the absence of sanitarians. These committees were made up of the band chief, an Indian Affairs representative, a nurse, and one member of the community who was not a member of the council or band, such as "influential private residents eg. the local missionary or resident clergyman, RCMP officer or Hudson Bay Post manager." The purpose of the committee was to "support, encourage and guide the worker."[147] In the end, all CHRs were supervised by a nurse and all functioned in relation to a committee.

In one of the promotional materials describing the CHR program, the philosophy of self-help was illustrated by a story about the Cambridge Bay training course:

> At the Cambridge Bay course no house rules were made for the men's residence. The candidates were all Eskimos but drawn from widely diverse communities and ranged from one who was nearly illiterate to a high school graduate. At first complete chaos reigned. The men were rowdy, did not use the facilities properly (one refused to remove his parka for any reason)[,] got drunk, did not turn up for meals or sessions, quarrelled and generally annoyed and angered each other. Finally they themselves requested they be regulated. Miss Martens' reply was "Make your own rules." They were taken-a-back, but, after some considerable argument, did, and [they devised] much more stringent and detailed rules than anyone else would have ventured to suggest

> and which they themselves enforced. One of them asked Miss Martens, "Would it not have saved a lot of fuss and bother if you had made these rules in the first place?" Miss Martens' reply was, "Possibly." But would you men have obeyed rules made by a woman?" She then went on to point out that the entire course was based on getting them first to see a need then figure out some action they could take to meet it. For a moment her questioner seemed puzzled then a sudden light dawned on him and he became delightedly enthusiastic.[148]

This story draws our attention to how the CHR program aimed to deal with recurring and gendered "chain of command" problems perceived by the MSB. In a telling write-up about the first training program, Ethel Martens noted that CHRs had expressed considerable insecurity about their jobs: "The Women asked, 'Are we going to be asked to do the work the nurse doesn't want to do?' The Men wanted to know, 'Can the nurse order us around?'"[149]

Community health work was envisioned to be qualitatively opposite to nursing work. Margaret Stott, a community development officer of the Indian Affairs branch, explained, "The Nurse in Charge of most stations...has come through a system where she has been expected to produce concrete results and to value such results.... It seems likely that she might not understand the Community Health Worker's job and might consciously or unconsciously desire results from his work which cannot be guaranteed if it is really up to the people to instigate changed health practices."[150] As personnel, nurses were seen as "newcomers," whereas CHRs were "of the community." As such, the CHR's job was, for nurses, most importantly to "improve the acceptance of the nurse through helping to interpret the nurse's role."[151]

Nurses relied on CHRs for this work, especially since most CHR work was done in communities rather than in centralized institutions such as hospitals and clinics. While the hospital and clinic were key visual and systemic elements of the expanding Medical Services Branch, they were not the only site of health care practice for First Nations and Inuit people at this time. Arguably, equally or even more important was patient care in the home. Home care was often advised because of a lack of hospital beds, because doctors felt patients could look after themselves, and, of course, because many patients preferred being at home to staying in the hospital, especially if the hospital was far from home.[152] As a result, home visiting was a central part of both CHR and nursing work, and together CHRs and nurses would fully treat some patients at home, provide follow-up care for patients who had been treated in hospital, and also give longer-term public health education. Dorothy Stranger recalls, "If there was somebody that had a sore or had an operation, that's when we'd both go and see. But if it was just somebody to go and visit… talk to, that's the one I would…that's what I liked. Yeah, it was nice."[153]

From today's perspective, home visiting could appear to carry some of the earlier connotations of nursing with domesticity and domestic service, which may have made it seem somewhat antiquated as nursing work professionalized. Moreover, no doubt some patients may have found the nature of home visiting invasive, regarding it as an extension of the government (represented by the nurse) into the intimate lives of Indigenous people, and therefore also as the intensification and personalization of state surveillance, judgement, and reform efforts not simply in its institutions (schools and hospitals), but also in the day-to-day lives of people in their homes. While CHRs did make a record of their visits and share monthly reports with nurses who read and signed off on them, creating an official, supervised administrative archive of personal and medical information, from the recollections of CHRs, home visiting characterized their responsibilities to community, which demanded that they know the people and document and attend to their needs as best they could. Many CHRs recall enjoying this aspect of their work, especially in visits with mothers with new babies and with elders. They are also remembered by community members for their work in this regard. While their work was to educate, many CHRs recalled that they were also educated and learned much from community members while home visiting, especially with respect to Indian medicine. Indeed, CHR work, and home visiting with elders in particular, has played an important role in the translation and preservation of traditional medicine and Indigenous knowledge.[154]

Home visiting and health education in general required that CHRs travel a great deal, especially if they were responsible for more than one community. Often this work was done with the nurse. Dorothy Stranger, who was responsible for Peguis, Jackhead, and Fisher River First Nations and the schools in the area, recalls, "[We'd g]o to school and I forget how many classrooms there were. But we'd do maybe one or two. Then we'd come back and maybe have to go someplace or somebody came home that was in the hospital. We'd always go and visit them right away. Not like now, they don't do that.… They were expecting us, because they knew that we would be coming around too.… And we pretty well did. But you know there wasn't as many people as there is now. You'd need about three people I guess."[155] With this emphasis on mobility and travel in their jobs, both CHRs and nurses faced many challenges and dangers, especially in cold weather. At times they were delayed because of getting stuck in the snow and often had to work late hours to ensure that they completed home visits. In addition, at times, CHRs and nurses also confronted community members who were unwilling to be treated, and who could threaten to, and sometimes did, become confrontational and violent. The provision of health care has shifted over time towards centralization in health centres, however, some feel that this has not made for better health care. Dorothy Stranger states, "I never see nurses traveling around now. I said, 'what kind of a program do they have now? I never see nurses travelling.' Cold weather like this, we'd go visiting anyway. But now they have a big health centre over there. I never go and ask them what they are doing. But you can see they're not working the way we did."[156]

Like all Indian health programming, the CHR program grew out of certain understandings that Indigenous people were inherently unhealthy and why. In the 1960s and 1970s, poor health in First Nations and Inuit populations was thought in large part to be because people were not "following the doctor's orders." In addition, a prevailing theory was that "(because of cultural differences and educational differences) Native people have little understanding of the meaning of good health."[157] A significant amount of material written about Indigenous health has been devoted to explaining the reasons for that perceived lack of understanding and how best to remedy it. Martens's solution, for example, was to teach Indians to "supervise" themselves. However, in the end, she still wanted to figure out how to get Indians to follow orders, and like those of all other Indian policy and programs, responsibilities of Indigenous CHRs were organized and supervised from above. In this, the program clung to a certain body of scholarship about the social dynamics of First Nations and Inuit communities in Canada.

Social science in the 1960s held two interconnected understandings about Indigenous people that were key to the supervisory aspects of the CHR program. First, Indigenous communities in Canada were "subordinate" and "dependent" on government protection. Second, and as a result, there was among Indians a "decline in the sense of responsibility for their own welfare."[158] To these, people responded in one of two ways. First, some degree of "indigenous defensive hostility" or "deep-rooted resentment against the white man" manifested in the "adoption of a pattern of behaviour displaying ignorance, lack of confidence and initiative and over-communication of their sickness, apathy, alcoholism and suicidal tendencies, over-communication of dependence on governmental assistance," an emphasis on "curative medicine,"[159] and a profound suspicion of government agencies, including the staff of the MSB. The second response was to become subordinate to "white man's culture" to the point that "Indian people will not accept the teachings of one of their own," especially if he or she was "in the pay of the white man and is attempting to spread the white man's ideas."[160]

While seemingly a genderless, "community-based" set of arguments, at the most fundamental level this theory relied on a postwar ideal of self-respecting manliness to explain why Indian men did not obey white men. "A man must have to work to be healthy," one CHR program evaluation explained, "for when jobs are not available depression, apathy, and the inability to secure proper food, clothing and housing act as preventatives to health and healthy conditions.... Welfare payments tend to inhibit work incentive. They foster a dependency relationship with the Indian dependent upon the white, and this is detrimental to the Indian's self-respect."[161] Martens explained,

> the Indians do not do what the doctor says just because he, a white man, said it, in fact they often deliberately do the exact opposite. They seem to think they are somehow "getting even" with him by defying him.... Rightly or wrongly they believe they have been exploited, defrauded, tricked by half understood promises and glib double talk and whatever a white man says is automatically regarded, at least until they get to know him particularly well, as likely to be another clever trap that will leave them holding the thin and sticky end of the stick. The problem is how to get them to accept the truths of modern hygiene which are not always self-evident even to the more sophisticated.[162]

Communities measured CHR work against "productive" Indian men's work. It was noted in 1967 that "the people are very aware that the Community Health Worker is getting a steady salary for his job so he should be doing something and doing something means something seen; for instance, cutting wood, netting fish, or making moccasins." It was also said that the type of work CHRs did made them suspicious to communities: the work had no immediate results compared to other work like hunting and fishing;[163] it relied on the "long process" of learning and involved not "doing" but "demonstrating"; it did not have the grand results that, for example, immunization had, but aimed instead to shift attitudes and behaviours.[164]

At the same time, when it came to men doing so-called "women's" work, particularly in child and maternal health, there was a lot more uncertainty. For example, during the 1970 training session for CHRs, Martens asked, "How do you get the importance of prenatal clinics across? And how would a male

CHW handle this?" The program material offered these answers:

- should be done through the women. Male CHW's could promote discussion through their wives or Health Committee or leave it to a female CHW if there is one in the community
- talk to husbands
- talk to community aide, if there is one in the community
- letters—not too effective but might work in a few cases
- hold a meeting with the nurse and invite all pregnant women. Doesn't have to be a home visit.
- visit mothers and leave books like "Mother and Baby" with them.[165]

The ability of male CHRs to relate to white men was of great interest to social scientists in the 1960s who argued that, while it was necessary for the job, working with white men could be seen to damage their authenticity in the eyes of their peers. In their 1964 analysis of the CHR program, Abramson, Arnold, and Piper stated, "Because they are now working to spread the ideas of the white culture and are being supervised by whites, they are looked upon with suspicion and jealousy by many of the more conservative members of their own group. Their new image of themselves as middlemen and their new familiarity with the ways of the dominant group often makes it less satisfying for them to relate socially with their own people alone." On the other hand, they stated, "the worker cannot allow himself to become so fully identified with the whites that he increases the suspicion in which he is held by the people of the reserve. This is likely to be an infrequent occurrence, at least in the short run, since the workers do not have the education or wage level of the whites, and often have had no opportunity to develop the same social behaviourisms. Particularly where the latter is true, they are unlikely to receive egalitarian treatment."[166]

A problem in the Foothills region in the mid-1960s arose when a CHR was viewed as not working a full forty hours per week on health program activities. Trainees in the Cambridge Bay program had been told that they could hunt when not busy with health work (likely to entice them to the positions). One worker was "losing the respect of the community" because his salary was unrelated to any observable work hours as a CHR. He himself was "not happy with a job which does not show any tangible results; he is becoming morose, sensitive and aware that there is much criticism in the settlement against him." The solution was to cut his hours (and pay) from forty to twenty per week.[167] Often, such stories about work patterns and local acceptance came through as arguments about modernity and whether Indians could or should access it—and, if so, how and when. Car ownership, for instance, was a recurring issue among CHRs and nurses. "To provide government transportation would tend to identify Indian health workers too much with other Federal employees," one regional superintendent argued, "and they will likely cease to be, in the minds of the Indians, 'one of them.' What they gain in status they will lose in their value as effective 'grass roots' health educators."[168]

The CHR position as a standardized civil servant position was short-lived. While originally a "permanent" position when the program started, the civil service commission needed to approve positions ahead of time before CHRs could be hired. It decided contracts were to be renewed on an annual basis. By the late 1960s, there was more of a push to surrender direct supervision of the community health representatives and have them be directly responsible to bands. By 1970, graduates of CHR training were no longer made public servants, but rather put on personal service contracts with the MSB. This was an interim step towards becoming band employees, and provided no security, none of the benefits received by public servants, and no compensation for overtime. In addition, personal service contracts were difficult to administer.[169] A move towards allocation agreements or twelve-month memorandums of agreement between bands and the federal government to cover CHR services meant that CHRs would increasingly be employed directly by bands. While it is clear that this form of labour contract was not preferred by CHRs—who were concerned that, in addition to the loss of benefits, their employment would become a matter of local politics—this was understood at the time to indicate the greater role bands were playing in planning and controlling health programs and delivering health care in their communities. In 1976, 280 CHRs worked for the MSB, while 50, or 15 percent, were employed by bands; by 1984, only 23 percent of the total 535 CHRs worked for the MSB, while 76 percent were employed by bands. Under contribution agreements, bands controlled the conditions of employment, hours of work, vacation leave, and sick benefits (although they were supposed to be comparable to those that applied to federal government employees in that province). Under these contracts, either party could terminate the contract with one month's notice.[170]

From the start, the MSB endeavoured to relinquish direct supervision and transfer responsibility for certain aspects of the CHR program to the provinces and individual bands.[171] As this occurred, serious labour concerns to do with the negotiation of fair and equitable band contracts arose.[172] For instance, leading CHRs in Manitoba and southern Alberta voiced concerns about being able to retain public service benefits (like job security, leave and sick benefits, and superannuation), so that the worker was not penalized in comparison with federal government employees.[173] CHR Alice Mancheese, who worked for thirty-nine years at Ebb and Flow Ojibway First Nation in Manitoba, was transferred to the band in about 1977. She writes, "When we were first with Medical Services, we had insurance and security, but when we transferred over to the band, we lost all our social advantages. We finally started getting insurance from the band and I am sad to say that after 39 years of service I am receiving $300 a month. Would I do it again? YES!"[174] The energy and commitment of CHRs for community health is even more pronounced when contrasted with potential workplace issues, remuneration, and benefits.

Conclusion

Voices of Community Health Representatives, a recent publication by NIICHRO, indicates some of the substantial changes in this field of work since the inaugural years of the program. Senior and retired CHRs recalled a time when they worked alongside very few health professionals (doctors or nurses) in their communities, and some observed that the work of CHRs in their community is currently being replaced by nurses or diffused into many different programs and undertaken by a range of workers who carry out specific initiatives, such as National Native Alcohol and Drug Abuse Program (NNADAP) workers and wellness workers. In some cases, CHRs have had new responsibilities added to their role as CHR. Most welcomed the expansion of personnel and physical infrastructure, including clinics and health centres, but remarked all the same that the work has become less demanding. Still, many CHRs continue to engage with the original objective of the position—to act as a cultural liaison between communities and health professions—and much of their health education work with elders, youth, babies, and families remains the same. Many CHRs surveyed for the publication saw themselves as providing necessary cultural orientation to new health professionals and vital translation services to clients and some health care professionals. They also remarked that a lot of CHR work was done after hours and on weekends, and many lamented that home visiting was not as common anymore.

Any federal Indian program developed in isolation from communities was and is suspected of being part of a long history of the Canadian government's attempts to evade treaty responsibilities, conserve federal funds, and erode services.[175] It is important, however, to also examine the gendered ways in which such a program was envisioned, enacted, and resisted. The CHR program in the early 1960s was built upon a distinct set of ideas about Indian people; in particular, that they were dependent, suspicious, stubborn, and disobedient as well as slow and uneducated. It was also built on the idea that men and women would work differently: men would plan and direct programs of health while women would report and consult about them. In addition, men were paid substantially more for the work that they did, even though men and women worked equally as CHRs. As the increasing number of women in the program suggests, for a variety of reasons, CHR work and the CHR position was feminized by both MSB staff and communities.

When I presented some of these details at an interdisciplinary gathering of scholars in the field of Aboriginal health, one respondent was shocked that originally there were more male than female CHRs, suggesting the extent to which the program has become associated with women's work. Ideas about work are socially and historically constructed, and in the case of CHRs, we have seen how notions about race and gender infused the Canadian government's patriarchal and colonial framework to circumscribe and devalue the labour of both male and female CHRs.

In the inaugural decade of the CHR program, there were three critical aspects of the program: selection of CHR candidates, CHR training, and CHR supervision. Ten years into the history of the CHR program, much had changed already. CHR training had and would continue to become more standardized and formalized. Employment would increasingly be governed by bands in contracts that would require professional development as a condition of continued employment and formal mechanisms for evaluating workers' performance and career progress. Moreover, the health care profession became more diversified and specialized, and the numbers of health workers increased. Recruitment efforts were also stepped up as a large program to encourage First Nations and Inuit people into health careers was developed. In spite of these challenges, CHRs constituted a significant number of the Indigenous workers within the MSB, which otherwise maintained a workforce that sorely lacked representation. In 1973, a Task Force on Community Health Auxiliaries (CHRs) estimated that less than 10 percent of MSB employees were Indigenous, while the number in "executive or administrative positions or employed in the health professions can be counted on the fingers of one hand."[176] It was noted at the same time that Indigenous people accounted for more than 50 percent of the U.S. Indian Health Service workforce, and they worked at all levels of the bureaucratic heirarchy and participated in all levels of decision-making affecting health programs.[177]

Nonetheless, the early CHR program is indicative of how the departments of Indian Affairs and Health and Welfare envisioned (and in some cases continue to envision) First Nations and Inuit labour—marginalized in terms of access to resources and professional development, under the supervision of white MSB professional staff, underpaid and unequally paid, and overworked. Whether this labour was formulated as "bridging a gap" between non-local health professionals and the Indian populations they "served" or as "helping people to help themselves," a CHR's work included paid federal employment in the health sector and voluntary community leadership. "Self-help" was about contemporary ways of dealing with inept colonial systems. The CHR program is in many ways postwar colonialism at work in Canada, as it takes its place in a long tradition of skirting the root causes of ill health in First Nations and Inuit communities, such as poverty, colonial policy, and institutionalization[178] as well as the state's evasion of its responsibility to fund health care for First Nations and Inuit people adequately and equally. High skills expectations from CHRs, such as cross-cultural communication, teaching, and the ability to function within two separate and varying systems, were not supported with adequate resources and appropriate remuneration. Their local leadership and skills were what got CHRs their jobs, but the MSB ultimately devalued the position and CHRs ranked well below nurses on the MSB hierarchy. That these nurses rarely came from Indigenous communities themselves was a point of contention that, in part, motivated a generation of Indigenous nurses in the 1970s to organize professionally for Indian control of Indian health.

CHAPTER FOUR

Gaining Recognition:
Labour as Activism among Indigenous Nurses

While employment with the Medical Services Branch was clearly racialized and gendered along a hierarchy that severely restricted the positions available to Indigenous women, not all Indigenous health workers fell into the lowest tiers of the system. A small but significant minority of Indigenous nurses also worked for the MSB. These nurses overcame considerable obstacles to attain nursing education and employment and did so in spite of educational policies that prepared Indigenous women for domestic work and generally discouraged them from pursuing higher education. The professional organization of Indigenous nurses in Canada—originally known as the Registered Nurses of Canadian Indian Ancestry (RNCIA)—was a culmination of Indigenous participation in modern health care labour and an important movement of resistance to patterns of Indigenous education and employment that disempowered Indigenous health care workers.

In 1975, Indigenous nurses assembled to hold the first conference of what would become RNCIA, now the Aboriginal Nurses Association of Canada.[1] RNCIA was the first organization of Aboriginal professionals in Canada, and its original objectives were unlike those of any other nursing organization. The primary goals of the organization were to improve the health of Aboriginal communities and to position professional Aboriginal nurses as critical components of the Indian health field. The organization also aimed to track and represent Aboriginal people in the profession; to bring to light problems related specifically to MSB nursing, including recruitment and retention of nurses; and to make visible the overwhelming under-representation of Aboriginal nurses in the profession. Another immediate goal of the organization was to promote health professions among Native students and improve their access to education. The founding of the organization was historically significant in terms of Aboriginal nursing, health, labour, and education, but it was not a starting point for the history of Aboriginal nurses. Rather, it was, as Jean Goodwill, a leading Cree RN from Saskatchewan and RNCIA organizer, put it, a "turning point."[2]

Currently, literature about RNCIA exists in two different forms. First, there is a significant but isolated collection of the organization's histories of itself. These histories outline the various efforts of Aboriginal nurses in the areas of Indian health research, community service, and nursing education. Their hagiographic style and tendency to focus on individual nurse profiles, however, make them less informative on the structures of and discourses on nursing, employment, and politics, either in the MSB or in other decolonization projects both within and outside of nursing.[3] RNCIA history also exists in brief paragraphs in chapters of books on Canadian nursing. In these, it is discussed as a recent "special interest" development—part of what is seen as a relatively new ethnic diversification in the nursing field—and characterized by a special interest in health problems associated with Aboriginal people.[4] In such renditions, RNCIA's capacity to address larger and longer-standing issues of racial discrimination in health service and health professions is obscured.

Together, these sources reveal the tendency to give only a cursory nod to Indigenous nursing in a story in which they otherwise do not participate that is common in historical scholarship—the depiction of Aboriginal history as either ancient and discontinued or recent and devoid of a past. The way that we perceive Aboriginal nurses as historically absent is illustrative of many of the problems with Aboriginal history, particularly when it comes to labour. In most versions, Aboriginal people are said to have "transitioned" to wage labour through a process of assimilation or integration, which suggests the impossibility of being Native *and* existing in the twentieth century simultaneously. For Aboriginal professionals, however, their labour history is conceived of as a single, swift moment of an individual "first."[5] Stories about the "first" are indeed compelling, and I have in this research been asked numerous times: "Who was the first Native nurse?" The "first" is a way of celebrating the monumental achievements made by those who were dramatically under-represented in their field. But the quest to find the first nurse seems inherently ahistorical. It relies on absence and a void of activity for the inspiration of a succession of path-breakers. In addition, it relies on modern institutional and professional definitions of "nurse" that are exclusive of the range of health work in which Indigenous people have historically engaged. While hinting at a past of struggle and resistance, it truncates larger contributions of Aboriginal women's work in our history and does little to explain absence in our reconstructions of the past. It is one of the ways in which we express a discomfort with Aboriginal modernity. The "absence" theory of twentieth-century Aboriginal labour history does not work well in Aboriginal nursing history. Employment—nursing in this case—became, in fact, a significant expression of postwar Indian identity. RNCIA was one development in a longer history of Aboriginal nurses, and it can be a conduit for telling a range of different stories about Aboriginal health and health services and about Aboriginal women, education, and employment.

This chapter is divided into three parts, starting with RNCIA objectives and early initiatives, then working backwards to analyze the broader history that produced or inspired them. I deal with the organization's objective to "improve Indian health," which originated from RNCIA's immediate context of political struggle for Indian control as well as Aboriginal nurses' longer historical engagement with caring for the health of Indigenous people, with federal health services for First Nations, and with colonial imposition in the health field. I also look at the historical context of RNCIA's aim to improve the recruitment and retention of Aboriginal nurses in the MSB, specifically their critique of a pattern of hiring non-local professional labour with local support staff. Finally, I put RNCIA goals to improve access to professional education for Native people in the historical context of postwar Indian education. This context included limited and highly regulated access to post-secondary education, an obscure and unpredictable system of funding, and the impact of the push for Bachelor of Nurse Entry to Practice on the professionalization of Aboriginal nurses. Putting Aboriginal nurse objectives at the centre of the analysis of change over time in the field of Aboriginal nursing history exposes their history of participation in health care, their critique of health services provided to Indigenous people and the employment practices of the MSB, and their engagement in post-secondary education and health human resources initiatives. Elsewhere, I have written about this history dating back to the turn of the century;[6] however, here my focus is on postwar nurses, that generation of registered nurses who founded RNCIA and who formed a particular kind of gendered, professional, Indigenous labour activism in the 1970s.

"Promoting and striving for better health for the Indian people": RNCIA, Nursing, and Indian Control of Indian Health

On 26 and 27 August 1975, more than forty Indigenous nurses from throughout Canada met at the Queen Elizabeth Hotel in Montreal to discuss the possibility of forming an association linking nurses of Native ancestry. The concept of an Indian nurses' association was conceived in 1974, and over the next year more than eighty nurses of Aboriginal ancestry were identified through personal contact, word of mouth, and networking.[7] Organizers estimated at the time that there were about 200 status Indian nurses, and even more counting those who were non-status.[8] Funds for the conference were granted by the Native Women's Program of the Native Citizens Directorate of the department of Secretary of State, the International Women's Year section of National Health and Welfare, and the Department of Indian and Inuit Affairs in Manitoba. The group also benefitted from the hospitality of Kahnawake.[9] At the meeting, nurses discussed matters like how to pool skills to improve Indian health and the role of Indian nurses in encouraging more Native people to enter the health professions. They also drafted a constitution and by-laws and established an executive committee consisting of three unpaid executive members and a board of directors consisting of elected provincial and territorial representatives. At this meeting, RNCIA also developed and adopted ten objectives.

The first objective of RNCIA was "to act as an agent in promoting and striving for better health for the Indian people, that is, a state of complete physical, mental, social, and spiritual well-being." Nurses in the organization asserted that Aboriginal health professionals, especially in MSB positions, would facilitate this goal. Significantly, several other nursing organizations formed at about the same time and with similar goals, including the American Indian Nurses Association, the National Alaska Native North American Indian Nurses Association,[10] the National Council of Maori Nurses,[11] and the US-based National Black Nurses Association. Clearly, both Indigenous nurses and other nurses of colour saw the nursing profession as a vehicle for improving their own people's wellness and achieving greater control over their own health services. Aboriginal nurses in Canada identified themselves as keen observers of health inequities because they saw them firsthand in their work. Moreover, they argued that as Native women they had a keen awareness of the needs of their own people and were thus better able to identify best practices and policies. RNCIA was part of a broader movement to identify and address inequities and systemic racism in health services and to address problems that were embedded in colonial ideologies and systems. It is important, then, to consider nursing as a site not only of colonization,[12] but also of resistance to it.

RNCIA was also founded in the context of distinct Indigenous politics and rights in the 1970s in Canada. RNCIA formed in a period during which First Nations, Métis, and Inuit peoples organized formally for unmitigated and constitutionally based rights to self-government and status as Aboriginal peoples in Canada. Self-determination in health was an integral aspect of these larger efforts. In 1969, the Canadian government proposed to dissolve the special status and rights of Aboriginal people and abandon the Indian Act. The proposal, called "The White Paper," moved to terminate federal responsibility and accountability and transfer all services to provinces in an effort to foster legal, social, and economic equality between Aboriginal and non-Aboriginal people in Canada. The vision of social equality was predicated on universal welfare programs. However, to Native people, social programs such as health and education are embedded in distinct historical relations and reciprocal treaty responsibilities between Indigenous people and the federal government. For example, the "Medicine Chest Clause," negotiated into Treaty Six, meant that a comprehensive health plan that incorporates all aspects of present-day health care should be available to all Native people; Aboriginal rights to health care thus predate and pre-empt universal welfare programming. Glaring health inequities and poor health services became important symbols not only of the neglected rights of Aboriginal people to adequate medical care, but also of how marginalized Aboriginal people had become and of the constraints on their capacity to deliver services to their own people.

In the mid-1970s, RNCIA was an important voice in an Indigenous political scene that was dominated by men. Indeed, it had to compete for its jurisdiction over health and struggled to gain legitimacy often without the support of mainstream Indigenous political groups: at least one "national Indian political group" blocked an early federal funding initiative.[13] RNCIA continued regardless, insisting that as health care providers and as Indigenous people, they were an informed and integral component of Indigenous political movements. Yet the organization seemed to walk a fine line in terms of Native women's politics and mainstream second-wave feminism, perhaps in part because of its interactions with larger, more formal Indian organizations. Despite being founded during International Women's Year and receiving funding from the Secretary of State through its directorate's Native Women's Program, RNCIA elected Tom Dignan, the only known male nurse of

Aboriginal ancestry at the time, as its first president (1975–1980). A non-status Mohawk who had been in the US Marines before becoming a nurse, Dignan achieved a baccalaureate in nursing and later trained and worked as a physician. His election as president of the new association was in part an effort to send the message that they were an organization open to both men and women of Indian ancestry.[14] Goodwill recalled, "The election of a male president during International Women's Year was questioned by feminists, but we persevered because we believed he had the qualities the group wished in a leader." The group "continued to welcome male nurses rather than compromise its professional status to achieve funding."[15]

In the context of the founding of the Native Women's Association of Canada in 1974 and provincially or locally organized Native women's groups and of various court challenges to gender discrimination in the Indian Act, RNCIA as an organization remained relatively silent on the issue of Indian women's rights in the early years, insisting that it was above all a "professional association."[16] Yet by the early 1980s, the organization began to express a firmer stance on women's issues. At a 1982 conference, RNCIA invited Myrna Whitehawk, an activist on Indian women's issues, and Kathleen Jamieson, who spoke about the involuntary enfranchisement of Indian women who married non-status men (Indian Act, Section 12 1b). The link between status and Indian women's poverty and ill health was clear. Ten years later, in 1992, the organization joined the Native Women's Association of Canada (NWAC) and Pauktuutit (the Inuit Women's Association) to protest their exclusion from the constitutional review process. (The government refused to fund any women's organization interested in the constitutional process, preferring instead to designate funding to male-dominated organizations.) Together, they eventually negotiated full participation, marking the first time that a federal process fully engaged Aboriginal women.[17] The RNCIA used its professional status to continue to articulate some of the most important arguments about the state of Indian health and health services on local, provincial and, national levels.

Indian Control

RNCIA's early history provides an important Aboriginal nurse perspective on Indigenous labour in the Medical Services Branch at a time when Native nurses believed that that system would eventually be theirs. "Indian Control" was an important organizing principle for Aboriginal nurses in these years. What did RNCIA nurses mean when they referred to "Indian Control"? First, Indian control expressed the goal of self-determination and

Figure 4.1. Indian and Inuit Nurses of Canada logo by Carol Prince: "The red maple leaf in geometric shape—stands for the Canadian Indian red maple leaf. The stem of the maple leaf has a feather in it—again to depict the North American Indian. The Ulu at the bottom of the stem joining the feather depicts the joining of the Inuit nurses with the Indian nurses. The flame on top represents the flame on Florence Nightingale's lamp." Indian and Inuit Nurse of Canada Newsletter, *Volume 1, Number 1, 1983.*

self-government in the field of health. Second, Indian control challenged the lack of consultation by governments with Aboriginal people in policies that affected them. Third, at a time when the federal government still sought integration, most pronounced perhaps in the 1969 White Paper,[18] Indian control articulated Indigenous peoples' difference in terms of their cultural and historical place within Canada and the rights and respect that derive from it. Indian control also took on more specific meanings within Aboriginal nursing; it referred to acting with authority in the areas of knowledge production, policy and planning, and education in Aboriginal health. The 1975 RNCIA objectives make it clear that "Indian Control" was about engaging in the myriad ways in which power is used in the field of health. Indian control was very much a verb.

Table 5. RNCIA Objectives, 1975.

1. To act as an agent in promoting and striving for better health for the Indian people, that is, a state of complete physical, mental, social and spiritual well-being.
2. To conduct studies and maintain reporting, compiling information and publishing of material on Indian health, medicine and culture.
3. To offer assistance to government and private agencies in developing programs designed to improve health in Indian communities.

4. To maintain a consultative mechanism whereby the association, bands, government, and other agencies concerned with Indian health may utilize.
5. To develop and encourage courses in the educational system of nursing and health professions on Indian health and cross-cultural nursing.
6. To develop general awareness of Indian and non-Indian communities of the special health needs of Indian people.
7. To generally encourage and facilitate Indian control of Indian health involvement and decision-making in Indian health care.
8. To research cross-cultural nursing and cross-cultural medicine and develop and assemble material on Indian health.
9. To actively develop a means of recruiting more people of Indian ancestry into the medical field and health professions.
10. To generally develop and maintain on an on-going basis, a Registry of Registered Nurses of Canadian Indian Ancestry.

Source: LAC, R11504, vol. 1, file 1-8, "History."

Most of the original goals of RNCIA had to do with moving into a central position within the Indian health system and extending Indigenous people's activity and influence as authorities in health and as advocates for Indigenous people. For example, RNCIA nurses sought influential positions in the areas where knowledge about Indigenous health was being formally produced, such as colleges, universities, and the MSB. They also acted as advocates for Indian health outside of the Medical Services Branch and consulted among various groups, including bands, government, and other health and nursing organizations. Jean Goodwill wrote of RNCIA: "We, the Indian people of Canada, are approaching a turning point in our history. We are actively seeking ways to govern ourselves, to set our own standards, and, ultimately to be responsible for and to learn from both our achievements and our mistakes. The association...is part of this trend."[19] As she was apt to do, Goodwill, in one phrase, crystallized the sentiments of most of her nursing colleagues and contextualized them within larger historical developments and the experiences of her people. As special adviser to minister of Health and Welfare Monique Bégin (c. 1980–1983) and president of RNCIA (1982–1989), Goodwill was a spokesperson for Native nurses and Indian health for many years.

Goodwill was a charismatic leader for the new organization and in many ways her life and work characterize the active pursuit for Indian control in health. Raised by her mother's sister, midwife, and medicine woman Harriet Cuthand, and her husband Jose on Little Pine (after her mother died of tuberculosis), Goodwill developed an interest in nursing early on. She spent several of her teenaged years hospitalized with tuberculosis, and at the sanatorium an interest in nursing grew.[20] A job as a nurse's aide in Saskatoon fed her interest and encouraged her further into the field of nursing.[21] Goodwill's formative years likely played an important role in her success at achieving higher education. A direct descendant of Chief Poundmaker and a fluent Cree speaker, Goodwill attended the reserve school at Little Pine up to eighth grade, and later Bedford Road Collegiate, Saskatoon. Goodwill was one of a small but growing number of Aboriginal people who achieved mainstream nursing education in the 1950s, graduating as a registered nurse from the Holy Family Hospital in Prince Albert. She then worked with Indian Health Services at Fort Qu'Appelle Indian Hospital and later the nursing station at La Ronge, Saskatchewan, with Public Health in Prince Albert and northern regions of Saskatchewan, and for a year at King Edward VII Memorial Hospital in Bermuda. Upon her return to Canada, she became involved in Aboriginal organizations. Her nephew, writer and storyteller Doug Cuthand, wrote, "She once told me that her work as a public health nurse was an exhausting and frustrating experience. The health problems in Indian communities were largely caused by poverty and poor living conditions. No amount of work on her part would change that. What was needed was changes to government policy and political action." In 1962 Goodwill became the executive director of the Winnipeg Indian Friendship Centre, and in 1966 she moved to Ottawa and worked for Indian Affairs in its Cultural Development section; she later worked as editor of the *Indian News* and on other projects.[22] When she helped to organize RNCIA, Goodwill was working with the Secretary of State and as a nursing consultant to the Medical Services Branch. In her various capacities, she had access to information about post-secondary-educated Native people and the skills and resources to locate and communicate with Aboriginal nurses and nursing students. This is significant because at the time Indigenous nurses were few and far between, many of them invisible minorities in their classrooms and workplaces. The difficult work of organizing requires individuals with the skills and connections to bring people together.[23]

Two other nurses are commonly acknowledged as critical to the organization of RNCIA and its early activities: Jocelyn Bruyere and Ann Callahan.

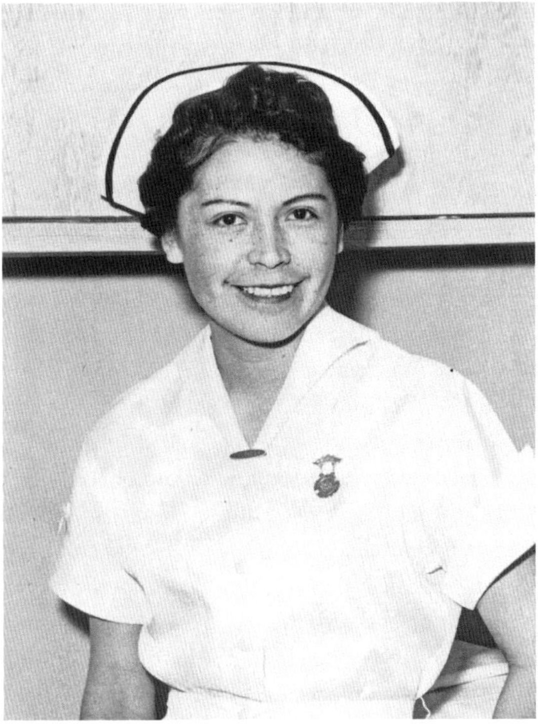

Figure 4.2. Jean Goodwill, leading Cree RN from Saskatchewan and RNCIA organizer.
Library and Archives Canada, E007140503.

Bruyere, from Opaskwayak Cree Nation, graduated in 1963 from the Victoria General Hospital in Winnipeg and obtained a Baccalaureate of Nursing in public health from the University of Saskatchewan in 1969. She also worked at the Manitoba Indian Brotherhood in various roles and with the Chiefs of Manitoba in developing the landmark position paper, "Wahbung: Our Tomorrows," a response to the 1969 White Paper. Ann Callahan, a Cree nurse from Peepeekisis Nation, Saskatchewan, attended a three-year RN training program at Winnipeg General Hospital in the 1950s and was recently honoured by Winnipeg's Health Sciences Centre with a building in the complex named after her. After she graduated as an RN, Callahan worked at the Winnipeg General for about fifteen years before obtaining a Diploma in Community Health Nursing from Assiniboine College, Brandon (1977). Together, Bruyere, Callahan, and Goodwill "not only wrote and developed the initial proposal to bring about a first conference but had to search this vast country for registered nurses of Indian ancestry."[24] These and other women formed a strong network of nurses who were mainly from the Prairies and who provided energy and structure to the early RNCIA.

While the organization's objectives were clear and well-understood, initial efforts to effect them stalled due to a lack of funds and credibility. According to one historical document, it was "a small miracle that this association survived the latter half of the '70s and the first half of the '80s."[25] Madeline Dion Stout, from Kehewin First Nation, was an early RNCIA organizer who trained as an RN at Edmonton General in 1968, and later earned her Bachelor of Nursing from Lethbridge. She worked at Charles Camsell and was a public health nurse at Peigan First Nation before becoming the special advisor on Native issues to the Minister of Health and Welfare and the Director of the Indian and Inuit Health Careers program of MSB. In a paper entitled "The Association of Registered Nurses of Canadian Indian Ancestry: Achievements and Future Prospects," Dion Stout recalls, "We weathered financial constraints and limitations posed by the geographical dispersal of our members (who presented the special problem of discovery in the first place). This distant removal from one another was a disadvantage to us...as we attempted to organize our efforts. Our group's thrust was... weakened because we were unable to give our undivided attention to the Association while our primary responsibilities lay to our respective positions and communities." During this time, MINA, also called "The Manitoba Group" of RNCIA (now Aboriginal Nurses Manitoba Inc.), was crucial for the momentum of the organization. Dion Stout credits "the determination of a few Indian nurses" who "nurtured the Association through periods of dormancy and uncertainty," including the "Manitoba nurses" who, she argues, "deserve a salute because their perseverance, solidarity, political awareness and ability assured the productivity of RNCIA during these trying years."[26]

Several attempts were made to obtain funds to run an office and staff, but in the early years, the organization was only able to get funding from the Secretary of State's office for one yearly board meeting and an annual national conference; RNCIA did not receive operational funds until the early 1980s, when the MSB provided funding for special projects, administrative staff, and day-to-day operational expenses.[27] The MSB justified this spending because liaison and educational work by RNCIA was of significant practical use to the MSB and Indian Affairs. With funding secured, RNCIA could carry out its objectives, and the results of this work increased their credibility with the MSB and other professional organizations. The paradox that Aboriginal nurses aimed for Indian control while relying on government funding for structural support must be understood in a much longer historical context of Aboriginal-government relations.

The Colonial History of Medical Services Branch

The objectives of RNCIA seem so reasonable as to be perhaps commonplace today: to improve Aboriginal health by fostering education, data collection, and Aboriginal nurse participation in MSB programming and health care provision. However, in the historical context of Aboriginal health systems and status, these goals were revolutionary. The goals of the organization were to transform the very nature of the relationships between Indigenous people and governments and reject the colonization of Aboriginal health.

Scholars have argued that colonization is not simply achieved through military operations, land appropriation, and legal submission, but also through "processes whereby the cultures and institutions of Indigenous peoples were demeaned, made illegal or displaced." Thus colonization involved a much broader social, cultural, and political agenda that included the organization of special services and programs for Indigenous people, including in the area of health. Colonization has had a physical impact on the health of Aboriginal people—most obviously in the decimation of Indigenous populations through imported diseases—and is now considered a "determinant" of Indigenous health. Yet the colonial history of Indigenous health also involved the replacement of Indigenous health and health care practices with European ones, and the undermining of Indigenous knowledge related to health. Limited and ineffectual medical and nursing services as well insured that while the health of Indigenous people declined, and Indigenous health knowledge was being replaced, newer services would justify and sustain Canadian imperial endeavours and internal colonial relations.[28]

From its earliest days, Indian submission and minimal service, rather than Indian control for Indian health, was the general principle around which Indian Health Services functioned. Around the turn of the twentieth century, the provision of medical services to Aboriginal people became the responsibility of the Department of Indian Affairs, which established a General Medical Superintendent in 1904 and a medical branch in 1927. The DIA's administrative structure for policy and planning and the provision of care did not involve Indigenous people. In addition to Indian agents, who supplied rations and some medical supplies, the health service relied heavily on non-Native women: "field matrons" were to supply simple remedies, educate people, and act in case of emergency and "travelling nurses" made inspection visits, held baby clinics, and travelled to schools and homes to give advice on healthy lifestyles. Their work in the area of health was to encourage the adoption of a Euro-Canadian lifestyle; Native medicines and practices were actively discouraged.

While these personnel were established, at the same time Indian Health Services was chronically underfunded and understaffed and thus health care remained very basic, if any existed at all. According to the Canadian federal government, the provision of health care to Indians was a "voluntarily assumed moral obligation on the part of the government" to serve an "obvious health need"[29] as opposed to a "statutory obligation." The Indian Health Service was meant to "fit the native people for what must be, eventually, an equal place in the community at large."[30] Thus, service was officially provided only to those recognized by the government as holding legal status as Indians and Inuit who could not afford to pay for it themselves. Others were to consult provincial services, although the federal government ultimately desired to devolve its responsibility for all registered Indians as well. Where IHS facilities did not exist, people relied on other health service providers, and by 1950 visits to non-IHS hospitals accounted for almost triple the number treated in departmental establishments.[31] Indeed, when we speak of the IHS in this period, we are looking at a minority of the treatment services accessed by Native people. Jean Goodwill, addressing Aboriginal nurses in 1982, stated, "Medical Services Branch has been set up in such a way that you could believe they did not have legal responsibility of health of Indian people...At the same time there is a responsibility according to what Indian people consider to be their treaty rights."[32]

In 1945, responsibility for the administration of health services to First Nations people was transferred to the Department of National Health and Welfare, and from this point the system expanded considerably, buoyed by increased government investment in the health and welfare of all Canadians through such programs as universal health care, unemployment insurance, and family allowances. This growth also coincided with a rise in public and academic interest in the health and welfare of those who were increasingly understood to be the "original" or the "oldest" Canadians. A broadly publicized tuberculosis crisis, high rates of infant mortality, and hard-hitting epidemics of influenza, mumps, typhoid, measles, chickenpox, and polio among Aboriginal communities, as well as the appalling treatment of Aboriginal veterans—still excluded from the rights of Canadian citizenship—stimulated public interest in Aboriginal people. A proliferation of anthropological, sociological, and economic studies on Native people in the postwar period, including studies of health services,[33] portrayed an Aboriginal population that was sicker, poorer, and less educated than the Canadian population at large. They also portrayed an Aboriginal population in need of sound management. At the same time, technological innovations in medicine (such as X-rays and vaccinations) and transportation (airplane travel) meant that studies, surveys, and treatment could be performed in Aboriginal communities more effectively, if with higher associated costs.[34] Expenditures by Indian Health Services alone rose from about $2.5 million in the 1945–46 fiscal year to more than $10 million in 1950–51.[35]

The administrative team at IHS expanded and consolidated in the 1950s as well and included the director; a regional medical superintendent, nursing consultant, and senior medical officer located at each regional headquarters (Vancouver, Edmonton, Regina, Winnipeg, and Ottawa); zone superintendents (usually located at a departmental hospital); and a number of medical officers. Graduate nurses, field nurses, medical officers, surgeons, full- and part-time physicians, and hundreds of others working on a fee basis joined the service in this period.[36] The country was divided into five regions, each of which was subdivided into zones. Each region and zone had its own administrative team, the nucleus of which was a medical superintendent, an administrative officer, and a nursing supervisor who was trained in public health nursing and also acted as a consultant to the hospital nursing directors in her area.

While the system employed surgeons, dentists, and full- and part-time private physicians, by far the main component of its staff, both ideologically and numerically, was nurses. Nurses were said to be the "frontline," the "heart" of the IHS, working both in the "field" and in Indian hospitals. The 1950s were the golden age of the nursing station and health centre; while the number of Indian hospitals did not increase considerably, the number of nursing stations rose from 18 in 1949 to 41 in 1959, and the number of health centres increased from 37 to 108 over the same period.[37] Nursing stations typically dealt with pre- and postnatal care, childhood illnesses, and minor accidents and were usually staffed by a graduate nurse, a practical assistant, and a fireman-labourer. Health centres consisted of a dwelling and an office staffed by a nurse, who provided medical attention within the limits of her resources. Her chief concerns were planning and implementing a public health program, home visiting, education, and inoculation.[38] The nursing service within IHS had expanded considerably. In 1927 there were about 38 nurses working for Indian Health Services in Canada;[39] by 1949, there were 54 graduate nurses in the field and 123 graduate nurses working in Indian hospitals.[40] Ten years later, the total number of graduate nurses was 604, a figure that is even more significant when compared to the numbers of other full-time IHS health and administrative personnel (106 medical officers, 20 dental officers, 38 senior administrators).[41] These numbers were, at the same time, severely inadequate to cover the territory and serve the people under this jurisdiction.

Health Services to Indigenous people in Canada were administered and controlled by the federal government, rather than by Indigenous people. Decisions were made from a top-down level, starting in Ottawa and working out to the regions. As such, IHS functioned as a colonial entity with respect to Indigenous people: it was a non-local authority that operated without consultation with the people most affected by the service. In addition, IHS provision followed paternalistic and assimilative policies and provided services that were inferior to those accessed by other Canadians. The expanded system in the postwar era did not radically alter the colonial nature of the IHS. Many of the nurses who formed RNCIA in the mid-1970s witnessed this system firsthand. They desired a profound transformation of the relationship between government and Indigenous people, and a system with a cross-cultural ethic that was controlled by Indigenous people themselves.

RNCIA Nursing Ethic

In light of the bureaucratic and non-local nature of IHS, it is significant that RNCIA had, and has, a very patient-centred nursing ethic. Dion Stout explained in the early 1980s that,

> As natives and as native health care providers, R.N.C.I.A. members are well acquainted with the grim picture of the health status of their people. They are aware of the statistics and the studies that substantiate this. Their awareness includes the government's admission of its failures which have rendered native people pathologically dependent on them. A curative health program, rent with communication problems, dominance over native community affairs and bureaucratic oppression have had crippling effects on the native people's general health. To compound these problems caused by powerful others, the native is influenced by a unique environment which is often times debilitating. Indian nurses know this is a culture of poverty. But they are confident that they can be instrumental in doing away with a great part of it so that alternatives can be implemented which will make life better for native people. Therefore, in their interactions with

> government, they have elected to be advocates for native clientele by bearing out existing problems and solutions. They have agitated for a review of government policies and programs, and they have called for incorporation of proper assessment and care into the planning of Indian health.[42]

RNCIA advocated for consultation and substantive participation of Indigenous people in decisions affecting the provision of their health care and for improving working conditions for all MSB nurses.

Another notable characteristic of the Aboriginal nursing ethic was RNCIA's commitment to a broad definition of health. Indeed, many spoke of a holistic approach to healing that considered mental, spiritual, and social as well as physical well-being. This ethic of nursing is most apparent in the organization's research and conference activities, which brought Aboriginal nursing into areas such as AIDS, alcohol and drug prevention, fetal alcohol syndrome, suicide, family violence, and mental health.[43] In their research, Aboriginal health issues were framed within cultural understandings and associated with colonization and the effects of poverty, discrimination, and social marginalization. In addition, significantly, for an organization of health professionals, Aboriginal nurses were not committed singularly to biomedical health care models, and traditional knowledge and medicine had an important place in their practice. From its inception, RNCIA articulated the need to respect and preserve "Indian medicine." In the 1970s, traditional medicine was perceived by some as key to the "empowerment" of Aboriginal people.[44] By the 1980s, traditional knowledge was being integrated into the training and practice of health professionals as a means to achieve both cultural sensitivity and culturally appropriate programming.

Identifying the problem of cultural alienation of Aboriginal patients in the health system, and of MSB nurses who worked with them, the organization proposed to improve health-care delivery practices by developing the field of cross-cultural nursing, or "transcultural nursing." Cross-cultural approaches permitted a discussion of the impact of cultural difference from both the patient's perspective and that of the care provider, and this early generation of Aboriginal nurses found in cross-cultural nursing a way to express and address many of the struggles they and their communities faced with regard to Western health care and health care providers. An anonymous "Indian Nurse" explained in a special 1978 edition of *The Canadian Nurse* that focused on Indian and Inuit health: "I often wonder how much the nurses working among Indians know about Indians—as opposed to what they think they know. More important, how many have any idea, any awareness of their own unconscious prejudices and stereotyped thinking? Whenever our people seek health care, they are vulnerable to the unconscious racism of health care workers and they suffer accordingly. It is dehumanizing and degrading to be stereotyped in this way—as any woman ought to know."[45]

Carol Prince, from Nisichawayasihk Cree Nation, has been an educator in the field of cross-cultural training and care. She earned her Registered Psychiatric Nurse diploma from Selkirk Hospital in 1965, an RN diploma from Winnipeg's Misercordia Hospital in 1972, and a BSc in Nursing from the University of Ottawa in 1987. Her career has spanned almost half a century and has included psychiatric, general duty, primary care, and community health nursing as well as advising and teaching; her teaching work has included cross-cultural training workshops. She argues that the objective of cross-cultural training is to improve the relationships between Native clients and health-care providers through mutual understanding. She has found that body language, shyness, and respect has often been misunderstood by health-care providers as apathy, and so cross-cultural training is about two groups understanding each other's language and values and relating to each other in a meaningful way. It is not one-sided, Prince argues, but involves an examination of all kinds of beliefs and backgrounds.[46]

Through concepts such as cross-cultural practice, *culture* and its study became integral to nursing education and work. Aboriginal nurses took on the work of defining, teaching, and practising cross-cultural care. One of the founding members of the Manitoba Indian Nurses Association, Pauline Wood Steiman, of St. Theresa Point First Nation, attended Misericordia Hospital School of Nursing in 1974, Red River College in 1986, the University of Manitoba in 1993 (BA), and later the University of Saskatchewan (Health Care Administration). Pauline Wood Steiman was a family practice and surgical nurse, health adviser, and rehab specialist in Winnipeg, northern Manitoba, Island Lake First Nation, and the Canadian Paraplegic Association. She also taught in the faculty of medicine in the field of Aboriginal health at the University of Manitoba.[47] In 1978, Steiman explained, "A native nurse is really a split personality. As a nurse, she must try to explain to her people what she has learned and understands of the new scientific world. To do this successfully, she must also maintain her identity as an Indian, remember and respect the psychological influences, beliefs and customs of the Native people. Our people desperately need better health care and education. The nursing profession can help us to achieve this goal if only they will continue to develop expertise in learning about the Indian people and their needs in the home and in the community."[48] The cross-cultural training RNCIA promoted paved the way for later developments in cultural safety and cultural competency, now considered fundamental elements in professional nursing in Canada.[49] Cultural competency is defined as the end result of a process of developing consciousness that includes cultural awareness, knowledge, understanding, and sensitivity, and then adapting care to be congruent with a client's culture. Cultural safety is a mutually interdependent concept that speaks to the client's perception within the health-care encounter. Developed by Māori nurses and midwives, and in particular by Māori nurse Dr. Irihapeti Ramsden, cultural safety recognizes the impact of nurses and their identities on nursing practices and defines as unsafe any practice that "diminishes, demeans, or disempowers the cultural identity and wellbeing of an individual."[50]

Cross-cultural care requires an understanding of illness not only within the patient's cultural context, but also within that patient's experience of colonialism and the power relationship between patients and health care providers. Marie Ross from Millbrook First Nation, near Truro, Nova Scotia, who graduated as a registered psychiatric nurse assistant in 1949 and a registered nurse in 1982 and later earned an Honours BA, explains the importance of understanding Aboriginal women patients' experience, and the importance of earning their trust: "Aboriginal women often have tragic histories of betrayal by authority figures, including their own parents. Some Aboriginal women have been subjected to further betrayals by relatives, teachers, priests, ministers and others in power positions who take advantage of the weak."[51] There are a range of consequences of a lack of trust in health care spanning treatment to program development; a lack of trust can make people hesitant to seek health care in the first place, or cause them to drop out of treatment before they are cured; in addition, a lack of trust has implications when trying to design and enact meaningful health programs, as trust is vital to their success.

As has been argued by historians elsewhere, Indian health was conceived of and dealt with largely by non-Native people.[52] For this reason, consultation has been central to RNCIA's nursing ethic. This role was substantiated in the government's 1979 New Indian Health Policy. This policy represented important shifts in the federal view of Indian health. First, the policy acknowledged that federal programs for Indian people are legal and traditional responsibilities of the federal government that arise from constitutional and statutory provisions, treaties, and practices. This act was also widely interpreted in practice to acknowledge the entitlement of all status Indians and Inuit to non-insured health benefits regardless of ability to pay or place of residence.[53] Second, the policy acknowledged the low levels of health experienced by First Nations communities as well as the importance of First Nations input into health programming to their communities. Following this policy, the federal government created the Advisory Commission on Indian and Inuit Health Consultation, headed by Justice Thomas Berger. One of RNCIA's first activities as advocates and consultants was to represent Native clientele and to advise Health Minister David Crombie on "methods of consultation that would ensure substantial participation of Indian people and Inuit people in decisions affecting the provision of health care to them and which of these methods ought the minister to adopt."[54] The commission argued that Indigenous control over Indigenous health programs was necessary to improve the health status of First Nations people, and it recommended that funding for health be given to the National Indian Brotherhood and Inuit Taparisat and to organizations and bands not affiliated with the Brotherhood and the Provincial Territorial (Aboriginal) Organizations. The commission also recommended that the Minister of National Health and Welfare convene a conference on Native health comprising predominantly Native people "with representation from organizations such as the Registered Nurses of Canadian Indian Ancestry."[55]

As minutes of RNCIA meetings attest, consultation activities continued throughout the history of the organization. Nurses met with a range of MSB officials, including the deputy minister, regional directors, and senior medical officers, to share their knowledge and offer solutions regarding the special health needs of Indian people, including recruiting more Native practitioners. The MSB formally acknowledged the consultative role of RNCIA in a 1981 document, "Development of Registered Nurses of Canadian Indian Ancestry," which declared the association to be "an increasingly valued source of professional advice on how to approach the task of encouraging and successfully graduating more nurses of native ancestry."[56] While it was a tribute to RNCIA and its members to have the confidence and trust of the government, Madeline Dion Stout argued that the MSB also benefited greatly because it had "co-opted a professional group of nurses. In order that this relationship remain reciprocal, mutually supportive and beneficial, effective communication will have to be maintained at all costs." She continues, "It is fair to assume that collaborative efforts with MSB can bring about improved statistics in the native employment in the civil service, especially in nursing."[57]

In the early 1980s, Aboriginal nurses moved into unprecedented positions in the government, which enabled them to advise more directly on health policy. In April 1980, Jean Goodwill became the Special Adviser on Indian and Inuit Health to the minister of National Health and Welfare. From 1980 to 1987, Carol Prince was the Special Adviser on Native Affairs to the assistant deputy minister of the Medical Services Branch, Health and Welfare. In 1983, Madeline Dion Stout was appointed Special Adviser on Indian Health to the Minister of Health and Welfare, taking over from Jean Goodwill. For some time, then, these and other First Nations nurses took on prime positions for consultation on Indian health policy and field operations. Aboriginal nurses also sat on a variety of committees ranging from Circumpolar Health, Status of Women, Canadian Nurses Association, Canadian universities' schools of nursing, and other national Aboriginal associations, to Medical Services Branch committees on such operations as epidemiology, nurse recruitment, regional nurse educators, health promotions strategies, and anti-smoking campaigns.

In the 1970s and 1980s, Aboriginal nurses gained growing recognition and RNCIA saw increased authority in the field of Aboriginal health. Throughout, the nurses prioritized the improvement of communication, understanding and respect and equalizing imbalances between nurses and patients and between government and Indigenous people. Despite this growing authority and centrality, however, there remained still relatively low numbers of Aboriginal nurses and, in the eyes of RNCIA, a great need for committed efforts to both recruit Indigenous nurses and to retain those who already worked in the MSB by advocating for better working conditions.

"To actively develop a means of recruiting more people of Indian ancestry": Labour Issues and the Medical Services Branch

A central and enduring objective of RNCIA was to bring more Indigenous people into nursing. In many ways, this objective spoke to the need to address a range of labour issues faced by Native nurses and to the particular kinds of skills Indigenous people brought to nursing work. One of the first initiatives of the RNCIA was to conduct a survey of Aboriginal nurses to identify barriers to employment faced by Aboriginal nurses in the Medical Services Branch and to make recommendations on how to improve Aboriginal nurse recruitment and retention.[58] One of the key questions in the survey was, "Do you, as an Indian nurse feel that health services for Indian/Inuit people should be delivered by Indian/Inuit nurses?" The overwhelming response was "yes." Many cited what Jean Goodwill called the "unique expertise" of Indian nurses, including cultural and linguistic communication skills. In the survey, 37 of 71 respondents spoke an Indigenous language as well as English or French.[59] Other reasons ranged from the desire to keep Native capital in Native communities, to the concept that Native nurses had a better awareness of and a "vested interest" in the needs of Indian health. It was also argued that Native nurses had a better capacity to inspire trust and understanding among Indian patients.

Thus recruitment was foremost on RNCIA's agenda. In the late 1970s and 1980s, the federal government developed several affirmative action policies to boost Aboriginal employment. These new policies were not in response to RNCIA, but RNCIA was certainly well aware of them, pointing to them to bolster their argument for hiring more Aboriginal nurses. They included the 1979 Indian Health Policy, the Canadian Human Rights Act (Section 15 of the Act provided for equal access for Aboriginal people to employment in the public services), the 1978 Treasury Board policy (which called for affirmative action in hiring Indian, Inuit, Métis, and non-status Indians in the public service), and a 1981 governor-in-council order that authorized Indian Affairs to tailor recruitment and selection for positions in the Indian and Inuit Recruitment and Development Program and the Native Development Program. But these did little more than earlier efforts by churches, the Department of Indian Affairs, and the Medical Services Branch to recruit Aboriginal nurses. In 1983, of the 800 nursing positions in the Medical Services Branch, only 31, or just under 4 percent, were filled by Native nurses, and none were reserved specifically for them.[60] Aboriginal nurses who worked in these positions faced "subtle" prejudices such as tokenism and paternalism as well as more outright discrimination. One such injustice was the MSB's practice of discouraging community members from visiting the living quarters of nursing stations, exacerbating the fact that nursing stations had housing units only for single nurses—a direct result of its long-standing practice of hiring non-local professional labour.[61]

The 1983 survey showed two additional labour issues affecting Aboriginal people in the Medical Services Branch. The first was the unwritten rule of employment whereby white or non-local women were hired in professional positions; Native people who worked in the system were largely its "support staff," trained for these positions in postwar federal initiatives such as the CHRs (see Chapter 3). The second issue, and one which affected Native registered nurses specifically, was location. Registered nurses complained of the limited choice of where they were able to obtain positions and the difficulties they faced when seeking employment in their own communities. Significantly, RNCIA talked about representation in the workforce in a way that made place matter—Aboriginal nurses wanted to bring their skills home and work to benefit their communities.

But the survey, not surprisingly, revealed other ongoing concerns about the Medical Services Branch. The MSB was perceived to have poor work environments and administration practices. Staff shortages, rapid rates of turnover, ineffectual communication, racism, and overwork led to many of the problems within the Indian Health Services of Indian Affairs, the Medical Services Branch of the Department of Health and Welfare, and later the First Nations and Inuit Health Branch. In many ways, the survey fits into what has become a significant body of literature about MSB nursing that has articulated issues in management and supervision, professional development and career advancement, salary and remuneration, lack of professional support, and poor working environments leading to burnout. While these are common issues in nursing work environments, the MSB faced additional operational problems that affected medical supplies and transportation of patients and health professionals because of its distinct cultural and geographical context. Due to understaffing, many nurses saw their role expand significantly; however, their increased responsibilities were often not met with increased authority or pay; most MSB nurses were young and female and faced discrimination on the basis of both gender and age, not to mention race. These issues are well-documented in *The Canadian Nurse* and by nurses and nurse historians.[62]

Additional problems with the MSB included the preparation and orientation of nurses for work, especially in places that were geographically isolated with respect to where many of the nurses came from. Moreover, the cross-cultural working environment demanded that nurses have cultural awareness skills and tolerance that they did not always have.[63] This in addition to understaffing led to particularly volatile working environments. Thus RNCIA voiced concerns of a broader group of nurses who worked in the north, expressing a need for recruitment but also specialized training. In an interview during his tenure as president of RNCIA, Tom Dignan explained,

> In the future...what we would like to do is encourage as many native people to become involved in the health professions so they could deliver a service to their people. But also to any registered nurse whether she be a Native or non-Native [we would like] to assist her in making a transition from working in the big city [to working in the north and dealing with the] problems that are there. As it stands right now, there is no real training period or even a short course in some of the problems that she may or he may encounter in the north. And it seems to be a trial and error process. And the turn over of nurses in Canada working in the

> north with Native people is so great that every year, a new nurse has to reinvent the wheel in terms of learning the community.[64]

Madeline Dion Stout described the "empathy" RNCIA displayed for their non-Aboriginal colleagues "who chose to practice in the challenging work world of Indian health." She also acknowledged the "unwholesome working conditions that many of them had to endure," including working in isolated or semi-isolated northern communities "without provisions for mental health breaks." In these workplace environments, where nurses were "out of sight out of mind" of the MSB administration, they often faced "undesirable and problematical situations," Dion Stout argued, and dealt with "tremendous responsibilities virtually on their own, often around the clock. Under-staffed conditions cause them to be over loaded with clinical treatments and disease outbreaks, on top of their regular duties. Further aggravations result from abuse by clientele, inadequate residence facilities, high cost of living and non-support by physicians they work with."[65]

On top of these conditions, many nurses were not being paid adequately. At the time, RNCIA nurses highlighted a trend in the MSB to hire what were called "underfills." Underfills were both Aboriginal and non-Aboriginal "nurses who lack necessary academic preparation for the positions they fill and who are least likely to be rewarded by satisfactory fee schedules and promotions, even if they have served MSB for years."[66] The problem was also articulated as "credentialism," or the failure to recognize experience as being of equal value to nursing credentials, particularly, the registered nurse diploma or bachelor degree. In the context of Indigenous labour, RNCIA saw this system as also failing to acknowledge cultural qualifications, experience, and perspective as of equal importance to professional qualifications, although of course the two need not be mutually exclusive.[67] One proposal to solve this problem of experienced but underpaid staff was to allow for promotion after two years, given a satisfactory job performance and a successful equivalency test result. The MSB also developed an internal creditation program by correspondence. In addition, RNCIA lobbied for the development of more Indian health professionals and the hiring of Native nurses irrespective of government educational standards, arguing that culturally qualified nurses could give a high standard of care while upgrading their credentials within the system.

With the transfer of administrative control over health care from the MSB to First Nations governments, or "Health Transfer," in the mid-1980s, nurses faced additional problems. As Wilma Doxtater, a Haudenosaunee nurse from Ontario who worked in British Columbia, pointed out, many band-employed nurses found that "new health administrators did not always have a health background and hence, did not always understand the role of the nurse."[68] Another issue was wage parity with nurses working in similar positions not under band authority. There were also concerns about a continuing lack of authority to make decisions and a lack of resources to run adequate services.[69] While RNCIA as a professional organization was committed to an improved health system that was controlled by and for Aboriginal communities, they were not willing to take a political stand on the health transfer issue. "We are always aware of the need to support Indian governments and the decisions of chiefs and Councils," one document stated, "but we must also uphold our professional standing and maintain a healthy working relationship with our colleagues and the clients who we serve."[70] Rather, the organization responded by advocating for band-employed nurses, developing important resource material on labour and transfer, and hosting workshops for band-employed nurses.[71]

While nursing labour issues of the late twentieth century were diverse, they tended to centre on nurses' lack of preparation for work in rural and northern communities, understaffing caused by poor working conditions, and the distinct cultural and geographical context of MSB nursing environments. Yet many of these labour issues were not new, as a more in-depth discussion of a longer history of First Nations in health care labour reveals.

A Long History of Health Care Labour

Indigenous people have always been active in the provision of spiritual, social, physical, and mental health care. Indian medicine was, however, broadly discouraged through assimilation policy and missionization and it was forcefully banned in the late nineteenth century with direct campaigns to prohibit traditional healing practices such as potlatches and Sun Dances in Aboriginal communities. These ceremonies were vital to Indigenous cultural and social cohesion and reaffirmed cultural and spiritual priorities. To the Department of Indian Affairs and the churches, however, they were "immoral"; they discouraged capitalism and the accumulation of private property; they were vehicles for mobilizing organized political activity; and they were seen to undermine the "civilizing" work of federal Indian education. They also blurred the vision of Canada as a politically and culturally homogeneous nation. Indian medicine was besieged because for Indigenous people, world view, ceremonial life, and social, economic, and political structures of the community are all connected. The repression of ceremonies—the spiritual underpinning of the Aboriginal world—was seen to be key to the modernization of Aboriginal societies. Despite being officially outlawed until the revised 1951 Indian Act, Indian medicine persisted, albeit underground.[72]

Aboriginal women's health work did not escape from such repression. Aboriginal medicine women and midwives, historian Kristin Burnett shows, were relied upon by First Nations and settler women alike, for their knowledge of medicinal plant use to address a variety of illnesses and injuries and knowledge of pregnancy and childbirth.[73] From the expressed frustrations of federal Indian health service employees it is clear that a persistent sector of the Indian population avoided Western approaches altogether and continued to seek traditional medicine. Because of the continuance and transformation of traditional healing practices in Aboriginal communities, many of the Aboriginal women who entered health care training and professions throughout most of the twentieth century would have been familiar with it, and, indeed, many had been delivered by midwives, were inspired in their youth by elders and traditional healers, and incorporated various practices in their own work. Others worked in the area of traditional medicines and adapted traditional knowledge and teachings in community health education and practices.

Some Aboriginal nurses, like Lea Bill, a Cree nurse from Pelican Lake Reserve in Saskatchewan, are widely recognized in First Nations communities as traditional healers.[74] However, most traditional healers worked outside of mainstream medical models, which nonetheless developed in relation to the work of medicine men and women. The rise of the modern medical profession was slow, and it involved standardizing medical education and practices and gaining exclusive support by the Canadian state. The modern profession inevitably gained momentum by distinguishing itself from "ineffective" and "unscientific" healers and by attaching itself to those with the most power in society. The definition of "nurse" was fashioned in the late nineteenth century, and the professionalization of the term carried with it class, imperial, and racial biases. It would exclude not only non-Western health care providers, but also the large number of women who assisted doctors and nurses and the even larger number of Aboriginal people working in various capacities at Canadian hospitals, clinics, and nursing stations throughout the twentieth century.

The definition of "nurse" did not exclude Aboriginal people outright, however. Aboriginal people have lobbied the federal government and bands for Aboriginal nurses since at least the early twentieth century. When RNCIA formed, the discussion centred on how increased representation in the nursing workforce and Indian control over Indian health would improve the health of Aboriginal people. However, for the first half of the twentieth century, the discussion had focussed on a range of other issues, including a "graduate problem" in Indian residential schools (too many graduates), a shortage of medical personnel, a need for public health provision, and the value of "good home girls" to communities.

In spite of the inferior education at Indian schools, by the 1910s there were a number of students who had graduated, and the department tried to find new schemes to help the graduates "establish themselves."[75] Their focus was not only on male students, and in fact, as Pamela White demonstrates, women were of special interest because of their influence in families and communities. For women, special effort was made to instil Euro-Canadian values of domesticity and standards and ways of living.[76] Various church and women's organizations involved themselves in efforts to further education opportunities for Aboriginal women, and they became a critical link for some who wanted to continue their education. These groups included the Imperial Order Daughters of the Empire, Women's Institutes, the Young Women's Christian Association, the Women's Christian Temperance Union, and Women's Auxiliaries. They were progressive, largely middle-class and Protestant church-affiliated groups that organized around issues such as temperance and prohibition, "universal" female suffrage, and missionary work, but they were also concerned with female education, public health, and the roles of women in society. While they most often engaged with Aboriginal people only on a philanthropic level (for example, sending clothing to reserves) and believed wholeheartedly in assimilation as a path towards equality, many encouraged post-secondary training and careers as a means towards this end. Groups offered medals, prizes, roses, and financial and moral support to Aboriginal women taking nursing courses. They reasoned that trained Aboriginal nurses would help in missionary work, undertake leadership roles in Aboriginal communities, assist in child and maternal health,[77] and help to combat serious tuberculosis and influenza epidemics.[78] Significantly, unlike Indian Affairs and Health Canada officials of the later twentieth century, missionary women involved in this work supported not only the further education of First Nations women, but also their employment as nurses in their own home communities, an argument that evaded IHS hiring practices, as we shall see below.[79]

By the postwar period, public discussion about Aboriginal nurses and Indian health had changed and was more formally undertaken by IHS and the DIA. Officially, the federal government expressed support for the education and employment of Native nurses so that they could serve the "true interests" of their own people. However, the federal government did not commit directly to securing jobs for qualified Aboriginal nurses in their own communities, but rather supported a much more vague notion of Indigenous labour. Their position was characteristic of policy that held that while First Nations should assimilate and integrate into the Canadian fabric of life, they should also maintain enough of a connection to Aboriginal people and communities to want to and be able to work among them. For example, the minister of National Health and Welfare stated in a 1946 session of the Joint Special Committee of the Senate and House of Commons to revise the Indian Act:

> It is proposed to make every effort to train Indians as doctors, nurses and sick attendants wherever possible. It is felt that the true interests of the Indian will best be served when they are taking an active part in looking after their own people. This may be taken as a necessary part of the development which is essential to the well-being of the Indians. What must be done is to encourage their natural pride in their own race and customs while at the same time learning the ways of life which will enable them to live in association with the white man.[80]

This recommendation for the training of Indigenous doctors and nurses was the last in a long list of suggestions made to the committee by the minister; in the mid-1940s, the training and employment of an Indigenous health care workforce was not yet directly equated with improving First Nations health. In the federal view, nursing was one option for education and employment that led to integration, which led to equality, which led to "well-being." It was, however, a limited option. While it was suggested that "doctors, nurses and sick attendants" be trained, in fact for women, there was an almost exclusive focus in these years on licensed practical nurses (LPN) and registered nurse assistant (RNA) programs. Medical school education was never discussed and registered nurse programs only rarely. This grew in part out of assumptions about women and work more generally, but also from perceptions that First Nations people had a limited capacity for education. In the 1950s and 1960s particularly, it was believed that the shorter and cheaper LPN and RNA programs would more rapidly solve what were becoming ongoing and systemic nursing shortages. Conveniently, however, this meant that modern systems of health care delivery would remain largely in the control of non-Native people.

Registered Nurses and the Medical Services Branch

Most of the nursing personnel in the MSB were non-Aboriginal women, many of them from outside of Canada. This recruitment was indeed one of the main issues RNCIA took on when it organized. It essentially criticized what it called the "indiscriminate employment of nurses"[81] by the Branch and especially its European recruitment efforts, arguing, "if they need to recruit from out of the country could it not be Indian Nurses from the United States where there are many Bachelor and Masters degree nurses?"[82] Aboriginal nurses pointed out that non-local employment led to high rates of turnover and poorer service. Moreover, it led to the hiring, in some instances, of nurses prejudiced against the very people they were meant to care for.[83] RNCIA tolerated the recruitment of foreign nurses to the MSB as a "necessary recourse to maintain the health care of native people"; however, they argued that "of all non-native nurses, it is generally the foreign nurses who have the most difficulty adjusting to the native culture and consequently are least likely to be embraced by native communities."[84]

RNCIA's activity on this front illuminates the long-standing issue of place for the few Native nurses who worked for the federal health service. In general, only 20 percent of all nurses in Canada before 1940 worked in hospitals; 80 percent were out in the community, working in private duty for individual clients and in public health. Yet most of the Aboriginal graduate nurses until the 1970s found jobs in hospitals.[85] In a 1975 interview at the first meeting in Montreal, Jocelyn Bruyere explained to the CBC, "there are [Aboriginal] nurses either practicing or non-practicing that have a potential to be a very valuable resource to the Indian community. And at the present time there was no kind of mechanism where this could happen."[86] Here she was very likely referring to the fact that most Aboriginal nurses retained positions in municipal hospitals when they graduated rather than filling positions as community and public health nurses within the MSB. A "mechanism" whereby Aboriginal nurses could be recruited to these positions, she argued, was needed in order to realize the full potential of Aboriginal nurses.

Aboriginal registered nurses have historically been discouraged from working as community health nurses. Officially, nurses in the MSB required a post-graduate public health course, and Indian Affairs agents often decided against funding higher education for Aboriginal nurses. However, many MSB nurses *also* lacked this qualification, so we must also look to other explanations for this trend. Historically, the federal government discouraged the employment of Native nurses in their own home communities. It is striking that in interdepartmental correspondence in the first half of the twentieth century, several letters from Indian Affairs stated that while it agreed to funding, it would not accept responsibility for arranging employment when the student completed her course.[87] Their insistence on this point is marked, particularly in comparison to contemporary efforts of missionary and women's organizations. Indeed, for most qualified Aboriginal registered nurses there were few opportunities to work in their communities, a situation described by Nora Gladstone, a registered nurse from Alberta whose education and work took her to Saskatchewan, Ontario, and British Columbia. "If I was to become a registered nurse today," Gladstone recalled in 2006, "I would stay at home and work among the people of the Blood Reserve. But back in the 1930s, there was no place for Native nurses on Indian reserves. For many years it was a struggle just to be responsible and to be the best in the profession I had chosen."[88]

Why was the department reluctant to commit to hiring Native women to work in the Indian Health Services and the Medical Services Branch? Some Indian agents were not, but the tone underlying most of the correspondence was that, once trained, Native nurses might not be willing to nurse in their own communities[89] because their education would somehow cause them to lose "affection or respect" for their own people.[90] In other versions, agents advised against returning Native women to their home communities because of a fear of so-called cultural backsliding and undesirable social and familial influences.[91] Non-local professionals maintained non-Aboriginal control and authority on reserves while furthering assimilation. Moreover, in many other cases, Aboriginal women were simply overlooked for these positions.

For their own part, many Aboriginal nursing students entered into programs with the clear intent of working among their own people. This was true despite, or perhaps because of, the fact that all federal services for Aboriginal people at that time operated without consultation with Aboriginal communities. Aboriginal nurses like Theresa Paupanekis of Norway House saw in nursing an important role in helping to improve health and living conditions for Native people.[92] Paupanekis, later Theresa Lang, took part in a 1955 documentary entitled *No Longer Vanishing* while she was in nurse training at St. Boniface. In the film, she stated: "Even when I was a little girl on the reserve I always wanted to be a nurse. I knew it wouldn't be easy and it wasn't. But now I'm getting there. Before I could enter the hospital at all I had to have more education than most of our people. Mother got her grade six but dad only went as far as grade two. And they both wanted me to get a real education. Being away from home was the hard part. Some kids called me "red Indian" or "savage" but I made a few close friends. I guess I was sensitive, but I stuck it out."[93] From Norway House, Paupanekis later worked at Norway House, Fisher River, and maybe Fort Qu'Appelle.

In an essay entitled "Why I Became a Nurse," Mrs. Wilma Strongeagle of The Pas, who had worked at St. Anthony's Hospital there and at Fort Qu'Appelle Indian Hospital, wrote: "It was a wonderful feeling to nurse some of my people. I really felt at home.... I am now in a position where I can care for my people. To see a sick person come back to health—whether the patient is Indian or not, is a wonderful experience."[94] The use of one's education for service to one's community was, for many, a strong impetus for wanting to work in the Indian Health Services. For some women who had lost Indian status, a career in Indian Health Services may even have been an opportunity to return to one's community.[95] While nursing has always been a profession loaded with gendered expectations of service, it symbolized considerably more than that for those of Aboriginal ancestry. The community service ethic became closely tied to the contemporary struggles and aspirations of Aboriginal communities and remains a continuing theme of RNCIA (now ANAC) membership.[96]

Maintenance, Housekeeping, "Helpers" and Paraprofessional Labour

The tendency to hire non-local professional labour did not mean that the IHS did not commonly hire Indian labour. Aboriginal labour, historian Laurie Meijer Drees argues, was "a nearly invisible backbone and significant interface with the Aboriginal patients in the [IHS] system."[97] Yet recurring observation of RNCIA and others was that Medical Service Branch positions that were the least well-paid, the least secure, and the least autonomous, were filled with Native people. Indeed, Aboriginal people were central to the functioning of IHS institutions, working as nurse's aides, cooks, laundry workers, firemen, janitors, ward aides, and housekeepers. Aboriginal support staff for the Medical Services Branch accounted for up to 25 percent of its employees by the 1950s.[98] As we have seen in Chapters 1 and 3, considerable efforts to train Indigenous nurse's aides and other health auxiliaries were underway and occurred across the country. In addition, many communities continued to practise traditional medicine despite efforts by government and missionaries to eliminate it. This meant that Indigenous people were not absent from the health care system. Their experiences of it at home and in hospitals, as students, patients, caregivers, and labourers contributed to their growing participation in nursing and the rise of RNCIA.

Indian Health Services, and later the Medical Services Branch, relied in every way upon the labour of Native people, such that it would be fair to say that its infrastructure relied equally on both sick and healthy aspects of Aboriginal communities prepared to use it on their own terms. "Case-finders" and "fact-finders," who supplied vaccines and took X-rays, blood samples, health data, and tubercular patients in the summer months, relied on community commitment and organization that brought Indigenous people together for events such as treaty days, festivals, summer gatherings, and ceremonies. Tuberculosis case-finding, or surveys to locate people with tuberculosis, depended upon the regular seasonal labour of hunting, trapping, fishing, and trading. Instruction in homes, schools, and churches involved the work of organizing, hosting, and incorporating knowledge in meaningful ways, and in many instances the IHS relied on already established groups, such as homemakers' clubs, to do this work for them. For every film, visual aid, and instructional booklet, there was also the invisible work of translators and interpreters, whose work should not be underestimated.[99] It is perhaps for this reason that each nursing station was staffed by not only a nurse but also at least two Aboriginal workers, a nurse's aide, and a caretaker.

Registered nurses have always been a notable minority among Aboriginal people working in the field of health care, especially those working at hospitals. For example, when asked if Aboriginal people were represented in all positions in her workplaces, Myrna Cruickshank, a Métis licensed practical nurse from near The Pas, who worked in Norway House, St. Vital Sanatorium, Beausejour, and South Indian Lake in the mid-twentieth century, responded, "No. Most were in menial jobs."[100] The IHS has historically drawn heavily on the uncertified or paraprofessional labour of Aboriginal people, including laundry workers, cooks, and cleaners, but most notably (at least for the purposes of this chapter) nurse's aides and ward aides, whose responsibilities ranged from making beds, cleaning rooms, and preparing food to patient care, including applying and changing dressings.

Cruickshank's observation is confirmed also in postwar federal surveys of Indigenous labour. While the most well-known of these studies focus on the labour of men (the *Hawthorn Report* and the *Lagasse Report*), there were a number of smaller labour surveys done for Indian Affairs that targeted certain fields of interest. These surveys are significant for a number of reasons. For one, they attest to federal efforts to manage Indigenous labour. For another, surveys were part of a pattern of social science approaches and federal surveillance in the employment of Aboriginal people. Importantly, one of the goals of Indian labour surveys was to find ways to encourage Native people into different fields, and in that respect they are helpful in illuminating the contemporary barriers to certain jobs as they appeared to and were explained by the federal government.

One such survey of Native nurses in the Medical Services Branch was taken in 1953. In the fall of 1952, H.M. Jones, the superintendent of welfare services in the Department of Indian Affairs, was inspired by a statement made in Parliament by Paul Martin (Sr.), then minister of National Health and Welfare. Martin, upon being questioned about the number of Indian employees in federal hospitals, promised, "where possible, we employ native personnel in all ranks."[101] In a poorly timed attempt to verify this statement, Jones asked department social workers to count all Indians who had undergone training and to comment on how to attract "girls" to this type of work.[102]

The survey is inconsistent and incomplete because the social workers did not canvass every Indian hospital and did not inquire about those who worked in the provincial system; however, the results were entirely predictable in that they showed the ubiquitous presence in the MSB of Indian labour, nearly exclusively at the lowest-level positions. For example, in Alberta the survey counted no Native graduate nurses, three nurse's aide graduates with five more in training, and "several" employed as ward aides and as kitchen and laundry help in departmental hospitals.[103]

Besides confirming that relatively few Aboriginal nurses worked for the department or were completing RN training, the survey participants also suggested why this was the case. In British Columbia, they noted that hospitals were "reluctant" to accept Indians as students or as employees.[104] In Saskatchewan, when the question of employing Indians arose, one matron replied: "Oh no, the Union wouldn't stand for it." The survey also revealed that "large wait lists" and "careful screening" were barriers for many students, Aboriginal students faced problems finding accommodation off reserve to attend schools, and many could not obtain the funding for tuition and living expenses. Some also noted that the high turnover rates among Aboriginal ward and nurse's aides and the failure of some students to complete the training was because the work was often rightly conceived of as temporary, poorly paid, and without opportunity for further advancement or higher wages.

The most oft-cited justification for the low numbers of Aboriginal nursing students, however, was that Aboriginal students did not have the appropriate discipline for nurse training and required "extra supervision"—particularly when they were "off duty." While maintaining that there was "little discrimination" against Indians, hospital administrators and social workers argued that it was "impossible to employ Indians because of poor educational standards and low standards of behaviour and personal cleanliness."[105] It is significant, but not surprising, that "culture" became blurred with "behaviour" and "work habits" in ways that explained why few Indians became nurses. Culture made Indianness and work incompatible. In British Columbia, for example, "Indian girls" were said to be "generally unreliable as hospital employees" because of their "lack of experience in accepting discipline and the fact that many of them are not interested in the work and take it because there is nothing else offered to them."[106]

Indeed, much of the surveying and writing about the specificities of Indigenous health labour represents a certain body of knowledge about the Aboriginal vocational student and worker, her capabilities and limitations, and her potential to work in health service. Assumptions about Aboriginal capacity to work and study were measured against the "high standard" of nursing, done presumably by non-Aboriginal people. Needing labour to supply its services, the federal government embraced vocational programs as a happy medium between the "discipline" of nursing school and the presumed lack thereof of the average Aboriginal person, and it became almost entirely committed to educating Aboriginal people for vocational rather than professional work. An earlier study done in 1949 by the Abitibi agency's Educational Survey Committee revealed that the "problems" found in this period were not which schools would permit Aboriginal students, but which schools were best "suited" to them, as Indian Affairs saw it. Indeed, the Indian nursing student was limited by the structural arrangements and programming that grew out of those assumptions about the "limited" capacities of Aboriginal "girls" to learn and to work.

Nursing assistant and nursing aide courses were favoured by the department in part because they did not require full matriculation or extended years of professional training. Provincially standardized Certified Nursing Assistant and Licensed Practical Nurse (LPN) programs involved about three months of theory and practice, followed by six months of practical work under trained supervisors. The prerequisites for these courses were: "An interest in nursing; good health; references; Age: 18–40 years; and Grade VIII (entrance certificate)."[107] Ruth Christie, a storyteller from Loon Straits, Manitoba, went through LPN training in the early 1960s. Describing the program at St. Boniface, Christie states, "It was a year, so you did four months of theory and eight months of practical and then you had to write a state-board exam. It was an all-day exam and there were 500 questions, and I think the minimum was 350 correct ones, and I had 448 correct. I can remember seeing this letter coming and I knew what it was because of the return address. I was nervous

Figure 4.3. Especially from the mid-1950s onwards, numerous women attended licensed practical nurse and registered nurse assistant programs, including Elizabeth Jonathan, Whitehorse, Yukon, (left) acting as patient, and Violet Harry, of Courtenay, British Columbia, students at the Vancouver Vocational Institute.
Library and Archives Canada, Vancouver Sun, *E002504561.*

about opening it up but, you know, I studied really hard because I thought how much my parents put into it, I wanted to make them proud of me."[108]

Especially from the mid-1950s onwards, numerous women who qualified applied for band or Indian Affairs loans to attend programs at the Vancouver Vocational Institute for practical nursing;[109] the nurse's aide course at the Provincial School of Practical Nursing in Calgary; the St. Boniface school for practical nursing in Winnipeg; the nursing assistant's courses in Sudbury, Hamilton, Toronto, Kingston, and London; and nurse's aide training at the Canadian Vocational Training Centre in Saskatoon, and others. In the 1960s, even more of these programs opened up.

Figure 4.4. Indian Affairs sponsored many First Nations women who wanted to attend licensed practical nursing and registered nurse assistant courses. Five First Nations students of twenty graduated in the 28th class of the Vancouver Vocation Institute: Marie Marchand, Okanagan Band, Maggie Campbell, Ahousat Band, Ann Allison, Lower Similkameen Band, Laurine Dixon, Canim Lake Band and Mina Hall, Bella Bella Band; they are with Mr. Ratcliffe from the Indian Affairs office in Vancouver. Library and Archives Canada, E00714051.

Marjorie Cantryn was one of the first people from her reserve, the Ohiet Band in Bamsfield, British Columbia, to pursue formal higher education and a trade. After eleven years in residential schools, she went to Vancouver for LPN training in 1955. "I never regretted that training," she stated in 1975. "It gave me a chance to work with people, especially my own people." For Cantryn, like many Aboriginal nurses, nursing was also a gateway into other fields of work, especially work involving social and cultural services to Aboriginal people.[110]

For many Aboriginal women, however, these programs were closed to them unless they had undertaken additional, preliminary training. Probationary courses were in line with the general philosophy of Indian Affairs that Indian girls were not "suited" to nursing training but could, with additional training, time, and effort, qualify for nurse's aide training. Extra probationary periods were also justified as a way of bringing Indian students up to the same level and non-Aboriginal students. For example, the IHS assisted in placing Aboriginal "girls" in short-term jobs to "provide the initial experience and help to put the Indian on an equal starting basis with the white girl."[111] It is likely that the additional preparation required of them was a deterrent for some students, since it deferred the point at which they earned their title and qualifications and the jobs and wages that went with them.

How much extra training was required often had to do with how far north the women had been born. In the early 1950s, "Indian girls" from the Northwest Territories, for example, had to take a preliminary ward aide course at the Whitehorse General Hospital before they qualified for the probationary program at Charles Camsell Indian Hospital in Edmonton, which was a prerequisite to determine Native students' "aptitude" for the nurse's aide program at Calgary.[112] The "elementary" course at Whitehorse consisted of helping the registered nurses, feeding patients (including infants), making beds, cleaning, and giving particular attention to Indian patients who had difficulty with English.[113] During that preliminary training for their probationary training at Camsell, students worked for three to eight hours a day at fifty cents per hour and received "one free meal daily."[114] The Vancouver Vocational Institute offered similar preparation at the Coqualeetza Indian Hospital, accepting three students at a time for a two-month internship to gain experience in tuberculosis and pediatric nursing.[115]

The Camsell Hospital offered "in-house" training for patients as orderlies, attendants, X-ray and lab technicians, and nurse's aides.[116] In addition, many women used the time they spent as patients in sanatoria to their advantage educationally and completed the educational requirements for nursing training and careers on their own.[117] Other women trained informally as nurse's aides; "Training on the Job" programs (or TOJ) formalized this type of apprenticeship training. In TOJ schemes, the department contracted with employers on behalf of Native people to place them in apprenticeship or trade training positions. The more stably funded vocational training and placement program run by Indian Affairs, the Placement and Relocation program (as discussed in Chapter 2), also placed a fair number of Aboriginal women in LPN programs.[118] As shown in Chapter 3, the Department of Health and Welfare had a training program of its own, run from the early 1960s, for community health representatives.

What significance, if any, does paraprofessional certification have for the history of Aboriginal nurses? Certified courses were strongly encouraged by the department in part because licensing enabled people to work off reserves and outside of Indian hospitals (which the earlier in-house IHS programs could not), and thus were seen to facilitate larger policies of integration by bridging the two labour markets of the Indian Health Services and the provincial health departments. Second, although nurse's aides critically assisted in the maintenance of the Indian Health Services hospitals, their work was couched in terms of its being for their own good, as a means to "self-improvement" and "self-sufficiency" rather than as "real" work in the "real" world. Third, licensed programs brought up an unexpected issue related in part to the question of segregated schooling for Aboriginal people. While the probationary programs for provincially certified courses were in many ways similar to the segregation of Native students in the earlier, uncertified ward aide and nurse's aide courses run for Indians at department hospitals, the department focussed on the opportunities offered in the postwar period for Indians to "learn to live with the white girls,"[119] as one departmental social worker stated in 1952. A brief scan of some of the LPN and RNA class photographs of the era reveals that they were in fact quite diverse in comparison to RN programs. Marjorie Cantryn explains that her school principal advised her to go into nursing because "there were lots of ethnic groups working in hospitals." Here, he argued, she would be less subject to discrimination than if she worked "in an office [as a secretary] where there would only be a few other Indian girls."[120]

From the point of view of Aboriginal women who worked in the hospitals, work was sometimes a transition from being a patient, sometimes even a means of accessing treatment.[121] For many, work at a hospital provided access not only to cash or payment in kind,[122] but also to relatives who were patients there. The standardization of nurse's aide courses may have improved the wages they earned, and for non-status Indians who were not funded by bands or the department, LPN or RNA courses were sometimes chosen because it was all they or their parents could afford. Ruth Christie recalls, "The reason I took LPN rather than RN was because I didn't want to be that much of a burden on my parents, you know, to provide, because I didn't have assistance like First Nations students do today. And my parents, you know, I don't think there were times when my Dad earned the amount of money they would have needed to support me." She completed her training with the help of her family: her dad gave her twenty-five dollars per month for rent, her brother gave her a television set, she visited with brothers and cousins in the city, and she got her sister's family allowance ($8 per month); in turn, she supported her sisters when they went to school.[123]

LPN education and employment were often no less intense than that for RNs. Myrna Cruickshank recalls that the LPN training experience was "intensive," with "not too much social life," and "very trying at times." She recalls that it was "quite hard work on the wards.... I was on nights and had to actually run to get all tasks finished by the time day staff came on."[124] This training was beneficial as in some places, where RNs were not available, LPNs did their work. When Eleanor Olson, a Cree woman from Norway House who trained in Winnipeg as an LPN in the 1950s, got a job in Peguis, she was the "doctor's nurse." She travelled around with doctors doing everything from delivering babies to community health. "I was the boss!" she recalls. She did a lot of work that RNs do today. "And I had to do it," she says, "because there weren't that many nurses—Aboriginal nurses—then. Not that many. There was some, but they all had their places to work."[125]

Yet professional standing held some currency among Aboriginal nurses. For example, RNCIA was open to all professional nurses of Canadian Indian ancestry, regardless of gender and status, as long as they were registered. However, even though RNCIA insisted it was above all a "professional" organization, its membership debated what qualified as Indian nursing labour and decided that association should be open to Aboriginal LPNs and RNAs though both only as non-voting members. Most likely, these stipulations had to do with securing funding and professional standing; however, it is significant that RNCIA opted for inclusivity in its membership, in terms of training and title or professional status. Moreover, RNCIA incorporated both status and non-status registered nurses and this inclusive objective is reflected in its subsequent name changes: in 1983 to the Indian and Inuit Nurses of Canada, and in 1992 to the Aboriginal Nurses Association of Canada, a title which recognizes nurses of all three distinct Aboriginal groups in Canada—First Nations, Inuit, and Métis. RNCIA also allowed for "honorary" non-Aboriginal members, though they could also not vote in the association's elections. Such inclusive measures made for a diverse membership; moreover, like any other labour force, Aboriginal nurses themselves were diverse, and they identified variably with a range of different issues. While they diverged on many, there were some issues that generated more intense agreement. Of these, education consistently brought RNCIA membership together. It is significant that unlike the IHS, the RNCIA recognized the skills, labour, and experience of those nurses who did not have formal RN qualifications. This reflects an understanding of the importance of tolerance and diversity and of the limited opportunities and enormous struggle of Aboriginal health workers. This also contrasts signifcantly with the education and employment ideologies of the government.

"To develop and encourage courses in the educational system... on Indian health": Aboriginal Nurse Education: From Barriers to Succession

The post-secondary training and employment of graduates of federal schools have received scant attention in the fields of medical history and the history of Indian education. And yet education is central to the history of Aboriginal nurses, including access to quality education, educating others about Aboriginal people, health career recruitment and retention through education, and culturally relevant training. While Aboriginal nurse education and recruitment continue to be framed as a "new" issue, Aboriginal nurses have a much longer history of education that can contextualize current debates.

RNCIA's earliest study on Aboriginal people and the nursing profession, *Barriers to Employment and Retention of Native Nurses*, showed that inadequate secondary school preparation, a lack of education funding, racial prejudice, and social and cultural isolation at school were all "barriers" to Aboriginal nursing students. The study was followed up by numerous initiatives to support Aboriginal nursing students and professionals. RNCIA promoted nursing at job fairs and gathered financial support for bursaries for Aboriginal nursing students. Like that of many studies on post-secondary education and Aboriginal people, RNCIA's approach was to identify "barriers" and then suggest ways of addressing them. In reality, many of the "barriers" identified were structural and pervasive, often interconnected in important ways, and in fact difficult to address. Indeed, primary and secondary education, language, cultural difference, and distance have all been identified as contributing factors, but Native students are still underrepresented in nursing programs. Lifting the overtly racial barriers has not translated to equal access. The enduring barriers are far more insidious, and it remains difficult to locate and identify the diffuse power that supports and sustains them. By looking at the tactics Native women used to access further education after federal schooling, we can historicize the barriers they faced and render their nature and power more visible.

Colour Bars, Funding, and Nursing Programs

Of the approximately forty registered nurses who attended the first RNCIA conference in 1975, most had become nurses after 1950, although some had trained during the 1930s and 1940s.[126] A time when Aboriginal nurses were barred from Canadian nursing schools was thus in living memory of many of the early members of RNCIA. So, too, was the opening up of educational opportunities for Aboriginal people—premised on a policy of "integration." There exists no history of colour bars and Native nursing in Canada; however, Indian Affairs records show that until the 1930s, only a minority of hospitals would accept Native students to train as nurses (the department kept lists of schools that were open—not closed—to Native people).[127] Nor does the lifting of restrictions on Aboriginal students at Canadian nursing schools exist as a specific historical moment, marked by legal statutes, celebrations, or a swift but significant change. In Canada, racism in post-secondary education was unofficial, and it was thus also difficult to formally identify and "remove." Yet some patterns in early Aboriginal post-secondary education help to elucidate strategies by which the exceptional student overcame barriers.

Federal records about nursing education do not account for all Aboriginal nurses. Many women chose not to reveal their heritage in an effort to increase their chances of acceptance and employment. Moreover, non-status Indians did not necessarily have access to loans or other funds for education, and some status Indians associated such funding with welfare reserved for those who were destitute and did not apply for it at all. There were actually far more Native nursing students during this period than we can ever know about.

In the early twentieth century, many Aboriginal nurses in Canada—particularly those from territories predating and straddling the border that separates Canada and the United States—went to American nursing schools, where they might not face the same ethnic barriers as they did in Canada.[128] Ontario Women's Christian Temperance Union activist Mrs. Ashcroft wrote as much after failing to get satisfactory responses from matrons of Canadian nursing schools to her appeal to admit Indian girls in 1918: "Those who have trained [as nurses] from the Brantford Reserve have trained in American Hospitals where they are glad to have them. It seems a pity that our Ontario Indian girls need to go to American Institutions...for their education." The failure of Canadian nursing schools to admit Indian students, she wrote, "is very discouraging to the girls. I am in communication with several Hospitals and earnestly hope to find places for those willing to take such training."[129] At the same time, relocation for school was often contingent upon the approval of Indian agents. One student from Sheshegwaning Band in northern Ontario attended nursing school at the Weston Sanatorium in the early 1920s in a program that required a term at a New York hospital for special training in obstetrics. Indian Affairs was reluctant to allow her to travel, and it was only because she was denied entrance at any other nursing school in Canada that they finally agreed. Upon this official approval, she wrote: "I'm going to New York at last at the end of this month. I'll be there on the 1st of April. My time has come at last."[130]

The only legislated aspect of Canadian colour bars vis-à-vis Native students was that, by the Indian Act, Aboriginal children were required to attend federal Indian schools, and it was only by exception to this rule that they accessed public education in Canada. Federal Indian schools did not have the capacity or inclination to educate students much past the sixth grade, and only a few actually provided the high-school courses required for nursing school. Moreover, the main goal of Indian female education was to prepare women for motherhood and/or domestic work, and the department considered few to be capable of attaining the two or three years of high school qualifications necessary for entrance to nursing school. For example, in 1936,one student from Round Lake Indian residential school in Saskatchewan expressed an interest in going to Vancouver to finish her schooling with a view to entering Vancouver Hospital for nurse training. The Indian department instead encouraged her to either go to Brandon to finish high school or work as a housekeeper.[131]

In *Topahdewin: The Gladys Cook Story*, Dakota elder Gladys Cook recalls her time at Elkhorn Residential School, Manitoba, where she experienced both physical and sexual abuse. When she turned sixteen, she was asked to leave. At that time, she had decided to apply to be a nurse, but in order to do so, she had to take a test to determine her level of education. She was unable to complete the grade 8, 7, 5, or even grade 4 tests. After twelve years of education at Elkhorn, she was deeply disappointed and angry to find that her grade 8 diploma at Elkhorn did not mean anything and that her education fell far short of that provided in non-Indian schools. In the end, she found a job working as housekeeping staff in a hospital in Yankton, South Dakota, and at the end of the Second World War, she volunteered to work on a hospital ship between Hawaii, Guam, and San Diego that brought wounded American soldiers back home.[132] After many difficult years spent in both the U.S. and Canada, Cook went on to become a strong community leader and counsellor on substance abuse, crime, and suicide, and helped many Native women, prisoners, and survivors of abuse. She has earned many awards and recognitions, including a Governor-General's Award for promoting women's rights, the Manitoba Premier's Award for volunteer work, a Health and Safety Promotion Award from the Manitoba Medical Association, and the Order of Manitoba. One commendation that she particularly valued was a tribute by her community of Sioux Valley.

Those wanting to attend non-Indian high schools required the approval of both the department and the "public" high schools—many of which had colour bars of their own. For example, Jennie Neilson, of the Blood Reserve in Alberta, attended St. Paul's residential school until 1942, when she was sixteen years of age. At the time, high school education was not offered at St. Paul's, so for further education, Neilson needed to attend a public high school. Cardston, Alberta, was the closest and most logical choice; however, attending public school off reserve in Alberta was difficult, as often public schools did not accept Aboriginal students. So with the help of a teacher and the support of her parents, she moved to Sault Ste. Marie in northwestern Ontario for high school. When she finished her exams there, she went to the St. Mary's training school for nurses, also in Sault Ste. Marie, and graduated three years later.[133] Neilson worked as an RN at the hospital in Cardston, Alberta, for more than a decade, later taking on a position as the public health nurse on the Blood Reserve from 1972 to 1995. She was recently honoured by the Blood Tribe Department of Health and the School of Health Sciences at the University of Lethbridge, along with Aboriginal nurses Isobel (Bella) Toth (née Hely) and Nora Baldwin (née Gladstone), both of whom had also attended St Paul's in the 1930s and gone on to nurse's training in BC.[134] These examples tell us something of the determination, relocation, and connections it took to be a nurse in those early years.

Common assumptions about Aboriginal people's health created another layer of discrimination. While all applicants to nursing schools had to undergo medical tests before they could register, just the assumption of ill health sometimes justified the disqualification of Aboriginal students from nursing schools, the withdrawal of financial support from Indian Affairs, and "special treatment" if they became ill at school. Overreaction to a simple bout of the flu cost one student from Munsee in southwestern Ontario. Hilda Miskokomon, who had graduated from the London Victoria Hospital in the late 1920s, was a "brilliant student; [and]...a universal favourite with nurses and doctors." She "was hoping to go back to nurse amongst her own people; was lady-like in manner and dress; and had never given a moment's anxiety since her arrival at the hospital," according to the supervisor of nurses. But when she added to her qualifications by taking a course in Public Health Nursing at the University of Western Ontario, a clerk at Indian Affairs noted that she had been admitted as a tubercular patient in London and immediately cancelled her funding. Later it was explained that she had actually only "had the flu.... This and her studies, had been a heavy strain; and considering her nationality, it was thought wise to give her a complete rest."[135] The same standards applied to non-Aboriginal nursing students when they fell ill; many who wanted to be nurses could not pass medical examinations to get into nursing school, and some had to withdraw from their program due to concerns about TB. However, for Aboriginal students, casual bureaucratic decisions with serious consequences were bolstered by popular ideology that bound together ideas about race and health. There was a widespread belief, explains historian Maureen Lux, that poor health among Aboriginal people was a biological expression of the struggle of "primitive" peoples with "civilization."[136] In addition, because for many students access to education was controlled by the department, decisions about withdrawal and re-entry into nursing programs were more remote for Aboriginal students than for the average nursing student. At the same time, many were inspired to go into nursing because of first-hand experience with health services and a drive to overcome whatever obstacles were put in their way.

Even as hospitals loosened their restrictions on training non-white students, Aboriginal people's access to training continued to be determined on a case-by-case basis and largely through the influence of department staff. School principals and teachers would write letters of reference to the superintendent of Indian Affairs[137] to request both permission and financial support to students they deemed worthy. This correspondence survives today at Library and Archives Canada in Ottawa. One example is the case of Rosabelle Ryder, who was an extraordinary woman in many ways and had a profound impact on Aboriginal nurses from Manitoba and Saskatchewan. A member of the Assiniboine Reserve from Carry The Kettle First Nation, Sintulta, Saskatchewan, she attended Round Lake Residential School in Saskatchewan in the 1930s. Here, one of her teachers noticed her strong academic capabilities and encouraged her to go into nursing. At the time, they could not find a nursing school that would accept First Nations students. Later in her education, while at Brandon Residential School, the subject came up again and by this time St. Boniface Hospital in Winnipeg offered a program that she could attend. As was most often the case in these early years, the superintendent of welfare and training for Indian Affairs decided on matters of post-secondary education for Native students. He received letters of reference from school principals, Indian agents, teachers, ministers, and sometimes judges. These letters made the case for federal support of individual students based on the student's health, ambition, hard work, determination, and academic ability. Ryder's school principal at Brandon (Dr. Doyle) wrote to Indian Affairs on her behalf. In this case, the superintendent decided in her favour. In Ryder's case, the department committed $75 to outfit her and an allowance of $6 per month—assuming that the allowance would only have to be made for the first year.[138] From the start, Ryder was committed to living and working among her people and to her career, which included work at one of the largest Indian hospitals in the country, Fort Qu'Appelle.

One of the most significant barriers to post-secondary education for Aboriginal people has been funding, and for many, the lack of funding rather than ability, commitment, or desire prevented access to higher education. Tracing the early history of First Nations post-secondary education funding in Canada is nearly impossible, as it appears to have been done largely on a case-by-case basis, decided by local authorities, school principals, Indian agents, and, ultimately, federal authorities at Indian Affairs. By 1917, however, western Canada had a loose system of assistance in place that consisted mainly of loans for cattle, horses, farm implements, building materials, sewing machines, and household furniture[139]—funding that continued federal schools' work of creating a domestic, agricultural settler population of Aboriginal peoples.[140] While the Indian Affairs annual report for that year recorded a "number of other ex-pupils" attending "colleges and universities," these students had been funded in a less than transparent manner, as indicated by the inquiries made on behalf of hopeful Native nurses. Indian Affairs had no clear policy for funding vocational training in these years. Superintendent of Indian Affairs Duncan Campbell Scott came closest to defining the department's position in a 1918 response to one inquiry: "the Department has, as you are aware, a number of institutions known as boarding and industrial schools in which children are reared and educated from the time of seven years. To those institutions we allow an annual per capita grant to cover the costs of maintenance.... [W]ith the consent of the department we would be prepared to allow the same grant for maintenance as we do to the institutions under our direct control" to students attending post-secondary institutions.[141] Scott clarified this statement in 1919: "It is of course to be understood each individual case will be considered on its merits, and full representation should be made to the Department when it is desired to take advantage of this offer."[142]

The per capita grant system came out of an order-in-council, and as John Milloy argues in *A National Crime*, the funding system relied on what he calls the "weakest link in the educational chain"—the ability of schools to acquire students.[143] That same system also ensured that the department would have ultimate authority over decisions made regarding Indian education. According to the department's 1928 annual report, for example, only 110 students were receiving some assistance from parliamentary appropriations for post-secondary education. The report did not record how many had applied for funding; however, it stated that grants were to be given "to the most promising, physically fit graduates of our own schools. If church and department representatives consider a graduate worthy a grant is allowed when the bona fide intention of the pupil is evident and provided proper supervision can be secured for the period of advanced study. These tuition grants are continued only when satisfactory reports are received."[144] In the mid-1930s, Methodist Reverend and Indian educator J.F. Woodsworth, who was not supportive of Native people's access to higher education, declared: "It may be stated that the Department has never turned down a pupil who has honestly sought a higher educational background—any failure has come from the Indian, through lack of application or appreciation, or inability to satisfy prescribed standards."[145] Correspondence relating to Aboriginal nurses demonstrates that Woodsworth was not fully informed on the matter.

The weight placed on Indian students' own "inabilities" is evident in the way nursing students accessed funding through to the mid-twentieth century. No assurances were made at all until acceptance by nursing schools was received by the Indian agent. The Indian agent or the student's past school principal then applied to the department with specific amounts for clothing and transportation, and, if approved, received the cheque and spent it on behalf of the student or sent it to the matron of the nursing school.[146] The department was most amenable to funding transportation, uniforms, and equipment, but would occasionally cover basic expenses as well. The expenditure of funds to train Aboriginal health professionals continued to be minimal, based on financial need and subject to the department's utmost priority of cost-saving. The timing of this lengthy process was critical only to the student, who, ironically, was the only one who never actually handled any money.[147] The reluctance of the department to send cheques ahead of time so that the student would be prepared before arriving at school led in some cases to a last-minute plea to the department for the cash.[148] Funding could also cease at any point, as it did when Hilda Miskokomon fell ill.

It is important to note that Indian rights to education were not part of this discussion until the 1970s. Before then, eligibility for post-secondary education funding was mostly talked about as a moral obligation to those who had suffered through Indian schools, or as a benefit voluntarily given to Indian people by the federal government. Loans were approved with the stipulation "until they are able to provide for themselves," which had two important meanings in the context of Aboriginal nursing students. As Aboriginal students, they were subject to a larger policy directive that discouraged government spending on Aboriginal people in favour of self-sufficiency. This policy was related in part to "dwindling" federal funds for undertaking fiscal responsibility for Aboriginal people, but it was also a way of blaming more structural problems of inequality on the "poor character" of Aboriginal people. The goal of self-sufficiency put Aboriginal students in a double bind. Those who were funded needed to portray both financial need on the one hand and "self-sufficiency" on the other in order to appear deserving of grants from the department. Loans could also be held against the student's parents or other family members and/or future treaty annuities owed to the individual or their family.

When the department chose to support nursing students, it maintained close control over funding throughout the course of study and monitored the progress of students through contact with nursing school matrons. When nineteen-year-old Irene Gaddie of Saskatchewan wanted to access nursing training in 1942, her principal at Brandon Indian Residential School, Reverend R.T. Chapin, made a special appeal to Indian Affairs for funding. Chapin argued that as a good, reliable, and ambitious student with "a good constitution and health and...a very pleasing manner," Gaddie was "the type that will make good and be a credit to the Indian Department." At the superintendent's request, the principal contacted the matron of the Brandon General Hospital, who agreed to accept Irene in the fall; she would require an initial grant of $25 for uniforms and $7.50 per month for maintenance, to which superintendent R.A. Hoey agreed. Hoey also requested a biannual report from the matron of the hospital. Throughout Gaddie's training, Indian Affairs transferred financial support to Brandon General through Chapin (and then Mr. Strapp, who replaced him as principal of the school). Along with funding came increased surveillance by Indian Affairs; while non-Native students normally had only to contend with matrons and perhaps their own parents, Aboriginal students in addition had to deal with Indian agents, the superintendent of welfare and training of Indian Affairs, and their former principals, all of whom were informed by the matrons of students' progress.[149]

On top of the burden of loans and the increased surveillance from the grant system, Aboriginal nursing students also faced active discouragement. While Cree elder Ann Callahan was at the Winnipeg General Hospital in training in the early 1950s, she claimed her tuition, books, and $25 dollars for spending money from Indian Affairs. She found the Indian agent, through whom her funding flowed, to be not at all supportive. When he filled out her clothing order, he told her "don't come back" and "you probably won't make it anyway."[150] She didn't get this kind of dismissal from everyone, though. She found that United Church missionaries in the community differed greatly from the ones she knew from residential schools, especially Miss Drake, a community advocate who Callahan said was "good to us."

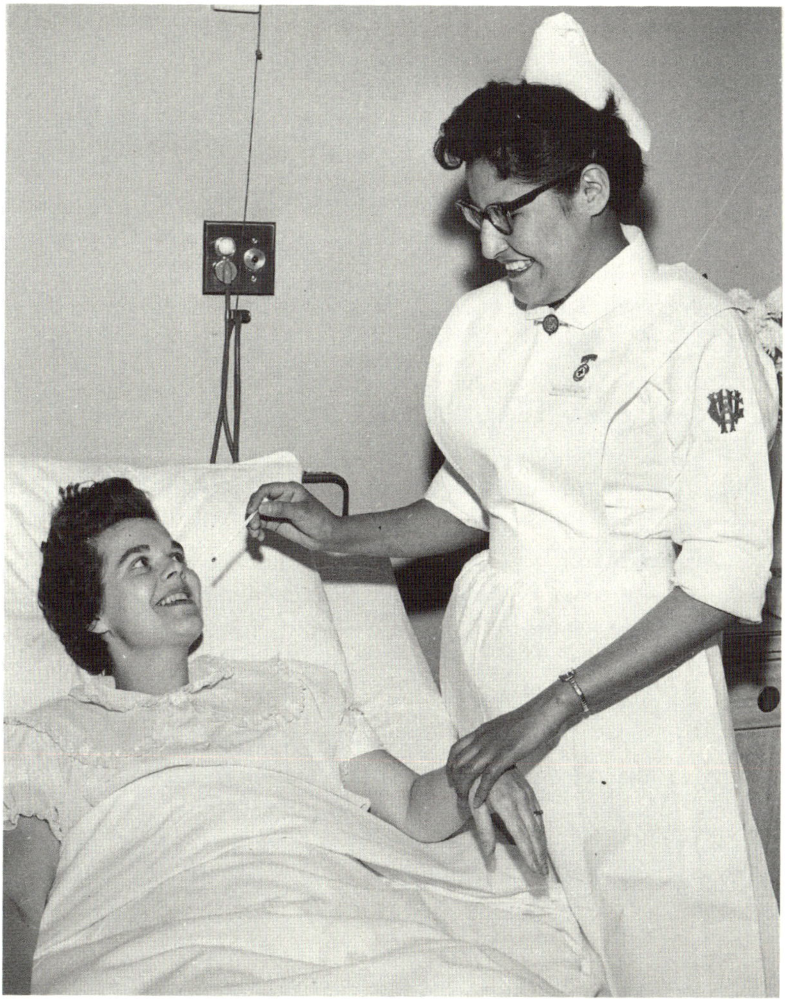

Figure 4.5. Ann Callahan (nee Thomas), one of the founding members of RNCIA, working as a registered nurse at the Women's Pavilion of the Winnipeg General Hospital, where she graduated in 1958.
Library and Archives Canada, Department of Citezenship and Immigration, PA-202475.

Irene Desjarlais (nee Gaddie), remembers a man who told her, "[you'll] be just like the rest of the Indians and quit, wasting the government's money." She decided then and there that "I'd show him that Indians are not quitters." On her first day of nursing school, she recalls feeling "so scared I felt like turning around and running down the steps and home. This was the first time away from my people."[151] But when Irene graduated in May of 1945, she did so with a first class standing, and Dr. P.E. Moore, the assistant superintendent of medical services to First Nations people, expressed interest in offering her a position in an Indian hospital.[152] In 1953, she became the head nurse at Fort Qu'Appelle Indian Hospital in Saskatchewan, and in 1967 she went into public health nursing, becoming the nurse in charge at Fort Qu'Appelle in 1972 and Assistant Zone Nursing Officer in 1978. Involved in the early development of RNCIA, Desjarlais also held a public health diploma from the University of Saskatchewan.

The Indian department was more amenable to funding registered nursing students by the 1950s, although it still did not have a policy to provide full access to post-secondary education to Aboriginal students. From 1957 onwards, the department offered some scholarships to Aboriginal students and had a special category for those who wanted to go into nursing.[153] There was near gender parity among the students getting awards; between 1957 and 1966, seventy-eight women and eighty men received scholarships. The amount of the awards differed, however. The scholarship program had $25,000 to award up to thirty-six scholarships annually, valued at $500 to $1,000 each, depending on the nature of the course: university courses, nursing, teacher training, vocational school progams, courses in agriculture, and "cultural scholarships."[154] The program reserved eight scholarships for those in non-degree registered nursing programs, one for each administrative region of the Indian Affairs department[155] It did the same for university scholarships. University students received between $750 and $1000, teachers in training received $750, and nursing students received $500. The program's evaluation in 1963 revealed that of a total of 119 awards to date, 33 went to university students, 21to nurses, 17 to those in technical programs, 33 to those in vocational programs, and 15 to those taking "cultural study."[156]

It is interesting to compare post-secondary funding before the 1970s with access to federal health services. While the department made no distinctions among registered Indians in its public health, preventative medicine, and health education campaigns, Native people could access clinical health services provided, first, that an individual was an Indian as defined by the Indian Act; second, that they followed "the Indian way of life, which for practical purposes means that he must be living on an Indian reserve or have been away from that reserve for a period of less than a year"; and, third, "that the individual is financially unable to arrange appropriate care for himself. If he is able, he is expected to do so."[157] These three criteria—registration, "an Indian way of life," and poverty—folded together colonial, cultural, and class identifiers of Aboriginal people. They reflected the government's intention to minimize federal responsibility by absorbing Indian populations, and they served simultaneously to identify and target Indian populations as pre-modern forms.

These criteria also guided decisions about funding for post-secondary education. Notably, funding remained contingent on the resources of the student's parents (if they were alive) and/or their extended family and community. One woman who trained in the mid-1950s received money from "Indian Affairs to purchase uniforms, aprons, collars, books, stockings" because her father was not "regularly employed and he states he is unable to help with the purchases."[158] The official line of Indian Affairs was that it would provide full access to post-secondary funding to any status Indian; in practice, funding for Indian students was contingent upon approval of the department, which had both explicit and invisible standards of its own. Its case-by-case approach was just one expression of the department's unwillingness to state an explicit and uniform policy on its responsibility to fund Indian education.

What was nursing education like for those Aboriginal women who were able to negotiate access to it? Until the early 1970s, nursing education was undertaken at hospitals in programs that combined labour and education. Nurse Jennie Neilson from the Blood Reserve in southern Alberta recalls that in her nursing program, students would wake up at 6 a.m. for a twelve-hour shift from 7 a.m. to 7 p.m. and be in bed by curfew at 10 p.m. There was little time for anything but nursing school, which in effect was working in a hospital. Students did not have much time for a social life. Nursing school was very physically demanding at this time, with a heavy load of courses and work, but, as Mi'kmaq nurse Marilyn Sark of the Lennox Island Band, Prince Edward Island, remarks, "we were all in the same boat." Also, she points out that, like many Aboriginal nurses in this period, she was a young woman when she graduated from the program.

Most of the women who went into nursing school were in their late teens and early twenties, and for some Aboriginal students it was not colour bar restrictions but age restrictions that limited their access to nursing education. Matriculation before the age of eighteen was common, and several had to wait a year before being eligible to go to nursing school. It was for this reason that Marilyn Sark went into a university program instead, and Wilma Strongeagle spent a year working as a ward clerk before beginning her nursing program. In nursing schools, and even within the profession, there was a fairly strict policy that nurses should be unmarried, and Aboriginal nurses were no exception. Most were single or unmarried. Nurses at the time were expected to represent restrained sexuality and virtue, and married women were generally excluded from the profession. This went on even into the 1960s, as Rosella McKay, a Saskatchewan community health nurse, recalls. As a student in the diploma nursing program at the University of Saskatchewan in the early 1960s, she found the university hospital was quite "liberal," as it did not judge nurses who were married or pregnant and who, at this time, were refused by other schools.[159]

For many Aboriginal nurses, studying to be a nurse often meant relocating. Their education, then, serves as an important reminder of the extraordinary mobility of Aboriginal women in this period: they moved for training and work within and between provinces, from reserves to urban centres, and sometimes they crossed international borders as well. At the same time, many could not attend training or had to cut their training short because of family responsibilities or homesickness. Due to the general isolation felt by students, it was common for siblings, cousins, or friends to travel together, for one to follow the other within a short time, or, when possible, for students to attend nursing school at hospitals near where they had a family or community connections. They often recall being the only Aboriginal student in their class and feeling lonely at school, far away from home, family, and community. This is ironic, as Carol Prince (and others) went into nursing expressly to get away from residential school. "There were few Aboriginal people residing in Winnipeg in the fifties," Callahan recalls. "If it were not for two or three families whose husbands were in the armed services, I would have been lonelier. Often times, they invited me to their homes to enjoy an Aboriginal meal, music, and their unique humour." Marilyn Sark also made close friends while at nursing school, some of whom she still keeps in contact with today.[160]

Some Aboriginal registered nursing students were able to take advantage of the specialization of nursing education at the time, including psychiatric nursing, nursing administration, and public health. Bachelor programs grew in this period, and some nurses went directly into degree programs or upgraded their qualifications. For example, Miss Edith Eileen Green, of Tyendinaga, graduated with her RN from the Toronto General School of Nursing, then worked in Belleville and Moose Factory before enrolling at the University of Toronto for an advanced course that would enable her to work as a public health nurse. When she completed the course in 1960, she worked at the Manitowaning Indian Hospital on Manitoulin Island, and then became the public health nurse in charge of the Nipissing Agency at Sturgeon Falls, Ontario.[161]

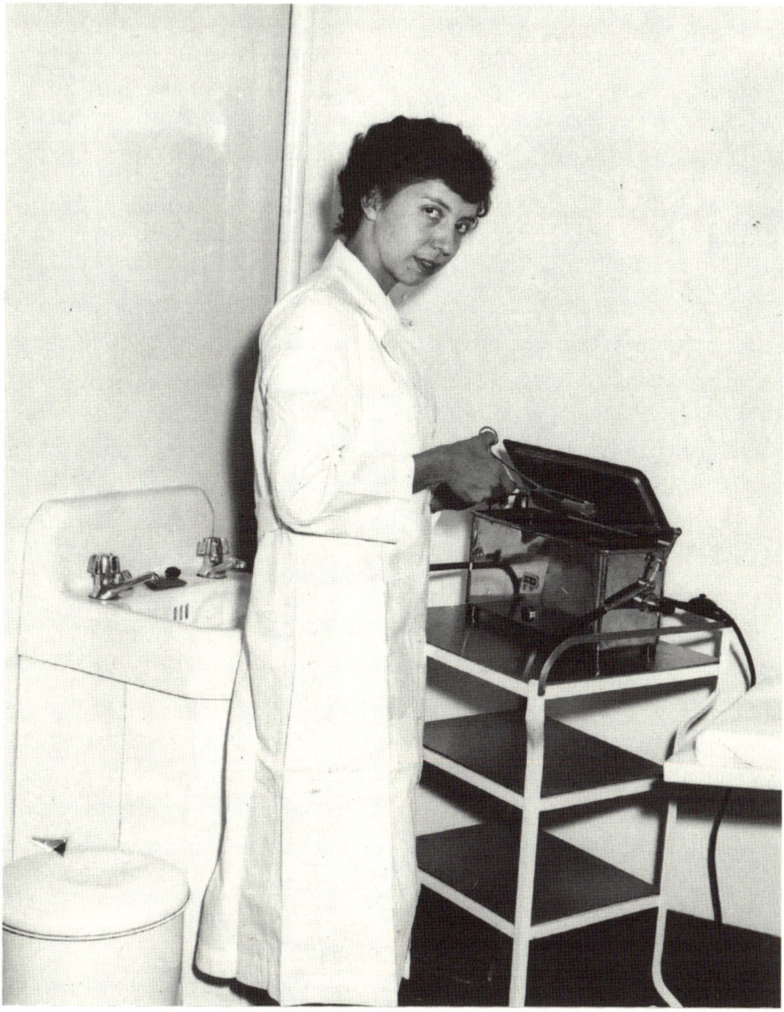

Figure 4.6. Edith Eileen Green, of Tyendinaga, Ontario, graduated as an RN from the Toronto General School of Nursing, and worked in Belleville and Moose Factory before enrolling at the University of Toronto for advanced training as a public health nurse. She completed the course in the spring of 1960 and, after working at Manitowaning Indian Hospital on Manitoulin Island, became the public health nurse in charge of the Nipissing Agency at Sturgeon Falls, Ontario, where she is shown here.
Library and Archives Canada, E011052444.

According to medical historian Kathryn McPherson, 148 graduated from basic baccalaureate programs in 1962, and it was heralded as a significant professional accomplishment.[162] Marilyn Francis (Sark) graduated from a four-year BSc (Nursing) program at Mount St. Vincent University in Halifax in the early 1960s. She became a nursing instructor at Hillsborough Hospital in Charlottetown, teaching psychiatric nursing and surgical nursing until 1965. She went on to be the Indian health liaison worker for Lennox Island and later the band welfare officer. Sark was also an Indian scholarship winner. She recalls feeling like a "feather in the cap" of the Indian department. Also in the 1960s, Mavis Brass, of Key Band, near Kamsack, Saskatchewan, earned a five-year nursing degree at the University of Saskatchewan. She wanted to specialize in nursing administration. Métis nurse Jean Isbister Ahenakew also chose a university program. She became a clinical and surgical nurse at Holy Family Hospital in Prince Albert, Saskatchewan.

Nursing curriculum for most of the twentieth century would have provided little information about Aboriginal people. Even as registered nursing programs moved out of hospitals and into colleges and universities, often the only skills development for nurses working with Aboriginal communities was the "In-Service Training Program" for community health nurses in the MSB. This training was not credited outside the MSB and was open only to nurses employed by the branch. Thanks to a range of Indigenous interventions into nursing education and issues faced in particular by Indigenous nursing students, much of this began to change, especially in the 1980s and beyond. It was one of RNCIA's goals to both make nursing education more accessible, and to make it much better for the next generation.

Indigenous Interventions into Nursing Education

For many Aboriginal nurses, their education began long before they entered nursing schools. Early childhood experiences and lessons learned among their families and communities often sustained them in the federal education system and prepared them for nurse's training. As a child, Ann Callahan was taught to believe in herself as "a child of creation." Well before she was sent to File Hills Residential School, she was constantly told that she was loved. For her, traditional ceremonies, visiting with elders, and connecting with her community were vital throughout her young years and today as well. Eleanor Olson, a Cree elder from Norway House and Peguis, was also prepared in these early years for a nursing career down the road. Until she was nine, she lived a traditional lifestyle, and was educated by her grandparents and great-grandparents, who would not permit her to attend residential school. She recalls that by the age of six, she knew all of her roles and responsibilities, which included knowing all the names of different fish, game, and birds. She knew how to fillet, tan hides, cure meats, and do quill and bead work. She also had to make sure that all the moss was washed and dried for diapers. Her grandmother taught her critical survival skills, and her aunties taught her how to read. Eleanor worked very hard when she was young, and it was this, she believes, that provided her with the work ethic she would need to undertake nursing training and a career in health care later in life. Many nurses recall the strong emphasis on education that was instilled in them by their families; for many, education was highly valued and prioritized. Additionally, nurses recall being prepared for hard work in their early years, preparation they felt had been necessary to endure the rigours of nursing school.

These recollections contradict more popular depictions of Aboriginal family life in the 1940s and 1950s, which has largely been pathologized in religious, sociological, bureaucratic, and economic interpretations. But the determination and success of Aboriginal nurses belie these interpretations and point instead to a solid foundation built from early family and community experiences. Many of the Aboriginal women who worked at hospitals in this period spoke their Indigenous language as well as English, which was invaluable for communicating with patients in the hospitals. Not only did many overcome the regimes and poor quality of federal schooling, but they also overcame the discrimination and racism so prevalent in Canadian society at that time. The skills and sense of self they learned, therefore, were crucial to their later survival and success as nurses.

In addition to early preparation, a number of changes were happening within education to support Indigenous nursing education reform. The RNCIA's first survey, held in 1983, indicates that Indian Affairs post-secondary funding, or partial funding, went to 68 percent of the respondents (only slightly less than the total number of status Indian respondents[163]). The survey reflects various developments in the 1970s, including the AFN's publication of *Indian Control of Indian Education* (1972), the articulation of treaty rights, the Post-Secondary Assistance Program for Indian Students, and the 1979 revision to the Indian Act,[164] each of which contributed to a more predictable and theoretically universal, if still inadequate, system of post-secondary funding for First Nations students.[165] To supplement these measures, RNCIA developed a number of incentives for Indigenous nurses.

The founding of RNCIA occurred during a significant turn in Indian education initiatives, and the association worked tirelessly to put nursing on that agenda. These efforts include the Baxter Fellowships. Baxter is a global producer of medical devices, pharmaceuticals, and other biotechnology. In 1985 Baxter "approached the association for assistance in attracting Aboriginal nurses to the north" and invited RNCIA to administer two annual scholarships to Aboriginal nursing students planning to pursue a nursing career in the north. In 1981, the Manitoba Indian Nurses Association established the Jean Goodwill Award "to honour IINC members for their contribution and dedication toward improving the health of our people."[166] It was awarded every two years to a nurse of Indian or Inuit ancestry who demonstrated the qualities for which Jean Goodwill was so admired. The Grace Easter Memorial Scholarship, established by the Aboriginal Nurses Manitoba in 1986, has been given to Aboriginal students enrolled in the first or second year of a nursing degree who demonstrate leadership skills and commitment to nursing within the Aboriginal community. This scholarship honours Grace Easter, a Swampy Cree nurse from Chemawawin Cree Nation (Easterville) who earned an RN from Red River in 1977 and worked for the Medial Services Branch Manitoba Region as a program director and First Nations Confederacy Health Advisor (1977–1982). Easter also served as the president of the Manitoba Indian Nurses Association, helped to develop Kekinan Centre (a housing complex for seniors in Winnipeg), and worked as the health coordinator and liaison for the Manitoba Indian Brotherhood.

In addition to financial support, RNCIA contributed to three further developments in the field of nursing education, the Indian and Inuit Health Careers Program (IIHCP), Access programs, and Native and Northern Nursing programs. Begun in 1984 and headed by the Department of National Health and Welfare with assistance from the Indian and Inuit Nurses of Canada, the IIHCP was a major impetus for Aboriginal people entering the profession and for innovations in nursing education for Aboriginal students. The program funded various initiatives, including Native-specific programs, bursaries and scholarships, and professional development. The main goals of the program were to "stimulate the interest of Indian and Inuit students in the health disciplines, to encourage them to choose health careers and then make it easier for them to achieve this goal." Additionally, IIHCP aimed to foster less alienating environments for Aboriginal students while educating students for work among Aboriginal people.[167]

The pursuit of "Indian control" was critically linked to the education and employment of Aboriginal professionals, and as the registered nursing diploma and the baccalaureate of nursing (BN) became benchmarks of success in the struggle for improved health and socio-economic status of Aboriginal people, RNCIA made great efforts to support all Aboriginal nurses who wanted to obtain these qualifications. This was especially important as the push for baccalaureate level "entry to practice" affected Aboriginal nurses in particular ways. Officially, the Medical Services Branch stipulated that only degree-educated nurses could take charge of a health centre or nursing station or practice public health in Aboriginal communities.[168] Native Nurses Access Programs, initiated first at the University of Saskatchewan and Lakehead University, aimed to train a new generation of Aboriginal nurses who would be prepared to take on these positions. The National Native Access Program to Nursing (NNAPN) at the University of Saskatchewan was a pre-nursing program created to assist Aboriginal students in gaining admission requirements to degree-granting nursing schools. Students attended a nine-week spring course in which they experienced the university environment, developed study, exam-writing, and library-research skills, and gained practical fieldwork experience. The program's success has led to its adoption in other universities.[169]

Urged by RNCIA to recruit as many Indian nurses as possible, the MSB met with RNCIA leadership in the 1980s to discuss how to improve the representation of Native nurses in the profession. The resulting document, *Resourcing Nursing Requirements for Indian Health* (March 1981), proposed Indian nurse training schools be instituted across the country based on certain criteria: "native commitment and control; location near native populations; cultural components to education; educational mandate from an established institution; special provisions for native students; establishment of day care facilities; utilization of existing plants and piggybacking to established educational facilities; and exploration of many resources for student funding."[170] The proposal for Indian nurse training schools was modelled on an educational institution owned and operated by the Blue Quills Native Education Council, near St. Paul, Alberta, now called Blue Quills First Nations College. This program operated under an agreement between the Blue Quills Native Education Council and the Grant MacEwan Community College in Edmonton to deliver a basic nursing diploma program consisting of an initial six-month qualifying course that met requirements for admission to any basic nursing program; a second full-year equivalent to the first-year program for any diploma course; and a year in Edmonton, where students completed their work at Grant MacEwan. When it opened, it was the only basic nursing program in Canada that catered especially to Native students.

It operated with seed funds from the MSB ($300,000 over three years) and private and provincial contributors. Already in 1982 there was interest in similar approaches in BC, Saskatchewan, and Manitoba.[171]

In 1986, Jean Goodwill, then president of the Indian and Inuit Nurses of Canada and director of the IIHC program in Saskatchewan, counted thirteen programs for Native nursing students across the country in a speech she gave at hearings on Indian Education at the Assembly of First Nations.[172] Many of these programs took a "community development approach" to nursing education. Pat Stewart, then a band nurse in The Pas who had helped to develop a Northern Bachelor of Nursing Program in Manitoba, explained in 1984, "A community development approach...bridges cultural difference; builds on existing knowledge, attitudes and skills; utilizes local resources; provides educational opportunities suited to the setting; develops personnel who already have roots in the region; provides training and employment opportunities that meet perceived native needs and priorities and, last, but not least, places an important service under local control."[173]

The key objectives were to educate people from reserves and northern areas who would return to these areas, a concept linked to the ongoing problems of high turnover rates and instability in the Medical Services Branch. Marilyn Tanner Spence, an RN from northern Manitoba, graduated with her nursing diploma in Thompson, Manitoba, in 1988. She chose this program specifically because it was "in the community that I lived in."[174] Although she had originally wanted to go to medical school, the nursing program was an Access program, and it was local and more affordable. Tanner Spence later went on to earn a nursing degree from the University of Manitoba in 1992 and a master's degree from the University of Victoria in 1998. She also worked as a nurse in hospital and nursing station settings at the Manitoba Keewatinowi Okimakanak, helped to develop university curriculum for an expanded role for nurses and to establish a nursing program at Norway House, and was a board member of the ANAC.

These programs were a significant departure from those targeted to Aboriginal nurses in earlier decades, which, in the 1950s and 1960s, had only supported paraprofessional training as nurse's aides and ward aides. First, they focussed on RN and BN as opposed to LPN and RNA training. Second, they were designed for Native nurses and intended to enable registered nurses to retain cultural integrity and sensitivity, thereby improving the quality of service provided in Aboriginal communities. While the programs sometimes struggled with competing objectives, inconsistent funding, and a lack of cooperation in terms of recruitment and regulation,[175] there was a consensus that nursing curriculum needed to change in order to prepare all nurses to better serve Aboriginal people and communities. This emphasis on cultural sensitivity in nursing education indicated the possibility of an ever-widening space for Aboriginal nurses in the profession. At the same time, an increase in their numbers was associated with an improvement in the quality of education and service of all nurses in Canada. Future health care workers will benefit as Aboriginal people join the ranks of teaching faculty in nursing education programs, where they can effectively challenge existing curriculas and direct the content of nursing education.

Conclusion

One striking characteristic of Aboriginal nursing history is the tradition of honouring energetic nursing leaders. In its written materials, RNCIA regularly seeks to promote Aboriginal nurses and to celebrate those who have made extraordinary contributions. Often in these tributes, nurses are positioned as role models whose careers have been exceptional or whose story is particularly inspiring, encouraging, or relatable. In doing so, the organization endeavours to ensure a succession of Indigenous health care professionals. In addition, in honouring its leaders, RNCIA acknowledges that advancements in the field of Aboriginal nursing have been guided and often also initiated by Aboriginal nurses themselves, many of them who are now considered senior nurses and elders. These nurses have combined a career in health services with their knowledge of Indigenous health to provide expertise on matters such as protocol and ethics, healing processes for communities and individuals, and programming for various Aboriginal populations, including prisons, residential schools survivors, health and social service workers, and others.

Culture, background, and education are intertwined in the labour history of Aboriginal women, and this is especially true for those who worked in Indian health. There were rifts between some professionals and paraprofessionals, and tensions between some Native and non-Native nurses. These differences sometimes served to justify the exclusion and unequal treatment of some nurses, especially as the demand for the labour of Indigenous nurses increased.[176] Yet community action consistently frames discussions of professionalism when it comes to Aboriginal nursing, and this is particularly clear when it comes to the ways that Aboriginal nurses are honoured. Significantly, in accounts about Aboriginal nurses, it is often the community work they do after their nursing career is over that is the focus, rather than the credentials they earned or their career itself. This reflects an Indigenous view of labour and can broaden paradigms of labour history, which focus merely on the formal working lives of individuals.

Three principle objectives of RNCIA—to improve the health of Indian people, to develop Aboriginal employment and professional standing, and to make post-secondary education more accessible—are central themes of twentieth-century Aboriginal history. To RNCIA, ideal Indian nurses were registered nurses working in their own communities for the MSB. They identified with Indian patients and had an inherent capacity to serve them best. Nursing, for Aboriginal people, was also about self-determination, good health for Aboriginal people, and creating and improving a dialogue with communities, nursing associations, health organizations, the federal government, and nursing schools.

Aboriginal nurses continue to be underrepresented, and the recruitment and retention of Aboriginal nurses remains a key area of research for nursing schools, federal agencies, and Aboriginal communities. All the same, the achievements of Aboriginal nurses are often underappreciated by those who are not directly involved in health care work—and sometimes even by those who are. Compared to other professions, nurses have made significant, sustained, and creative efforts to effect change in Aboriginal health, nursing work, and nursing education. Earlier in the century, Aboriginal women were often subject to paternal, top-down programs that steered them into domestic service. Few had other opportunities for post-secondary education, and for those who did, it was equated with assimilation and integration rather than service to one's community. Yet, by the 1980s, Aboriginal nurses across the country had articulated how nursing work by Aboriginal people could affect self-determination and had made the nursing profession responsible for shouldering in part the enormous responsibilities of decolonizing health care in Canada.

Conclusion

The Wages of Whiteness and the Indigenous Historian

I have argued that the politics of modernity and the state shaped twentieth-century Aboriginal women's wage labour. In the case studies of Aboriginal women's labour examined here, the state's offer of training and employment for Native women was premised on the regulation of labour and discipline of personal lives and identities. But, as we have seen, Native women also used labour as a strategy of cultural persistence and a means to gain recognition and control within modernity, challenging conventional narratives of Aboriginal absence and displacement in modern Canadian history. I have attempted to balance the tendency in history to present Aboriginal women's lives either as managed federally to the point of invisibility or as static and unchanging to the point of exclusion from modernity altogether.

The themes of labour, modernity, and the state interconnect in twentieth-century Aboriginal women's history. While many historians have overlooked Native women's involvement in domestic labour, especially in the modern era, it was clearly in high demand. The state played a central role in training Native women to work as domestic servants by making domestic training central to girls' curriculum in federal Indian schooling. Schools became vital sources of Indian labour for federal institutions and private individuals. Not only did the state play a role in training, it also directly recruited, contracted, and regulated Native women's domestic labour and supervised the working and leisure lives of workers themselves.

From the point of view of the Department of Indian Affairs, both domestic labour and the domestic workspace were to have a disciplinary effect on Indigenous women. The department's insistence on the need to regulate workers' recreational time highlights how the state perceived Native women who engaged in wage labour outside of reserves as somehow vulnerable and in need of management. We cannot dismiss the intervention of the state in the lives of working Native women because in many cases it had profound and long-lasting impacts, not only on their lives but also on the lives of other Native women and families and on the perpetuation of stereotypes of Indian women in mainstream society. The attention paid to Indigenous women's working lives also highlights the state's investment in and attempts to control the process by which Native people engaged in, failed to engage in, obtained, quit, and were released from employment.

The historical literature on Native labour (mostly men's) has focussed on the nature, timing, and effects of Native people's so-called difficult and ultimately disastrous transition to wage work after the fur trade period. Yet Native women's domestic labour history demonstrates the persistent demand for Native labour and the continuing patterns of Native women's engagement in it. Native women who worked as domestics often did so for only a short period of time, and many moved or returned home after one or two years. This was because of the nature of that work, which was often both mobile and temporary, in spite of the department's objective of permanent employment. Still, Native women did take part in domestic work in significant numbers; even short-term, transitory experiences had a meaningful effect. There exists a "secret history" of twentieth-century domestic work among Native women that deserves to be made known and more fairly positioned within our understandings of both Aboriginal and labour history.

There was a marked shift in postwar Indian policy from a vision of isolation for civilization on reserves to one of integration for invisibility in the broader Canadian nation. But this did not mean that the state abandoned its claim to the management of Indigenous populations. The Department of Indian Affairs' Placement and Relocation program was one means by which the state attempted to use employment to enact federal goals of integration by permanent urban settlement. The Placement and Relocation program reflected a variety of mid-twentieth-century imperatives and developments, including tuberculosis rehabilitation programs, vocational skills training, discipline and self-sufficiency through full-time permanent employment, enfranchisement and assimilation, and the ultimate dissolution of the Indian department. For Native women, hairdressing, with its relatively short and inexpensive program of study and seemingly limitless and immediate possibilities for work, was a popular option in the program.

Aboriginal women who worked as hairdressers in the late 1950s and 1960s were seen to be confronting and conquering cosmic cultural extremes, solitudes that were often presented as temporal and spatial in nature. They were cast as women working in extraordinary circumstances, bridging the strange and overwhelming city and rustic simplicity, exchanging tradition for modernity. But hairdressers were not the only Aboriginal women engaging in modern labour; Native women chiefs, welfare officers, Homemakers' Club women, artisans, shopkeepers, musicians, restaurant owners, dressmakers, bank cashiers, stewardesses, waitresses, secretaries and stenographers, nurses and nurse's aides, and radio presenters and hosts were, too. These other fields of work for Aboriginal women deserve investigation as well.

Aboriginal women also have a history of salon labour that speaks to issues of race, class, entrepreneurship, and the role of urban beauty cultures in expressions of Indian resistance. Hairdressing is an urban, technological, and self-styled "scientific" occupation that emphasizes modern femininity, deportment, beauty, and aesthetics; for Aboriginal women in the trade, this challenged contemporary expectations at mid-century. While shop ownership was impossible for most Aboriginal women in the beauty industry, Aboriginal women put urban beauty culture to the task of furthering Indian politics of rights, equality, race relations, and nation building. At the same time, Indian princess contests regularly celebrated a particular kind of idealized traditional femininity that displaced women from modernity.

It is this idea of displacement by the modern and the contemporary that informed many of the programs for "community" and "economic" development in the 1960s and 1970s. The early history of the Community Health Representatives program helps to illuminate how the state fashioned Indigenous labour as paraprofessional, gendered, and racialized, and then put it into service as such. Three aspects of the program illuminate how federal ideals about gendered division of Indigenous labour and about Indian and white labour informed the CHR program in its inaugural decade: the selection of CHR candidates, the training program, and supervision during and after the employee probationary period. Originally, the selection process favoured men by disqualifying women who were under the age of 35, had young children, or were unmarried. The training curriculum, wage structure, and supervision made CHR work appear highly gendered, but this was an imposed structure that inherently devalued women's work in relation to men's. It is ironic that Ethel Martens, the program's founder, argued that devaluing women's work suited the culture of Indigenous communities and thus also the larger goals of creating non-paternalistic, culturally sensitive federal programming. The labour of Indian women was also devalued within a larger, extremely hierarchical federal department of the Canadian government, the Medical Services Branch of the Department of National Health and Welfare.

As the CHR program's early history makes clear, major decision-making in Indian health was not in the hands of those most directly affected—Aboriginal people. This lack of responsibility to Aboriginal people was addressed head-on in the mid-1970s by the Registered Nurses of Canadian Indian Ancestry, or RNCIA (now the Aboriginal Nurses Association of Canada, or ANAC). Yet the moment when the organization formed did not signal an entrance into history from "irrelevance," but instead marked the culmination of a number of grievances Aboriginal nurses had with the state—particularly its systems of health, employment, and education. Nineteen seventy-five was indeed an important turning point, rather than a starting point in the history of Native nurses.

Working back through time, it is clear that the RNCIA's founding goals spoke to much broader discussions about Aboriginal health, employment, and education history in the twentieth century. Aboriginal nurses positioned themselves as experts in health care for Aboriginal people, as advocates for their health, and as keen critics of the inadequate and racist discriminatory health services available to them. The RNCIA also voiced many of the issues that Aboriginal nurses had with the MSB's employment practices. Finally, RNCIA members were active in and supportive of some of the early education initiatives that were meant to improve Native people's access to post-secondary education, funding, and professional careers. It is significant that, together, both nursing and Indian ancestry were seen as a site of powerful resistance. The idealized Indian nurse was in possession of an RN degree, worked for Indian Health Services, identified "first-hand" with Indian patients, and had an inherent capacity to best serve Aboriginal communities. As such, importantly, the history of the RNCIA also illuminates how Native labour both influenced and was influenced by the changing politics of being Native in the last half of the twentieth century.

There is much that can be learned from this story of labour, modernity, and the state in Aboriginal women's history. In the professional discipline of history, ideas about modernity and the state can play a role in the exclusion and invisibility of Native labour. This concern has remained with me through the writing of this book and has encouraged me also to think critically about training and employment in the academy. In the following pages I would like to historicize the twentieth-century English Canadian historical profession using what I have learned about the Indian history of post-secondary education and labour. This conclusion is not meant to offer well-supported and decisive arguments about the profession, but rather to raise and document some serious questions and concerns about it. I want to do so by problematizing the nearly homogeneous working culture in the Canadian historical profession, the profession's contradistinctions between authentic Aboriginal historical figures and modern professional historians, and the position of the Canadian state in Aboriginal history writing and practice.

Indigenous critique of historical scholarship has a history of its own. Aboriginal scholars have challenged the ways (non-Native) historians have depicted Native people as non-literate and therefore non-historical. They have deconstructed colonial mythologies that represented Indigenous people as static relics of an earlier stage of evolution. They have shown how Western reason, objectivity, and knowledge construct their opposites, which then get imposed on Aboriginal people. They have analyzed how Indigenous knowledge, ethics, and subjectivities have been fashioned, and to what ends. They have discussed how sexism compounded with racism has left Native women academics particularly vulnerable both within and outside of their communities. They have questioned if professional training makes Indigenous academics somehow inauthentic. In terms of academic professionalism, Aboriginal critiques have shifted from a discussion of access to knowledge to a discussion of its production, translation, use, protection, and ownership.[1]

Historical knowledge production is in all ways a project in which Native people are profoundly and politically invested, but in their critiques Indigenous scholars often use "history" and sometimes "History" as shorthand for colonization, misrepresentation, dispossession, antiquated and racist approaches, and as a powerful force of continuing oppression. However, rarely do these investigations inquire about how the professionalization of history as a discipline has served to reduce, exclude, and obscure the work of Native scholars in this field. This is the irony of claims that you have to be Native to do accurate historical scholarship about Native people, as if the process by which professional history is made and recognized is transparent and unproblematic and not itself profoundly political, whoever is doing it.

Allied scholars are also engaged in this question of exclusion, often in the context of offering intellectual, political, and administrative support to Aboriginal students. Several Canadian women's and gender historians have raised the question of equity and diversity in their history departments in the context of discussions on the status of women in the history profession.

Some historians of Aboriginal history have also offered constructive criticism about the eurocentrism of Canadian institutions of higher learning.[2] The focus has often been on Aboriginal undergraduate students, their "problems" within the education system, family and community priorities, a lack of material resources, issues with work and study conditions at the post-secondary level, and, ultimately, their failure to see that, as one scholar put it, "Canadian history can train them for their current struggles over politics and land-claim issues."[3] A lack of interest or investment in the historical profession on the part of Indigenous people is thus popularly explained as a bewildering oversight, something related intrinsically to "Nativeness," or the unfortunate result of social inequality. Rarely do these investigations of absence and exclusion inquire about how professional history itself works as an agent that discourages and marginalizes Indigenous historical labour.

It is significant that in Aboriginal nursing, professional identity developed in ways that insisted upon presence and representation, while in Aboriginal history, this has not happened. Nursing is a larger, more popular, and more accessible profession, but when considering its history of professionalization—safeguarding privilege and power among white women[4]—Aboriginal nurses' insistence on inclusion is significant. It is important to note that Native doctors, too, have made a place for themselves. Recently the Indigenous Physicians Association of Canada (IPAC) has insisted on working with the Association of Faculties of Medicine of Canada (AFMC) to restructure curriculum for *all* medical students in Canada so that it is culturally relevant and safe and includes material on Indigenous health.[5] In addition, capacity-building projects, including Aboriginal health student centres and internships, have been initiated across the country. In many ways, professional history has isolated itself from ongoing Indigenous scholarly critique, questions of equity and access in academia, and other developments in the fields of Indigenous education and professionalism elsewhere in academia. This isolation has left professional history largely unaffected by other changes in the institution, and so there is much historians can learn about ways to make a profession that is not inevitably non-Indian.

One assumption underlying recent professional conversations about Aboriginal history seems to be that Aboriginal people are not only absent from professional dialogue about Aboriginal history, but also oblivious to history's professional culture altogether. The practice in history of referring to the professional (and presumed white) "we" as distinct and separate from the Aboriginal (and presumed non-academic) "them" is but one manifestation of this trend. By envisioning an "us" utterly devoid of "them" and a "them" that is not in the audience, historians leave the impression that Aboriginal people do not read, write, and think historically. The result is the sense that their role in the production of scholarly history is a matter of performance; they are either "playing Indian" or, as Susan M. Hill has articulated, we are "playing historian."[6]

In history, as in other forms of work, there is a significant and seemingly irreconcilable dualism that divides Native people as the target or object of labour and Native people as workers. In the field of history, this split divides Native people as history and Native people as historians. We are reminded here of Philip Deloria's arguments about expectation and expectedness. He argues that part of the project of understanding Indian modernity is to take as a subject of investigation the ideological and discursive frames non-Indians used to explain and contain Indian people. One of these frames is professional history. We cannot take the profession's presumption of absence to be meaningless and incidental. It is the result of the ways in which familiar categories like Indian and white, traditional and assimilated, savage and civilized, authentic and "tainted," and advocacy and objectivity are made by and in turn create and materially enforce certain expectations.[7] When many of us consider ourselves to be Aboriginal historians, or those who look at history from an Aboriginal perspective, how did "history" become something that is self-consciously non-Native, "outside," or apart from us? How did the discipline and the profession develop in ways that excluded the presence and the possibility of Aboriginal historians? Moreover, how and why does it continue to do so?

The assumption of cultural homogeneity among historians is a recent development. One hundred and fifty years ago, the idea that, as the language used by historians suggests, historians are de facto non-Aboriginal, would not have made any sense. Maureen Konkle and Robin Jarvis Brownlie locate the mid-nineteenth century as a significant period of Aboriginal history writing in the works of, for example, George Copway and Peter Jones.[8] While we might think of these individuals as "Indians in unexpected places," they were not particularly viewed that way by their contemporaries, and they joined a cadre of Indian intellectuals, political organizers, poets, and philosophers in the nineteenth century. In their research, lectures, and publications, these historians used history to counter misrepresentations of Native people and to affirm, among other things, Native people's political autonomy and human equality.

History by Aboriginal people, however, is distinctly silenced in the twentieth century. (Brownlie argues until 1969, but I would argue, with a few exceptions, for the entire century.) While Konkle does not address this silencing in her account, Brownlie argues that it was "due, no doubt, to a relative lack of public interest in the reading public and, in Canada, a general shortage of publishing opportunities."[9] The silencing of Aboriginal historians' voices seems to have had other causes, however, since, as so many scholars have shown, there has never been a scarcity of interest in Indians.[10] Importantly, neither author subscribes to a model of Aboriginal decline, so popular in history, to locate and then explain the silencing of Aboriginal histories. Neither author either, however, addresses professional history's role in this process.

Around the turn of the century, history became a modern profession. As history moved towards "a career for university-trained, university-based professionals," historians engaged in a process of erecting and policing the boundaries that determined who could and who could not know, teach, and practise history.[11] They developed, as Donald Wright argues, "a set of common assumptions, questions, methods, and values," an "association to articulate and defend its interests," and "prolonged training in a definable body of knowledge, a credential system, a code of ethics, self-government, and legislated access to a particular labour market," as well as a privileged access to financial and social rewards for services.[12] That shift made professional history writing indelibly entwined with access to education and thus circumscribed not only white women's participation, as Wright and others argue,[13] but also that of Aboriginal women and men. Whereas Native people could be and were historians before history professionalized, as of February 2014, there are only perhaps five Aboriginal professors in tenured or tenure-track positions in history departments in Canada,[14] most of whom were hired in the last three years.

When I discuss this figure with other historians, what is offered is a generalized discourse that conflates and deflects structural and disciplinary issues as Indigenous peoples' difficult "cultural" confrontation with post-secondary education—and sometimes modernity. Yet Indian assimilation policy impeded, or even precluded, Indigenous participation in the modernization of the historical profession. By section 86(1) of the 1876 Indian Act, a university-educated Indian could automatically be stripped of Indian status. Blair Stonechild shows that the policy was in fact broadened in scope in 1927 to coerce the enfranchisement of any Indian or Indians seen fit for Canadian citizenship, but the law was never successfully imposed.[15] However, it no less serves as an important and profoundly pervasive narrative about how higher education was associated with "civilization" and, later, integration, and how, in Devon Mihesuah's phrase, "Natives and Academics" get made to be opposing categories of inquiry and identity.[16] As discussed in Chapter 1, for over half of the twentieth century, official Indian school curricula maintained a focus on manual as opposed to academic training. This limited Native people's ability to pursue post-secondary education, and students were often hastily shuttled directly into the workforce in "suitable" vocations like domestic service. The DIA did have a measured and case-by-case system of spending discretionary funds[17] on post-secondary education; however, by the 1950s, as shown in Chapter 2, that system advocated cheaper, shorter adult education or vocational training programs like the Placement and Relocation Program. The department ultimately envisioned training and education as a step signalling a longer voyage towards equality by way of disintegrating Indian legal status. Even into the 1960s, higher education for Aboriginal people was often spoken about in terms of a "transition" to modernity: wildlife was often mentioned, as was a vanishing way of life of the hunter and trapper, white settlement, and industrial progress.[18] This narrative of transition is, importantly, the master narrative of Indian history as it has been professionally written and taught in Canada.

Historiography is a way of understanding the accumulation of theories, sources, methods, and principles of professional history, and its purpose is to organize and explain how a certain body of knowledge developed over time. It is significant that historiographies of Aboriginal history by Canadian historians do not normally begin by examining the works of people like Copway and Jones and their discussions of the customs, characteristics, and traditions of Native nations, their documentation of colonization and settlement, and their political struggles for sovereignty.[19] Rather, "our" historiography commonly begins in one of two ways. The first is by way of early to mid-twentieth-century economic histories of Canadian national development. Here, Native people are depicted as the preludes to a national story and as backward or clever customers of a fur trade who quickly or slowly fall prey to superior technology, railroads, and reserves. Aboriginal historiography is also framed as a late 1960s "newcomer" to history, arising from "relative obscurity"[20] and blossoming some time after Canadian national, political, economic, military, intellectual, regional, business, labour, social, women's, and ethnic history. This second origin is fashioned as a consequence of the civil rights movement, second-wave feminism, the Second World War, Aboriginal protest against the 1969 White Paper, and urban migration, which, J.R. Miller argues, brought "Native peoples into the presence and consciousness of non-Natives, including academics."[21] It was at this time that historians, in growing history departments,[22] began to challenge evolutionary linear progressive history and question the truths about the moral, intellectual, technical, and spiritual supremacy of Europeans. They also sought to "interpret" the "perspectives" of Native people, but only those who lived long, long ago and who had either "declined" in the face of, or "persisted" in spite of, change over Canadian time. These two cohorts of historians form the basis of our understanding of the origins of Aboriginal history in Canada.

Aboriginal historiography plays a significant role in the normalization of the exclusion of Aboriginal people from professional history. Because it is conceived of as a progression of remote/objective/non-Aboriginal historians through time, each of whom "pushed the boundaries" of historical scholarship, we are obliged to revere historians in those two crucial cohorts for arguing ("in splendid obscurity") that Native people mattered at all.[23] Aboriginal history students are told of the "first" Aboriginal historians that they wrote at a time of determinism, a period of salvage ethnology when a desire to develop grand theories to justify Western global hegemony was "the way people did things." But we cannot approach the history of the professionalization of Aboriginal history as an absent-minded "way of doing things." Historians actively produced histories that served to protect the boundaries of the historical profession in ways that eliminated not just the presence of Indian intellectuals, but also even the possibility of that presence.

Aboriginal history was not just "relatively obscure" before the 1960s, it was *made* so. The "original" or "founding" historians of Aboriginal people wrote their fantasies of Native acquiescence to national development just after the tail end of the treaty and reserve period, during the Indian residential school system, and while Indian political movements struggled for treaty rights, religious freedoms, the halting of land surrenders, and, of course, improved health and education. Harold Innis, for example, would have been aware of this as he took part in an important University of Toronto–Yale University conference in 1939, which brought together representatives of "the governments of Canada and the United States, as well as Indians, missionary societies, and scientists" to discuss such wide-ranging topics as Indian education, Indian policy, "land issues," health, arts and craft production, and "racial tension" in Canadian society.[24] While some early anthropologists like James A. Teit became involved in Indian political struggles through their work, however problematically,[25] it is historiographical doctrine to point to the "sympathy" of professional historians in the 1970s and the expert witness scene in the 1990s when discussing the origins of Aboriginal history.[26] We also need to investigate how professional historians engaged when, in the 1970s and

1980s, Aboriginal students organized for greater access to education and when other disciplines like nursing worked to restructure their programs in ways that appealed to Aboriginal students.

It is important to recognize the work and commitment of individual historians in these years who sought to study and teach Aboriginal history as well as the limits within which they toiled, such as the real scarcity of historical material they themselves could refer to and the myriad ways they too were marginalized in the profession. But there is a way in which this second cohort of historians is celebrated not simply because they made progressive contributions, but also because they were alone in doing so. Yet the ethno-historians from the late 1960s and historians by the 1970s and 1980s onwards talked about ethnocentrism, cultural pluralism, and culture clash *while* Indians continued to write about history in the context of contemporary struggle either outside of the academy as creative writers, journalists, politicians, and activists, or in other fields like anthropology, sociology, English, law, education, and Native studies.[27] These Aboriginal histories are too often merely footnoted out of the discipline. Those who celebrate the contributions of this generation of historians often overlook the discipline's more widespread refusal of Indigenous topics at this time and the longer-term effects of diverting students interested in Aboriginal history.[28]

Historians have recently been congratulating themselves on the significant shifts in professional Aboriginal history, as they "find" Aboriginal women, stereotypes, the Indian Affairs department and Indian Health Services, and are "shocked" by histories of legal and social regulation, discrimination, mistreatment, experimentation, as well as culpable, capitalist settlers. Ted Binnema and Susan Neylan argue, in a subtle yet important distinction of terms, that such "academics soon learned that doing Native history had real consequences for the lives of Aboriginal people."[29] In spite of this marvellous accomplishment, they still cannot "find" Aboriginal historians. Within the discipline of history, scholarship by Native people is still largely considered primary source material. Olive Dickason's meticulous histories of Indian image-making, colonial encounter both at the core and periphery of empire, French colonialism, and Canadian First Nations stand as an important exception and continue to be referred to by historians throughout the country.[30] Having been forced to retire in 1996, however, Dickason was, until 2010, also the last tenured Aboriginal person to work in a history department in Canada, and, while no less vitally important, her work is also emblematic of hard times for Native people in the profession.

As Aboriginal scholarship is made distinct from Aboriginal historiography, so too are Aboriginal people alienated from history departments. In the Aboriginal history field alone, problematic hiring practices and limited training opportunities in part explain why few Aboriginal people commit to history at the graduate level and beyond. For the few positions in Aboriginal history, the circular and self-referential credentials required by history departments often substantially narrow the diversity of potential candidates by excluding candidates with interdisciplinary PhDs in fields like Native studies. Distinct skills demanded of Aboriginal historians, such as Indigenous language skills, training in history from an Indigenous perspective, and Indigenous historical knowledge, are also rarely prioritized or recognized. In terms of the current state of professional training, it is still rare that a history department in Canada offers graduate courses or comprehensive exams in the field of Aboriginal history,[31] and there is resistance to permitting graduate courses or supervision from interdisciplinary fields. This suggests not so subtly that Aboriginal history is not professional history, or not Canadian history, in spite of the fact that it is recognized (even by the Canadian Historical Association) to be just that.[32]

Aboriginal history remains a marginalized field in part because it is perceived to be subsumed within national histories (Canadian, American) or imperial ones (French, British). This reflects the way history professionalized in Canada as an exercise in nation building; the idea that Canadian history should fashion, foster, and defend the Canadian nation and the identity of Canadians is foundational to its existence as a profession. But the use of the nation-state as an organizing principle subtly and unsubtly presents history, and more particularly Canadian history, as not the project of Aboriginal people and non-white people more generally. Organized nationally, historians meet, practise, and standardize the profession largely in the absence of other Native scholarship that is itself often unwilling to call itself history, much less "Canadian" history. In the classroom, Canadian history courses introduce Aboriginal people's history in preliminary lectures, only to abandon it for the rest of the school year to make way for the "real stuff." In thematic history courses such as women's history or education history (normally also oriented around the nation), Aboriginal people's history is often confined to a single lecture; for example, "Women in the Fur Trade" or "Residential Schools."

Affixing Aboriginal history to the study of Canada alone where it is subordinated and isolated as a "special focus" is as colonizing as it is ahistorical, and there are a number of related implications for students of history, professional historians, history departments, and professional history itself.

First, it leaves the impression that there is no continuum of Aboriginal history. Second, the habitual isolation of Aboriginal experience from broader historical inquiries tends to limit its wider relevance. There is currently no professional understanding within Canadian history that demands we consider how well we are teaching and researching Aboriginal history. We continue to think of Aboriginal history as a specialized and segregated subsection of history with a limited range of knowledge and expertise. Here, Aboriginal history tends to be used to exemplify and reproduce rather than challenge central debates in professional history, including the nature of national narratives[33] and "advocacy" and "objectivity."[34] Rather, Aboriginal history can and should radically alter the entire discourse of Canadian history itself.

The development of useful and fair methodologies has been key to the professionalization of history, and the focus of many recent professional Aboriginal histories has been on how to treat Aboriginal people and Aboriginal knowledge as subjects of inquiry.[35] The emphasis on methods stems in part from critiques of the erasure of Aboriginal people and epistemologies from history as historians are currently "doing" it.[36] But rather than inquiring about how professional historians came to know Aboriginal histories, Aboriginal people and their views of history are often essentialized in ways that ultimately secure the good old professional "we." This focus on methodology often and perhaps inadvertently poses Aboriginal history as "something else," not history, while building another boundary around those who can and cannot "do" it. Notably, the dynamics in much of this research are similar to the 1960s' Community Health Representatives program explored in Chapter 3, whereby Native people participate again as paraprofessionals, as "informants" and "collaborators"—both *extremely* loaded terms—to career historians.

Other ways historians come to know Aboriginal history also trap and contain Indigenous historians; for instance, the emphasis on culture clash and difference, on authenticity instead of content, and on decline and/or persistence as being the only expressions of change over time.[37] The authentic self, in academia and elsewhere, creates its opposite—those who are deemed to be in-the-closet, slippery, or even un-Indian. Identities real, imposed, and imagined are sites of power and expectation within race scholarship, as are racialized academic identities within the history department and the history profession more generally. In addition to being hit by what one scholar calls the History Stick[38] (in our case the weapon that tells us what we do is not "real" history), Aboriginal historians are also hit by the Identity Stick. Identity in many ways precedes what we write and reinforces a schism that makes Aboriginal people invisible as scholars and scholars invisible as Aboriginal people. The split makes Indigenous academic labour vulnerable in ways that non-Native labour is not. It is also a re-articulation of Indian Act policies of segregation and assimilation.

Instead of being part of a larger inquiry about human relations, for Aboriginal people identity is a tool that disengages and detaches labour into a singular, predetermined, identifiable, and much-coveted commodity. There is a prevailing notion that there is one kind of Indian scholar, and those who labour outside of this mould do so at their own peril. This singular kind of scholar makes their labour suitable for only certain positions, conversations, questions, and discussions, and not others. Within the university, Indigenous scholarship is reduced in a number of other ways as well. Susan Page and Chirstine Asmar find in their study of Australian Indigenous researchers that their research productivity represents only the tip of the iceberg of their labour, which includes community commitments, informal support roles, and their duties as "instant experts in all things Indigenous across institutions." For many, the result is that completed degrees, published work, and seniority (the recognized products of academic accomplishment) take longer or are never achieved. Narrowly defined terms of research productivity continue to exclude the diverse nature of the academic labour of many Indigenous scholars.[39]

An awareness of identity among non-Native scholars, on the other hand, serves to reinforce the boundaries of history as a place for them. For example, in conversation with non-Aboriginal history graduate student colleagues, more than once I have encountered the argument that non-Native historians should not compete for and "take away" jobs in Indigenous studies and Native studies. Why would they assume that Native academics would only want to work in a Native studies department and not in a history department? What assumptions about the limits of representation of Aboriginal people in universities are evident here?

What is the price of exclusion and absence in history departments? What are, as labour historian David Roediger puts it, the "wages of whiteness?"[40] The effects of the ways in which Native labour is understood as absent are evident not only in hair salons, hospitals, and the health care system, but also in classrooms where Aboriginal people confront suspicion concerning their ability to work and their ability to know and fairly teach history. Also, a continuing expectation of absence leaves the university floor open to racism of the most overt nature.[41] The professionalization of history has wider implications beyond classrooms and universities in determining how our historical resources are preserved, protected, accessed, and used in places like museums, archives, and parks, and in publishing and skilled historical rights and claims research. These are important domains of both popular and professional Aboriginal history in Canada, and they continue to be, with few exceptions, organized along the lines and objectives of professional historical models. While some of these fields have been variably "receptive" to Indigenous knowledge, none have been seriously confronted by Indigenous historical labour.[42]

While taking my undergraduate degree at McMaster University, I had conversations with an education counsellor about my fields of interest. "History? How is that going to help our people?" he asked. Another counsellor urged me strongly into the nursing field, where there was a "real" employment need. Even while I surveyed other Aboriginal academics about the presence of Aboriginal scholars in history departments, I was asked, "Why does this matter?" When I approached one Aboriginal nurse for an interview about the history of Aboriginal nursing, she asked, "Why would we want a historian to do this?" While history has always been and continues to be one of the ways we document our lives, understand our change over time, and protect our rights, it appears to be seen as a less and less relevant field to the project of mounting of a full challenge to colonialism, racism, and oppression. This is the cost of Aboriginal exclusion—the wages of whiteness—paid by professional history.

From the 1940s to the 1980s and beyond, Aboriginal women's lives inescapably involved modern labour that was highly regulated by the Canadian nation-state. Taking a job as a domestic was commonplace, and it was often the most readily available way to earn some money in part because at school Indigenous girls were trained exclusively for manual domestic labour. Relocating to urban areas to work for wages full-time was equally common, and, while they were often depicted as people "displaced" by modernity for whom labour signalled integration and, ultimately, invisibility, these women forged lives that remained distinctly Indigenous. Other Indigenous women chose careers that enabled them to serve reserve communities directly, such as the CHRs, who balanced the demands of federal health authorities and community priorities while taking on the most important health concerns of the day. Aboriginal nurses, who confronted racism both in school and in the workplace, even forged an association that aimed to document their concerns and to work with the state in order to address them. Yet the lives of Aboriginal women in these years have been largely obscured, with distressing consequences for our history. Fortunately, the actions and experiences of Aboriginal women remain accessible through oral histories and archival research, and rich histories of domestics, community health representatives, hairdressers, nurses, and others can be uncovered and reintegrated into a fuller understanding of Aboriginal people's lives and work in the twentieth century.

Notes

Introduction

1 Mary Bletcher, "Indian Girls Pave the Way for Others," Real Manitobans, *Winnipeg Free Press*, 18 January 1958, 7.

2 Chadwick Allen, "Unspeaking the Settler: 'The Indian Today' in International Perspective," *American Studies* 46, 3–4 (Fall/Winter 2005): 39–57.

3 Mary Jane McCallum, "To Make Good Canadians: Girl Guiding in Indian Residential Schools" (MA thesis, Trent University, 2002).

4 Other variants of the decline/persist debate include continuity, equality, co-operation, the middle ground, self-sufficiency/autonomy, accommodation and partnership as well as coercion, dependence, and dominance. See Arthur J. Ray, *Indians in the Fur Trade, 1660–1870* (Toronto: University of Toronto Press, 1974); Robin Fisher, *Contact and Conflict: Indian-European Relations in British Columbia, 1774–1890* (Vancouver: University of British Columbia Press, 1978); Rolf Knight, *Indians at Work: An Informal History of Native Indian Labour in British Columbia, 1853–1930* (Vancouver: University of British Columbia Press, 1978); Gerald Friesen, *The Canadian Prairies: A History* (Toronto: University of Toronto Press, 1987); J.R. Miller, *Skyscrapers Hide the Heavens: A History of Indian-White Relations in Canada* (Toronto: University of Toronto Press, 1989); Richard White, *The Middle Ground: Indians, Empires, and Republics in the Great Lakes Region, 1650–1815* (Cambridge: Cambridge University Press, 1991); and Colin Calloway, *New Worlds for All: Indians, Europeans and the Remaking of Early America* (Baltimore: Johns Hopkins University Press, 1997). For a gendered formulation of the decline/persist debate, see Theda Perdue, *Cherokee Women: Gender and Culture Change, 1700–1835* (Lincoln: University of Nebraska Press, 1998).

5 Steven High, "Native Wage Labour and Independent Production during the 'era of irrelevance,'" *Labour/Le Travail* 37 (Spring 1996): 243–64.

6 Maureen K. Lux, *Medicine That Walks: Disease, Medicine, and Canadian Plains Native People, 1880–1940* (Toronto: University of Toronto Press, 2001); Elizabeth Vibert, *Traders' Tales: Narratives of Cultural Encounters in the Columbia Plateau 1807–1946* (Norman: University of Oklahoma Press, 1997); Carolyn Podruchny, "Unfair Masters and Rascally Servants? Labour Relations Among Bourgeois, Clerks, and Voyageurs in the Montreal Fur Trade, 1870–1821," in *Labouring Canada: Class, Gender, and Race in Canadian Working-Class History*, ed. Bryan D. Palmer and Joan Sangster (Don Mills, ON: Oxford University Press, 2008), 4–16; Paige Raibmon, *Authentic Indians: Episodes of Encounter from the Late Nineteenth-Century Northwest Coast* (Durham: Duke University Press, 2005); Clyde Ellis, "Five Dollars a Week to Be 'Regular Indians': Shows, Exhibitions, and the Economics of Indian Dancing, 1880–1930," in *Native Pathways: American Indian Culture and Economic Development in the Twentieth Century*, ed. Brian Hosmer and Colleen O'Neill (Boulder: University Press of Colorado, 2004), 184–208; Andy Parnaby, "'The best men that ever worked the lumber': Aboriginal Longshoremen on Burrard Inlet, BC, 1863–1939," *Canadian Historical Review* 87, 1 (March 2006): 53–78; and Robin Jarvis Brownlie, "'A better citizen than lots of white men': First Nations Enfranchisement—An Ontario Case Study, 1918–1940," *Canadian Historical Review* 87, 1 (March 2006): 29–52.

7 Andrea Smith, "Native American Feminism, Sovereignty, and Social Change," in *Making Space for Indigenous Feminism*, ed. Joyce Green (Halifax: Fernwood Publishing, 2007), 98.

8 Karen Flynn, *Moving Beyond Borders: A History of Black Canadian and Caribbean Women in the Diaspora* (Toronto: University of Toronto Press, 2011). See also Jennifer Blythe and Peggy Martin McGuire, "The Changing Employment of Cree Women in Moosonee and Moose Factory," in *Women of the First Nations: Power, Wisdom, and Strength*, ed. Christine Miller and Patricia Chuchryk (Winnipeg: University of Manitoba Press, 1996), 131–50.

9 Carol Williams, "Between Doorstep Barter Economy and Industrial Wages: Mobility and Adaptability of Coast Salish Female Labourers in Coastal British Columbia, 1858–1980," in *Native Being, Being Native: Identity and Difference, Proceedings of the 5th North American Symposium*, ed. Mark B. Spencer and Lucretia Scoufos (Durant: Southeastern Oklahoma State University, 2005) and Tressa Berman, *Circle of Goods: Women, Work and Welfare in a Reservation Community* (Albany: State University of New York, 2003).

10 Kathy M'Closkey, *Swept Under the Rug: A Hidden History of Navajo Weaving* (Albuquerque: University of New Mexico Press, 2002); Colleen O'Neill, *Working the Navajo Way: Labour and Culture in the Twentieth Century* (Lawrence: University Press of Kansas, 2005); and Sherry Farrell Racette, "Don't Get Me Started! Absence, Tokenism, and Missed Opportunities? Aboriginal Women and Public History in Canada," (paper presented at the 86th Annual Meeting of the Canadian Historical Association, Saskatoon, SK, 30 May 2007); "Looking for Stories and Unbroken Threads: Museum Artifacts as Women's History and Cultural Legacy," in *Restoring the Balance: First Nations Women, Community, and Culture*, ed. Gail Guthrie Valaskakis, Madeleine Dion Stout, and Eric Guimond (Winnipeg: University of Manitoba Press, 2009), 283–312.

11 Some of the contributions in Carol Williams, ed., *Indigenous Women and Work: From Labor to Activism* (Urbana: University of Illinois Press, 2012) challenge this chronology.

12 Ruth Roach Pierson, *"They're Still Women After All": The Second World War and Canadian Womanhood* (Toronto: McClelland and Stewart, 1986); Wendy Mitchinson, Paula Bourne, Alison Prentice, Gail Cuthbert Brant, Beth Light, and Naomi Black, eds., *Canadian Women: A Reader* (Toronto: Harcourt Brace, 1996); Jennifer A. Stephen, *Pick One Intelligent Girl: Employability, Domesticity, and the Gendering of Canada's Welfare State, 1939–1947* (Toronto: University of Toronto Press, 2007).

13 Patty Leow, "The Back of the Homefront: Black and American Indian Women in Wisconsin during World War II," *Wisconsin Magazine of History* 82, 2 (Winter 1998–1999): 82–103.

14 Mary Louise Adams, *The Trouble with Normal: Postwar Youth and the Making of Heterosexuality* (Toronto: University of Toronto Press, 1997); Mona Gleason, *Normalizing the Ideal: Psychology, Schooling, and the Family in Postwar Canada* (Toronto: University of Toronto Press, 1999); and Elaine Tyler May, *Homeward Bound: American Families in the Cold War Era* (New York: Basic Books, 1988).

15 The work of Nancy Janovecik and Heather Howard profoundly challenges this image by exploring Native women's voluntarism and organization in the 1960s to the 1980s: Nancy Janovicek, "'Assisting our own': Urban Migration, Self-Governance, and Native Women's Organizing in Thunder Bay, Ontario, 1972–1989," *American Indian Quarterly* 27, 3–4 (Summer/Fall 2003): 548–65, and Heather Howard-Bobiwash "Women's Class Strategies as Activism in Native Community Building in Toronto, 1950–1975," *American Indian Quarterly* 27, 3–4 (Summer/Fall 2003): 566–82.

16 Joan Sangster, *Regulating Girls and Women: Sexuality, Family, and the Law in Ontario, 1920–1960* (Toronto: Oxford University Press, 2001), 170.

17 Carolyn Kenny, *North American Indian, Métis, and Inuit Women Speak about Culture, Education, and Work* (Ottawa: Status of Women Canada, 2002), available at Government of Canada Publications, http://publications.gc.ca/collections/Collection/SW21-90-

2001E.pdf (accessed 5 February 2014), and Julie Guard, "Authenticity on the Line: Women Workers, Native 'Scabs,' and the Multi-Ethnic Politics of Identity in a Left-led Strike in Cold War Canada," *Journal of Women's History* 15, 4 (Winter 2004): 117–40.

18 The growing field of the history of nursing, one of the most traditionally white and feminized professions, has been very useful to this research. Work on migrant nurses of colour articulates many of the forms of combined sexual and racial discrimination experienced also by Native women. Dea Birkett, "The 'White Woman's Burden' in the 'White Man's Grave': The Introduction of British Nurses in Colonial West Africa," in *Western Women and Imperialism: Complicity and Resistance*, ed. Nupur Chaudhuri and Margaret Strobel (Bloomington: Indiana University Press, 1992), 177–88; Kathryn McPherson, *Bedside Matters: The Transformation of Canadian Nursing, 1900–1990* (Toronto: Oxford University Press, 1996), and "Nursing and Colonization: The Work of Indian Health Services Nurses in Manitoba, 1945–1970," in *Women, Health, and Nation: Canada and the United States since 1945*, ed. Georgina Feldberg, Molly Ladd-Taylor, Alison Li, and Kathryn McPherson (Montreal: McGill-Queen's University Press, 2003), 223–46; Helen Gilbert, "Great Adventures in Nursing: Colonial Discourse and Health Care Delivery in Canada's North," *Jouvert: A Journal of Postcolonial Studies* 7, 2 (Winter/Spring, 2003), http://english.chass.ncsu.edu/jouvert/v7i2/gilber.htm (accessed 31 January 2014); and Karen Flynn, "Race, Class, and Gender" and "Race, the State, and Caribbean Immigrant Nurses, 1950–1962," in *Women, Health, and Nation*, Felberg et al., 247–63.

19 T.J. Jackson Lears, *No Place of Grace: Antimodernism and the Transformation of American Culture 1880–1920* (Chicago: University of Chicago Press, 1983).

20 Philip J. Deloria, *Indians in Unexpected Places* (Lawrence: University Press of Kansas, 2004) and *Playing Indian* (New Haven: Yale University Press, 1998).

21 Colleen O'Neill, "Rethinking Modernity and the Discourse of Development in American Indian History, an Introduction," in *Native Pathways: American Indian Culture and Economic Development in the Twentieth Century*, ed. Brian Hosmer and Colleen O'Neill (Boulder: University Press of Colorado, 2004), 1–24, and *Working the Navajo Way: Labour and Culture in the Twentieth Century* (Lawrence: University Press of Kansas, 2005).

22 Andrea Smith, "Indigenous Women and Violence: Rethinking the Nation-State" (lecture, University of Manitoba, Winnipeg, MB, 10 March 2008) and Audra Simpson "On Ethnographic Refusal: Indigeneity, 'Voice' and Colonial Citizenship," *Junctures*, December 9, 2007, 67-80.

23 See, for example, Bryan Palmer, *Working Class Experience: The Rise and Reconstitution of Canadian Labour* (Toronto: Butterworths, 1983).

24 Keith Thor Carlson, Melinda Marie Jette, and Kenichi Matsui, "An Annotated Bibliography of Major Writings in Aboriginal History, 1990–99," *Canadian Historical Review* 82, 1 (2001): 123, and Ken Coates, "Writing First Nations into Canadian History: A Review of Recent Scholarly Works," *Canadian Historical Review* 81, 1 (2000): 99–114.

25 See, for example, Birkett, "The 'White Woman's Burden'"; Laurie Meijer Drees and Lesley McBain, "Nursing and Native People in Northern Saskatchewan, 1930s–1950s," *Canadian Bulletin of Medical History* 18, 1 (2001): 43–65; McPherson, "Nursing and Colonization"; and Gilbert, "Great Adventures in Nursing."

26 Patricia Jasen, "Race, Culture, and the Colonization of Childbirth in Northern Canada," in *Rethinking Canada: The Promise of Women's History*, ed. Veronica Strong-Boag, Mona Gleason, and Adele Perry (Don Mills, ON: Oxford University Press, 2002), 355–66; Mary-Ellen Kelm, *Colonizing Bodies: Aboriginal Health and Healing in British Columbia, 1900–1950* (Vancouver: University of British Columbia Press, 1998); James B. Waldram, D. Ann Herring, and T. Kue Young, *Aboriginal Health in Canada: Historical, Cultural, and*

Epidemiological Perspectives (Toronto: University of Toronto Press, 1995); John and Jean Comaroff, "Medicine, Colonialism, and the Black Body," chap. 8 in *Ethnography and the Historical Imagination* (Boulder: Westview Press, 1992); and Lux, *Medicine That Walks.*

27 For a discussion of gender discrimination in the Indian Act and Native women's resistance to it, see Bonita Lawrence, *"Real" Indians and Others: Mixed-Blood Urban Native Peoples and Indigenous Nationhood* (Vancouver: University of British Columbia Press, 2004). See also Sylvia Van Kirk's discussion of how intermarriage was regulated in fur trade and settler colonial contexts in "From 'Marrying-In' to 'Marrying-Out': Changing Patterns of Aboriginal/Non-Aboriginal Marriage in Colonial Canada," *Frontiers: A Journal of Women Studies* 23, 3 (2002): 1–11.

28 For a more elaborate discussion of oral history method, see Julie Cruickshank, *Life Lived Like a Story: Life Stories of Three Yukon Native Elders* (Vancouver: University of British Columbia Press, 1990)

29 Andrea Smith, "Native American Feminism," 96.

30 Jennifer Nez Denentdale, "Chairmen, Presidents, and Princesses: The Navajo Nation, Gender, and Politics of Tradition," *Wicazo Sa Review* 21,1 (Spring 2006), 26n46.

Chapter One
Sweeping the Nation: Indigenous Women and Domestic Labour in Mid-Twentieth-Century Canada

1 Denise Rudniki, "Digger," *The Forgotten People* (Summer 1972): 3.

2 See, for example, Jennifer S.H. Brown, "A Cree Nurse in a Cradle of Methodism: Little Mary and the Egerton R. Young Family at Norway House and Berens River," in *First Days, Fighting Days: Women in Manitoba History*, ed. Mary Kinnear (Regina: Canadian Plains Research Center, 1987), 18–40, and *Strangers in Blood: Fur Trade Company Families in Indian Country* (Vancouver: University of British Columbia Press, 1980); Sylvia Van Kirk, *"Many Tender Ties": Women in Fur-Trade Society, 1670–1870* (Winnipeg: Watson and Dwyer, 1980), and "From 'Marrying-In' to 'Marrying-Out': Changing Patterns of Aboriginal/Non-Aboriginal Marriage in Colonial Canada"; Patricia A. Roome, "'From One Whose Home Is among the Indians': Henrietta Muir Edwards and Aboriginal Peoples," in *Unsettled Pasts: Reconceiving the West through Women's History*, ed. Sarah Carter, Lesley Erickson, Patricia Roome, and Char Smith (Calgary: University of Calgary Press, 2005), 47–78; Joan Sangster, "Constructing the 'Eskimo' Wife: White Women's Travel Writing, Colonialism, and the Canadian North, 1940–60," in *Creating Postwar Canada: Community, Diversity, and Dissent, 1945–75*, ed. Magda Fahrni and Robert Rutherdale (Vancouver: University of British Columbia Press, 2007), 23–44; and Myra Rutherdale, *Women and the White Man's God: Gender, Race, and the Canadian Mission Field* (Vancouver: University of British Columbia Press, 2002).

3 Margaret Whitehead, "'A Useful Christian Woman': First Nations' Women and Protestant Missionary Work in British Columbia," *Atlantis* 18 (1994): 142–66; Carol J. Williams, "'She Was the Means of Leading into the Light': Photographic Portraits of Tsimshian Methodist Converts," chap. 3 in *Framing the West: Race, Gender, and the Photographic Frontier in the Pacific Northwest* (Don Mills, ON: Oxford University Press, 2003).

4 See, for example, Patricia Albers and Beatrice Medicine, eds., *The Hidden Half: Studies of Plains Indian Women* (Lanham, MD: University Press of America, 1983); Ellice B. Gonzales, *Changing Economic Roles for Micmac Men and Women: An Ethnohistorical Analysis*, National Museum of Man Mercury Series, Paper 72 (Ottawa: National

Museums of Canada, 1981); Somer Brodribb, "The Traditional Roles of Native Women in Canada and the Impact of Colonization," *Canadian Journal of Native Studies* 4, 1 (1984): 85–103; Laura Klein and Lillian Ackerman, eds., *Women and Power in Native North America* (Norman: University of Oklahoma Press, 1995); Nancy Shoemaker, ed., *Negotiators of Change: Historical Perspectives on Native American Women* (New York: Routledge, 1995); Theda Perdue, *Cherokee Women*; and Colleen O'Neill, "The 'Making' of the Navajo Worker: Navajo Households, the Bureau of Indian Affairs, and Off-Reservation Wage Work, 1948–1960," *New Mexico Historical Review* 74, 4 (October 1999): 375–405.

5 Victoria Haskins, *Matrons and Maids: Regulating Indian Domestic Service in Tucson 1914–1934* (Tucson: University of Arizona Press, 2012); Jane E. Simonsen, *Making Home Work: Domesticity and Native American Assimilation in the American West, 1860–1919* (Chapel Hill: University of North Carolina Press, 2006); Margaret D. Jacobs, *Engendered Encounters: Feminism and Pueblo Cultures, 1879–1934* (Lincoln: University of Nebraska Press, 1999), and "Working on the Domestic Frontier: American Indian Domestic Servants in White Women's Households in the San Francisco Bay Area, 1920–1940," *Frontiers* 28, 1–2 (2007): 165–99; Adele Perry, *On the Edge of Empire: Gender, Race, and the Making of British Columbia, 1849–1871* (Toronto: University of Toronto Press, 2001); Joanne Scott and Raymond Evans, "The Moulding of Menials: The Making of the Aboriginal Female Domestic Servant in Early Twentieth-Century Queensland," *Hecate* 22, 1 (1996): 139–57; Victoria Haskins, "On the Doorstep: Aboriginal Domestic Service as a 'Contact Zone,'" *Australian Feminist Studies* 16, 34 (2001): 13–25, and "Domestic Service and Frontier Feminism: The Call for a Woman Visitor to 'Half-Caste' Girls and Women in Domestic Service, Adelaide, 1925–1928," *Frontiers* 28, 1–2 (2007): 124–94; Albert L. Hurtado, "Hardly a Farm House—A Kitchen without Them: Indian and White Households on the California Borderland Frontier in 1860," *Western Historical Quarterly* (July 1982): 245–70; Pamela Margaret White, "Restructuring the Domestic Sphere—Prairie Indian Women on Reserves: Image, Ideology, and State Policy, 1880–1930" (PhD diss., McGill University, 1987); Sarah Carter, *Capturing Women: The Manipulation of Cultural Imagery in Canada's Prairie West* (Montreal: McGill-Queen's University Press, 1997); and Devon A. Mihesuah, *Cultivating the Rosebuds: The Education of Women at the Cherokee Female Seminary, 1851–1909* (Urbana: University of Illinois Press, 1993).

6 See Stephen High, "Native Wage Labour and Independent Production during the 'Era of Irrelevance,'" *Labour/Le Travail* 37 (Spring 1996): 243–64; Robin Jarvis Brownlie, "'Living the Same as the White People': Mohawk and Anishinabe Women's Labour in Southern Ontario, 1920–1940," *Labour/Le Travail* 61 (Spring 2008): 41–68; O'Neill, *Working the Navajo Way*; Tressa Berman, *Circle of Goods: Women's Work and Welfare in a Reservation Community* (Albany: State University of New York Press, 2003); and Williams, "Between Doorstep Barter Economy and Industrial Wages."

7 George Beaulieu, comp., *Sandy Bay Anishinabek: The Elders Tell Their Stories* (Manitoba: Sandy Bay Education Foundation, Manitoba, 1996).

8 Janet Silman, *Enough Is Enough: Aboriginal Women Speak Out* (Toronto: Women's Press, 1987), 19–30. See also Kim Anderson, *Life Stages and Native Women: Memory, Teachings, and Story Medicine* (Winnipeg: University of Manitoba Press, 2011), and Brenda Child, *Holding Our World Together: Ojibwe Women and the Survival of Community* (New York: Penguin, 2013).

9 Genevieve Leslie, "Domestic Service in Canada, 1880–1920," in *Women at Work: Ontario, 1850–1930*, ed. Janice Acton, Penny Goldsmith, and Bonnie Shepard (Toronto: Canadian Women's Educational Press, 1974), 71–125, and Alison Prentice et al., eds. *Canadian Women: A History* (Toronto: Harcourt Brace, 1988).

10 See, for example, Sedef Arat-Koc, "From 'Mothers of the Nation' to Migrant Workers: Immigration Policies and Domestic Workers in Canadian History," in *Rethinking Canada: The Promise of Women's History*, ed. Veronica Strong-Boag, Mona Gleason, and Adele Perry, 4th ed. (Toronto: Oxford University Press, 2002), 283–98.

11 Lisa Chilton, *Agents of Empire: British Female Migration to Canada and Australia, 1860s–1930* (Toronto: University of Toronto Press, 2007).

12 Perry, *On the Edge of Empire*, 21, 73, and 145–46.

13 Nandita Sharma, *Home Economics: Nationalism and the Making of 'Migrant Workers' in Canada* (Toronto: University of Toronto Press, 2006); Daiva K. Stasiulis and Abigail B. Bakan, *Negotiating Citizenship: Migrant Women in Canada and the Global System* (New York: Palgrave MacMillan, 2003); and Abigail B. Bakan and Daiva Stasiulis, eds., *Not One of the Family: Foreign Domestic Workers in Canada* (Toronto: University of Toronto Press, 1997).

14 Brownlie, "'Living the Same as the White People.'"

15 Pierrette Hondagneu-Sotelo, *Domestica: Immigrant Workers Cleaning and Caring in the Shadows of Affluence* (Berkeley and Los Angeles: University of California Press, 2001).

16 Agnes Calliste, "Canada's Immigration Policy and Domestics from the Caribbean: The Second Domestic Scheme," in *Race, Class, Gender: Bonds and Barriers. Socialist Studies* 5 (1989): 133–65. See also Franca Iacovetta, "'Primitive Villagers and Uneducated Girls': Canada Recruits Domestics from Italy, 1951–52," *Canadian Woman Studies* 7, 4 (Winter 1986): 14–18.

17 White women's politics did not entirely ignore non-white domestic labour issues prior to the 1980s; in fact, some individuals were quite active. For example, Beatrice Bridgden, a CCF candidate in 1936 and United Church worker who followed domestics around Winnipeg in the 1950s, and Mrs. Asta Oddson, an Indian Affairs social worker who also ran in the 1936 election for the Social Credit Party, were not involved as a "movement," but Native domestic labour was part of their politics and their work.

18 Indigenous people were also in this era erroneously called "the oldest Canadians" and "refugees in their own homes." For more on Canadians "new" and "original," see Heidi Bohaker and Franca Iacovetta, "Making Aboriginal People 'Immigrants Too': A Comparison of Citizenship Programs for Newcomers and Indigenous Peoples in Postwar Canada, 1940s–1960s," *Canadian Historical Review* 90, 3 (September 2009): 427–61.

19 In the records, "rural" and "local" are often used interchangeably, suggesting that "rural" in fact just meant within or close to an Indian agency.

20 INAC file 601/25-2, vol. 2, R.F. Davey, Residential Schools Past and Future, 8 March 1968. Cited in Report of the Royal Commission on Aboriginal Peoples, vol. 1, *Looking Forward, Looking Back* (Ottawa: Canada Communication Group Publishing, 1996), 323.

21 John Milloy, *A National Crime: The Canadian Government and the Residential School System, 1879–1986* (Winnipeg: University of Manitoba Press, 1999); J.R. Miller, *Shingwauk's Vision: A History of Native Residential Schools* (Toronto: University of Toronto Press, 1997); Brian Titley, "Indian Industrial Schools in Western Canada," in *Schools in the West: Essays in Canadian Educational History*, ed. Nancy M. Sheehan, J. Donald Wilson, and David C. Jones (Calgary: Detselig Enterprises, 1986), 133–53; Elizabeth Furniss, *Victims of Benevolence: The Dark Legacy of the Williams Lake Indian Residential School* (Vancouver: Arsenal Pulp Press, 1995); Agnes Grant, *No End of*

Grief: Indian Residential Schools in Canada (Winnipeg: Pemmican Publications, 1996); and Isabelle Knockwood, *Out of the Depths: The Experiences of Mi'kmaw Children at the Indian Residential School of Schubenacadie, Nova Scotia* (Lockeport, NS: Roseway Publishing, 1992).

22 Veronica Strong-Boag, *The New Day Recalled: Lives of Girls and Women in English Canada, 1919–1939* (Toronto: Copp Clark Pitman, 1993).

23 David Wallace Adams, *Education for Extinction: American Indians and the Boarding School Experience, 1875–1928* (Lawrence: University Press of Kansas, 1995), and Jean Barman, "Separate and Unequal: Indian and White Girls at All Hallows School, 1884–1920," in *Children, Teachers and Schools in the History of British Columbia*, ed. Jean Barman, Neil Sutherland, and J. Donald Wilson (Calgary: Detselig Enterprises, 1995), 343. Work on Indigenous education and female domestics in Australia is also insightful. Scott and Evans show that their federal schools for Indigenous people aimed to create an "underclass of obedient underpaid labourers, both on reserves and missions and in private employment," that education was "utilitarian rather than intellectual," and that Indigenous students were "schooled for lifetimes of drudgery. Scott and Evans, "The Moulding of Menials," 139–57.

24 Milloy, *A National Crime*, 169.

25 Jean Barman, Yvonne Hébert, and Don McCaskill, eds., *Indian Education in Canada, vol. 1, The Legacy* (Vancouver: University of British Columbis press, 1986), and Verna J. Kirkness, *Evaluation Report: Education of Indians in Federal and Provincial Schools in Manitoba* (Ottawa: Department of Indian Affairs and Northern Development, 1978), 176.

26 Mary Jane Logan McCallum, "'I Would Like The Girls At Homes': Domestic Labour and the Age of Discharge at Canadian Indian Residential Schools," in, *Colonization and Domestic Service: Historical and Contemporary Perspectives,* ed. Victoria Haskins and Claire Lawrie (New York: Routledge, Forthcoming, 2014).

27 Jane Willis, *Geniesh: An Indian Girlhood* (Toronto: New Press, 1973), 105.

28 Miller, *Shingwauk's Vision*, 255–57.

29 Library and Archives Canada (hereafter LAC), Record Group 10 Indian Affairs (hereafter RG 10), Volume 8414, File 1/21-1 pt. 3, Correspondence Regarding the Placement of Indian Labour 1955–1956, "The Deputy Minister" Ottawa, 27 June 1955.

30 Willis, *Geniesh*, 177–81.

31 LAC, Record Group 29 Health Canada (hereafter RG 29), vol. 2912, file 851-1-A501 pt. 1, Indian and Northern Health Services—Manitoba Regional Office—Winnipeg, MB, 1914/10-1940/12, "Health and Disease at the Norway House Indian Agency," 26 April 1925. Cowall Farrell and Alivaktuk find that Pannirtuuq hospital workers' salaries were paid by nurses through a "barter and trade system." Emily Cowall Farrell and Meeka Alivaktuk, "The Work We Have Done: Relationship, Investment, and Contribution. The Inuit Workers at St. Luke's Hospital Pannirtuuq 1930–1972," unpublished paper, 11–12. The maid at Island Lake Nursing Station in 1951 was paid by order of credit on the HBC. LAC, RG 29, vol. 2782, file 823-1-A501, Nursing and Dispensing Arrangements, Manitoba Regional Headquarters, Winnipeg, MB, September 1906 - November 1952, letter to the Director IHS from W.J. Wood, 25 June 1951.

32 Archives of the Diocese of Rupertsland, Rupert's Land Diocesan Board of the Women's Auxiliary to the Missionary Society of the Church of England in Canada, *Annual Reports*, 1918, 1924, 1925, and 1931.

33 Ann Callahan, interview with author, 26 March 2006.

34 Eleanor Olson, interview with author, 14 July 2006.

35 Other apprenticeship and in-service courses were undertaken at Clearwater Sanatorium and elsewhere, and they were promoted at other hospitals like Lytton, Tranquille Sanatorium, and perhaps Kamloops Hospital as well. LAC, RG 10, vol. 8767, file 1/25-7-5, pt. 1, General Correspondence Regarding Vocational Training for Indian Nurses and Nurse's Aides Throughout Canada 1941-1952, Superintendent of Education, "Training of Indians as Nurses and Nurses' Helpers," by C.A.F. Clark, Educational Survey Officer, 9 August 1949.

36 Laurie Meijer Drees, "Training Aboriginal Nurses: The Indian Health Services in Northwestern Canada, 1939–1975," in *Caregiving on the Periphery: Historical Perspectives on Nursing and Midwifery in Canada*, ed. Myra Rutherdale (Montreal: McGill-Queen's University Press, 2010), 181–209.

37 Yukon Archives, Whitehorse, RG 85, C-1-a, vol. 791, file 6210, probably Dr. J.A. Urquhart to R.A. Gibson, Director, Lands Parks and Forests Branch, Department of Mines and Resources, 19 February 1940, as cited in Meijer Drees, "Training Aboriginal Nurses," 194.

38 Meijer Drees, "Training Aboriginal Nurses," 195.

39 LAC, RG 10, vol. 8414, file 1/21-1, pt. 3, Memorandum to the Director Re: Training Farm Labourers and Domestic Workers, R.F. Davey, Superintendent of Education, 17 June 1955.

40 LAC, RG 10, vol. 8413, file 1/21-1, pt. 1, Correspondence Regarding the Placement of Indian Labour 1933–1954, letter to Colonel Jones, Director, Indian Affairs Branch, from J. D'Astoust, Regional Supervisor of Indian Agencies, Re: Nursing Station Personnel, Pointe Bleue Indian Agency, 19 January 1954; letter to P.E. Moore from H.M. Jones, Ottawa, 22 January 1954; and letter to Colonel Jones from P.E. Moore, 5 February 1954.

41 Ron Laliberte, "The 'Grab-a-Hoe' Indians: The Canadian State and the Procurement of Aboriginal Labour for the Southern Alberta Sugar Beet Industry," *Prairie Forum* 31, 2 (Fall 2006): 305–24, and Ron Laliberte and Vic Satzewich, "Native Migrant Labour in the Southern Alberta Sugar-beet Industry: Coercion and Paternalism in the Recruitment of Labour," *Canadian Review of Sociology and Anthropology* 38, 1 (1999): 65–86.

42 Beaulieu, *Sandy Bay Anishinabek*, n.p.

43 LAC, RG 10, vol. 8767, file 1/25-7, pt. 8, General Correspondence Regarding Vocational Training of Indians Throughout Canada 1961–1963, Circular No. 59 re: On-The-Job Training to Indian Commissioner for BC, Regional Supervisors from H.M. Jones, Director, 20 March 1961, and letter to Regional Supervisor, Alberta, from R.F. Battle, Chief, Economic Development Division, 23 June 1961.

44 LAC, RG 10, vol. 8767, file 1/25-7, pt. 8, letter to Chief, Education Division, Indian Affairs Branch, from Regional Supervisor, Manitoba, 29 September 1961, and Memorandum to Indian Affairs Branch from Winnipeg Regional Office Re: On-the-Job Training Program by A.G. Leslie, 7 November 1961.

45 LAC, RG 10, vol. 8767, file 1/25-7, pt. 8, Progress Report "On-the-job" trainees Indian residential schools.

46 "Long Range Planning and Financial Forecasting," Education Division, Indian Affairs Branch, December 1966, as quoted in Kirkness, *Evaluation Report*, 181.

47 Milloy, *A National Crime*, 206.

48 Willis, *Geniesh*, 194–97.

49 Mary Kinnear, *A Female Economy: Women's Work in a Prairie Province 1870–1970* (Montreal: McGill-Queen's University Press, 1998), 110.

50 LAC, RG 10, vol. 3199, file 504 178-5, Headquarters Correspondence Concerning the Employment of Indian Girls as Domestic Servants 1941–1945, Report on Shubenacadie Indian Agency for the Month of May 1943, H.C. Rice, Indian Agent. Rice unfortunately finished this sentiment with "which appears to me a good argument against the suggestion that the inertia, characteristic of the male Indian, results from a dietary deficiency." Report for the Month of February 1943, St. Mary's Reserve, York Co., N.B. by Indian Agent Edward J. Whalen, 6 March 1943; Report for the Month of March 1944, Edward J. Whalen, Indian Agent; Report of Rama Indian Agency for the Month of March 1944, H. J. Featherston, Indian Agent; Personal Report for the Month of October 1941, Sarnia, Ontario, November 6, 1941, Geo. W. Down, Indian Agent; Report on Sturgeon Falls Agency for the Month of November 1943, J.A. Marleau, Indian Agent; Report for the Month of February 1943, Chapleau, Ontario, 1 March 1943, F. Matters, Indian Agent; Report on Clandeboye Indian Agency for the Month of May 1944, E. McPherson, Indian Agent; Report on File Hills Indian Agency for the Month of April 1944, Frank Booth, Indian Agent; Report on Touchwood Indian Agency for October 1943, R.S. Davis, Indian Agent; Report on Touchwood Indian Agency for the Month of April 1944, R.S. Davis, Indian Agent; Report on Duck Lake Agency for the Month of December 1943, S.H. Simpson, Indian Agent; Letter to Mr. Henry, National Selective Service Mobilization Section, Ottawa, from C. W. Jackson, Chief Executive Assistant, Department of Mines and Resources, 20 October 1943.

51 LAC, RG 10, vol. 3199, file 504, 178-5, letter to J.E. Morris, Welfare Division, from C.A. Primeau, Principal, Indian Residential School, Spanish, Ontario, 1 February 1943.

52 LAC, RG 10, vol. 3199, file 504 178-5, letter to C.A. Primeau from R.A. Hoey, Superintendent of Welfare and Training, 5 February 1943.

53 The connection to Shingwauk and Spanish probably developed out of two causes: first, in southern Ontario many ex-students could get work and better-paid work closer to home; second, there seems to be a personal connection formed at these schools between the principals, the agents, and individuals in Ottawa like Senator Cairine Wilson.

54 These lists included over thirty names in 1943. LAC, RG 10, vol. 3199, file 504 178-5, letter to M.S. Blanchard, Principal, The Mackay School, Montreal, from R.A. Hoey, 10 September 1942.

55 LAC, RG 10, vol. 6033, file 150-61, pt. 1, Headquarters - Monthly Reports - Welfare-Training Services Division 1941-1945, Memorandum, Ottawa, 31 January 1943.

56 This was probably less indicative of contemporary concerns about venereal disease than it was about fear of the spread of tuberculosis from Native people to whites, but at the time, both shared the status of being highly associated with those marginalized by class and race.

57 LAC, RG 10, vol. 3199, file 504 178-5, letter to J.W. Daley, Indian Agent, from R.A. Hoey, 14 June 1944.

58 LAC, RG 10, vol. 3199, file 504 178-5 contains all of the substantive documentary information about the Ottawa Experiment.

59 LAC, RG 10, vol. 3199, file 504 178-5, letter to R.A. Hoey from Principal Laferriere, Girls School, Spanish, Ontario, 31 June 1943. In one case, a great-grandfather recommended his granddaughters to the agents, wanting them to have the "opportunity" to be domestics. Still, the agent needed to convince the parents to let them go. LAC, RG 10, vol. 3199, file 504 178-5, letter to C.R. Johnston, Indian Agent, Manitowaning, from R.A. Hoey, 28 June 1943.

60 LAC, RG 10, vol. 3199, file 504 178-5, letter to F. Matters, Indian Agent, Chapleau, from R.A. Hoey, Superintendent Welfare and Training, 26 February 1943, and letter to Indian Affairs Branch from F. Matters, 3 March 1943.

61 LAC, RG 10, vol. 3199, file 504 178-5, letter to R.A. Hoey from C.A. Primeau, 10 August 1943.

62 This period of time, six months, may be significant. By the Indian Act, people absent from the reserve could be stricken from the register and had six months to protest their loss of Status.

63 LAC, RG 10, vol. 3199, file 504 178-5, letter to R.A. Hoey, from F. Matters, 15 April 1943; letter to F. Matters from R.A. Hoey, 17 April 1943; and letter to F. Matters from R.A. Hoey, 27 April 1943.

64 LAC, RG 10, vol. 3199, file 504 178-5, letter to H.P. Ruddy, Indian Agent, Golden Lake, from R.A. Hoey, Supt. Welfare and Training, 12 September 1943, and letter to Indian Affairs Branch from H.P. Ruddy, 2 October 1943.

65 LAC, RG 10, vol. 3199, file 504 178-5, letter to R.P.G. Laurence from R.A. Hoey, Ottawa, 5 July 1943.

66 LAC, RG 10, vol. 3199, file 504 178-5, letter to J.W. Daley, Indian Agent, Walpole Island, from R.A. Hoey, 26 June 1943; letter to Mr. C. R. Johnston, Indian Agent, Manitowaning, Ontario, from R.A. Hoey, 27 July 1943; letter to Mr. Hoey from F. Matters, 15 April 1943; and letter to F. Matters from R.A. Hoey, 17 April 1943.

67 Statistics Canada, Historical Statistics of Canada, Section E: Wages and Working Conditions, Series E41-135, Table E60-68, "Average annual, weekly and hourly earnings, male and female wage-earners, manufacturing industries, Canada, 1934 to 1969," http://www.statcan.gc.ca/pub/11-516-x/sectione/4147438-eng.htm (accessed 5 February 2014); Canada, Department of Labour, Canadian Labour Market (June 1946), 20–21, as cited in Ann Porter, "Women and Income Security in the Postwar Period: The Case of Unemployment Insurance, 1945–1962," in *Canadian Working-Class History: Selected Readings*, 3rd ed., ed. Laurel Sefton MacDowell and Ian Radforth (Toronto: Canadian Scholars' Press, 2006), 308.

68 Hoey informed Blanchard that they would be unable to "obtain three girls" for his school: "We now have over thirty names of persons who are in need of domestics and it is very doubtful if we will be able to obtain one-third of this number in the next twelve months." Blanchard had already telephoned the Indian Agent at Cauganawaga to inquire about domestics, but Hoey mentioned that he should try him again in person. LAC, RG 10, vol. 3199, file 504 178-5, letter to Mr. Morris from M.S. Blanchard, Principal, The MacKay Institution for Protestant Deaf Mutes, Montreal, 4 September 1943; letter to Mr. M.S. Blanchard from R.A. Hoey, 10 September 1943.

69 Essential needs in household work were defined as:

Where illness in the home prevents a man or woman in essential employment from attending at his or her work

Where aged people require a housekeeper

Where both husband and wife are employed. Particularly where there is a local labour shortage and the wife is employed in high priority work for which she is especially qualified (e.g. nursing, day nurseries, social service, personnel work).

Where there are small children in the home and where the burden upon the mother, particularly in times of illness of the children, becomes too great. In instances such as those outlined above women can be persuaded that by accepting domestic work they are rendering essential service to their country.

LAC, Record Group 27, Department of Labour (herafter RG 27), vol. 1523, file X5-12, pt. 1, Domestic Services — Labour Requirements.

70 In a letter to all Regional Superintendents and Managers from the National Selective Service Circular, Unemployment Insurance Commission Employment Service and

Unemployment Insurance Branch, Department of Labour, December 30, 1942 that all women persuaded to accept work under certain circumstances would be rendering "essential service" to their country. LAC, RG 27 Vol 1523 File X5-12 pt. 1, Letter to All Regional Superintendents and Managers from the National Selective Service Circular, Unemployment Insurance Commission Employment Service and Unemployment Insurance Branch, Department of Labour, 30 December 1942. "All Kinds of Help Wanted Now: 103 Domestic Help Wanted," *Globe and Mail*, 2 October 1942, 23.

71 LAC, RG 10, vol. 3199, file 504 178-5, letter to J.E. Morris from C.A. Primeau, 11 June 1943.

72 LAC, RG 10, vol. 3199, file 504 178-5, letter to C.A. Primeau from R.A. Hoey, 14 June 1943.

73 LAC, RG 10, vol. 3199, file 504 178-5, letter to F. Matters, Indian Agent, Chapleau, from R.A. Hoey, Superintendent Welfare and Training, 26 February 1943, and letter to Indian Affairs Branch from F. Matters, 3 March 1943.

74 LAC, RG 10, vol. 3199, file 504 178-5, letter to R.P.G. Laurence, Indian Agent, Sault Ste. Marie, from R.A. Hoey, 7 July 1943.

75 LAC, RG 10, vol. 3199, file 504 178-5, letter to J.E. Morris from A.C. Hardy, 30 April 1943.

76 LAC, RG 10, vol. 3199, file 504 178-5, letter to Reverend James Howitt, Principal Indian Residential School, Spanish, from R.A. Hoey, Superintendent of Welfare and Training, 26 March 1942; letter to Sister St. Jacob, Superintendent, Ottawa General, from R.A Hoey, 26 March 1942; letter to Sister St. Jacob from R.A. Hoey, 6 May 1942; letter to Sister St. Jacob from R.A Hoey, 26 June 1942; letter to C.A. Primeau, Principal, Indian Residential School, Spanish, from Philip Phelan, Chief, Training Division, 12 June 1942; and letter to Philip Phelan from C.A. Primeau, 13 June 1942.

77 Unsuccessful applicants for domestics through this Indian Affairs program included the St. Charles (nursing) Home, the Good Shepherd Refuge in Sudbury, and the Mackay Institution for Protestant Deaf Mutes.

78 LAC, RG 20, vol. 6206, file 468-1 (1-3), MR C 7937, letter to Dr. McGill from R. Hoey, 9 November 1942, as cited in Milloy, *A National Crime*, 192.

79 Milloy, *A National Crime*, 263–64.

80 LAC, RG 10, vol. 3199, file 504 178-5, letter to Mr. Morris from a domestic, 1 July 1943, and letter to a domestic from Mr. Morris, 5 July 1943.

81 LAC, RG 10, vol. 3199, file 504 178-5, letter to J.W. Daley from R.A. Hoey, 26 June 1943.

82 LAC, RG 10, vol. 3199, file 504 178-5, letter to Indian Affairs Branch from C.R. Johnston, 9 July 1943, and letter to C.R. Johnston from R.A. Hoey, 20 July 1943.

83 LAC, RG 10, vol. 3199, file 504 178-5, letter to C.A. Primeau from R.A. Hoey, 7 July 1943.

84 LAC, RG 10, vol. 3199, file 504 178-5, letter to R.A. Hoey from Sister Marcelline, Superior, St. Charles Home, Ottawa, 10 May 1942; letter to Sister Marcelline from R.A. Hoey, 18 May 1942; letter to Several Agents from R.A. Hoey, 18 May 1942; and letter to the Reverend Sister from Indian Agent, St. Regis, 22 June 1942.

85 LAC, RG 10, vol. 8421, file 501/21-1, Manitoba Region—General Correspondence Regarding Placement of Indian Labour 1954–1965, letter from H.G. Sprott to Labour Temple, International Hod Carriers, Common Labourers Union of America, 14 July 1959.

86 LAC, RG 10, vol. 3199, file 504 178-5, letter to Indian Affairs Branch from C. Roberts, 21 February 1944, and letter to C. Roberts from R.A. Hoey, 23 February 1944.

87 Laliberte, "The 'Grab-a-Hoe' Indians," and Laliberte and Satzewich, "Native Migrant Labour in the Southern Alberta Sugar-beet Industry."

88 LAC, RG 10, vol. 3199, file 504 178-5, letter to Indian Affairs Branch from F. Matters, 15 July 1943; letter to F. Matters from R.A. Hoey, 19 July 1943; letter to Indian Affairs Branch from F. Matters, 21 July 1943; letter to Mr. Morris from Secretary, Elmwood, 3 March 1944; letter to F. Matters from R.A. Hoey, 29 April 1944; letter to Indian Affairs Branch from F. Matters, 4 May 1944; Office of the Indian Agent, Toronto, Ontario, Signed Statement, 10 August 1944; letter to F. Matters, 10 August 1945; Memorandum, Superintendent, Reserves and Trusts, Mr. A.G. Leslie, from C. Roberts, 17 August 1945; letter to F. Matters from D.J. Allan, 22 August 1945; letter to D.J. Allan from C. Roberts, 22 August 1945; and letter to Mrs. Buck, Matron, Elmwood School, from C. Roberts, Welfare Division, 31 August 1945.

89 LAC, RG 10, vol. 3199, file 504 178-5, Memorandum to Indian Affairs Branch, Ottawa, 4 May 1944.

90 LAC, RG 10, vol. 3199, file 504 178-5, Department of Mines and Resources letter, 18 November 1943. This was before universal health care coverage.

91 Kinnear, *A Female Economy*, 23.

92 Anne McClintock, *Imperial Leather: Race, Gender and Sexuality in the Colonial Context* (New York: Routledge, 1995).

93 M. Elise Marubbio, *Killing the Indian Maiden: Images of Native American Women in Film* (Lexington: University Press of Kentucky, 2006).

94 LAC, RG 10, vol. 3199, file 504 178-5, letter to R.A. Hoey from Principal Strapp, Mount Elgin, 13 March 1943; letter to Principal Strapp from R.A. Hoey, 16 March 1943; letter to Tuffnell, Indian Agent, from R.A. Hoey, 13 July 1943; letter to Frederick Tuffnell from R.A. Hoey, 28 July 1943; letter to Indian Affairs Branch from F.W. Tuffnell, 17 August 1943; letter to F.W. Tuffnell from R.A. Hoey, 20 August 1943; letter to Indian Affairs Branch from F. Matters, 1 September 1942; letter to F. Matters from R.A. Hoey, 4 September 1943; letter to Indian Affairs Branch from Matters, 30 September 1943; letter to F. Matters from R.A. Hoey, 6 October 1943; letter to F. Matters from R.A. Hoey, 17 January 1944; and letter to Indian Affairs Branch from F. Matters, 2 January 1944.

95 See also Velma Demerson, *Incorrigible* (Waterloo, ON: Wilfrid Laurier University Press, 2004).

96 Lynne Marks, *Revivals and Roller Rinks: Religion, Leisure, and Identity in Late Nineteenth Century Small Town Ontario* (Toronto: University of Toronto Press, 1996); Margaret Jane Hillyard Little, *No Car, No Radio, No Liquor Permit: The Moral Regulation of Single Mothers in Ontario, 1920–1997* (Toronto: Oxford University Press, 1998); and Kathy Peiss, *Cheap Amusements: Working Women and Leisure in Turn-of-the-Century New York* (Philadelphia: Temple University Press, 1986).

97 Margaret D. Jacobs, "Diverted Mothering among American Indian Domestic Servants, 1920–1940," in *Indigenous Women and Work* ed. Williams, 179–92.

98 Sarah Carter, *The Importance of Being Monogamous: Marriage and Nation Building in Western Canada to 1915* (Edmonton: University of Alberta Press, 2008).

99 LAC, RG 10, vol. 3199, file 504 178-5, letter to R.A. Hoey from F. Matters, 15 April 1943; letter to F. Matters from R.A. Hoey, 17 April 1943; letter to Indian Affairs Branch from F. Matters, 24 April 1943; letter to F. Matters from R.A. Hoey, 26 April 1943; and letter to F. Matters from R.A. Hoey, 27 April 1943.

100 Sangster, *Regulating Girls and Women*, 186. See also Jean Barman, "Taming Aboriginal Sexuality: Gender, Power, and Race in British Columbia, 1850–1900," *BC Studies* 115–16 (Fall/Winter 1997–98): 237–67.

101 LAC, RG 10, vol. 3199, file 504 178-5, letter to C.A. Primeau from J.E. Morris, 30 July 1943; letter To Whom It May Concern from J.E. Morris, 30 July 1943; letter to J.E. Morris from Chief Constable, 31 July 1943; letter to C.A. Primeau from R.A. Hoey,

5 August 1943; letter to The Commanding Officer, Camp Borden, from R.A. Hoey, 5 August 1943; letter to R.A. Hoey from C.A. Primeau, 10 August 1943; letter to C.A. Primeau from R.A. Hoey, 12 August 1943; and letter to R.A. Hoey from Colonel Commandant, 11 August 1943.

102 LAC, RG 10, vol. 8413, file 1/21-1, pt. 1, letter to Col. H.M. Jones, Superintendent—Welfare Services, from G.H. Gooderham, Regional Supervisor of Indian Agencies, 14 August 1952.

103 LAC, RG 10, vol. 8424, file 701/21-2, Alberta Region—Consultation for Employment and Placement of Indian Labour 1954–1965, letter to Indian Affairs, Ottawa, from Regional Supervisor, Alberta, R.D. Ragan, Re: Placement of Indian Domestics, 24 March 1965.

104 LAC, RG 10, vol. 8424, file 701/21-2, letter to Superintendent Stoney/Sarcee Indian Agency from Development Officer, Calgary, A.J. Karch, Re: Continuation of Placement Services, Southern Alberta, 19 March 1965.

105 *Indian News*, March 1964, 7.

106 LAC, RG 10, vol. 8427, file 601/21-3, letter to Chief, Economic Development Division, from Regional Supervisor, Saskatchewan re: Housekeeping Training—Prince Albert, 4 January 1961 and Memorandum to Chief, Economic Development Division from Regional Supervisor, Saskatchewan Re: Housekeeper Training – Prince Albert, Dec. 9, 1960.

107 LAC, RG 10, vol. 8425, File 1/21-3, pt. 3, Correspondence Regarding the Relocation of Indians for Employment, Memorandum to Indian Affairs Branch from Regional Supervisor – District of Mackenzie Re: Vocational Adjustment of Training Graduates, 21 April, 1961.

108 LAC, RG 10, vol. 8413, file 1/21-1, pt.1 extracted from the Monthly Report of the Alberta Social Worker, Wills R. Broderick, April 1952.

Chapter Two
The Permanent Solution: The Placement and Relocation Program, Hairdressers, and Beauty Culture

1 LAC, RG 10, vol. 8421, file 501/21-1, pt. 2, Manitoba Region—General Correspondence Regarding Placement of Indian Labour, 1957–1959, Placement Forms, 1 October 1957 to 31 March 1958.

2 In government documents, the program was variously called the Indian Placement and Rehabilitation Program, the Urban Integration Program, the Employment Placement and Rehabilitation Program, the Urban Placement Program, the Indian Employment Placement Program, the Placement Program, and often also referred to as "a" placement program. For the purposes of this chapter it will be referred to singularly as the "Indian Placement and Relocation Program" or the "placement program," as I am investigating placement operations with respect to the objectives of employment and relocation. In an early study of the program, social worker Carl Latham noted that several of the candidates he interviewed were unaware of being included in the Indian Placement and Relocation Program: "It would seem that the name conveys little meaning to participants and that the latter had selected what was of interest to them, that is, how the program could help them." Carl R. Latham, "Indian Placement Programme Administered by the Indian Affairs Branch of the Department of Citizenship and Immigration" MA thesis, University of Toronto, 1958, 132.

3 "2 Leaders, 11 Delegates at Citizenship Seminar," *Indian News* 5, 2 (December 1961): 3.

4 The department undertook an increased number of employment surveys, inventories of Indian labour potential, and studies and task forces on Native employment, which continued into the 1970s and beyond. Helen Buckley, *The Indians and Métis of Northern Saskatchewan: A Report on Economic and Social Development* (Saskatoon: Centre for Community Studies, 1963); Harold Cardinal, *Unjust Society* (Edmonton: M.G. Hurtig, 1969); Edgar Dosman, *Indians: The Urban Dilemma* (Toronto: McClelland and Stewart, 1972); D.B. Sealey and V.K. Kirkness, eds., *Indians without Tipis: A Resource Book by Indians and Métis* (Winnipeg: William Clare, 1973); D.B. Sealey and A.S. Lussier, *The Metis: Canada's Forgotten People* (Winnipeg: Manitoba Metis Federation Press, 1975); H.B. Hawthorn, C.S. Belshaw, and S.M. Jamieson, *The Indians of British Columbia: A Study of Contemporary Social Adjustment* (Toronto: University of Toronto Press, 1960); and Jean H. Lagasse, *A Study of the Population of Indian Ancestry Living in Manitoba* (Winnipeg: Department of Agriculture and Immigration, 1959).

5 In 1951, the BIA expanded its unofficial relocation program by creating a new Branch of Placement and Relocation in the BIA. This program was modelled after the War Relocation Authority, which had succeeded in relocating Japanese-Americans from the California coast to inland areas. Initiated in Oklahoma, New Mexico, California, Arizona, Utah, and Colorado, the first urban Indian relocates arrived in Chicago, Los Angeles, and Denver in the early 1950s. This comprehensive program was organized to meet three main priorities: on-the-job training and apprenticeship, adult vocational training, and direct employment. Its objectives were to desegregate the reserve population and to assimilate Native Americans through integration. By 1973, more than 100,000 people had been relocated through the program.

6 LAC, RG 10, vol. 8414, file 1/21-1, pt. 4, Correspondence Regarding the Placement of Indian Labour, 1956, Memorandum to the Director, 25 October 1956.

7 Stephen, *Pick One Intelligent Girl*, 19.

8 Latham, "Indian Placement Programme," 59.

9 House of Commons, Debates (Hansard), 24th Parliament, 7-8 Elizabeth II, Volume III, Second Session, May 15, 1959, 3713.

10 Bohaker and Iacovetta, "Making Aboriginal People 'Immigrants Too.'"

11 LAC, RG 10, vol. 8414, file 1/21-1, pt. 4, Memorandum to the Director, 25 October 1956.

12 Latham, "Indian Placement Programme," 52–53. This meeting included Director of Immigration C.E. Smith and L.M Hunter, chief of the Settlement Division.

13 LAC, RG 10, vol. 8424, file 401/21-2, Ontario Regional Headquarters - Consultation for Emplyment Opportunities and Placement of Indian Labour, letter to W.R. Baskerville, director of Immigration, Department of Citizenship and Immigration, from H.M. Jones, director of Indian Affairs, 1 October 1958.

14 Latham, "Indian Placement Programme", 101, 109. Only three of the organizations were known to hire other Indians. At this time, Carl Latham, Delaware social worker, was covering Saskatchewan for the Indian Affairs Branch. He had a BA from the University of Western Ontario and had obtained his BSW and MSW at the University of Toronto. His study of the placement program was part of the requirements for his degree.

15 Latham, "Indian Placement Programme," 52–53.

16 Programs of rehabilitation and placement and relocation are often mentioned together or one after the other. Department of Citizenship and Immigration, "The Indian People of Canada," *Citizen* 4, 1 (February 1958): 18.

17 "Case finding" is a term used by Indian Health Services to describe its various efforts to locate, usually by X-ray surveys, Native individuals who had tuberculosis, and to remove them to tuberculosis sanatoria.

18 This suggests that Denise may have had some training in hairdressing as well. "The Tanches: A Story of Courage," *Indian News* 4, 4 (April 1961): 8.

19 The Sanatorium Board of Manitoba conducted a study in this period looking at rehabilitants'"unemployment" rates and paid income tax to show how the treatment was about "investment" rather than philanthropy. Archives of Manitoba, Sanatorium Board of Manitoba, Aisle L, Bay 11, Shelf 7, Temp Box 22, Scrapbooks Newspaper Clippings November 1960–January 1962 and January 1962–February 1963.)

20 Latham, "Indian Placement Programme," 66.

21 "Many Take Vocational Training: Employment Horizon Broadens for Indians, New Placement Service Aids Job Hunters," *Indian News* 2, 4 (September 1957): 2.

22 Latham, "Indian Placement Programme,"37.

23 Ibid., 1.

24 Indian Affairs distinguished placement candidates from "ordinary welfare relief cases" and those more "suited" to casual employment. The program also differed from the Revolving Loan Fund program, which provided loans lasting a maximum of five years to individuals and groups wanting to start new business ventures on and off reserves to purchase agricultural machinery, fishing gear, livestock, and equipment. The government decided that the Revolving Loan Fund was inadequate and ineffective and replaced it with the Indian Economic Development Fund in 1970. These funds were available to Indians and non-Indians who could not meet the requirements of conventional lending agencies but whose businesses benefited Indian communities. Canada, Department of Indian and Northern Affairs, *Annual Report,*1972–73, 51. Bands' trust funds—or an individual band's funds made up of annuities and monies derived from Indian assets, like the sale of land, leases, timber, oil and gas exploration, and gravel—were used in some instances for vocational training, even though federal funding for placement and relocation was broadly considered a new source of Indian money.

25 "Speech by Superintendent-General: 'The Future of the Canadian Indian,'" *Indian News* 2, 2 (May 1956): 2.

26 LAC, RG 10, vol. 8415, file 1/21-1, pt. 8, Correspondence Regarding the Placement of Indian Labour and Publication 1960–1962, meeting of the representatives of the Forest Industry in Northwestern Ontario, Ontario Department of Lands and Forests, and Indian Affairs Branch, 27 September 1962, Appendix No. 2.

27 LAC, RG 10, vol. 8426, file 401/21-3, pt. 3, Ontario Regional Headquarters - Relocating Indians for Employment 1959, "Indian Employment Placement Program," n/d.

28 J.J. Fransen, "Employment Experiences and Economic Position of a Selected Group of Indians in Metropolitan Toronto" (MA thesis, University of Toronto, 1964), 44.

29 Canada, Department of Citizenship and Immigration, Indian Affairs Branch, *Annual Report* 1956–57, 50.

30 Donald Fixico, *Termination and Relocation: Federal Indian Policy, 1945–1960* (Albuquerque: University of New Mexico Press, 1986) and *The Urban Indian Experience in America* (Albuquerque: University of New Mexico Press, 2000). See also Kathryn Leilani MacKay, "Warrior into Welder: A History of Federal Employment Programs for American Indians, 1878–1972," (PhD diss., University of Utah, 1987).

31 "Speech by Superintendent-General," 2.

32 LAC, RG 10, vol. 8427, file 501/21-3, Manitoba Regional Office—Relocation of Indians for Employment, 1958–1963, letter to R.D. Ragan, Regional Supervisor of Indian Agencies, Manitoba, from J.H. Gordon, Chief, Welfare Division, Re: Placement Information Record Forms, 12 September 1958.

33 MacKay, "Warrior into Welder," 179.

34 LAC, RG 10, vol. 8427, file 501/21-3, letter to Regional Supervisor, Manitoba, from Jules D'Astous, Chief, Economic Development Division, 24 July 1963.

35 LAC, RG 10, vol. 8426, file 401/21-3, pt. 4, letter to Regional Supervisor, North Bay, from R.F. Battle, Chief, Economic Development Division, 19 December 1961.

36 One assessment of the program observed, "all candidates [in the placement program] were approached by the Branch rather than came to the Branch to receive help towards establishment." LAC, RG 10, vol. 8424, file 401/21-2, letter from Carl Latham to J.H. Gordon, 16 April 1958, and letter to Carl Latham from H.M. Jones, 25 April 1958. The department worried that the study might reflect poorly on the branch and restricted access to it until Indian Affairs itself agreed to release it. I could not find a copy of the original report, only reference to it in correspondence.

37 Latham, "Indian Placement Programme," 91–92.

38 LAC, RG 10, vol. 8426, file 401/21-3, pt. 4, Ontario Regional Headquarters—Relocation of Indians for Employment, 1960–1962, "Indian Employment Placement Program."

39 John Borrows, "Physical Philosophy: Mobility and the Future of Indigenous Rights," in *Indigenous Peoples and the Law: Comparative and Critical Perspectives*, ed. Benjamin J. Richardson, Shin Imai, and Kent McNeil (Portland, OR: Hart Publishing, 2009), 403–419.

40 LAC, RG 10, vol. 8414, file 1/21-1, pt. 3, Correspondence Regarding the Placement of Indian Labour, 1955–1956, Memorandum to the Minister: "A Step Towards Integration," 13 January 1956.

41 "Speech by Superintendent-General," 1–2.

42 LAC, RG 10, vol. 8473, file 1/23-35, pt. 2, Statistical Report on the Indian Employment Placement Program 1962–64, "Examples of Employment."

43 E.P. Thompson, *The Making of the English Working Class* (London: Gollancz, 1963).

44 Hugh Shewell, *"Enough to Keep Them Alive": Indian Welfare in Canada, 1873–1965* (Toronto: University of Toronto Press, 2004).

45 See, for example, Employment and Immigration Canada, *The Development of an Employment Policy for Indian, Inuit and Metis People* (Ottawa: Employment and Immigration Canada, 1978), 10. "The federal government funds a number of programs with a potential for directly affecting the employment of native people.... All have to strive for success in the context of an open economic market.... All operate with the realization that the long-term solution to native unemployment must come in the form of jobs in the private sector operating in national and international markets that are open and competitive."

46 The Placement and Relocation program distinguished between "rural" and "urban" employment, and separate personnel were assigned to each, with "field" officers operating the former and "placement" officers the latter.

47 J.J. Fransen, the first placement officer in southern Ontario serving primarily the Toronto area, even returned to school after working in this field for several years in order to get his master's degree in social work.

48 Mr. John Rayson, for example, Manitoba's first placement officer, had served six years with the Army Service Corps during the Second World War. He moved to the DIA from Veterans Affairs and was appointed Indian Agent of the Portage la Prairie agency in 1950.

49 They were located at Vancouver, Whitehorse, Prince George, Fort Smith, Nanaimo, Edmonton, Calgary, Saskatoon (two), Winnipeg (two), The Pas, Regina, Thompson, Port Arthur, North Bay, London, Toronto, Quebec City, and Amherst. Department of

Indian Affairs and Northern Development, *The Indian in Transition: The Indian Today* (Ottawa: Queen's Printer, 1964), 10, and "Some 1,500 Find Jobs: Placement Program Successful," *Indian News* 6, 3 (February 1963): 3.

50 Haskins, *Matrons and Maids*, 4–6.

51 Counselling Foundation of Canada, *A Coming of Age: Counselling Canadians for Work in the Twentieth Century* (Toronto, 2002).

52 "Speech by Superintendent-General," 1–2.

53 Department of Indian Affairs and Northern Development, *The Indian in Transition: The Indian Today*, 12.

54 Latham, "Indian Placement Programme", 25 and 26.

55 Ibid.

56 Department of Citizenship and Immigration, *The Canadian Indian* (Ottawa: Queen's Printer, 1964), 14.

57 Department of Indian Affairs and Northern Development, *The Indian in Transition: The Indian Today*, 11-12.

58 LAC, RG 10, vol. 8426, file 401/21-3, pt. 4, "Indian Employment Placement Program."

59 LAC, RG 10, vol. 8427, file 501/21-3, letter to Indian Affairs Branch from R.D. Ragan, Regional Supervisor of Indian Agencies, 1 December 1958, re: Voucher #420 Placement Assistance.

60 LAC, RG 10, vol. 8424, file 401/21-2, letter to the Secretary, Treasury Board, from Laval Fortier, 5 August 1958. In 1962, placement officer J.J. Fransen noted that the placement program is "not geared to family relocation and placement." Fransen, "Employment Experiences and Economic Position of a Selected Group of Indians," 39.

61 The focus on men is also reflected in three studies of the program. The first study, by the regional supervisor of Toronto in March 1961, excluded Indian women who married and returned home to live with their husbands who never had been in Toronto. Apart from this, it was argued that the selection of nine men and three women was a "fairly representative group for this study." In this study all twelve were unmarried. LAC, RG 10 vol. 8426, file 401/21-4, pt. 4, Memorandum to Indian Affairs Branch from Regional Supervisor, Toronto, on Evaluation—Employment Placement Program, 6 April 1961.

62 LAC, RG 10, vol. 8426, file 401/21-3, pt. 4, "Indian Employment Placement Program."

63 Department of Indian Affairs and Northern Development, *The Indian in Transition: The Indian Today*, 11.

64 Latham, "Indian Placement Programme," 55.

65 Ibid., 57.

66 LAC, RG 10, vol. 8426, file 401/21-3, pt. 4, "Indian Employment Placement Program."

67 Franca Iacovetta and Wendy Mitchinson, "Social History and Case Files Research," in *On the Case: Explorations in Social History*, ed. Franca Iacovetta and Wendy Mitchinson (Toronto: University of Toronto Press, 1998), 3.

68 LAC, RG 10, vol. 8421, file 501/21-1, pt. 2, Placement Files.

69 LAC, RG 10, vol. 8424, file 401/21-2, letter to the Secretary, Treasury Board, from Laval Fortier, 5 August 1958, Appendix A, "Assistance Under the Urban Placement Program."

70 Costs included "transportation to the centre of employment, and meals and accommodation on route where necessary; room and board, or alternatively house rental, services, and food costs, at prevailing rates for the area, which will normally be for a period of less than two months; personal allowances of $15 per month for individuals, or $25 per month for families, normally for a period of two months or less; Clothing where necessary, normally amounting to $100 or less; Assistance in purchasing furniture and

household effects, normally amounting to $250 or less; Provision of tools where necessary to affect placement, normally amounting to $150 or less; On-the-job training contracts with employers on behalf of placement candidates, where required for permanent placement on a pre-apprenticeship or trade training basis, normally for a period of six months but in any case not to exceed one year." LAC, RG 10, vol. 8424, file 401/21-2, letter to the Secretary, Treasury Board, from Laval Fortier, 5 August 1958. Monthly Report of Expenditures of the Indian Employment and Placement Program recorded Room and Board, Personal Allowance, Clothes, On-the-Job Training, Miscellaneous (tools etc.), Total, and Repayments.

71 LAC, RG 10, vol. 8424, file 401/21-2, letter to the Secretary, Treasury Board, from Laval Fortier, 5 August 1958, Appendix A, "Assistance Under the Urban Placement Program."

72 LAC, RG 10, vol. 8426, file 401/21-3, pt. 4, letter to Regional Supervisor, North Bay, from Chief, Economic Development Division, R.F. Battle, 19 December 1961.

73 "Chattels" in these files normally referred to bedroom suites, kitchen suites, refrigerators, electric ranges, chairs, and other miscellaneous items.

74 LAC, RG 10, vol. 8426, file 401/21-3, pt. 5, Ontario Regional Headquarters—Relocation of Indians for Employment, 1963–1965, Lien Note.

75 LAC, RG 10, vol. 8426, file 401/21-3, pt. 4, letter to Indian Affairs Branch from Regional Supervisor, North Bay, 27 December 1961.

76 Twenty-five percent of placement funds in the Alberta region went to the Family Services Association of Edmonton in 1965–66.

77 Terrance Pelletier, "Cowessess First Nation, the Town of Broadview, and the City of Regina: A Study of Historical Relationships, 1870–1995" (paper presented at the 85th annual meeting of the Canadian Historical Association, York University, Toronto, ON, May 2006). Pelletier points out that urban homes were attractive because running water and electricity were not readily accessible on reserves by the mid-1960s.

78 For more information on later employment programs, see Canada, Employment and Immigration Canada, *The Development of an Employment Policy for Indian, Inuit and Metis People* (Ottawa: Employment and Immigration Canada, 1978); Impact Research, *Native People and Employment in the Public Service of Canada* (Ottawa: Office of Native Employment, Public Service Commission, 1976); Stewart J. Clatworthy, *The Effects of Education on Native Behaviour in the Urban Labour Market* (Ottawa: Labour Market Development Task Force, 1981); and Canada Employment and Immigration Advisory Council, *Employment Services to Natives* (Ottawa: The Council, 1982).

79 Latham, "Indian Placement Programme," 132.

80 Canada, Department of Citizenship and Immigration, Indian Affairs Branch, *Annual Report*, 1958-59, 77.

81 Department of Indian Affairs and Northern Development, *The Indian in Transition*, 19.

82 Canada, Department of Citizenship and Immigration, Indian Affairs Branch, *Annual Report*, 1959-60, 47.

83 LAC, RG 10, Volume 8426, File 401/21-3, pt. 4, "Indian Employment Placement Program."

84 Canada, Department of Citizenship and Immigration, Indian Affairs Branch, *Annual Report*, 1964-65, 28.

85 "More Indians in City Than On Reservations," *Winnipeg Free Press*, 27 January 1958, 22.

86 LAC, RG 10, vol. 8426, file 401/21-3, pt. 4, "Help Young Indians to Fit into City Life," *Globe and Mail*, 1 April 1961.

87 L. Zeitoun, *Canadian Indians at the Crossroads: Some Aspects of Relocation and Urbanization in Canada* (Ottawa: Department of Manpower and Immigration, 1969), 11–18.

88 Other tests used by the NES include the Kuder Interest Test, the Test of Learning Capacity, the Dominion Vocabulary Test, and the Dominion Group Test of Learning Capacity.

89 Canadian Broadcasting Corporation, *Wojeck*, "The Last Man in the World," dir. Ron Kelly, 1966.

90 Examples of these films include the National Film Board of Canada's *The Transition* (1964), *High Steel* (1965), *Charley Squash Goes to Town* (1969), *Because They Are Different* (1964), *No Longer Vanishing* (1955), and *The Longer Trail* (1956). *No Longer Vanishing* and *The Longer Trail* were shown on the first day of the training course for placement officers. LAC, RG 10, vol. 8427, file 901/21-3, British Columbia and Yukon Regions– Relocation for Employment, "One Week's Training Course in Ottawa for Indian Placement Officers."

91 See, for example, Judith Walkowitz, *City of Dreadful Delight: Narratives of Sexual Danger in Late-Victorian London* (Chicago: University of Chicago Press, 1992); Carolyn Strange, *Toronto's Girl Problem: The Perils and Pleasures of the City 1880–1930* (Toronto: University of Toronto Press, 1995); Kathy Peiss, Cheap Amusements: *Working Women and Leisure in Turn-of-the-Century New York* (Philadelphia: Temple University Press, 1986); and Kay Anderson, *Vancouver's Chinatown: Racial Discourse in Canada, 1875–1980* (Montreal: McGill-Queen's University Press, 1991).

92 Sherene H. Razack, "Gendered Racial Violence and Spatialized Justice: The Murder of Pamela George," in *Race, Space and the Law: Unmapping a White Settler Society*, ed. Sherene H. Razack (Toronto: Between the Lines, 2002), 121–56.

93 However, at some times and in some places the numbers of women were closer to equal with those of men. For example, in the 1 October 1957 to 31 March 1958 report for Manitoba, seven men and six women were placed. Four of the women were single and three had children. The numbers shifted as candidates married, moved, changed jobs, and looked for other opportunities.

94 United Church Archives, 509/2/1-4 no. 7, G. McMillan, Social And Economic Research 1947–1959, G.M. Grieve, Report on Indian Work, Winnipeg, Manitoba, January 1957–August 1957.

95 LAC, RG 10, vol. 8426, file 401/21-3, pt. 5, letter to Mr. Bonnah from R.H. Biddle, Placement Officer, 22 May 1963.

96 *The Transition*, dir. Mort Ransen, National Film Board of Canada, 1964. The lead character of the film, Jimmy Robinson, age nineteen, from "a reserve not too far from the city," explained, "they had arranged for a room there before I had arrived in the city. It's a nice house, lots of space, and Mrs. Gray seems like a nice lady. For the first time I'll have a room of my own. Don't know if I like it without my brothers in the house and all their noise. I suppose it'll be lonesome sometimes."

97 LAC, RG 10, vol. 8426, file 401/21-3, pt. 5, letter to Mr. Bonnah, Regional Supervisor, Toronto, from Mr. Biddle, Southern Ontario Placement Officer, 22 May 1963.

98 LAC, RG 10, vol. 8463, file 1/23-21, pt. 1, General—Social Workers' Reports, 1953–1960, "Urban Hostels for Indian Youth" by Supervisor of Social Workers F. Grant.

99 United Church Archives, Woman's Missionary Society Notes, Blue Scrapbook, pl. 195. 505/1-1. Oddson was responding to a popular liberal middle-class sentiment that boarding homes for Indians would tend to segregate them from the rest of the urban population. She was also responding primarily to what she saw as her responsibilities to Indian mothers of girls who moved to cities.

100 For more primary source information on the lodge, the United Church Archives in Winnipeg holds a substantial and organized file on the matter. United Church Archives 509/1/5-1, Conference of Manitoba and Northwest Ontario, Conference Home Missions, Indian and Métis Reception Lodge, 1959–1979, Lodge Proposal/Director's Report/Articles. See also "How Placement Program Helped Couple Find Work," *Indian News* 4, 2 (May 1960): 1.

101 LAC, RG 10, vol. 8426, file 401/21-3, pt. 4, Ontario Regional Headquarters Relocation of Indians for Employment 1960–1962, Memorandum to Regional Supervisors, Maritimes, from Chief, Economic Development Division, 26 June 1962.

102 LAC, RG 10, vol. 8426, file 401/21-3, pt. 4, letter to Indian Affairs Branch, from McKinnon, 18 July 1962.

103 Heather Howard-Bobiwash, "Women's Class Strategies as Activism in Native Community Building in Toronto, 1950–1975," *American Indian Quarterly* 27, 3/4 (2003): 566.

104 United Church Archives, 509/2/1-4, no. 7, G. McMillan, Social And Economic Research 1947–1959. G. M. Grieve, Report on Indian Work, Winnipeg, Manitoba, January 1957–August 1957.

105 Latham, "Indian Placement Programme," 148.

106 Ibid., 130.

107 "Indian Women of Today," and "At Work in Whitehorse," *Indian News* 4, 3 (December 1960): 1 and 2.

108 Pamela White, "Restructuring the Domestic Sphere," 261-7.

109 Department of Citizenship and Immigration, Indian Affairs Branch, "Conference on Indian Employment: First Combined Conference of Placement and Field Officers," Ottawa, December 7-10, 1959, 28.

110 Lilianne Ernestine Krosenbrink-Gelissen, "The Native Women's Association of Canada," in *Native Peoples in Canada: Contemporary Conflicts*, ed. James S. Frideres, 5th ed. (Toronto: Prentice Hall, 1998), 302, as cited in Janovicek, "'Assisting our own.'"

111 RG 10, Volume 8426, File 401/21-3, pt. 4, Virginia Etherington, "Help Young Indians to Fit Into City Life," *Globe and Mail*, April 1961.

112 Department of Labour, *Women at Work in Canada: A Fact Book on the Female Labour Force* (Ottawa: Queen's Printer, 1965), 26 and 32.

113 Marvel advertisement, *Globe and Mail*, 3 January 1957, 30.

114 "The Labor Scene: University Degree Not Always a Must," *Winnipeg Free Press*, 9 September 1967, 29.

115 LAC, RG 10, vol. 8426, file 401/21-3, pt. 4, "Training Opportunities for Young People" by A.J. Boisvert, Northern Ontario Placement Officer, June 1961.

116 LAC, RG 10, vol. 8421, file 501/21-1, pt. 2, Placement Forms.

117 Ibid.

118 "Hairdresser at Portage: How Louise Found Her Job," *Indian News* 4, 2 (May 1960): 4.

119 Malcolm Davidson, "Indian Economic Development in 'the *Indian News*' (1954–1982)," *Canadian Journal of Native Studies* 3, 2 (1983): 321–40.

120 Barbara Brookes and Catherine Smith, "Technology and Gender: Barbers and Hairdressers in New Zealand, 1900–1970," *History and Technology* 25, 4 (2009): 365–86.

121 Julie A. Willet, *Permanent Waves: The Making of the American Beauty Shop* (New York: New York University Press, 2000); Julia Kirk Blackwelder, *Styling Jim Crow: African American Beauty Training during Segregation* (College Station: Texas A and M University Press, 2003); Kathy Peiss, *Hope in a Jar: The Making of America's Beauty Culture*

(New York: Metropolitan Books, 1998); and Tiffany M. Gill, "Civic Beauty: Beauty Culturists and the Politics of African American Female Entrepreneurship, 1900–1965," *Enterprise and Society* 5, 4 (2004): 583–93.

122 Flynn, *Moving Beyond Borders*.

123 Deloria, *Indians in Unexpected Places*, 7.

124 Adele Perry, "Fair Ones of a Purer Caste: White Women and Colonialism in Nineteenth-Century British Columbia," *Feminist Studies* 23, 3 (Fall 1997), and Sarah Carter, "Categories and Terrains of Exclusion: Constructing the 'Indian Woman' in the Early Settlement Era in Western Canada," *Great Plains Quarterly* 13, 3 (Summer 1993): 147–61.

125 "Okanagan Girl Leads Class," *Indian News* 4, 4 (April 1961): 4.

126 Maria Campbell, personal communication, 26 April 2006.

127 Job advertisements for workers of "any nationality" signalled tolerance and inclusivity, yet "English-speaking" qualified this open-mindedness significantly.

128 LAC, RG 10, vol. 8427, file 501/21-3, Placement Forms.

129 LAC, RG 10, vol. 8427, file 501/21-3, Permanent Placements, March 1961.

130 Table 36: "Women Wage Earners in Leading Personal Service Occupations, by Earnings, Canada, Year Ending June 1, 1961," in *Women at Work in Canada* (Ottawa: Department of Labour, 1965), 9.9.

131 "Head of Hairdressers Speaks Against Tips," *Winnipeg Free Press*, 17 March 1966, 14.

132 LAC, RG 10, vol. 8426, file 401/21-3, pt. 4, Memorandum to Indian Affairs Branch from Regional Supervisor Toronto, Re: Evaluation—Employment Placement Program, 6 April 1961, Appendix "B."

133 Latham, "Indian Placement Programme," 142.

134 Ibid, 123. Likewise the department's 1961 survey of the southern Ontario candidates showed that of the three women included in the survey, two had grade 12, and the other had grade 8. LAC, RG 10, vol.8426, file 401/21-3, pt. 1.

135 Department of Labour, *Women at Work in Canada*, 53 and 58.

136 LAC, RG 10, vol. 8426, file 401/21-3, pt. 4, Memorandum to Indian Affairs Branch from Regional Supervisor, Toronto, J.E. Morris, Re: Evaluation—Employment Placement Program, April 6, 1961.

137 Fransen, "Employment Experiences and Economic Position of a Selected Group of Indians," 41.

138 Ibid., 57.

139 Maria Campbell, personal correspondence, 26 April 2006, and *Halfbreed* (Toronto: McClelland and Stewart, 1977), 132–35.

140 Constance Backhouse, *Colour-Coded: A Legal History of Racism in Canada, 1900–1950* (Toronto: University of Toronto Press, 1999), 226–71.

141 Viola Desmond's paternal grandfather was a hairdresser in Halifax's north end. Barbering was a means of carving out a successful living in the late nineteenth and early twentieth centuries because of racial segregation in many parts of the country. Viola went to mixed elementary and secondary schools, then taught at segregated schools for Black students. She saved her money, knowing from the outset that she wanted to set up a hairdressing business of her own. Training facilities in Halifax were closed to Black women in the 1930s, but Viola was able to enrol in Montreal and then train in New York and Atlantic City. Backhouse, *Colour-Coded*, 226–71. See also Julie Willett, "'Hands Across the Table': A Short History of the Manicurist in the Twentieth Century," *Journal of Women's History* 17, 3 (2005): 59–80.

142 Brownlie, "'Living the Same as the White People,'" and *A Fatherly Eye: Indian Agents, Government Power, and Aboriginal Resistance in Ontario, 1918–1939* (Toronto: Oxford University Press, 2003) .

143 Indian and Northern Affairs Economic Development—Operations, "Chez Hair is Open for Business to Men and Women," *Ideas* 4, 1 (Spring 1976): 14–5.

144 Grace Poulin, *Invisible Women: WWII Aboriginal Servicewomen in Canada* (Thunder Bay, ON: D.G. Poulin/Ontario Native Women's Association, 2007), 57–60 and 105–8.

145 LAC, RG 10, vol. 8426, file 401/21-3, pt. 4, Memorandum to Indian Affairs Branch, from Regional Supervisor, Toronto Re: Evaluation—Employment Placement Program, 6 April 1961.

146 "Mother of Five Runs Beauty Salon," *Indian News* 4, 3 (December 1960): 4. Mrs. Genevieve Julian, 28 and widowed, operated a beauty shop out of her "welfare house" on the Millbrook Reserve near Truro. She had trained at the Trans-Canada Beauty Industries School of Moncton, NB, and received some financial help toward her fees, but paid for her own board and lodging while in Moncton.

147 "Iroquoian Women Adjust to Changes," *Indian News* 10,5 (February 1968): 4, 5.

148 See, for example, Janice Acoose, *Iskwewak—Kah' Ki Yaw Ni Wahkomakanak: Neither Indian Princesses Nor Easy Squaws* (Toronto: Women's Press, 1995); Daniel Francis, *The Imaginary Indian: The Image of the Indian in Canadian Culture* (Vancouver: Arsenal Pulp Press, 1997); and Rayna Green, "The Pocahontas Perplex: The Image of Indian Women in American Culture," *Massachusetts Review* 16 (1975): 698–714.

149 Wendy Kozol, "Miss Indian America: Regulatory Gazes and the Politics of Affiliation," *Feminist Studies* 31, 1 (Spring 2005): 64–94.

150 These competitions date back to the early twentieth century at the Hudson Bay Dog Derby and the Trappers' Festival. The competition apparently became "more competitive" in the late 1940s, "with women gaining 'points' throughout the festival for their beauty, poise, personality and talent." Contestants were sponsored by groups in and around The Pas, and the funds raised were used as prize money for the World Championship Sled Dog Race. The winner of this contest (underwritten by two fur auction houses in Winnipeg) received a crown, a parka, and a trip to Chicago. "Speed, Brawn and Beauty: The History of the Northern Manitoba Trappers' Festival Fur Queen," at the Virtual Museum website: http://www.museevirtuele- virtualmuseum.ca/sgc-cms/histoireees_de_chez_nous-communitymemories/pm_v2.php?id=story_line&lg=English&fl=O&e=x382&sl=3162&pos=1 (accessed 6 Feb. 2014). Jean Goodwill, a Cree Nurse from Saskatchewan and founder of the Aboriginal Nurses Association of Canada was the Fur Queen in 1959.

151 The Miss Manitoba Indian Princess pageant was open to girls eighteen to twenty-five years of age and of Indian descent. At the contest, participants wore two "native costumes" and gave a three- to five-minute speech on a subject relating to Indian history or present-day life. The local winner competed for the Miss Indian Princess of Canada title. "Seek Manitoba Indian Princess," *Winnipeg Free Press*, 29 May 1970, 3.

152 Marina Assu and Darlene Campbell were crowned Miss Totem Princess in 1956 and 1962 respectively.

153 "Angeline Monkman Fur Queen Entry," *Winnipeg Free Press*, 8 January 1965, 20.

154 *Indian News* 5, 2 (December 1961): 8; 5, 1 (June 1961): 8; 4, 3 (December 1960): 2.

155 LAC, RG 10, vol. 7189, file 1/2-11-2, pt. 4, Correspondence Regarding the Departmental Staff Association and the Civil Service Recreation Association 1963–4. Janet Morris was also a Hostess of the Indian Pavilion at Expo '67.

156 Mark Cronlund Anderson and Carmen L. Robertson, *Seeing Red: A History of Natives in Canadian Newspapers* (Winnipeg: University of Manitoba Press, 2011): 195–96.

157 "Indian Princess Keeps Cool in Beaded Cape," *Winnipeg Free Press*, 19 July 1967, 19.

158 Bob Lowrey, "Named Manitoba Indian Princess," *Winnipeg Free Press*, 3 July 1969, 50.

159 "Indian Princess Keeps Cool in Beaded Cape," 19; "Manitoba Princess Crowned," *Brandon Sun*, 17 July 1967, 2.

160 Myra Rutherdale and J.R. Miller, "'It's Our Country': First Nations' Participation in the Indian Pavillion at Expo '67," *Journal of the Canadian Historical Association* 17, 2 (2006): 148–73.

161 "Mohawk Girl Chosen Miss Indian Affairs," *Indian News* 4, 3 (December 1960): 2.

162 "This Time She Really Is!" *Indian News* 8,1 (July 1965): 1.

163 Janet Morris, "Living in Ottawa," *Micmac News* 1, 2 (7 March 1966): 1–2.

164 Gretchen M. Bataille and Laurie Lisa, eds. *Native American Women: A Biographical Dictionary* (New York: Taylor and Francis, 2001).

165 "Council Meeting Fake: Princess vows fight over Indian Crown," *Globe and Mail*, 6 June 1964, 1.

166 Patrizia Gentile, "'Government Girls' and 'Ottawa Men': Cold War Management of Gender Relations in the Civil Service," in *Whose National Security? Canadian State Surveillance and the Creation of Enemies*, ed. Gary Kinsman, Dieter K. Buse, and Mercedes Steedman (Toronto: Between the Lines, 2000), 131–41.

167 Laila Haidarali, "Is it True What They Say about Models?: Modelling African American Womanhood on the Eve of the Civil Rights Era," *Atlantis: A Women's Studies Journal* 32, 1 (2007): 144–55.

168 Jennifer Nez Denetdale, "Chairmen, Presidents, and Princesses: The Navajo Nation, Gender, and Politics of Tradition," *Wicazo Sa Review* 21, 1 (Spring 2006): 10.

169 Ibid., 27n49.

170 Jo-Anne Fiske argues that colonialism "dislocates women as producers, undermines their social position, and discredits their abilities as public leaders and decision makers." "Fishing Is Women's Business: Changing Economic Roles of Carrier Women and Men," in *Native Peoples, Native Lands: Canadian Indians, Inuit and Metis*, ed. Bruce Cox (Ottawa: Carleton University Press, 1987), 186.

171 For more on the photos of contest winners, see Kozol, "Miss Indian America." She studies pose and form in the photos of Miss Indian America and local powwow princesses, arguing that the photos contain Indian identity with the gender politics of fashion photography, among other things.

172 Linda Lafreniere, secretary, Manitoba Indian Brotherhood, also Miss Folklorama; Valerie Klyne, secretary, Manitoba Métis Federation, also 1969 Manitoba Indian Princess; Eileen Fitzner, payroll clerk and part-time student who had a modelling assignment at Garden City shopping centre; Pauline Wood, receptionist at the Manitoba Rehab Hospital, 1970 Manitoba Indian princess; Mabel Sinclair, former legal secretary and Red River College social work graduate; Shirley Fontaine, secretary at National Indian Brotherhood. "First Indian Models Gorgeous at Graduation," *Winnipeg Free Press*, 15 August 1970.

173 Jo-Anne Fiske, "The Womb Is to the Nation as the Heart Is to the Body: Ethnopolitical Discourses of the Canadian Indigenous Women's Movement," in *Feminism, Political Economy and the State: Contested Terrain*, ed. Pat Armstrong and M. Patricia Connelly

(Toronto: Canadian Scholars' Press, 1999), 293–325; Sarah Banet-Weiser, *The Most Beautiful Girl in the World: Beauty Pageants and National Identity* (Berkeley and Los Angeles: University of California Press, 1999); and Elwood Watson and Darcy Martin, "*There She Is, Miss America": The Politics of Sex, Beauty and Race in America's Most Famous Pageant* (New York: Palgrave MacMillan, 2004).

174 See Rutherdale and Miller, "It's Our Country."

175 See "Shelley Niro," in *A Time of Visions: Interviews by Larry Abbott*, http://www.britesites.com/native_artist_interviews/sniro.htm (accessed 6 February 2014).

176 LAC, RG 10, acc 1999-01431-6, box 56, file 1/211-2, pt. 1, Placement of Indian Labour. Consultations for Employment opportunities 1954–1968, "Employment and Relocation Program." At this point, counsellors worked with the Department of Manpower, provincial programs, and interested community organizations.

177 The Task Force on Manpower for Native People, assigned to study how Native people could benefit more from Manpower Programs, included Employment and Relocation Services among Indian Affairs' existing programs, and noted that Indian Affairs' programs would decrease as Manpower's expanded.

178 Department of Indian Affairs and Northern Development, *Indian Education Program* (Ottawa, Indian Affairs and Northern Development, 1972), 32, 35.

179 LAC, RG 10, Acc 2001–0093–x, Box 14, File 501-21-2-3. Minutes of the Fourth National Advisory Council Meeting, 22–24 March 1976.

180 Leah Cohen, Discussion Paper: Employment of Native Women, "Manpower Programs and Special Needs of Native Women," in *Task Force on Manpower Services to Native Peoples*, Papers, 1975, 3–4.

181 Indian Affairs Branch, Department of Citizenship and Immigration, *The Indian in Transition: Indian Education* (Ottawa: Queen's Printer, 1962), 18.

182 *The Transition.*

183 Deloria, *Indians in Unexpected Places*, 14.

184 See Cathleen Cahill, *Federal Fathers & Mothers: A Social History of the United States Indian Service, 1869–1933* (Chapel Hill: University of North Carolina Press, 2011).

Chapter Three
An Early Labour History of Community Health Representatives, 1960–1970

1 The five other services were: Civil Aviation Medicine, Public Service Health, Quarantine Division, Immigration Medical Services, and Sick Mariners' Service. See Catherine L. Cook, "Jurisdiction and First Nations Health and Health Care" (MSc thesis, University of Manitoba, 2003); Melanie MacKinnon, "A First Nations Voice in the Present Creates Healing in the Future," *Canadian Journal of Public Health* (January–February 2005): 513–16; Waldram, Herring, and Young, *Aboriginal Health Canada*.

2 There were other terms such as "Native Health Worker," "Settlement Worker," "Community Health Worker," "Health Aide," "Nurse's Aide," "Sanitation Aide," "Community Health Auxiliary/Aide," and "Community Aide," which sometimes carried different duties and responsibilities. Community health is now undertaken under a number of different titles, including not only "Community Health Representative," but also "Community Health Worker," "Community Health Educator," "Community Wellness Worker," and more specialized titles in prenatal care, diabetes, and drug and alcohol addiction.

3 Some exceptions include McPherson, "Nursing and Colonization," and Laurie Meijer Drees, "Indian Hospitals and Aboriginal Nurses: Canada and Alaska," *Canadian Bulletin of Medical History* 27, 1 (2010): 139-161.

4 Analytic literature on the CHR program actually quite closely follows the primary source material, most of which comes from the Department of National Health and Welfare, its affiliates, or its contractors and was therefore federally approved before being released to the public. Waldram, Herring, and Young's study in many ways typifies this work by dealing only momentarily with the CHR program. They argue that it "smacked of tokenism, since at the time there were no efforts to train Aboriginal people for the more advanced medical positions." *Aboriginal Health in Canada*, 253. Chantelle Richmond's work, which examines CHRs and Aboriginal Community Structure, stands apart: "Social Support as it Shapes Aboriginal Health" (PhD diss., McGill University, 2007).

5 Debbie Dedam-Montour et al., *Voices of Community Health Representatives* (Kahnawake, QC: National Indian and Inuit Community Health Representatives Organization [NIICHRO], 2010), 13.

6 LAC, RG 29, vol. 2704, file 804-4-1, pt. 1, Community Health Representatives, June 1958 to May 1973, Ethel G. Martens, "Training Public Health Auxiliary Workers in Community Development" (paper prepared for seminar at University of North Carolina, Chapel Hill, 5–9 May 1963).

7 LAC, RG 29, vol. 2704, file 804-4-1, pt. 1, Anne Grant, "Health Education at the Top of the World," reprinted from *International Journal for Health Education* 8, 1.

8 LAC, RG 29, vol. 2704, file 804-4-1, pt. 1, Ethel G. Martens, "Planning and Implementation of a Health Programme" (paper presented at the annual meeting of the Canadian Public Health Association, Winnipeg, MB, 28 May 1963).

9 "The Native people" were apparently "less apt to be appalled by the poverty and ignorance which often immobilizes someone from a more prosperous culture." Martens, "Training Public Health Auxiliary Workers in Community Development."

10 Health and Welfare Canada, *Task Force on Community Health Auxiliaries* (Ottawa: Medical Services Branch, 1973), 116.

11 Leonard Bluebird and Dorothy Krasaukas, "Canadian First Nation Control of Health: A Successful Case Study," in *Circumpolar Health 90: Proceedings of the 8th International Congress on Circumpolar Health, Whitehorse, Yukon, 20–25 May 1990*, ed. B. Postl, et al. (Winnipeg: University of Manitoba Press for the Canadian Society for Circumpolar Health, 1991). In this era, CHRs were also not invited to attend meetings about recruiting and training Community Health Workers. Not until 1977 did First Nations have the opportunity to be involved in the program, when they were invited to a meeting to develop a National CHR Curriculum Guide. Assembly of First Nations, "Community Health Representatives Proposal for Enrichment and Expansion" (background paper, 30 May 1988), 5.

12 Ethel Martens, *Mexico and Canada: A Comparison of Two Programs Where Indians are Trained in Community Development* (Ottawa: Department of National Health and Welfare, 1966), 31.

13 By 1966, it was noted that "several women were band councillors." Ethel G. Martens, "Culture and Communications—Training Indians and Eskimos as Community Health Workers," *Canadian Journal of Public Health* 57, 11(November 1966): 499.

14 LAC, RG 29, vol. 2705, file 804-4-2, pt. 1, Community Health Representatives Training, August 1956 to December 1961, "Progress Report Community Health Worker Training Programme," 15 December 1961.

15 LAC, RG 29, vol. 2706, file 804-4-2, pt 3, Community Health Representatives, Training, January 1962 to August 1967, Minute Sheet—Indian and Northern Health Services, Department of National Health and Welfare: Subject, Evaluation Study on the First Health Worker Training Program, Preliminary Report, 13 April 1964, and letter to Medical Services from Regional Superintendent, Medical Services, Central Region, 8 May 1964, Re: Preliminary Report of CHWs. See also Martens, *Mexico and Canada.*

16 Dedam-Montour et al., *Voices of Community Health Representatives*, 59.

17 Meijer Drees, "Training Aboriginal Nurses." See also Aboriginal Nurses Association of Canada, *Twice as Good: A History of Aboriginal Nurses* (Ottawa: Aboriginal Nurses Association of Canada, 2007).

18 In the job description and terms of reference for Community Health Workers, "To act as interpreter when necessary" was the seventh and last in a list of "duties." LAC, RG 29, vol. 2704, file 804-4-1, pt. 2, Community Health Workers, Medical Services, Department of National Health and Welfare. Translators not only worked in instructional capacities, but also had critical roles with respect to patients, physicians, and nurses, who may have held very disparate views of both illness and treatment. As others have argued, they are not objective, neutral intermediaries, but advocates mediating conflicting values. While unaccredited as professional or paraprofessional work, the job involves taking on multiple and sometimes conflicting roles, including that of direct translator, informant, biomedical interpreter, and patient advocate. Joseph M. Kaufert and William W. Koolage, "Role Conflict among 'Culture Brokers': The Experience of Native Canadian Medical Interpreters," *Social Science and Medicine* 18, 3 (2005): 283–86, and Joseph M. Kaufert, Robert W. Putsch, and Margaret Lavallee, "Experience of Aboriginal Health Interpreters in Mediation of Conflicting Values in End-of-Life Decision Making," *Circumpolar Health* 96 (1998): 44–45.

19 Health and Welfare Canada, *Task Force on Community Health Auxiliaries.*

20 LAC, RG 29, vol. 2709, file 804-4-x 200, pt. 1, Community Health Representatives, Manitoba Region, Winnipeg, Man. "July 1965 Narrative" by CHR Eliza English, Brochet. See also Monthly Report, Community Health Worker, Draft, September 1962, stating that people requested advice about "commercial fishing, mining, prospector licensing."

21 LAC, RG 29, vol. 2706, file 804-4-2, pt. 3, "Problems Raised by Community Health Workers—Norway House Course."

22 Valerie Galley, "Indigenization as Neoliberal Rule: The Case of the Canadian Aboriginal Head Start Initiative" (MA thesis, Trent University, 2004).

23 Martens was actually reprimanded for not following the approved lines of communication, which started with zone superintendents. Representatives of Indian Affairs and Indian Health Services met with bands and councils, gave them an "itinerary," asked for their opinion, explained their work, left posters, and requested bands to pick their own applicants. The cost per student was estimated at $55 for meals, $15 for accommodation in staff quarters, and $30 "for personal requirements." LAC, RG 29, vol. 2706, file 804-4-2, pt 2, Minutes of Meeting—Training of Eskimos, 10 August 1962; and letter to Miss E. Martens from O.J. Bath, MD, Regional Superintendent (Central), 2 April 1962.

24 LAC, RG 29, vol. 2705, file 804-4-2, pt. 1, Community Health Representatives, Training, "Native Health Worker Programme—Indian and Northern Health Services," n.d.

25 Cambridge Bay, NT (1963), Norway House, MB (1963), Fort Qu'Appelle, SK (1964), Hobbema, AB (1965), Inuvik, NT 1965), Norway House (1967), Fort Churchill, MB (1967–68), Fort Qu'Appelle (1970); Brandon, MB (1970), Moose Factory, ON (1971), Coqualeetza, BC (1971–72). There was also a two-day gathering in Thunder Bay in 1972 to discuss alcoholism, and a "Health Animator Program" began in Quebec around 1975.

26 Department of National Health and Welfare Canada, *Community Health Worker Program Analysis and Evaluation* (Ottawa: Medical Services Branch, 1967).

27 Health and Welfare Canada, *Task Force on Community Health Auxiliaries*, 116.

28 LAC, RG 29, vol. 2705, file 804-4-2, pt. 1, Community Health Representatives, Training, "Native Health Worker Programme—Indian and Northern Health Services," n/d.

29 Department of National Health and Welfare, *The Community Health Worker in Indian and Eskimo Communities Canada* (Ottawa: Medical Services Branch, 1970).

30 Dedam-Montour et al., *Voices of Community Health Representatives*, 12.

31 LAC, RG 29, vol. 2705, file 804-4-2, pt. 1, Progress Report of the Sub-Committee on the Native Health Worker Training Program, n/d.

32 LAC, RG 10, vol. 2706, file 804-4-2, pt. 4, Community Health Worker Training Program, 1965.

33 LAC, RG 29, vol. 2706, file 804-4-2, pt. 3, General Comments—Community Health Worker Programme.

34 Dorothy Stranger, interview by author, 20 January 2012.

35 Ibid.

36 LAC, RG 29, vol. 2704, file 804-4-1, pt. 2, Community Health Workers, Medical Services, Department of National Health and Welfare; RG 29, vol. 2706, file 804-4-2, pt. 2, letter to the Director, Medical Services, from O.J. Rath, Regional Superintendent, Central Region, 20 February 1963.

3 LAC, RG 29, vol. 2706, file 804-4-2, pt. 3, Community Health Representative Training July 1963–August 1964.

38 The maximum age for CHRs was 64. Martens, "Culture and Communications," 497.

39 LAC, RG 29, vol. 2704, file 804-4-1, pt. 2, Medical Services, Department of National Health and Welfare, Community Health Workers, September 1965.

40 Edward J. Abramson, Robert Arnold, and Gerald Piper, *The Community Health Worker Program: A Critical Analysis and Evaluation* (Ottawa: Medical Services, National Department of Health and Welfare, 1964), 28–29.

41 Martens, "Training Public Health Auxiliary Workers in Community Development," 12.

42 Northern Affairs paid for Inuit CHR training, and eventually the process was run through Manpower. LAC, RG, vol. 2704, file 804-4-1, pt 2, Medical Services, Department of National Health and Welfare, Community Health Workers, September 1965.

43 Stranger, interview.

44 Dedam-Montour et al., *Voices of Community Health Representatives*, 20.

45 LAC, RG 29, vol. 2706, file 804-4-2, pt 4, Memorandum to Director, Medical Services, from Regional Superintendent, Foothills Region, M. Matas, 13 July 1965.

46 Adams, *The Trouble with Normal.*

47 Cora J. Voyageur, "The Community Owns You: Experiences of Female Chiefs in Canada," in *Out of the Ivory Tower: Feminist Research for Social Change*, ed. Andrea Martinez and Meryn Stuart (Toronto: Sumach Press, 2003), 228–47.

48 Abramson, Arnold, and Piper, *Community Health Worker Program*, 16–17.

49 Dave Quance, "Nancy Ferguson, 27, is Nurse to 1,400 Saskatchewan Indians," *Winnipeg Tribune*, 12 January 1957,clipping in the 10, 5 (January–February 1957).

50 Susan Hartman, "Women's Employment and the Domestic Ideal in the Early Cold War Years," in *Not June Cleaver: Women and Gender in Postwar America, 1945–1960*, ed. Joanne Myerowitz (Philadelphia: Temple University Press, 1994).

51 There is a lot of material from which to draw here; for example, see Bureau of Northwest Territories and Yukon Affairs, *The Book of Wisdom for Eskimo* (Ottawa: Lands, Parks and Forest Branch, Department of Mines and Resources, 1947) and Department of National Health and Welfare, *A Book for Mother* and *The Pre-Schooler* (Ottawa: Indian and Northern Health Services, 1958). Felt boards were popular teaching tools for children in the 1960s and 1970s. They looked like blackboards, but were made of felt and displayed images and words also made of felt.

52 See, for example, Elaine Tyler May, *Homeward Bound: American Families in the Cold War Era* (New York: Basic Books, 1988); Adams, *The Trouble with Normal;* and Mona Gleason, *Normalizing the Ideal: Psychology, Schooling, and the Family in Postwar Canada* (Toronto: University of Toronto Press, 1999).

53 Stacey O'Brien, "Jennie Nielsen," *Lethbridge Herald*, 5 June 2006, A3.

54 Helen Gilbert, "Great Adventures in Nursing." Meijer Drees and McBain argue that nurses in northern Saskatchewan "spent little of their social time within the Aboriginal communities they served." They suggest that a "prevailing attitude of superiority and the social distance some nurses felt from the communities they served...could also have been related to the fact that most were unmarried during their terms of service in the north, and that their service hours were long." Laurie Meijer Drees and Lesley McBain, "Nursing and Native Peoples in Northern Saskatchewan: 1930s–1950s," *Canadian Bulletin of Medical History* 18, 1 (2001): 56, 58.

55 Joan Sangster, "Constructing the 'Eskimo' Wife: White Women's Travel Writing, Colonialism, and the Canadian North, 1940–60," in *Creating Postwar Canada: Community, Diversity, and Dissent 1945–1975*, ed. Magda Fahrni and Robert Rutherdale (Vancouver: University of British Columbia Press, 2007), 23–44, and Chrys Ingraham, *White Weddings: Romancing Heterosexuality in Popular Culture* (New York: Routledge, 1999).

56 Intermarriage was discussed by the MSB in remote terms, as something that happened in "former times" between fur traders and Native women. See, for example, LAC, RG 29, vol. 2912, file 851-1-A501, pt 1, "Health and Disease at the Norway House Indian Agency." Otherwise, the MSB spoke of the biology of mixed-race children, focussing on their capacity to be healthier, smarter, and with "admirable qualities" (for which the "white blood" accounted). Elsewhere, encounters between white men and Native women were sexualized as deviant, dangerous, and coerced, while intermarriage between Native men and white women factored into the First and Second World War experience of Aboriginal men while "away."

57 Elijah became a CBC radio announcer and was part of the Eskimo Affairs Committee in 1958; while Elijah was in Ottawa, two nieces visited and were placed by a social worker as au pairs. Later, it was said that "Government officials are proud of the two marriages. Northern experts regard them as the best possible advertising for their claim that full integration is a realistic objective." Bruce Phillips, "Fraternization Has Happy Ending" and "Two Girls Happily Wed to Eskimos," in "Officials Approve Women Marry Eskimo Husbands," *Camsell Arrow* 13, 3 (January–March 1960), 74.

58 LAC, RG 29, vol. 2705, file 804-4-2, pt. 1, letter to Regional Superintendent, Foothills Region, INHS Edmonton, from Zone Superintendent, Yukon Zone, NDD MacKinnon, 24 September 1958.

59 LAC, RG 29, vol. 2705, file 804-4-2, pt. 1, letter to Regional Superintendent, Eastern Region, from H.B. Sabeen, MD, Medical Officer, Pangnirtung, 2 May 1958.

60 Abramson, Arnold, and Piper, *The Community Health Worker Program*, 16–17.

61 LAC, RG 29, vol. 2706, file 804-4-2, pt 4, Minutes of the Meeting of Committees to Plan Community Health Worker Training Program, Northwest Territories, 1966.

62 LAC, RG 29, vol. 2706, file 804-4-2, pt. 3, letter to Regional Superintendent, Medical Services, Central Region, from Zone Superintendent, Southern Manitoba Zone, J.G. Nicholas, Re: Health Aide Evaluation Study, 15 May 1964.

63 LAC, RG 29, vol. 2706, file 804-4-2, pt. 3, letter to Medical Services from Regional Superintendent, Medical Services, Central Region, Re: Preliminary Report of CHWs, 8 May 1964.

64 LAC, RG 29, vol. 2706, file 804-4-2, pt. 4, Minutes of the Meeting of Committees to Plan Community Health Worker Training Program, Northwest Territories, 1966.

65 LAC, RG 29, vol. 2706, file 804-4-2, pt. 2, Community Health Worker Training Program, Foothills Region Meeting, 26 November 1962.

66 LAC, RG 29, vol. 2706, file 804-4-2, pt 4, Minutes of the Meeting of Committees to Plan Community Health Worker Training Program, Northwest Territories, 1966.

67 LAC, RG 29, vol. 2705, file 804-4-2, pt. 1, letter to Regional Superintendent, Eastern Region, from H.B. Sabeen, MD, Medical Officer, Pangnirtung, 2 May 1958.

68 LAC, RG 29, vol. 2705, file 804-4-2, pt. 1, Progress Report of the Sub-Committee on the Native Health Worker Training Program, n.d., Ethel G. Martens, Chairman.

69 LAC, RG 29, vol. 2707, file 804-4-2, pt. 7B, "Community Health Worker Training Programme Fort Churchill, Manitoba."

70 LAC, RG 29 vol. 2705, file 804-4-2, pt. 1, letter to Regional Superintendent, Eastern Region, from H.B. Sabeen, MD, Medical Officer, Pangnirtung, 2 May 1958.

71 By 1973, it was noted that only in the Manitoba, Saskatchewan, and "Northern regions" did training programs have more men than women.

72 Nancy Marian Gerein, "The Community Health Representative in Alberta: A Program Evaluation" (MSc thesis, University of British Columbia, 1977), 21.

73 Health and Welfare Canada, *Task Force on Community Health Auxiliaries*, Appendix B.

74 RG 29, vol. 2706, file 804-4-2, pt. 4, Minutes of the Meeting of Committees to Plan Community Health Worker Training Program, Northwest Territories, 1966.

75 RG 29, vol. 2706, file 804-4-2, pt. 3, news release, "Self Help Programme for Indians," 21 April 1964. As the program became more standardized, CHRs were to undertake three projects during their orientation: make a map of their community showing houses and facilities; do a "community appraisal," which included the populations of various age groups, types of housing available, and health statistics; and undertake an interview survey of their people's health knowledge. Department of National Health and Welfare, *The Community Health Worker.*

76 Stranger, interview.

77 Health and Welfare Canada, *Task Force on Community Health Auxiliaries*, 69.

78 Travel expenses for staff were covered by their own department headquarters. LAC, RG 29, vol. 2705, file 804-4-2, pt. 1, Intradepartmental Correspondence to the Director, Indian and Northern Health Services, from Central Regional Office, Winnipeg, 17 November 1961.

79 If CHRs were receiving relief assistance, then it was deducted from their wages drawn from training. LAC, RG 29, vol. 2706, file 804-4-2, pt. 3, letter to John Joseph Leveque, Indian Hospital Fort Qu'Appelle, from A.G. Leslie, Regional Supervisor of Indian Agencies, 28 April 1964.

80 LAC, RG 29, vol. 2706, file 804-4-2, pt. 2, Community Health Worker Meeting, 29 October 1962. The one hundred dollars was based on the amount Indian Affairs paid to students taking technical training: $64 per month for maintenance allowance, $15 per month spending allowance, and $20 per month clothing allowance. It was noted in this

meeting that it was necessary to pay the men as much as a caretaker. RG 29, vol. 2705, file 804-4-2, pt. 1, Minutes of a Meeting of the Regional Committee on the Native Health Worker Training Program, held in Indian Health Services Office, Winnipeg, 9 March 1961.

81 LAC, RG 29, vol. 2707, file 804-4-2, pt. 7B, "1970 Community Health Worker Training Programme, Fort San, Saskatchewan," 5.

82 The program materials for the CHR course at Fort Qu'Appelle outlined the activities that had to be performed by each of the students, which included: give a two-minute talk to a group; give a five-minute talk to a group; use a filmstrip projector; use a 16-mm movie projector; give a talk using a filmstrip; introduce a movie; prepare a felt-board display; give a presentation using a felt-board display; prepare a flip chart; give a presentation using a flip chart (i.e. teaching); prepare a poster; prepare a bulletin board display; use the duplicator; lead a discussion; write a letter; fill in a report form; use the tape recorder; give a chalk talk; prepare a lesson plan; introduce a speaker; plan for a meeting; and give a fifteen-minute talk to a group. LAC, RG 29, vol. 2706, file 804-4-2, pt. 3, General Comments—Community Health Worker Programme.

83 LAC, RG 29, vol. 2706, file 804-4-2, pt. 3, General Comments—Community Health Worker Programme; RG 29, vol. 2704, file 804-4-1, pt. 1, Grant, "Health Education at the Top of the World."

84 LAC, RG 29, vol. 2706, file 804-4-2, pt. 2, Community Health Worker Training Program for Cambridge Bay, NWT.

85 LAC, RG 29, vol. 2704, file 804-4-1, pt. 1, Grant, "Health Education at the Top of the World."

86 LAC, RG 29, vol. 2706, file 804-4-2, pt. 3, Community Health Worker Training Program, Cambridge Bay Progress Report, 20 July 1963.

87 Illness topics covered impetigo, lice, scabies, gastrointestinal disorders, rabies, diabetes, alcohol and drug addiction, and also surveys of hepatitis, venereal disease, polio, X-rays, immunizations, and tuberculosis. "Germ theory" organized much of these discussions. Child and maternal health topics included pre- and postnatal care, bathing the baby, feeding (breast and formula), well-baby clinics, and neglected children. Food topics included diet, vitamins, nutrition, shopping, and budgeting. Water and waste management topics included garbage disposal, privy construction, spring clean-ups, and water testing and purification. Pest control focussed on but was not limited to dogs and flies.

88 Health and Welfare Canada, *Task Force on Community Health Auxiliaries*, 144.

89 LAC, RG 29, vol. 2704, file 804-2-1, Native Education and Training. "Community Health Workers For Indian and Northern Health Services Department of National Health and Welfare," 1961.

90 LAC, RG 29, vol. 2707, file 804-4-2, pt. 7B, Memorandum to Regional Director, Ontario from Regional Sanitarian F. Cayer, 14 October 1970.

91 Paule McNicoll, Frank Tester and Peter Kulchyski, "Arctic Abstersion: *The Book of Wisdom for Eskimo*, Modernism and Inuit Assimilation," *Etudes Inuit Studies* 23, 1–2 (1999): 199–220.

92 This was also the case for health aides in Alaska. Meijer Drees, "Indian Hospitals and Aboriginal Nurses."

93 LAC, RG 29, vol. 2705, file 804-4-2, pt. 1, letter to Director, Indian Affairs Branch, from P.E. Moore, Re: Indian Adult Health Education and the Training of Health Workers, 28 October 1958. Moore conceded that "generally speaking, the bands that require the services of health workers are probably those bands which are the most impoverished and hence most likely in need of household and community hygiene." RG 29, vol. 2705,

file 804-4-2, pt. 1, letter to P.E. Moore, Indian and Northern Health Services, from H.M. Jones, 21 November 1960.

94 LAC, RG 29, vol. 2705, file 804-4-2, pt. 1, letter to P.E. Moore, Indian and Northern Health Services, from H.M. Jones, 21 November 1960.

95 LAC, RG 29, vol. 2704, file 804-4-1, pt. 2, Community Health Workers, Medical Services, Department of National Health and Welfare.

96 LAC, RG 29, vol. 2706, file 804-4-2, pt. 3, "Problems Raised by Community Health Workers—Norway House Course."

97 LAC, RG 29, vol. 2704, file 804-4-1, pt. 2, Community Health Workers, Medical Services, Department of National Health and Welfare.

98 LAC, RG 29, vol. 2704, file 804-4-1, pt. 1, Community Health Workers for Indian and Northern Health Services, Department of National Health and Welfare, c. 1961.

99 LAC, RG 29, vol. 2704, file 804-4-1, pt. 1, Extract from the minutes of a meeting of the Treasury Board, held in Ottawa, on 11 March 1963.

100 LAC, RG 29, vol. 2705, file 804-4-2, pt. 1, Minutes of a Meeting of the Regional Committee on the Native Health Worker Training Program, held in Indian Health Services Office, Winnipeg, 9 March 1961.

101 LAC, RG 29, vol. 2705, file 804-4-2, pt. 1, Minutes of a Meeting of the Committee on the Native Health Worker Training Program, 14 February 1961.

102 LAC, RG 29, vol. 2706, file 804-4-2, pt. 3, letter from J.H. Wiebe, incomplete, n.d.; and Minute Sheet, Indian and Northern Health Services, Department of National Health and Welfare, Subject: Reports on Follow-up Visit on Community Health Worker Training Program, 29 January 1964. "Allowances for dependents" was argued as a justification for higher wages for Indian men CHRs.

103 LAC, RG 29, vol. 2705, file 804-4-2, pt. 1, Minutes of a Meeting of the Committee on the Native Health Worker Training Program, 14 February 1961.

104 LAC, RG 29, vol. 2706, file 804-4-2, pt. 3, letter to Regional Superintendent, Medical Services, Central Region, from Zone Superintendent, Southern Manitoba Zone, J.G. Nicholas, Re Health Aide Evaluation Study, 15 May 1964.

105 LAC, RG 29, vol. 2706, file 804-4-2, pt. 4, letter to the Regional Superintendent, Foothills Region, Medical Services, from Regional Dietitian, W. Roscoe, Foothills Region, 18 May 1965.

106 Dedam-Montour et al., *Voices of Community Health Representatives*, 72.

107 LAC, RG 29, vol. 2706, file 804-4-2, pt. 2, Community Health Worker Training Program, Foothills Region, 26 November 1962.

108 LAC, RG 29, vol. 2704, file 804-4-1, pt. 1, Extract from the minutes of a meeting of the Treasury Board, held at Ottawa on 11 March 1963.

109 Abramson, Arnold, and Piper, *Community Health Worker Program*, 27.

110 LAC, RG 29, vol. 2704, file 804-4-1 pt. 2, "Medical Services Department of National Health and Welfare Community Health Workers," September 1965.

111 Canadian Human Rights Commission, *Public Service Alliance of Canada v Treasury Board*, T.D. 4/91, 19 March 1991, p. 19, http://decisions.chrt-tcdp.gc.ca/chrt-tcdp/archive/en/item/7053/index.do?r=AAAAAQAycHVibGljIHNlcnZpYZUgYWx saWFuY2Ugb2YgY2FuYWRhIHYgdHJlYXN1cnkgYm9hcmQAAAAAAQ (accessed 14 January 2014).

112 Ibid., 20.

113 Ibid., 31. The Canadian Human Rights Commission complaint came from the Public Service Alliance, which alleged that the wages paid to CHRs contravened the Human

Rights Act (sec. 7, 10, and 11) on the grounds of "systemic discrimination" resulting in unequal pay between men and women. At the time, it was argued that CHRs participated in "women's work" and were thus compensated on a different scale. The problem with the 1987 decision (besides the seemingly arbitrary date of 1980, which cuts off almost twenty years worth of CHR labour history) was that it compensated only those who had worked and were still working as public servants. NIICHRO pursued the issue, arguing that no CHRs who worked on band contracts would benefit from this wage-parity decision. Thus, if they were excluded from compensation because they were employed by Indians, then in a very real way, this was a case not only about gender but also about racial discrimination. Compensation forms, available through NIICHRO, continue to be filed by the over 1,000 CHRs.

114 LAC, RG 29, vol. 2706, file 804-4-2, pt. 2, Community Health Worker Meeting held 29 October 1962 at the regional office to discuss the number of delegates, place, time, and feasibility for this program for Eskimos in the Foothills Region.

115 For example, for the training program to be held at Cambridge Bay, two daily meals were prepared for CHRs by one of two local women. They had been allocated $300 for four hours daily per month for a cook to prepare meals for eight people. LAC, RG 29, vol. 2706, file 804-4-2, pt. 2, Meeting Concerning Community Health Workers Training Program, 29 March 1963. It was suggested that cooks and housekeepers hired for the 1965 CHW program at Hobbema, AB, be "two Eskimo girls" in an on-the-job training plan. It was hoped that three cooks could be obtained from Family Institute courses in Hobbema, to be paid salaries of $310 to $375 per month. In addition, a cook's helper was to be paid $250 per month. Cleaning of the classroom was arranged locally (hired from among the clinic and residence cleaning staff) at a wage of $1.25 per hour for a kitchen maid and housemaid. Miss Martens also requested part-time secretarial help for the duration of the training program. LAC, RG 29, vol. 2706, file 804-4-2, pt. 4, Community Health Workers Training Program 1965, Regional Planning Committee Minutes, 28 June 1965.

116 Patricia Verge, *Angus, from the Heart: The Life of Counsellor Angus Cowan* (Cochrane, AB: Springtide Publishing, 1999).

117 Jennifer A. Stephen, *Pick One Intelligent Girl.*

118 In her comparative work on a similar program in Mexico, it is clear that Martens was partial to Mexican programming, which involved all government agencies cooperatively working in the area, as opposed to the situation in Canada, in which Indian services were relegated to either Indian Affairs or Health Canada. Martens was also involved in the Navajo Cornell Field Health Project, which trained Navajo women as health workers, and had researched a program of "sanitation aides" in Alaska.

119 LAC, RG 29, vol. 2705, file 804-4-2, pt. 1, "Self-help for Canadian Indians," Ethel G. Martens, *International Journal of Health Education.*

120 LAC, RG 29, vol. 2704, file 804-4-1, pt. 1, Martens, "Planning and Implementation of a Health Programme."

121 LAC, RG 29, vol. 2705, file 804-4-2, pt. 1, "Native Health Worker Programme, Indian and Northern Health Services."

122 LAC, RG 29, vol. 2709, file 804-4-x200, pt. 1, letter to Miss Voth, Nurse in Charge Island Lake Nursing Station from Ethel Martens, Health Educator, 19 March 1962.

123 According to the Department of Labour, "Under these laws a woman employee who considers that her rate of pay is not equal to that paid to a male fellow employee doing the same kind of work may make a complaint to the Department of Labour which administers the Act, and there is a provision for investigation of the complaint and for redress if it is well founded." Department of Labour, *Women at Work in Canada* (Ottawa: The Queen's Printer, 1959), 70.

124 LAC, RG 29, vol. 2704, file 804-4-1, pt. 1, Programme Suggestions for Community Health Workers, 1–6, and Suggested Programme for Community Health Workers (Women), 1–2.

125 Dedam-Montour et al., *Voices of Community Health Representatives*, 20.

126 LAC, RG 29, vol. 2704, file 804-4-1, pt. 1, Martens, "Planning and Implementation of a Health Programme."

127 Department of National Health and Welfare, *The Community Health Worker*, 3.

128 Stranger, interview.

129 The program required the cooperation of sympathetic field nurses, but the region was also chosen because it had a large population with a high incidence of disease. Health and Welfare Canada, *Task Force on Community Health Auxiliaries*, 117.

130 LAC, RG 29, vol. 2706, file 804-4-2, pt. 2, Meeting concerning the Community Health Workers Training Program, 29 March 1963. One of the concerns of CHRs in the late 1960s was that nurses could fire them at will if they could not get along, treating them akin to "casual workers." LAC, RG 29, vol. 2704, file 804-4-1, pt. 2, letter to Director General, Medical Services, from Adviser, Health Education, Medical Services, 11 July 1969.

131 LAC, RG 29, vol. 2706, file 804-4-2, pt. 2, letter to Mr. J. Staunton, Superintendent Indian Affairs Branch, Rossville, Manitoba, from Martens, 27 March 1962; RG 29, vol. 2704, file 804-4-1, pt. 1, Martens, "Training Public Health Auxiliary Workers"; and RG 29, vol. 2706, file 804-4-2, pt. 3, General Comments—Community Health Worker Programme.

132 Standardized forms assessed CHR work in eight parts: *Home visits* (alone and with nurse); *Meetings* (including details on the subject, attendance, and teaching aids used; *Projects* (including pre- and postnatal care; housing and sanitation; social events; dental health; and substance abuse programs); *Teaching and teaching aids used*; *Films and filmstrips shown*; *How many people came to ask for advice? Explain information given*; and *Plans for the next month*. Another form outlined the "correct" answers to the eight sections and raised questions if the CHR's actual response did not conform. There were also personal appraisal reports to be filled out by the nurse regarding the evaluation of the functioning of the CHR. LAC, RG 29, vol. 2711, file 804-4-X300, pt. 1, Community Health Representatives, Saskatchewan Region, Regina, May 1966 to February 1978, Review of Community Health Worker Monthly Reports, 1971; RG 29, vol. 2704, file 804-4-1, pt. 1, Evaluation of Community Health Worker Report and Programme in General; and author's review of monthly CHR reports.

133 Between 1949 and 1959, nursing stations rose in number from 18 to 41, and health centres from 37 to 108. Nursing stations dealt with maternity cases, childhood illness, and minor accidents. They were usually staffed by a graduate nurse, a practical assistant, and a fireman-labourer. Health centres consisted of a dwelling and an office and were staffed by a nurse, who provided medical attention within the limits of her resources. Her chief concerns were the planning and implementation of a public health program, home visiting, educating, and inoculating. Canada, Department National Health and Welfare, *Annual Report*, 1948–49, 1954–55, and 1958–59.

134 LAC, RG 29, vol. 2704, file 804-4-1, pt 2, "Questionnaire on Role of Community Health Workers as Seen by Field Nursing Staff," November 1965.

135 High rates of turnover also, as Abramson explains, meant little development of "personal knowledge by the white personnel of the Indian people. This limits their ability to serve in selection or supervision of the community health worker, particularly when consideration of the many types of social work that are likely to accrete to the basic functions of the worker is involved." Abramson, Arnold, and Piper, *Community Health Worker Program*, 11.

136 LAC, RG 29, vol. 2704, file 804-4-1, pt 2, "Some Observations on the Community Health Worker Program" by Margaret Stott.

137 Department of National Health and Welfare, *The Community Health Worker*, 1970.

138 While the image of the MSB nurse has her working in an undefined vast wilderness, one of her original and primary tasks was to visit the domestic sphere of Indian people, where, it was hoped, she would teach about housekeeping and child care. The domestic work of IHS nurses has been interpreted more as a factor of white women's disciplinary, colonial, and scientific gaze than as a factor of earlier associations of nursing with domesticity and domestic work. How could the Indigenous home, as opposed to the hospital or clinic, be the workspace of the professionalizing nurse?

139 Department of National Health and Welfare, *Community Health Worker*, 1970; and LAC, RG 29, vol. 2704, file 804-4-1, pt. 2, "Questionnaire on Role of Community Health Workers as Seen by Field Nursing Staff," November 1965.

140 Health and Welfare Canada, *Task Force on Community Health Auxiliaries*, 124.

141 Abramson, Arnold, and Piper, *Community Health Worker Program*, 28.

142 LAC, RG 29, vol. 2706, file 804-4-2, pt. 3, letter to Regional Superintendent, Medical Services, Central Region, from Zone Superintendent, Southern Manitoba Zone, J.G. Nicholas, Re: Health Aide Evaluation Study, 15 May 1964.

143 LAC, RG 29, vol. 2706, file 804-4-2, pt. 3, letter to Medical Services from Regional Superintendent, Medical Services, Central Region, Re: Preliminary Report of CHWs, 8 May 1964.

144 LAC, RG 29, vol. 2706, file 804-4-2, pt. 3, letter to Medical Services from Regional Superintendent, Medical Services, Central Region, Re: Preliminary Report of CHWs, 8 May 1964.

145 LAC, RG 29, vol. 2706, file 804-4-2, pt. 4, Memorandum to all Regional Superintendents, Medical Services, from Director, Medical Services, Re: Committee on Community Health Workers, 20 July 1965.

146 LAC, RG 29, vol. 2706, file 804-4-2, pt 2, to Mr. J. Staunton, Superintendent, Indian Affairs Branch, Rossville, Manitoba, from Martens, 27 March 1962.

147 LAC, RG 29, vol. 2704, file 804-2-1, "Community Health Workers for Indian and Northern Health Services, Department of National Health and Welfare," 1961.

148 LAC, RG 29, vol. 2704, file 804-4-1, pt 2, Medical Services Department of National Health and Welfare Community Health Workers, September 1965, 3.

149 LAC, RG 29, vol. 2704, file 804-4-1, pt. 1, Ethel G. Martens, "Training Public Health Auxiliary Workers in Community Development," 9.

150 LAC, RG 29, vol. 2704, file 804-4-1, pt. 2, "Some observations on the Community Health Worker Program" by Margaret Stott.

151 LAC, RG 29, vol. 2704, file 804-4-1, pt. 2, "The Community Health Worker in Indian and Eskimo Communities, A New Member of the Health Team," 7.

152 LAC, RG 29 vol. 2707 file 804-4-2 pt. 7B, "1970 Community Health Worker Training Programme, Fort San, Saskatchewan," 5.

153 Stranger, interview.

154 Dedam-Montour et al., *Voices of Community Health Representatives.*

155 Stranger, interview.

156 Stranger, interview.

157 Health and Welfare Canada, *Task Force on Community Health Auxiliaries*, 9.

158 Ibid., 121.

159 Ibid., 123.

160 Abramson, Arnold, and Piper, *Community Health Worker Program*, 10–11.

161 Ibid., 10–11.

162 LAC, RG 29, vol. 2704, file 804-4-1, pt. 2, Medical Services Department of National Health and Welfare Community Health Workers, September 1965.

163 Notably, hunting and fishing seasons posed problems for recruitment, as well as for the "effectiveness" and "efficiency" of CHRs.

164 LAC, RG 29, vol. 2704, file 804-4-1, pt. 2, "Some Observations on the Community Health Worker Program," by Margaret Stott.

165 LAC, RG 29, vol. 2707, file 804-4-2, pt. 7B, Community Health Worker Training Programme Fort San, Saskatchewan, 1970.

166 Abramson, Arnold and Piper, *Community Health Worker Program*, 12.

167 LAC, RG 29, vol. 2706, file 804-4-2, pt. 4, letter to Dr. Matas, Regional Superintendent, Foothills Region, from Steering Committee, 7 October 1964.

168 LAC, RG 29, vol. 2706, file 804-4-2, pt. 3, letter to Regional Superintendent, Medical Services, Central Region, from Zone Superintendent, Southern Manitoba Zone, J.G. Nicholas, Re: Health Aide Evaluation Study, 15 May 1964.

169 Health and Welfare Canada, *Task Force on Community Health Auxiliaries*, 28.

170 LAC, RG 29, vol. 2711, file 804-4-X300, pt. 1, Contract for CHRs. Band contracts raised several important questions about CHR work: for example, should nurses be involved in negotiating contracts, and how; could CHRs drive Crown-owned vehicles for their work; who paid for insurance, and who was responsible in the event of an accident; was a contract employee a Crown employee; could Métis people be paid for orientation allowances; and were band employees by definition federal public servants?

171 LAC, RG 29, vol. 2704, file 804-4-1, pt. 2, letter to Director General, Medical Services, from Adviser, Health Education, Medical Services, 11 July 1969. In at least one monthly report, CHRs were involved in placing a child in a foster home and inquiring about welfare for orphans.

172 LAC, RG 29, vol. 2704, file 804-4-1, pt. 2, letter to Director General, Medical Services, from Adviser, Health Education, Medical Services, 11 July 1969.

173 LAC, RG 29, vol. 2704, file 804-4-1, pt. 2, Memorandum to Director General, Medical Services, from Adviser, Health Education, Medical Services Re: Community Health Worker Project, 11 July 1969.

174 Dedam-Montour et al., *Voices of Community Health Representatives*, 55.

175 LAC, RG 29, vol. 2705, file 804-4-2, pt. 1, letter to P.E. Moore, Indian and Northern Health Services, from H.M. Jones, 21 November 1960.

176 Health and Welfare Canada, *Task Force on Community Health Auxiliaries*, 9.

177 Ibid., 95.

178 See, for example, Kelm, *Colonizing Bodies*; Lux–*Medicine That Walks;* Waldram, Herring, and Young, *Aboriginal Health in Canada*; Patricia Jasen, "Race, Culture, and the Colonization of Childbirth in Northern Canada"; and Milloy, *A National Crime*.

Chapter Four: Gaining Recognition: Labour as Activism Among Indigenous Nurses

1 The organization has gone through a number of name changes: Registered Nurses of Canadian Indian Ancestry (1975–1983), Indian and Inuit Nurses of Canada (1983–1992), and Aboriginal Nurses Association of Canada (1992–present).

2 Jean Goodwill, "Nursing Canada's Indigenous People," Editorial, *Canadian Nurse* 80, 1 (January 1984): 6.

3 See, for example, Mary-Ellen Kelm and Aboriginal Nurses Association of Canada, *Thirty Years of Community: Aboriginal Nurses Association of Canada* (Ottawa: Aboriginal Nurses Association of Canada, 2005), and Aboriginal Nurses Association of Canada, *Aboriginal Nurses Association of Canada: Working Together for Quality Nursing Care and Healing, 1975–1995* (Ottawa: Aboriginal Nurses Association of Canada, 1995).

4 See, for example, Alice J. Baumgart and Jenniece Larsen, *Canadian Nursing Faces the Future: Development and Change* (Toronto: C.V. Mosby, 1988), and Marjorie McIntyre, Elizabeth Thomlinson, Carol McDonald, eds., *Realities of Canadian Nursing: Professional, Practice, and Power Issues*, 2nd ed. (Philadelphia: Lippincott, Williams and Wilkins, 2006).

5 For example, Jean Goodwill, an influential Cree nurse critical to the founding of the organization, has been celebrated as the "first Aboriginal woman in Canada to complete her nursing training." Meijer Drees and McBain, "Nursing and Native Peoples in Northern Saskatchewan: 1930s to 1950s," 61–62. The authors mark the date of Goodwill's graduation as the starting point at which Aboriginal people entered the medical system as nurses. Earning her RN in 1954, Goodwill was not the first Aboriginal nurse, but she represents in many ways a generation of Aboriginal nurses inasmuch as a large number of people identified with her and with the issues in Native nursing that she talked about.

6 Aboriginal Nurses Association of Canada, *Twice As Good.*

7 LAC, Record Group R11504 - Aboriginal Association of Canada (Heareafter R11504), vol. 1, file 1-8, no author, "History of the Indian and Inuit Nurses of Canada," n.d., c. 1990. By 1990, RNCIA had grown to approximately 400 members.

8 Jocelyn Bruyere and Tom Dignan, "Taking the Power Back: Native Women Organize," interview by Johnny Yesno, host, *Our Native Land*, Canadian Broadcasting Corporation, 30 August 1975, http://www.cbc.ca/archives/discover/programs/o/our-native-land-1/taking-the-power-back-native-women-organize.html (accessed 4 February 2014).

9 LAC, R11504, vol. 1, file 1-8, no author, "History," no date, ca 1980.

10 In 1982, RNCIA member Carol Prince met with the American Indian Nurses Association, then struggling under the Reagan administration. Aboriginal Nurses Association of Canada Records at Headquarters (hereafter ANAC), Registered Nurses of Canadian Indian Ancestry, conference proceedings, "How Poverty Affects Indian Women and Their Health," Winnipeg, MB, 11–13 June 1982, 9-10. The American Indian Nurses Association disbanded in 1984, but led to the founding of the National Native Alaska North American Indian Nurses Association. Organizationally, the ANAC also cultivated significant ties with provincial and national registered nurse associations, as well as feminist organizations and Aboriginal political organizations.

11 The Congress of Aboriginal and Torres Straight Islander Nurses (CATSIN) was founded in 1997.

12 For analyses of nursing and colonization, see Dea Birkett, "The 'White Woman's Burden' in the 'White Man's Grave': The Introduction of British Nurses in Colonial West Africa," in *Western Women and Imperialism: Complicity and Resistance*, ed. Nupur Chaudhuri and Margaret Strobel (Bloomington: Indiana University Press, 1992), 177–88;

Meijer Drees and McBain, "Nursing and Native People in Northern Saskatchewan"; Kathryn McPherson, "Nursing and Colonization: The Work of Indian Health Services Nurses in Manitoba, 1945–1970," and Gilbert, "Great Adventures in Nursing."

13 Jean Cuthand Goodwill, "Indian and Inuit Nurses of Canada," *Canadian Woman Studies* 10, 2–3 (1989): 119, and Aboriginal Nurses Association of Canada, *Working Together*, 4–5. In an early history of the organization it was recorded that, "To date, the RNCIA has made several sincere efforts to try to get their objectives underway as stated in the constitutions…nothing materialized for the RNCIA but during this time the National Indian Brotherhood was able to get funding from Medical Services to set a National Commission Inquiry on Indian Health consisting of representatives from each of the provincial and territorial associations. In addition to their Health Coordinator they hired a Medical Consultant. This commission has held a series of meetings since November 1978 which has generated a lot of interest on health related activities in most provinces and at the national level. One RNCIA member, Grace Easter, sits on the commission representing Four Nations Confederacy." LAC, R11504, vol. 1, file 1-8, "History."

14 Aboriginal Nurses Association of Canada, *Working Together*, 3.

15 LAC, R11504, vol. 1, file 1-8, Jean Goodwill, "History of IINC," no date, ca. 1990, 6 and 7.

16 Kelm and Aboriginal Nurses Association of Canada, *Thirty Years of Community*, 7.

17 Fiske, "The Womb Is to the Nation as the Heart Is to the Body," 84; Aboriginal Circle of the Canadian Panel on Violence Against Women, *Changing the Landscape: Ending Violence—Achieving Equality* (Ottawa: Minister of Supply and Services, 1993), 143.

18 The White Paper proposed to terminate the Indian Act, disintegrate treaties, dismember tribal communities, and dissolve Indian status in Canada.

19 Jean Cuthand Goodwill, "Organized Political Action: Indian and Inuit Nurses of Canada," in Baumgart and Larsen, *Canadian Nursing Faces the Future*, 501.

20 Cheryl Petten, "Jean Goodwill: Health Care Worker Encouraged Youth," *Windspeaker*, Footprints, http://www.ammsa.com/content/jean-goodwill-footprints (accessed 4 February 2014).

21 "Profiles: Jean Cuthand Goodwill," *Canadian Woman Studies* 10, 2–3 (1989): 121.

22 It was recorded in 1971 that Goodwill had been "a member of the following: the Indian-Eskimo Association of Canada, the National Indian Council, the National Indian Princess Pageant Committee, the National Native News Service Committee, and was a consultant on the committee for the Canadian Correction Association report 'Indians and the Law.' She toured with the Canadian Prairie Inter-Tribal Dancers in Holland and France in 1969. Lately she has been involved in the study for the Royal Commission on the Status of Women, with particular reference to recommendations concerning Indian and Eskimo women; has assisted in the planning and co-ordination of the National Indian Cultural Conference, 1970–1; has reviewed textbooks for the Ontario Department of Education; and has served as Chairman of the Steering Committee for the formation of a National Native Women's Association." Jean Goodwill, "A New Horizon for Native Women in Canada," in *Citizen Participation: Canada: A Book of Readings*, ed. James A. Draper, (Toronto: New Press, 1971), 369–70.

23 Petten, "Jean Goodwill"; Doug Cuthand, "Saskatchewan Loses Esteemed Health Advocate," *Saskatchewan Indian* 27, 4 (Winter 1997): 21. Doug Cuthand, "Goodwill, Jean Cuthand (1928–97)," *The Encyclopedia of Saskatchewan*, http://esask.uregina.ca/entry/goodwill_jean_cuthand_1928-97.html (accessed 4 February 2014).

24 LAC, R11504, vol. 1, file 1-8, No Author, No Title, "Draft," No Date, ca. 1988.

25 LAC, R11504, vol. 1, file 1-8, "History of the Indian and Inuit Nurses of Canada."

26 LAC, R11504, vol. 1, file 1-8. Madeleine Stout, "The Association of Registered Nurses of Canadian Indian Ancestry: Achievements and Future Prospects," unpublished paper prepared for Dr. J. Scholdra, University of Lethbridge (14 April 1982), 9.

27 LAC, R11504, vol. 1, file 1-8, No Author, "For N.T." No Date, ca. 1990.

28 McPherson, "Nursing and Colonization," 225–26.

29 Canada, Department of National Health and Welfare, *Annual Report*, 1947–48, 40–41.

30 Canada, Department of National Health and Welfare, *Annual Report*, 1948–49, 107.

31 Canada, Department of National Health and Welfare, *Annual Report*, 1949–50.

32 ANAC, Registered Nurses of Canadian Indian Ancestry, conference proceedings, "How Poverty Affects Indian Women and Their Health," Winnipeg, MB, 11–13 June 1982, 7.

33 Shewell, *"Enough to Keep Them Alive."*

34 Mary Jane McCallum, "This Last Frontier: Isolation and Aboriginal Health," *Canadian Bulletin of Medical History* 22, 1 (2005): 103–20.

35 Canada, Department of National Health and Welfare, *Annual Report*, 1945–6 and 1950–1.

36 To this was added the services of provincial Public Health Nursing Services, the Red Cross, and the Victorian Order of Nurses.

37 Canada, Department of National Health and Welfare, *Annual Report*, 1948–49 and 1958–59.

38 Canada, Department of National Health and Welfare, *Annual Report*, 1954–55.

39 Canada, Department of Indian Affairs, *Annual Report*, 1926–27, 10–11.

40 Canada, Department of National Health and Welfare, *Annual Report*, 1948–49, 42.

41 Canada, Department of National Health and Welfare, *Annual Report*, 1958–59, 21.

42 LAC R11504, vol. 1, file 1–8, Stout, "Association of Registered Nurses of Canadian Indian Ancestry," 3-4.

43 Themes of Aboriginal nurse conferences have included:

1977: MINA: Indian nurse education, Indian health, Indian medicine, Indian nursing (including a questionnaire to focus on the special needs of Indian patients), and cross-cultural nursing.

1982: Winnipeg: How Poverty Affects Indian Women and Their Health

1983: Brantford: Native Health Professionals for Better Health

1984: Vancouver: Women, Health, and Development

1986: Victoria: Transcultural Nursing

1987: Charlottetown: Alcohol: A Family Disease

1988: Hobbema: Family Violence

1989: Wikwemikong: Women and Abuse

1990: Whitehorse: Child Sexual Abuse

1991: Learning Paths: Reducing Family Violence in Aboriginal Communities

(LAC, R11504, vol. 1, file 1-8, "History"; "For N.T." and No Author, "History 1992-3," c. 1993).

44 LAC, R11504, vol. 1, file 1-17, Jean Goodwill, "Traditionalism for Empowerment," ca. 1985.

45 "Focus on Native Health," *Canadian Nurse* 74, 9 (October 1978): 8.

46 ANAC, "Carol Prince," profile, created as part of the *Twice as Good: A History of Aboriginal Nurses* (ANAC: March 2007) interview and project, 16 August 2006.

47 "Board of Directors," at the Aboriginal Nurses Manitoba Inc. http://www.aboriginalnurses.ca/board-of-directors/ (accessed 4 February 2014).

48 Pauline Steiman, "Caring for Indian Outpatients," *Canadian Nurse* 74, 9 (October 1978): 40.

49 Scholars have continued to work on the concepts of cross-cultural training, cultural safety, and cultural competency in the field of nursing, more recently challenging if, how, and to what ends these concepts engage with essentialist and fixed notions of culture. See Patricia Gray and Debera J. Thomas, "Critical Reflections on Culture in Nursing," *Journal of Cultural Diversity* 13, 2 (Summer 2006): 76–82.

50 Dianne Wepa, preface to *Cultural Safety in Aotearoa New Zealand* (Auckland: Pearson, 2004), cited in ANAC *Aboriginal Health Nursing Project: Initiating Dialogue* (31 March 2006), 21.

51 John Soosaar, *Daily News* (Halifax), 5 February 2006, Local News section, 8.

52 See for example Kelm, *Colonizing Bodies,* and Lux, *Medicine That Walks.*

53 Waldram, Herring, and Young, *Aboriginal Health in Canada*, 185.

54 Thomas Berger, *Report of the Advisory Commission on Indian and Inuit Health Consultation* (Ottawa: Health and Welfare Canada, 1980).

55 LAC, R11504, vol. 1, file 1-8, "History."

56 LAC, R11504, vol. 1, file 1-8, Stout, "Association of Registered Nurses of Canadian Indian Ancestry," 11.

57 Ibid., 12.

58 LAC, R11504, vol. 32, file 32-5, and Jean Goodwill, *Survey of Native Nurses to Determine and Identify the Barriers to Employment and Retention of Native Nurses Within Medical Services Branch of National Health and Welfare* (ANAC, 1984). A random selection of one hundred nurses were asked to take part in the study; seventy-one responded with completed questionnaires from all parts of Canada except Newfoundland and the Northwest Territories: Ontario (twenty-seven), Manitoba (ten), Quebec and Alberta (eight each), Nova Scotia, Saskatchewan, and British Columbia (five each), New Brunswick, Prince Edward Island, and the Yukon Territory (one each). Of the respondents, fifty were Status Indians, sixteen were non-Status Indians, and five were Métis. Forty-eight of the seventy-one belonged to RNCIA.

59 Goodwill, *Survey of Native Nurses.*

60 Ibid.

61 LAC, R11504, vol. 32, file 32-4, Registered Nurses of Canadian Indian Ancestry Survey, 1983. In at least one case, housing was denied to an Aboriginal nurse on the basis that MSB staff accommodations were reserved for nurses with no families.

62 See, for example, Brenda Canitz, "A Study of Turnover in Northern Nurses: Isolation, Control and Burnout," MHSc Thesis, University of Toronto 1991 and "Nursing in the North: Challenge and Isolation," in M. Crnkovich, ed. *'GOSSIP': A Spoken History of Women in the North* (Ottawa: Canadian Arctic Resources Committee), 193–212; McPherson, "Nursing and Colonization," and Waldram, Herring, and Young, *Aboriginal Health in Canada*, 187–190.

63 Waldram, Herring, and Young, *Aboriginal Health in Canada*, 188.

64 Bruyere and Dignan, "Taking the Power Back."

65 LAC, R11504, vol. 1, file 1-8, Stout, "Association of Registered Nurses of Canadian Indian Ancestry," 5–6.

66 Ibid., 6.

67 Ibid., 7–9.

68 Kelm, and Aboriginal Nurses Association of Canada, *Thirty Years of Community*, 15.

69 LAC, R11504, vol. 1, file 1-8, No Author (Jean Goodwill?), "History of IINC," no date, ca. 1988, 14-17.

70 LAC, R11504, vol. 1, file 1-8, "History of IINC," 14.

71 LAC, R11504, vol. 1, file 1-8, "For N.T."

72 Katherine Pettipas, *Severing the Ties That Bind: Government Repression of Indigenous Religious Ceremonies on the Prairies* (Winnipeg: University of Manitoba Press, 1994); Lux, *Medicine That Walks*; and Waldram, Herring, and Young, *Aboriginal Health in Canada*.

73 Kristin Burnett, *Taking Medicine: Women's Healing Work and Colonial Contact in Southern Alberta, 1880-1930* (Vancouver: University of British Columbia Press, 2010).

74 Aboriginal Nurses Association of Canada, *Working Together*.

75 Aboriginal Nurses Association of Canada *Twice as Good*.

76 White, "Restructuring the Domestic Sphere."

77 LAC, RG 10, vol. 3199, file 504, 178, Headquarters—Correspondence Concerning the Training of Indian Girls as Nurses, 1917–1941, letter to "Indian Girls," from Mrs. B.C. Ashcroft of the Patriotic and Missionary Board of the Ontario Woman's Christian Temperance Union, 9 October 1917, and "Announcement" by Mrs. W.C. Ashcroft, Superintendent of Work among Indians, Ontario WCTU.

78 LAC, RG 10, vol. 3199, file 504, 178, Correspondence, letter to Sir, from Lily Bool, Indian Work, British Columbia Women's Christian Temperance Union, 6 May 1919. The influenza epidemic was so severe that at their 1918 general meeting the Ontario WCTU made three resolutions to assist: "Our Supt. of Indian work reported the conditions among the Indians as very serious especially since the 'flu' epidemic. Many of the mothers of families having died, in very many cases for lack of suitable nursing and medical attention. It was therefore RESOLVED that we ask the Indian Department at Ottawa to formulate some reputation to provide short terms of training for Indian girls that would prepare them for nursing amongst their own people especially as there are so many tuberculosis patients among the Indian people"; also, "That we ask the government to establish sanitoriums on Indian reserves where Indian girls could be trained in nursing"; and "That we appeal to the government to [?] a dept. of Medical Inspection Indian Schools to be supervised by professional nurses." Letter to Minister of the Interior, from Mrs. H.M. Detlor, Corresponding Secretary of the Ontario Woman's Christian Temperance Union, North Bay, 14 December 1918.

79 An excellent source of information on missionary women's support of local Aboriginal employment is the records of the Committee on Follow-Up Work among Indian Girls of the Women's Auxiliary of the Anglican Church Missionary Society, led by Mrs. Shirley R.O. Taylor. As head of this committee, Mrs. Taylor wrote to girls who graduated from Anglican residential schools in order to inquire about their further education, home lives, and work. Over three hundred ex-pupils from across Canada corresponded with her between the years 1931 and 1957. Anglican Archives of Canada, General Synod Archives, *The Living Message* (December 1931–November 1958).

80 Special Joint Committee of the Senate and House of Commons Appointed to Continue and Complete the Examination of the Indian Act, *Minutes of Proceedings and Evidence*, (No. 3, 6 June 1946), 69.

81 LAC, R11504, vol. 1, file 1-8, Stout, "Association of Registered Nurses of Canadian Indian Ancestry, 8.

82 LAC, R11504, vol. 1, file 1-8, "History of IINC," 9. All the same, they insisted that an Indian nurse attend recruitment efforts meant to deal with unbearable shortages in Indian and Northern Health Services.

83 "Focus on Native Health," *Canadian Nurse* 74, 9 (October 1978): 8.
84 LAC, R11504, vol. 1, file 1-8, Stout, "The Association of Registered Nurses of Canadian Indian Ancestry," 9.
85 For those interested in working among their own people, a few hospitals seem to have been more open to Native nurses. In particular, the hospitals of File Hills, Fort Qu'Appelle, Cardston, and Lady Willingdon were popular options, as were urban hospitals and sanatoria treating Aboriginal people in the south, such as Ottawa Civic, St. Boniface in Winnipeg, and Charles Camsell in Edmonton, Dynevor in Selkirk, Toronto Hospital for Incurables, and St. Bartholomew's in Lytton.
86 Bruyere and Dignan, "Taking the Power Back."
87 LAC, RG 10, vol. 3199, file 504, 178, letter to E.A.W.R. McKenzie, Indian Agent, from A.F. MacKenzie, 6 November 1936.
88 J. Kulig and S. Grypma, "Breaking Down Racial Barriers: Honouring Pioneer Aboriginal Nurses from the Blood Reserve," *Alberta RN* 62, 8 (October 2006): 16.
89 LAC, RG 10, vol. 3199, file 504, 178, letter to J.R. MacGregor, Esq., Acting Indian Agent, Gore Bay, Ontario, from Asst. Deputy and Secretary, Ottawa, 10 May 1919.
90 LAC, RG 10, vol. 3199, file 504, 178, letter to Mr. J.D. McLean, Asst. Deputy and Secretary, Department of Indian Affairs, from E. MacK. Dickson, Lady Superintendent, Toronto Free Hospital for Consumptives, 3 March 1921.
91 LAC, RG 10, vol. 3199, file 504, 178, letter to the Secretary, Indian Affairs, from Col. C.E. Morgan, Supt. Six Nations, 8 June 1933.
92 "Nurse-in-Training Will Serve in North," *Indian News* (January 1955): 4.
93 *No Longer Vanishing*, dir. Grant McLean, National Film Board of Canada, 1955.
94 Wilma Strongeagle, "Why I Became a Nurse," *Indian News* (October 1962): 4.
95 Many of the the women in the 1983 survey were funded by Indian Affairs, but were non-Status, meaning that they had lost their band membership.
96 See, for example, "Profiles" in Aboriginal Nurses Association of Canada, *Working Together*.
97 Meijer Drees, "Training Aboriginal Nurses".
98 Canada, Department of National Health and Welfare, *Annual Report*, 1952–53, 34. "Supporting the medical officers and nurses were 1,150 valued employees whose skills and efforts make a medical service possible. Of these 295 were Indians or Eskimos. The additions during the year included 138 positions of appropriate classifications."
99 Kaufert and Koolage, "Role Conflict among 'Culture Brokers'" and Kaufert, Putsch, and Lavallee, "Experience of Aboriginal Health Interpreters in Mediation of Conflicting Values in End-of-Life Decision Making."
100 Myrna Cruickshank, personal correspondence, 2 April 2006.
101 House of Commons, *Debates*, vol. 3, 60th session, 21st Parliament (Ottawa: Queen's Printer, 1952), 2988.
102 LAC, RG 10, vol. 8767, file 1/25-7-5, pt. 1, letter to Miss M.S. Payne, Miss B. Fortin, Miss H. Martins, Miss J. Bartlett, Mrs. A. Oddson, Miss H.M. Heseltine, Miss W.R. Broderick, and Miss P.F. Grant, from H.M Jones, 13 August 1952.
103 LAC, RG 10, vol. 8767, file 1/25-7-5, pt. 1, letter to H.M. Jones, Superintendent of Welfare Services, Indian Affairs Department, from W.R. Broderick, Social Worker, 15 August 1952.
104 LAC, RG 10, vol. 8767, file 1/25-7-5, pt. 2, letter to Indian Affairs Branch from W.S. Arneil, Indian Commissioner for BC, 6 October 1952.

105 LAC, RG 29, vol. 8767, file 1125-7-5, pt. 2, letter to Mr. H.M. Jones, Superintendent of Welfare, Indian Affairs Branch, from H. Margaret Heseltine, Social Worker, Regina, 18 October 1952.

106 LAC, RG 10, vol. 8767, file 1125-7-5, pt. 2, letter to Indian Affairs Branch from W.S. Arneil, Indian Commissioner for BC, 6 October 1952.

107 LAC, RG 10, vol. 8767, file 1/25-7-5, pt. 1, letter from B. Davidson, Reg. N. Inspector, ca. 1952.

108 Ruth Christie, interview with author, 18 March 2006.

109 According to the *Indian News*, in 1962, the Vancouver Vocational Institute had trained over 250 Indian students, and "some 20 Indian girls are trained as practical nurses each year." *Indian News* (October 1962): 8.

110 Jean Goodwill, ed., *Speaking Together: Canada's Native Women* (Ottawa: Secretary of State, 1975), 12. Cantryn went on to become president of the Coqualeetza Fellowship in Vancouver and later helped to found the Vancouver Aboriginal Friendship Centre, even acting as vice-president of the national organization of Friendship Centres. Cantryn was also the founding president of the Allied Indian and Métis Society, setting up a halfway house for Aboriginal ex-inmates, and the first woman to sit on the Vancouver Police Commissioner's Board. She also sat on the board of the BC Association of Non-Status Indians.

111 Indian and Northern Health Services, Directorate Report (Ottawa, 1960), 13, as cited in Meijer Drees, "Training Aboriginal Nurses," 196.

112 LAC, RG 10, vol. 8767, file 1/25-7-5, pt. 2, "Training of Indian Girls as Nurses Aides," course offered in Alberta, literature enclosed in a letter to Superintendent, Welfare Service, from Willa R. Broderick, Social Worker, 31 October 1952.

113 LAC, RG 10, vol. 8767, file 1/25-7-5, pt. 2, letter to Indian Affairs Branch, from W.S. Arneil, Indian Commissioner for BC, 19 February 1954.

114 LAC, RG 10, vol. 8767, file 1/25-7-5, pt. 2, letter to Indian Affairs Branch, from W.S. Arneil, Indian Commissioner for BC, 19 February 1954.

115 Meijer Drees, "Training Aboriginal Nurses," 195–6.

116 Meijer Drees found that the "Directorate of IHS did state openly that '...as soon as our patients are able, they engage in rehabilitation employment around the hospital. This is carried out on a selective basis.'" Meijer Drees, "Training Aboriginal Nurses," 197.

117 Rita Gilboche, a Métis woman from Camperville, Manitoba, completed grade eight at home, and when she was sent to a tuberculosis sanatorium for two years, she finished grade nine by correspondence. This experience clearly had an impact on her, as she worked as a practical nurse in sanatoriums across the country from James Bay to Vancouver. Tuberculosis nursing became her specialty. Goodwill, *Speaking Together*, 68–69.

118 For example, between February and May 1962, the Vancouver placement officer reported that Elizabeth Jonathan, Freda Hanna, Marion Dixon, and Mary Aquinas were placed in Practical Nurse training at Vancouver General Hospital; Marcy Nelson was placed at Miller Bay Indian Hospital; and Vera Derrick at Prince George General Hospital. Vera, from Kitwancool, BC, took employment as a hospital aide at the Indian and Northern Health Services hospital at Miller Bay. LAC, RG 10, vol. 8473, file 1/23-35, pt. 1, Statistical Report on the Indian Employment Placement Program, 1959–1962, Placement Officer's Worksheet for Quarter ending 28 February 1962; and RG 10, vol. 8473, file 1/23-35, pt 2, Statistical Report on the Indian Employment Placement Program, 1962–1964 Quarterly Report for BC Region, Vancouver, ending 31 May 1962.

119 LAC, RG 10, vol. 3199, file 504, 178, "Training of Indian Girls as Nurses Aides."

120 Goodwill, *Speaking Together*, 12.

121 LAC, RG 10, vol. 8767, file 1/25-7-5, pt. 1. For example, one young woman entered into a position at an Ontario sanatorium to allow her to access pneumothorax treatments.

122 Cowall Farrell and Alivaktuk, "The Work We Have Done." Cowall Farrell and Alivaktuk find that hospital workers' salaries were paid by nurses through a "barter and trade system."

123 Christie, interview.

124 Cruickshank, personal correspondence.

125 Eleanor Olson, interview with author, 14 July 2006.

126 Of a sample of fifteen at the first meeting, one had graduated in the 1930s, three in the 1940s, four in the 1950s, six in the 1960s, and one in the 1970s.

127 Training facilities open to Aboriginal students included: Toronto General Hospital, Ottawa Civic, St. Boniface Hospital, Good Samaritan Hospital in Brandon, Toronto Hospital for Incurables, Midland General, London Hospital, McKellar General Hospital in Fort William, and Nelson General Hospital, BC. After surveying hospitals in Ontario in 1930, A.F. MacKenzie, the acting assistant deputy and secretary of Indian Affairs, found that only fifteen hospitals in Ontario were "open to receive Indian girls in training as nurses." LAC, RG 10, vol. 3199, file 504, 178, letter to Rev. T.B. R. Westgate, from A.F. MacKenzie, Acting Asst. Deputy and Secretary, 12 May 1930.

128 Meijer Drees, "Training Aboriginal Nurses," 189.

129 LAC, RG 10, vol. 3199, file 504, 178, letter to "Dear Sir" from Mrs. B.C. Ashcroft, Supt. Indian Work, October 1918; Memorandum, Department of Indian Affairs Canada, to Mr. Scott from Accountant, 26 May 1919; letter to Mr. J.D. McLean, Asst. Deputy and Secretary, Dept of Indian Affairs, from E. MacK. Dickson, Lady Superintendent, Toronto Free Hospital for Consumptives, 3 March 1921.

130 LAC, RG 10, vol. 3199, file 504, 178, letter from Agnes Sampson, 19 March 1921. See also Cynthia Toman, "'My chance has come at last!': The Weston Hospital, the Women's Christian Temperance Union, and Indian Nurses in Canada, 1917–1929," *Native Studies Review* 19, 2: 95–120.

131 LAC, RG 10, vol. 3199, file 504, 178, letter to A.F. McKenzie, Indian Agent, Broadview, from Deputy Superintendent General, 14 November 1936.

132 *Topahdewin: The Gladys Cook Story*, dir. Lisa Berry, Anglican Church of Canada, 2004.

133 Stacy O'Brien, "Jennie Neilsen," *Lethbridge Herald*, 5 June 2006, A3. See also Kulig, "Breaking Down Racial Barriers," 14–16.

134 Toth had completed high school at St. Paul's school in the early 1930s and, under sponsorship of the Anglican Church, went to Kootenay Lake Training School for Nurses in Nelson, BC. When Gladstone graduated from St. Paul's in 1938, the school no longer offered high school courses, and her father, future senator James Gladstone, arranged for her to complete high school at Bedford Road Collegiate in Saskatoon. She went on to nursing school at the Royal Jubilee Hospital in Victoria, BC.

135 LAC, RG 10, vol. 3199, file 501, 178, letter to Duncan C. Scott from Ontario Women's Christian Temperance Union, 6 May 1929; letter to Mrs. May R. Thornley, Ontario WCTU from Deputy Superintendent General, 14 May 1929; letter to Duncan Campbell Scott from May R. Thornley, 13 May 29; and letter to Mrs Bycroft from Hilda Miskokomon, 25 June 1929.

136 Lux, *Medicine That Walks*.

137 See, for example, LAC, RG 10, vol. 3199, file 504, 178.

138 LAC, RG 10, vol. 3199, file 504, 178, correspondence between R.A. Hoey, Superintendent of Welfare and Training and A.G. Hamilton, Inspector of Agencies, 1936–7.

139 Canada, Department of Indian Affairs, *Annual Report*, 1916–17, 14.

140 Sarah Carter, *Lost Harvests: Prairie Indian Reserve Farmers and Government Policy* (Montreal: McGill-Queen's University Press, 1990).

141 LAC, RG 10, vol. 3199, file 504, 178, letter to Mrs. Ashcroft from Scott, Deputy Superintendent General, 24 October 1918.

142 LAC, RG 10, vol. 3199, file 504, 178, letter to Lily Bool from Duncan C. Scott, 5 June 1919.

143 Milloy, *A National Crime*, 67.

144 Canada, Department of Indian Affairs, *Annual Report*, 1927–28, 12 and 18.

145 J.F. Woodsworth, "Problems of Indian Education in Canada," in *The North American Indian Today: University of Toronto—Yale University Seminar Conference, Toronto, September 4–16, 1939*, ed. C.T. Loram and T.F. McIlwraith (Toronto: University of Toronto Press, 1943), 270–71.

146 Some students' education funds did not flow through Indian agents or principals. One nursing student from Sheshegwaning was funded on 4 January 1944 directly by the Superintendent of Indian Affairs, who sent cheques through the DIA accountant to the matron of her school. "The Department will contribute to the extent of $125.00 per annum if necessary toward the purchase of clothing, books, etc., payment to be made upon presentation of accounts certified by the Superintendent of the institution." The funding went to the Lady Superintendent Miss E.F. Baker at St. Andrews Hospital. This was also the only case that I came across where the department actually paid the entire amount of a per-capita grant for education. LAC, RG 10, vol. 3199, file 504, 178, correspondence to Mr. Creighton, Esq. Law Clerk of the Senate, from Duncan C. Scott Deputy Superintendent General, Department of Indian Affairs, 6 March 1926.

147 LAC, RG 10, vol. 3199, file 504, 178, correspondence to J.R. MacGregor, Esq., Acting Indian Agent, Gore Bay, Ontario, from Assistant Deputy and Secretary, Ottawa, 10 May 1919.

148 LAC, RG 10, vol. 3199, file 504, 178, correspondence to Indian Affairs from Acting Indian Agent, Gore Bay, 13 May 1919, and correspondence to J.R. MacGregor, Esq., Acting Indian Agent, Gore Bay, from Assistant Deputy and Secretary, Indian Affairs, 21 July 1919.

149 LAC, RG 10, vol. 8767, file 1/25-7-5, pt. 1, correspondence between R.T. Chapin, Brandon Indian Residential School Principal; Christina Macken, Superintendent, Brandon General Hospital; R.A. Hoey, Superintendent of Welfare and Training; O.B. Strapp, Principal, Brandon Indian Residential School; and Philip Phelan, Chief, Training Division, 20 April 1942, 4 May 1942, 18 May 1942, 22 May 1942, 9 January 1943, 4 January 1944, 12 October 1945, 19 October 1945.

150 Callahan, interview.

151 Goodwill, *Speaking Together*, 46.

152 LAC, RG 10, vol. 8767, file 1/25-7-5, pt. 1, letter to Mr. Strapp, Principal, Indian Residential School, Brandon, Manitoba, from Philip Phelan, Chief, Training Division, 19 October 1945. See also Goodwill, *Speaking Together*, 46.

153 "Twenty-Nine Awarded Scholarships," *Indian News* 6, 3 (February 1963): 4.

154 Cultural scholarships were for training in art, music, drama, carving, or similar artistic work.

155 "Indians to Share Valuable Scholarships," *Indian News* 2, 3 (March 1957): 1, 4. There were eight separate university scholarships, one for each of the Indian administrative regions, to be awarded to the Indian students attaining the highest senior matriculation

standing in each of the eight regions (at least 60 percent). These students could choose any course of study they wished, except for nursing or teacher training, and received $750 or $1,000. In addition, eight nursing students received $500 scholarships each, eight teachers received $750 each, eight commercial/technical students received between $400 and $750, and two agriculture students received $500 and $750 each.

156 "Prove Value of Scholarships: High Percentage Successful," *Indian News* 6, 3 (February 1963): 7. See also "Twenty-six Young People Win Indian Affairs Scholarships," *Indian News* 5, 2 (December 1961): 4–6.

157 Canada, Department of National Health and Welfare, *Annual Report*, 1955–56, 84.

158 LAC, RG 10, vol. 8767, file 1/25-7-5, pt. 2, letter, to Indian Affairs branch, from J.D. MacPherson, 23 September 1955.

159 ANAC, "Rosella McKay," profile, created as part of the *Twice As Good: A History of Aboriginal Nurses* (ANAC: March 2007) interview and project, 31 July 2006.

160 Callahan, interview; ANAC "Carol Prince," profile, and "Marilyn Sark," profile, created as part of the *Twice As Good: A History of Aboriginal Nurses* (ANAC: March 2007) interview and project, 6 September 2006.

161 ANAC, "Marilyn Sark," profile, and "Faye North Peigan," profile, created as part of the *Twice As Good: A History of Aboriginal Nurses* (ANAC: March 2007) interview and project, 3 August 2006. "Mohawk Girl Is Nurse-in-Charge at Nipissing," *Indian News* 4, 4 (April 1961): 3.

162 McPherson, *Bedside Matters*, 221.

163 The high percentage of funded students may have been influenced by the selection process, which included the use of the DIAND post-secondary students registry, chiefs from some Indian communities, members of RNCIA, and the two major national conferences.

164 For more on this, see Winona L. Stevenson, "Prairie Indians and Higher Education: An Historical Overview, 1876 to 1977," and Darlene Lanceley, "The Post-Secondary Assistance Program for Indian Education: The Vehicle for Change and the Voice of Opposition," in *Hitting the Books: The Politics of Educational Retrenchment*, ed. Terry Wotherspoon (Toronto: Garamond Press, 1991), 215–48.

165 Respondents to the survey argued that DIAND funding was "very often inadequate," needing to be "supplemented from other sources," Goodwill, *Survey of Native Nurses*.

166 LAC, R11504, vol. 1, file 1-8, "Draft."

167 "A New Federal Program: Indian-Inuit Professional Health Career Development," *IINC Newsletter* 1,1: 3.

168 LAC, R11504, vol. 2, folder 2-10, "Field Trip to Winnipeg — 17–21 May, Jean Goodwill."

169 Waldram, Herring and Young, *Aboriginal Health in Canada*, 251–52.

170 LAC, R11504, vol. 1, file 1-8, Stout, "The Association of Registered Nurses of Canadian Indian Ancestry," 11.

171 The Northern Bachelor of Nursing Program in Manitoba, for example, was envisioned in 1982 as a four-year program and a partnership among the Swampy Cree Tribal Council, the University of Manitoba, and the Province of Manitoba. It aimed to create a cadre of Aboriginal health professionals without forcing them to relocate for school—a trend which, along with the MSB hiring policy, had drawn Aboriginal nurses largely to urban areas. It had changed by the time it was implemented in 1990 to a two-year post-RN Bachelor of Nursing program for "northerners" and closed its doors four years later. The program's demise revealed the differing visions and outcomes of "partnerships" between First Nations, universities, and the provincial and federal governments and the extent to which governments were willing to share control over education with the

other partners. It also revealed a pattern among nurses of professional accreditation; rather than promoting the BN first, most had to get a diploma in nursing and upgrade later. David Gregory, Mary Jane McCallum, Brenda Elias, and Karen Grant, "Self-Determination and the Swampy Cree Tribal Council: A Case Study Involving Nursing Education in Northern Manitoba," *Canadian Journal of Nursing Research* 40, 2 (June 2008): 132–49.

172 LAC, R11504, vol. 33, file 33-17, Hearings on Indian Education—Assembly of First Nations, 6 October 1986, tape transcript: Jean Goodwill. These included the Blue Quills/Grant MacEwan Community Diploma Nursing Program, the Inner City Nursing Project/Red River Community College in Winnipeg, the Northern Nursing Education Program in Thompson, Manitoba/Red River Community College, the Native Health Careers Access Program at Caribou College in Kamloops BC (now Thompson Rivers University), and the Native Nurses Entry Program/Lakehead University.

173 Pat McCormick Stewart, "Helping People to Help Themselves: A Community Development Approach to Nursing Education," *Canadian Nurse* 80, 1 (January 1984): 36.

174 Aboriginal Nurses Association of Canada, Marilyn Tanner-Spence, profile, created as part of the *Twice As Good: A History of Aboriginal Nurses* (ANAC: March 2007) interview and project, 25 July 2006.

175 For example, see literature on Manitoba programs: G. Connell, R Flet, and P Stewart, "Implementing Primary Health Care through Community Control: The Experience of Swampy Cree Tribal Council," and E. Thomlinson, D. Gregory, and J. Larsen, "The Northern Bachelor of Nursing Program: One Solution to Problems in Health Care Provision," *Circumpolar Health 90: Proceedings of the 8th International Congress on Circumpolar Health, Whitehorse, Yukon, May 20-25, 1990* (Winnipeg, University of Manitoba Press, 1991), 44–46, 145–48; E. Thomlinson, "Northern Bachelor of Nursing Program: Issues in the Implementation of a Curriculum to Meet Community and Nursing Needs," *Redressing the Imbalance: Health Human Resources in Rural and Northern Communities: Proceedings from a Conference Hosted by the Northern Health Human Resources Research Unit, Thunder Bay, Ontario, October 21–24, 1993* (Thunder Bay, ON: Lakehead University Centre for Northern Studies, 1995), 489–95; and Gregory et al., "Self-Determination and the Swampy Cree Tribal Council."

176 LAC, R11504, vol. 1, file 1-8, "History of IINC," 12–13.

Conclusion: The Wages of Whiteness and the Indigenous Historian

1 See, for example, Olive Dickason, *The Myth of the Savage and the Beginnings of French Colonialism in the Americas* (Edmonton: University of Alberta Press, 1984); Patricia Monture-Agnus, *Thunder in My Soul: A Mohawk Woman Speaks* (Halifax: Fernwood Press, 1995); Emma LaRocque, "The Colonization of a Native Woman Scholar," in *Women of the First Nations: Power, Wisdom, and Strength*, ed. Christine Miller and Patricia Chuchryk, with Marie Smallface Marule, Brenda Manyfingers, and Cheryl Deering (Winnipeg: University of Manitoba Press, 1996); Devon A. Mihesuah, ed., *Natives and Academics: Researching and Writing about American Indians* (Lincoln: University of Nebraska Press, 1998); Linda Tuhiwai Smith, *Decolonizing Methodologies: Research and Indigenous Peoples* (London: Zed Books, 1999); David Long and Olive Dickason, *Visions of the Heart: An Introduction to Canadian Aboriginal Issues*, 2nd ed. (Toronto: Harcourt Brace, 2000); Beatrice Medicine, *Learning to Be an Anthropologist and Remaining "Native"* (Urbana: University of Illinois Press, 2001); Philip Deloria, "Thinking about Self in a Family Way," *Journal of American History* 89, 1 (June 2002); Devon A. Mihesuah and Angela C. Wilson, eds., *Indigenizing the Academy: Transforming Scholarship and Empowering Communities* (Lincoln: University of Nebraska Press, 2004); Kathy Absolon and Cam Willett, "Putting Ourselves Forward: Location in Aboriginal Research," in *Research as Resistance: Critical, Indigenous, and Anti-oppressive Approaches*, ed. Leslie Brown and Susan Strega (Toronto: Canadian Scholars' Press/Women's Press, 2005), 97–126; and Dale Turner, *This Is Not a Peace Pipe: Towards a Critical Indigenous Philosophy* (Toronto: University of Toronto Press, 2006).

2 An example of this kind of critique was a discussion on aspects of race and history at the 2004 Fort Garry Lectures. Robin Jarvis Brownlie, Adele Perry, Franca Iacovetta, and Kathryn McPherson, "Roundtable Discussion" (panel at the Fort Garry Lectures in History, University of Manitoba, Winnipeg, MB, May 2004).

3 Franca Iacovetta summarizes many of these positions in her response to Linda K. Kerber's essay on women historians and historical practice, "Towards a More Human Academy? Some Observations from a Canadian Feminist Historian," *Journal of Women's History* 18, 1 (2006): 141–46.

4 See, for example, McPherson, *Bedside Matters*; Shula Marks, *Divided Sisterhood: Race, Class, and Gender in the South African Nursing Profession* (London: Macmillan Press, 1994); and Darlene Clark Hine, *Black Women in White: Racial Conflict and Co-operation in the Nursing Profession, 1890–1950* (Bloomington: Indiana University Press, 1989).

5 See, for example, Marcia Anderson and Barry Lavallee, "The Development of the First Nations, Inuit and Métis Medical Workforce," *Medical Journal of Australia* 186, 10 (2007): 539–40, and reports gathered at "Medical Education: Aboriginal Health Needs" at the Association of Faculties of Medicine of Canada website, http://www.afmc.ca/social-aboriginal-health-e.php (accessed 5 February 2014). This material identifies key areas for improvement and a "Core Competencies" framework.

6 Susan M. Hill, personal communication, 15 September 2007.

7 Deloria, *Indians in Unexpected Places*.

8 Maureen Konkle, *Writing Indian Nations: Native Intellectuals and the Politics of Historiography, 1827–1863* (Chapel Hill: University of North Carolina Press, 2004), and Robin Jarvis Brownlie, "First Nations Perspectives and Historical Thinking in Canada," in *First Nations, First Thoughts - New Challenges*, ed. Annis May Timpson (Vancouver: UBC Press, 2009), 21–50. See also Bernd C. Peyer, ed., *American Indian Nonfiction: An Anthology of Writings, 1760s–1930s* (Norman: University of Oklahoma Press, 2007); and Gretchen M. Bataille and Kathleen Mullen Sands, *American Indian Women Telling Their Lives* (Lincoln: University of Nebraska Press, 1987).

9 Brownlie, "First Nations Perspectives and Historical Thinking in Canada," 27.

10 See, for example, Peyer, *American Indian Nonfiction*; Deloria, *Indians in Unexpected Places* and *Playing Indian*; Daniel Francis, *The Imaginary Indian*; and Shewell, *"Enough to Keep Them Alive"*.

11 Donald Wright, "Gender and the Professionalization of History in English Canada before 1960," *Canadian Historical Review* 81, 1 (March 2000): 29, 35.

12 Donald Wright, *The Professionalization of History in English Canada* (Toronto: University of Toronto Press, 2005), 3–6.

13 Wright, "Gender and the Professionalization of History"; Bonnie Smith, *The Gender of History: Men, Women, and the Historical Practice* (Cambridge, MA: Harvard University Press, 1998); and Beverly Boutilier and Alison Prentice, *Creating Historical Memory: English-Canadian Women and the Work of History* (Vancouver: University of British Columbia Press, 1997).

14 This statistic is drawn from an informal survey of Indigenous and other scholars in various departments at Canadian universities as well as a database of Aboriginal PhD students and faculty at Canadian universities and colleges collected by Marie Battiste, Aboriginal Education Research Centre, University of Saskatchewan. It relies on self-identification.

15 Blair Stonechild, *The New Buffalo: The Struggle for Aboriginal Post-Secondary Education in Canada* (Winnipeg: University of Manitoba Press, 2007), 21–23.

16 Mihesuah, *Natives and Academics*.

17 Funds amounted to what annual parliamentary appropriations would allow.

18 For an example of 1960s Indian education philosophy, see Indian Affairs Branch, *The Indian in Transition: Indian Education*.

19 One exception is J.R. Miller's "Bringing Native People in from the Margins" in his *Reflections on Native-Newcomer Relations: Selected Essays* (Toronto: University of Toronto Press, 2004): 13–35. He begins his historiography with an examination of English-Canadian writing on Aboriginal people produced outside of the academy in the nineteenth century.

20 Keith Thor Carlson, Melinda Marie Jette, and Kenichi Matsui, "An Annotated Bibliography of Major Writings in Aboriginal History, 1990–99," *Canadian Historical Review* 82, 1 (2001): 123.

21 Miller, *Reflections on Native-Newcomer Relations*, 19.

22 There was a well-noted expansion of history departments across the country in the 1960s and 1970s.

23 Ken Coates, "Writing First Nations into Canadian History: A Review of Recent Scholarly Works," *Canadian Historical Review* 81, 1 (March 2000): 99. See also, for example, James W. St. G. Walker, "The Indian in Canadian Historical Writing," *Canadian Historical Association Historical Papers* 6, 1 (1971): 21–51; and "The Indian in Canadian Historical Writing, 1972–1982" in *As Long as the Sun Shines and Water Flows: A Reader in Canadian Native Studies*, ed. Ian A.L. Getty and Antoine S. Lussier (Vancouver: University of British Columbia Press, 1983), 340–57; and Carlson, Jette, and Matsui, "An Annotated Bibliography." See also Arthur Ray's introduction in Harold A. Innis, *The Fur Trade in Canada: An Introduction to Canadian Economic History*, with an introduction by Arthur J. Ray (Toronto: University of Toronto Press, 1999); and Ted Binnema and Susan Neylan, "Arthur J. Ray and the Writing of Aboriginal History," in *New Histories for Old: Changing Perspectives on Canada's Native Past* (Vancouver: University of British Columbia Press, 2007), 1–17.

24 C.T. Loram and T.F. McIlwraith, *The North American Indian Today* (Toronto: University of Toronto Press, 1943), x.

25 Wendy Wickwire, "'They Wanted...Me to Help Them': James A. Teit and the Challenge of Ethnography in the Boasian Era," in *With Good Intentions: Euro-Canadian and Aboriginal Relations in Colonial Canada*, ed. Celia Haig-Brown and David A. Nock (Vancouver: University of British Columbia Press, 2006), 297–320.

26 See, for example, Binnema and Neylan, "Arthur J. Ray," 8–9.

27 An incomplete list of contributions in these years would include Howard Adams, *Prison of Grass: Canada from a Native Point of View* (Toronto: New Press, 1975); Harold Cardinal, *The Unjust Society: The Tragedy of Canadian Indians* (Edmonton: M.G. Hurtig, 1969), and *The Rebirth of Canadian Indians* (Edmonton: M.G. Hurtig, 1977); Patricia Albers and Beatrice Medicine, eds., *The Hidden Half: Studies of Plains Indian Women* (Lanham, MD: University Press of America, 1983); Kirkness, *Evaluation Report;* Sealey and Kirkness, *Indians without Tipis;* Emma LaRocque, *Defeathering the Indian* (Agincourt, ON: Book Society of Canada, 1975); and Manitoba Indian Brotherhood, *The Shocking Truth about Indians in Textbooks: Textbook Evaluation* (Winnipeg: Manitoba Indian Cultural Education Centre, 1977). Journals such as the *Native Studies Review* (1984–), *Canadian Journal of Native Education* (1980–), *American Indian Quarterly* (1974–), *Wicazo Sa Review* (1985–), and the *Canadian Journal of Native Studies* (1981–) were committed to publishing Native scholars at this time.

28 In his response to the panel "Power, Culture, and Place: Aboriginal Historians in Aboriginal History" at the 2008 Canadian Historical Association, Dr. John Milloy told a story about his own experiences studying the Aboriginal history of the fur trade at Oxford, where he was asked, "Indians, John? Should you not be over in the Anthropology department?" John Milloy, "Power, Culture, and Place: Aboriginal Historians in Aboriginal History" (facilitator/respondent at the annual meeting of the Canadian Historical Association, University of British Columbia, Vancouver, BC, 2–4 June 2008). My mom, who also wanted to study Aboriginal history, had to reckon with the same closed-mindedness in history; however, she indeed had no choice in the matter. She earned a B.A. in anthropology in the 1980s, mostly by night and summer school classes offered through distance education at a local community college.

29 Binnema and Neylan, "Arthur J. Ray," 8.

30 Olive Patricia Dickason's works have been published in several editions; these are the first (and English language) editions of her most popular monographs: *The Myth of the Savage: And the Beginnings of French Colonialism in the Americas* (Edmonton: University of Alberta Press, 1984); *Canada's First Nations: A History of Founding Peoples from Earliest Times* (Toronto: Oxford University Press, 1992); and *Visions of the Heart: Canadian Aboriginal Issues* (Toronto: Harcourt Brace, 1996).

31 From my own experience, McMaster University stands out as having no undergraduate or graduate courses in Aboriginal history or professors who specialize in Aboriginal history. There needs to be a survey of history departments in Canada for more detailed information about their course offerings, fields of study, hiring practices, and priorities.

32 For example, the *Canadian Historical Review* has regularly listed works in Aboriginal history in its catalogue of "Recent Publications relating to Canada" at least since 1990.

33 For a discussion of national narratives, see, for example, J.L. Granatstein, *Who Killed Canadian History?* (Toronto: HarperCollins 1998), and responses such as Franca Iacovetta, "Gendering Trans/National Histories: Feminists Rewriting Canadian History," *Journal of Women's History* 19, 1 (2007): 206–13.

34 For a discussion of objectivity and advocacy in Aboriginal history, see Carlson, Jette, and Matsui, "An Annotated Bibliography," and Kerry Abel, "Tangled, Lost and Bitter? Current Directions in the Writing of Native History in Canada," *Acadiensis* 26, 1 (Autumn 1996). To expand on this, the debates over "advocacy" and "objectivity"

in professional history tended to be in fact about an individual historian's position with regard to the state, and they were yet another way of engaging in a project of how to improve on a profession by building boundaries that exclude Native people. Often "advocacy" is used to subtly undermine an argument; for example, in this review of Shewell: "The advocacy that runs through the book adds to the intensity of the argument but raises concerns about its partisanship." Ken Coates, review of *"Enough to Keep Them Alive": Indian Social Welfare in Canada 1873–1965*, by Hugh Shewell, *Journal of Interdisciplinary History* 37, 4 (2007): 658. "Advocacy" is used here to critique not the book's argument, but the author's position with regards to the imperial Canadian state. Consider Alvin Finkel's review of the same work: "Shewell's account is one that focuses heavily on original sin, in this case the government's dispossession of Native people." This critique was made to highlight important alternatives to advocacy—"agency" and "Native voice"—however, reducing Shewell's work to a discussion of "original sin" undermines, obscures, and even makes light of the very real content of the book, which *is* a critique of the federal government. Alvin Finkel, review of *"Enough to Keep Them Alive": Indian Social Welfare in Canada 1873–1965*, by Hugh Shewell, *Labour/Le Travail* 55 (Spring 2005): 325.

35 See, for example, essays in John Sutton Lutz, ed., *Myth and Memory: Stories of Indigenous-European Contact* (Vancouver: University of British Columbia Press, 2007).

36 "Doing Aboriginal History" (panel presented at the annual meeting of the Canadian Historical Association, Saskatoon, SK, May 2007).

37 Audra Simpson's "On Ethnographic Refusal" has been useful in thinking about how history, like anthropology, has particular "methods of knowing" Indigenous people.

38 Antoinette Burton, "Who Needs the Nation? Interrogating 'British History,'" *Journal of Historical Sociology* 10, 3 (1997): 272–82.

39 Susan Page and Christine Asmar, "I Don't Want to Be a Black White Academic: Reconsidering Indigenous Academic Teaching Roles in 'Mainstream' Universities," (paper presented at the World Indigenous Peoples' Conference on Education, Melbourne, Australia, 9 December 2008).

40 David Roediger, *The Wages of Whiteness: Race and the Making of the American Working Class* (New York: Verso, 1996).

41 A brief survey of Indigenous university professors who teach history in other departments on RateMyProfessor.com revealed these expectations. While it is not reliable information about professors, the website is revealing of students' expectations of them. In reviews of Indigenous professors, particularly women, there is notable suspicion of their ability to know, evaluate, and teach history, and also their ability to be impartial.

42 Antoinette Burton, "Archive Stories: Gender in the Making of Imperial and Colonial Histories," in *Gender and Empire*, ed. Philippa Levine (Oxford: Oxford University Press, 2004), 281–93.

Bibliography

Unpublished Primary Sources

Archival Collections

RG 10 Indian Affairs (Library and Archives Canada)

RG 29 National Health and Welfare (Library and Archives Canada)

R11504 Aboriginal Nurses Association of Canada (Library and Archives Canada)

ANAC Aboriginal Nurses Association of Canada Records (ANAC Headquarters, Ottawa)

Archives of the Diocese of Rupert's Land (Winnipeg, Manitoba)

Sanatorium Board of Manitoba (Archives of Manitoba)

United Church Archives (Winnipeg, Manitoba)

Anglican Archives of Canada, General Synod Archives (Toronto, Ontario)

Interviews and Correspondence

Ann Callahan, Interview with Author, 26 March 2006.

Eleanor Olson, Interview with Author, 14 July 2006.

Ruth Christie, Interview with Author, 28 March 2006.

Maria Campbell, Personal Correspondence, 26 April 2006.

Myrna Cruickshank, Personal Correspondence, 2 April 2006.

Dorothy Stranger, Interview with Author, 20 January 2012.

Published Primary Sources

Radio, Film and Television

"Our Native Land," August 30, 1975, Interview with Jocelyn Bruyere and Tom Dignan, Announcer, Lloyd Heanderson, Host, Johnny Yesno, CBC radio archives: http://www.cbc.ca/archives/discover/programs/o/our-native-land-1/taking-the-power-back-native-women-organize.html.

Because They Are Different. Dir. Richard Gilbert. National Film Board, 1964.

Cold Journey. Dir. Martin Defalco. National Film Board, 1975.

Loyalties. Dir. Anne Wheeler. Alberta Motion Picture Development Corporation, 1987.

"The Last Man in the World." *Wojeck.* Dir: Ron Kelly. Canadian Broadcasting Corporation, 1966.

The Longer Trail. Dir. Fergus McDonell. National Film Board, 1956.

The Transition. Dir. Mort Rensen. National Film Board, 1964.

No Longer Vanishing. Dir. Grant McLean. National Film Board, 1955.

Print Media

Camsell Arrow (Charles Camsell Indian Hospital)

Citizen (Department of Citizenship and Immigration)

Health and Welfare Canada (Department of National Health and Welfare)

Ideas (Indian and Northern Affairs Economic Development)

Indian News (Department of Indian Affairs)

The Canadian Nurse (Canadian Nurses Association)

The Aboriginal Nurse (Aboriginal Nurses Association of Canada)

The Forgotten People (Native Council of Canada)

Winnipeg Free Press

Globe and Mail

Brandon Sun

Government Documents

Abramson, Edward J., Robert Arnold and Gerald Piper. *The Community Health Worker Program: A Critical Analysis and Evaluation.* Ottawa: Medical Services, National Department of Health and Welfare, June 1964.

Assembly of First Nations. "Community Health Representatives Proposal for Enrichment and Expansion." Background Paper, 30 May 1988.

Canada. Bureau of Northwest Territories and Yukon Affairs. *The Book of Wisdom for Eskimo.* Ottawa: Department of Mines and Resources, Lands, Parks and Forest Branch, 1947.

____. Department of Citizenship and Immigration. Indian Affairs Branch, *Annual Reports, 1950–1965.* Ottawa: Queen's Printer, 1950-1965.

____. Department of Citizenship and Immigration. Indian Affairs Branch. "Conference on Indian Employment: First Combined Conference of Placement and Field Officers." Ottawa, December 7–10, 1959.

____. Department of Citizenship and Immigration. *The Canadian Indian.* Ottawa: Queen's Printer, 1964.

____. Department of Citizenship and Immigration, Indian Affairs Branch. *The Indian in Transition: Indian Education.* Ottawa: Queen's Printer, 1962.

____. Department of Indian Affairs. *Annual Report,* 1916–1929. Ottawa: Queen's Printer, 1916–1929.

____. Department of Indian and Northern Affairs. *Annual Report,* 1973. Ottawa: Information Canada, 1973.

____. Department of Indian Affairs and Northern Development. *The Indian in Transition: The Indian Today.* Ottawa: Queen's Printer, 1964.

____. Department of Labour. *Women at Work in Canada: A Fact Book on the Female Labour Force.* Ottawa: Queen's Printer, 1958, 1964 and 1965.

____. Department of Mines and Resources. *Annual Reports.* Ottawa: Queen's Printer, 1940-1950.

____. Department of National Health and Welfare. *Annual Reports,* 1945–1952. Ottawa: King's Printer, 1945–1952.

____. Department of National Health and Welfare. *A Book for Mother.* Ottawa: Indian and Northern Health Services, 1958.

____. Department of National Health and Welfare. *The Community Health Worker in Indian and Eskimo Communities Canada.* Ottawa: Medical Services Branch, 1970.

____. Department of National Health and Welfare. *Community Health Worker Program Analysis and Evaluation.* Ottawa: Medical Services Branch, 1967.

____. Department of National Health and Welfare. *The Pre-Schooler.* Ottawa: Indian and Northern Health Services, 1958.

____. Department of National Health and Welfare. *Annual Reports,* 1953–1968. Ottawa: Queen's Printer, 1953–1968.

____. Department of National Health and Welfare. *Annual Reports,* 1969–1973. Ottawa: Information Canada, 1969–1973.

____. Employment and Immigration Advisory Council. "Employment Services to Natives." Ottawa: The Council, 1982.

____. Employment and Immigration Canada. *The Development of an Employment Policy for Indian, Inuit and Metis People.* Ottawa: Employment and Immigration Canada, 1978.

____. Employment and Immigration Canada. *Native Women – Labour Force Development.* Ottawa: Joint Canada Employment and Immigration Commission/Native Women's Association of Canada Working Group on Native Women's Employment, 1981.

____. Health and Welfare Canada. *Task Force on Community Health Auxiliaries.* Ottawa: Medical Services Branch, 1973.

____. Manpower and Immigration. *Canadian Indians at the Crossroads: Some Aspects of Relocation and Urbanization in Canada.* Ottawa: Queen's Printer, 1969.

____. Manpower and Immigration. *Task Force on Manpower Services to Native Peoples.* 1975.

____. Manpower and Immigration. *Task Force on Manpower Services to Native Peoples.* 1976.

____. *Royal Commission on Aboriginal Peoples.* Volume 1, Looking Forward, Looking Back. Ottawa: Canada Communications Group Publishing, 1996.

____. Secretary of State. *Speaking Together: Canada's Native Women.* Ottawa: Secretary of State, 1975.

Clatworthy, Stewart J. "The Effects of Education on Native Behaviour in the Urban Labour Market." Ottawa: Department of Employment and Immigration, Task Force on Labour Market Development, 1981.

____. *Issues Concerning the Role of Native Women in the Winnipeg Labour Market.* Winnipeg: Institute of Urban Studies, 1981.

Impact Research. *Native People and Employment in the Public Service of Canada.* Ottawa: Office of Native Employment, Public Service Commission, 1976.

Kenny, Carolyn. *North American Indian, Métis and Inuit Women Speak about Culture, Education and Work.* Ottawa: Status of Women Canada, 2002. publications.gc.ca/collections/Collection/sw21-90-2001E.pdf. Accessed 9 February 2014.

Kirkness, Verna J. Evaluation Report: *Education of Indians in Federal and Provincial Schools in Manitoba.* Ottawa: Department of Indian Affairs and Northern Development, 1978.

Lagasse, Jean H. *A Study of the Population of Indian Ancestry Living in Manitoba.* Winnipeg: Department of Agriculture and Immigration, 1959.

Martens, Ethel. *Mexico and Canada: A Comparison of Two Programs Where Indians Are Trained in Community Development.* Ottawa: Department of National Health and Welfare, 1966.

Theses, Dissertations, Unpublished Papers, and Websites

Brownlie, Robin Jarvis, Adele Perry, Franca Iacovetta and Kathryn McPherson. "Roundtable Discussion." Panel at the Fort Garry Lectures in History, University of Manitoba, Winnipeg, May 2004.

Cook, Catherine L. "Jurisdiction and First Nations Health and Health Care," MSC thesis, University of Manitoba, 2003.

Cowall Farrell, Emily, and Meeka Alivaktuk. "The Work We Have Done: Relationship, Investment and Contribution The Inuit Workers at St. Luke's Hospital, Pannirtuuq, 1930–1972." Unpublished paper, 2003.

Farrell Racette, Sherry. "Don't Get Me Started! Absence, Tokenism, and Missed Opportunities? Aboriginal Women and Public History in Canada." Paper presented at the annual meeting of the Canadian Historical Association, Saskatoon, May 2007.

Flynn, Karen. "Race, Class and Gender: Black Nurses in Ontario, 1950–1980." PhD diss., York University, 2000.

Fransen, J.J. "Employment Experience and Economic Position of a Selected Group of Indians in Metropolitan Toronto." MA thesis, University of Toronto, 1964.

Galley, Valerie. "Indigenization as Neoliberal Rule: The Case of the Canadian Aboriginal Head Start Initiative." MA thesis, Trent University, 2004.

Gerein, Nancy Marian, "The Community Health Representative in Alberta—A Program Evaluaiton," MA thesis, University of British Columbia, 1977.

Gregory, David, Mary Jane L. McCallum, Karen R. Grant and Brenda Elias. "Self-Determination and the Swampy Cree Tribal Council: A Case Study Involving Nursing Education in Northern Manitoba." Paper presented at the Manitoba First Nations Centre for Aboriginal Health Research, Health Services Research Project Symposium, Opaskwayak Cree Nation, March 2006.

Harris, Aroha. "Dancing with the State: Māori Creative Energies and Policies of Integration 1945–1967." PhD diss., University of Auckland, 2007.

Innes, Robert Alexander, Susan M. Hill and Mary Jane McCallum. "Power, Culture and Place: Aboriginal Historians in Aboriginal History." Panel at the annual meeting of the Canadian Historical Association, University of British Columbia, Vancouver, British Columbia, June, 2008.

Latham Carl R., "Indian Placement Programme Administered by the Indian Affairs Branch of the Department of Citizenship and Immigration," MA thesis, University of Toronto 1958.

MacKay, Kathryn Leilani. "Warrior into Welder: A History of Federal Employment Programs for American Indians, 1878–1972." PhD Diss., University of Utah, 1987.

McCallum, Mary Jane. "To Make Good Canadians: Girl Guiding in Indian Residential Schools." MA thesis, Trent University, 2002.

McNab, Miriam, Robert Alexander Innes, Rebecca Major and Anne Mease. "Territory, Movement and Theory: Towards a Critical Native Studies Pedagogy II." Panel presented at the Native American and Indigenous Studies Conference, Athens, Georgia, 10–12 April 2008.

Monture, Rick. "Teionkwakhashion tsi Niionkwariho:ten: "we share our matters": A literary history of Six Nations of the Grand River," PhD diss., McMaster University, 2010.

Pelletier, Terrance. "Cowesses First Nation, the Town of Broadview, and the City of Regina: A Study of Historical Relationships, 1870–1995." Paper presented at the annual meeting of the Canadian Historical Association, Toronto, May 2006.

Poulin, Grace. "Invisible Women: WWII Aboriginal Servicewomen in Canada." MA thesis, Trent University, 2007.

Richmond, Chantelle. "Social Support as it Shapes Aboriginal Health." PhD diss., McGill University, 2007.

Smith, Andrea. "Indigenous Women and Violence: Rethinking the Nation-State." Paper presented at the University of Manitoba, Winnipeg, March 2008.

White, Pamela. "Restructuring the Domestic Sphere—Prairie Indian Women on Reserves: Image, Ideology and State Policy 1880–1930." PhD diss., McGill University, 1987.

Secondary Sources

Abbott, Larry. "Shelley Niro," in "A Time of Visions: Interviews by Larry Abbott." http://www.britesites.com/native_artist_interviews/sniro.htm.

Abel, Kerry. "'Tangled, Lost and Bitter?' Current Directions in the Writing of Native History in Canada." *Acadiensis* XXV:1 (1996): 92–101.

Aboriginal Circle Canadian Panel on Violence Against Women Changing the Landscape: Ending Violence—Achieving Equality. Ottawa: Minister of Supply and Services, 1993.

Aboriginal Nurses Association of Canada. *Aboriginal Nurses Association of Canada: Working Together for Quality Nursing Care and Healing, 1975–1995.* Ottawa: Aboriginal Nurses Association of Canada, 1995.

_____. *Twice As Good: A History of Aboriginal Nurses.* Ottawa: Aboriginal Nurses Association of Canada, 2007.

Absolon, Kathy, and Cam Willett. "Putting Ourselves Forward: Location in Aboriginal Research." In *Research as Resistance: Critical, Indigenous and Anti-oppressive Approaches*, edited by Leslie Brown and Susan Strega, 97–126. Toronto: Canadian Scholars' Press/Women's Press, 2005.

Acoose, Janice. *Iskwewak—kah'ki yaw ni wahkomakanak: Neither Indian Princesses Nor Easy Squaws.* Toronto: Women's Press, 1995.

Adams, David Wallace. *Education for Extinction: American Indians and the Boarding School Experience 1875–1928.* Lawrence: University Press of Kansas, 1995.

Adams, Mary Louise. *The Trouble with Normal: Postwar Youth and the Making of Heterosexuality.* Toronto: University of Toronto Press, 1997.

Albers, Patricia, and Beatrice Medicine, eds. *The Hidden Half: Studies of Plains Indian Women.* New York: University Press of America, 1983.

Allen, Chadwick. "Unspeaking the Settler: 'The Indian Today' in International Perspective." *American Studies* 46:3/4 (Fall/Winter 2005): 39–57.

Anderson, Kay. *Vancouver's Chinatown: Racial Discourse in Canada, 1875–1980.* Montreal: McGill-Queen's University Press, 1991.

Anderson, Kim. *Life Stages and Native Women: Memory, Teachings, and Story Medicine* (Winnipeg: University of Manitoba Press, 2011).

Anderson, Marcia, and Barrie Lavallee. "The development of the First Nations, Inuit and Métis medical workforce." *Medical Journal of Australia* 186:10 (2007): 539-540.

Arat-Koc, Sedef. "From 'Mothers of the Nation' to Migrant Workers: Immigration Policies and Domestic Workers in Canadian History." In *Rethinking Canada: The Promise of Women's History*, edited by Veronica Strong-Boag, Mona Gleason and Adele Perry, 283–98. 4th ed. Toronto: Oxford University Press, 2002.

Backhouse, Constance. *Colour-Coded: A Legal History of Racism in Canada, 1900–1950.* Toronto: University of Toronto Press, 1999.

Bakan, Abigail B. and Daiva Stasiulis, eds. *Not One of the Family: Foreign Domestic Workers in Canada.* Toronto: University of Toronto Press, 1997.

Banet-Weiser, Sarah. *The Most Beautiful Girl in the World: Beauty Pageants and National Identity.* Berkeley: University of California, 1999.

Barman, Jean. "Separate and Unequal: Indian and White Girls at All Hallows School, 1884–1920." In *Children, Teachers and Schools in the History of British Columbia,* edited by Jean Barman, Neil Sutherland and J. Donald Wilson, 333–357. Calgary: Detselig Enterprises, 1995.

____. "Taming Aboriginal Sexuality: Gender, Power, and Race in British Columbia, 1850-1900." *BC Studies* 115–16 (Fall-Winter 1997–98): 237–67.

Barman, Jean, Y. Hébert, and D. McCaskill, eds. *Indian Education in Canada. Volume 1: The Legacy.* Vancouver: University of British Columbia Press, 1986.

Bataille, Gretchen M., and Kathleen Mullen Sands. *American Indian Women Telling Their Lives.* Lincoln: University of Nebraska Press, 1987.

Bataille, Gretchen M., and Laurie Lisa, eds. *Native American Women: A Biographical Dictionary.* New York: Taylor and Francis, 2001. Available at http://www.netlibrary.com.proxy2.lib.umanitoba.ca/Reader/. Accessed 6 May 2008.

Baumgart, Alice J., and Jenniece Larsen. *Canadian Nursing Faces the Future: Development and Change.* Toronto: C.V. Mosby Company, 1988.

Beaulieu, George, Comp. *Sandy Bay Anishinabek: The Elders Tell Their Stories.* Manitoba: Sandy Bay Education Foundation, 1996.

Bederman, Gail. *Manliness and Civilization: A Cultural History of Gender and Race in the U.S. 1880–1917.* Chicago: University of Chicago Press, 1995.

Berman, Tressa. Circle of Goods: *Women, Work and Welfare in a Reservation Community.* Albany: State University of New York, 2003.

Binnema, Ted, and Susan Neylan, eds. *New Histories for Old: Changing Perspectives on Canada's Native Pasts.* Vancouver: Unviersity of British Columbia Press, 2007.

Birkett, Dea. "The 'White Woman's Burden' in the 'White Man's Grave': The Introduction of British Nurses in Colonial West Africa." *In Western Women and Imperialism: Complicity and Resistance,* edited by Nupur Chaudhuri and Margaret Strobel, 177–88. Bloomington: Indiana University Press, 1992.

Blackwelder, Julia Kirk. *Styling Jim Crow: African American Beauty Training during Segregation.* College Station, TX: Texas A&M University Press, 2003.

Bluebird, Leonard, and Dorothy Krasaukas. "Canadian First Nation Control of Health: A Successful Case Study." In *Circumpolar Health 90: Proceedings of the 8th International Congress on Circumpolar Health,* edited by B. Postl et al., 59–62. Winnipeg: University of Manitoba Press, 1991.

Blythe, Jennifer, and Peggy Martin McGuire. "The Changing Employment of Cree Women in Moosonee and Moose Factory." In *Women of the First Nations: Power, Wisdom, and Strength,* edited by Christine Miller and Patricia Chuchryk, 131–50. Winnipeg: University of Manitoba Press, 1996.

Bohaker, Heidi, and Franca Iacovetta. "Making Aboriginal People 'Immigrants Too': A Comparison of Citizenship Programs for Newcomers and Indigenous Peoples in Postwar Canada, 1940s–1960s." *Canadian Historical Review* 90, 2 (September 2009) 427–461.

Boutilier, Beverly, and Alison Prentice. *Creating Historical Memory: English-Canadian Women and the Work of History.* Vancouver: UBC Press, 1997.

Brodribb, Somer. "The Traditional Roles of Native Women in Canada and the Impact of Colonization." *Canadian Journal of Native Studies* 4, 1 (1984): 85–103.

Brookes, Barbara, and Catherine Smith. "Technology and Gender: Barbers and Hairdressers in New Zealand 1900–1970." *History and Technology* 25, 4 (2009): 365–86.

Brown, Jennifer S.H. "A Cree Nurse in a Cradle of Methodism: Little Mary and the Egerton R. Young Family at Norway House and Berens River." In *First Days, Fighting Days: Women in Manitoba History,* edited by Mary Kinnear, 18–40. Regina: Canadian Plains Research Center, University of Regina, 1987.

____. *Strangers in Blood: Fur Trade Company Families in Indian Country.* Vancouver: University of British Columbia Press, 1980.

Brown, Jennifer S.H., and Elizabeth Vibert, eds. *Reading Beyond Words: Contexts for Native History.* Toronto: Broadview Press, 1996.

Brownlie, Robin Jarvis. "First Nations Perspectives and Historical Thinking in Canada." In *First Nations, First Thoughts—New Challenges,* edited by Annis May Timpson, 21-50. Vancouver: UBC Press, 2009.

____. "'Living the same as the white people': Mohawk and Anishinabe Women's Labour in Southern Ontario in the 1920s and 30s." *Labour/Le Travail* 61 (Spring 2008): 41–68.

____. "'A better citizen than lots of white men': First Nations Enfranchisement—An Ontario Case Study, 1918–1940." *Canadian Historical Review* 87:1 (March 2006): 29–52.

____. *A Fatherly Eye: Indian Agents, Government Power, and Aboriginal Resistance in Ontario, 1918–1939.* Don Mills, ON: Oxford University Press, 2003.

Brownlie, Robin Jarvis, and Mary-Ellen Kelm. "Desperately Seeking Absolution: Native Agency as Colonialist Alibi?" *Canadian Historical Review* 75, 4 (December 1994): 543–56.

Buckley, Helen. *The Indians and Metis of Northern Saskatchewan: A Report on Economic and Social Development.* Saskatoon: Centre for Community Studies, 1963.

Burton, Antoinette. "Archive Stories: Gender in the Making of Imperial and Colonial Histories." In *Gender and Empire*, edited by Phillipa Levine, 281–93. Oxford: Oxford University Press, 2004.

____. "Who Needs the Nation? Interrogating 'British History.'" *Journal of Historical Sociology* 10, 3 (1997): 272–282.

Burton, Antoinette, ed. *Gender, Sexuality and Colonial Modernities.* New York: Routledge, 1999.

Cahill, Cathleen. *Federal Fathers and Mothers: A Social History of the United States Indian Service,* 1869-1933. Chapel Hill: University of North Carolina Press, 2011.

Calliste, Agnes. "Antiracism Organizing and Resistance in Nursing: African-Canadian Women." *Canadian Review of Sociology and Anthropology* 33, 3 (August 1996): 361–90.

____. "Canada's Immigration Policy and Domestics from the Caribbean: The Second Domestic Scheme." *Race, Class, Gender: Bonds and Barriers Socialist Studies* 5 (1989): 133–65.

____. "Women of Exceptional Merit: Immigration of Caribbean Nurses to Canada." *Canadian Journal of Women and the Law* 6, 1 (1993): 85–102.

Calloway, Colin. *New Worlds for All: Indians, Europeans and the Remaking of Early America.* Baltimore: The Johns Hopkins University Press, 1997.

Campbell, Maria. *Halfbreed.* Toronto: McClelland and Stewart, 1977.

Cardinal, Harold. *Unjust Society.* Edmonton: M.G. Hurtig Ltd., 1969.

Carlson, Keith Thor. *The Power of Place, the Problem of Time: Aboriginal Identity and Historical Consciousness in the Cauldron of Colonialism.* Toronto: Unviersity of Toronto Press, 2010.

Carlson, Keith Thor, Melinda Marie Jette, and Kenichi Matsui. "An Annotated Bibliography of Major Writings in Aboriginal History, 1990–99." *Canadian Historical Review* 82, 1 (2001): 122–71.

Carter, Sarah. *Capturing Women: The Manipulation of Cultural Imagery in Canada's Prairie West.* Montreal: McGill-Queen's University Press, 1997.

____. "Categories and Terrains of Exclusion: Constructing the 'Indian Woman' in the Early Settlement Era in Western Canada." *Great Plains Quarterly* 13, 3 (Summer 1993): 147–61.

____. *Lost Harvests: Prairie Indian Reserve Farmers and Government Policy.* Montreal: McGill-Queen's University Press, 1990.

Child, Brenda. *Holding our World Together: Ojibwe Women and the Survival of Community.* New York: Penguin, 2013.

Chilton, Lisa. *Agents of Empire: British Female Migration to Canada and Australia, 1860s–1930.* Toronto: University of Toronto Press, 2007.

Coates, Ken. "Writing First Nations into Canadian History: A Review of Recent Scholarly Works." *Canadian Historical Review* 81, 1 (March 2000): 99–114.

Coates, Ken, and Robin Fisher, eds. *Out of the Background: Readings on Canadian Native History.* 2nd ed. Toronto: Copp Clark, 1999.

Cobb, Daniel M., and Loretta Fowler. *Beyond Red Power: American Indian Politics and Activism since 1900.* Santa Fe: School for Advanced Research Press, 2007.

Comaroff, John, and Jean Comaroff. *Ethnography and the Historical Imagination.* Boulder: Westview Press, 1992.

Connell, G., R. Flett, and P. Stewart. "Implementing Primary Health Care through Community Control: The Experience of Swampy Cree Tribal Council." In *Circumpolar Health 90: Proceedings of the 8th International Congress on Circumpolar Health,* edited by B. Postl et al., 44–6. Winnipeg: University of Manitoba Press, 1991.

Cuthand, Doug. "Saskatchewan Loses Esteemed Health Advocate." *Saskatchewan Indian* 27:4 (winter 1997): 21.

____."Goodwill, Jean Cuthand (1928–97)." *The Encyclopedia of Saskatchewan* http://esask.uregina.ca/entry/goodwill_jean_cuthand_1928-97.html. Accessed 12 April 2014.

Davidson, Malcolm. "Indian Economic Development in 'the Indian News' (1954–1982). *Canadian Journal of Native Studies* 3, 2 (1983): 321–40.

Dedam-Moutour, Debbie, Marcel Tessier, et al. *Voices of Community Health Representatives.* Kahnawake QC: National Indian and Inuit community Health Representatives Organization (NIICHRO), 2010.

Deloria, Philip J. *Indians in Unexpected Places.* Lawrence: University Press of Kansas, 2004.

____. *Playing Indian.* New Haven, CT: Yale University Press, 1998.

____. "Thinking about Self in a Family Way." *Journal of American History* 89, 1 (June 2002): 25–9.

Denetdale, Jennifer Nez. "Chairmen, Presidents, and Princesses: The Navajo Nation, Gender, and Politics of Tradition." *Wicazo Sa Review* 21:1 (Spring 2006): 9–28.

Dickason, Olive. *Canada's First Nations: A History of Founding Peoples from Earliest Times.* 3rd ed. Don Mills, ON: Oxford University Press, 2002.

____. *The Myth of the Savage and the Beginnings of French Colonialism in the Americas.* Edmonton: University of Alberta Press, 1984.

Dosman, Edgar. Indians: *The Urban Dilemma.* Toronto: McClelland and Stewart, 1972.

Dubinsky, Karen. *Improper Advances: Rape and Heterosexual Conflict in Ontario 1880–1929.* Chicago: University of Chicago Press, 1993.

Ellis, Clyde. "Five Dollars a Week to Be 'Regular Indians': Shows, Exhibitions, and the Economics of Indian Dancing, 1880–1930." In *Native Pathways: American Indian Culture and Economic Development in the Twentieth Century,* edited by Brian Hosmer and Colleen O'Neill, 184–208. Boulder: University Press of Colorado, 2004.

Epp, Marlene, Franca Iacovetta, and Frances Swyripa, eds. *Sisters or Strangers? Immigrant Women, Minority Women, and the Racialized 'Other' in Canadian History.* Toronto: University of Toronto Press, 2004.

Farrell Racette, Sherry. "Looking for Stories and Unbroken Threads: Museum Artifacts as Women's History and Cultural Legacy." In *Restoring the Balance: First Nations Women, Community, and Culture,* ed. Gail Guthrie Valaskakis, Madeleine Dion Stout, and Eric Guimond, 283–312. Winnipeg: University of Manitoba Press.

Feldberg, Georgina, Molly Ladd-Taylor, Alison Li and Kathryn McPherson, eds. *Women, Health and Nation: Canada and the United States since 1945.* Montreal: McGill-Queen's University Press, 2003.

Fisher, Robin. *Contact and Conflict: Indian-European Relations in British Columbia, 1774–1890.* Vancouver: University of British Columbia Press, 1978.

Fiske, Jo-Anne. "Fishing Is Women's Business: Changing Economic Roles of Carrier Women and Men." In *Native Peoples, Native Lands: Canadian Indians, Inuit and Metis,* edited by Bruce Cox, 186–98. Ottawa: Carleton University Press, 1987.

____. "The Womb Is to the Nation as the Heart Is to the Body: Ethnopolitical Discourses of the Canadian Indigenous Women's Movement." In *Feminism, Political Economy and the State: Contested Terrain,* edited by Pat Armstrong and M. Patricia Connelly, 293–325. Toronto: Canadian Scholars' Press, 1999.

Fixico, Donald. *Termination and Relocation: Federal Indian Policy, 1945–1960.* Albuquerque: University of New Mexico Press, 1986.

____. *The Urban Indian Experience in America.* Albuquerque: University of New Mexico Press, 2000.

Flynn, Karen. "Race, the State, and Caribbean Immigrant Nurses, 1950–1962." In *Women, Health and Nation: Canada and the United States Since 1945,* edited by Georgina Felberg, Molly Ladd-Taylor, Alison Li, and Kathryn McPherson, 247–63. Montreal: McGill-Queen's University Press, 2003.

____. *Moving Beyond Borders: a History of Black Canadian and Caribbean Women in the Diaspora.* Toronto: University of Toronto Press, 2011

Francis, Daniel. *The Imaginary Indian: The Image of the Indian in Canadian Culture.* Vancouver: Arsenal Pulp Press, 1997.

Freeman, Carla. *High Tech and High Heels in the Global Economy: Women, Work and Pink-Collar Identities in the Caribbean.* Durham: Duke University Press, 2000.

Friesen, Gerald. *The Canadian Prairies: A History.* Toronto: University of Toronto Press, 1987.

Froman, Karen. "The Undercover Indian: Explorations in Urban Aboriginal Identity." In *Intersecting Worlds: Rural and Urban Aboriginal Issues,* edited by Denise Fuchs and Mary Jane McCallum, 13–22. Winnipeg: St. John's College Press, 2005.

Furniss, Elizabeth. *Victims of Benevolence: The Dark Legacy of the Williams Lake Indian Residential School.* Vancouver: Arsenal Pulp Press, 1995.

Gentile, Patrizia. "'Government Girls' and 'Ottawa Men': Cold War Management of Gender Relations in the Civil Service." In *Whose National Security? Canadian State Surveillance and the Creation of Enemies,* edited by Gary Kinsman, Dieter K. Buse, and Mercedes Steedman, 131–141. Toronto: Between the Lines, 2000.

Getty, Ian A.L., and Antoine S. Lussier, eds. *As Long as the Sun Shines and Water Flows: A Reader in Canadian Native Studies.* Vancouver: University of British Columbia Press, 1983.

Gilbert, Helen. "Great Adventures in Nursing: Colonial Discourse and Health Care Delivery in Canada's North." *Jouvert: A Journal of Postcolonial Studies* 7, 2 (Winter/Spring, 2003). Available at: http://english.chass.ncsu.edu/jouvert/v7i2/gilber.htm. Accessed 12 April 2014.

Gill, Tiffany M. "Civic Beauty: Beauty Culturists and the Politics of African American Female Entrepreneurship, 1900–1965." *Enterprise and Society* 5, 4 (2004): 583–93.

Gleason, Mona. *Normalizing the Ideal: Psychology, Schooling and the Family in Postwar Canada.* Toronto: University of Toronto Press, 1999.

Gonzales, Ellice B. *Changing Economic Roles for Micmac Men and Women: An Ethnohistorical Analysis.* National Museum of Man Mercury Series: Paper 72. Ottawa: National Museums of Canada, 1981.

Gooderham, Kent. *I Am an Indian.* Toronto: J.M. Dent and Sons Ltd., 1969.

Goodwill, Jean Cuthand. "Indian and Inuit Nurses of Canada." *Canadian Woman Studies* 10, 2–3 (Summer/Fall 1989): 117–23.

____."Indian and Inuit Nurses of Canada." *Saskatchewan Indian Federated College Journal 4, 1* (1988): 93–104.

____."Organized Political Action: Indian and Inuit Nurses of Canada." In *Canadian Nursing Faces the Future: Development and Change,* edited by Alice J. Baumgart and Jenniece Larsen, 501–10. Toronto: C.V. Mosby Company, 1988.

____. "Nursing Canada's Indigenous People." Editorial, *The Canadian Nurse* 80, 1 (January 1984): 6.

____."A New Horizon for Native Women in Canada." In *Citizen Participation: Canada: A Book of Readings,* edited by James A. Draper, 369-70. Toronto: New Press, 1971.

Grant, Agnes. *No End of Grief: Indian Residential Schools in Canada.* Winnipeg: Pemmican Publications Inc., 1996.

Gray, Patricia D. and Debera J. Thomas. "Critical Reflections on Culture in Nursing." *Journal of Cultural Diversity* 13, 2 (Summer 2006): 76–82.

Gregory, David, et al. *Against the Odds: An Update on Aboriginal Nursing in Canada.* Available at the University of Lethbridge Institutional Repository, https://www.uleth.ca/dspace/handle/10133/522.

Gregory, David, Mary Jane L. McCallum, Karen R. Grant, and Brenda Elias. "The Swampy Cree Tribal Council and Aboriginal Governance: A Case Study of Nursing Education in Northern Manitoba." *Canadian Journal of Nursing Research* 40, 2 (June 2008): 132–149. Accessed 12 April 2014.

Green, Joyce, ed. *Making Space For Indigenous Feminism.* Black Point, NS: Fernwood Publishing, 2007.

Green, Rayna. "The Pocahontas Perplex: The Image of Indian Women in American Culture." *Massachusetts Review* 16 (1975): 698–714.

Grygier, Pat Sandiford. *A Long Way from Home: The Tuberculosis Epidemic among the Inuit.* Montreal: McGill-Queen's University Press, 1994.

Guard, Julie. "Authenticity on the Line: Women Workers, Native 'Scabs' and the Multi-ethnic Politics of Identity in a Left-Led Strike in Cold War Canada." *Journal of Women's History* 15, 4 (Winter 2004): 117–40.

Haidarali, Laila. "'Is It True What They Say About Models?': Modelling African American Womanhood on the eve of the civil rights era." *Atlantis: A Women's Studies Journal* 32, 1,(2007): 144–155.

Harris, Cole. *Making Native Space: Colonialism, Resistance, and Reserves in British Columbia.* Vancouver: University of British Columbia Press, 2002.

Hartman, Susan M. "Women's Employment and the Domestic Ideal in the Early Cold War Years." In *Not June Cleaver: Women and Gender in Postwar America, 1945–1960,* edited by Joanne Myerowitz, 84–101. Philadelphia: Temple University Press, 1994.

Hart-Wasekeesikaw, Fjola. "Nurse Profile: Jocelyn Bruyere." *The Aboriginal Nurse* 15, 1 (April 2000): 1, 10.

Haskins, Victoria. *Matrons and Maids: Regulating Indian Domestic Service in Tucson, 1914–1934.* Tucson, University of Arizona Press, 2012.

____. "On the Doorstep: Aboriginal Domestic Service as a 'Contact Zone.'" *Australian Feminist Studies* 16, 34 (2001): 13–25.

____. "Domestic Service and Frontier Feminism: The Call for a Woman Visitor to 'Half-Caste' Girls and Women in Domestic Service, Adelaide, 1925–1928," *Frontiers* 28, 1–2 (2007): 124–94.

Haskins, Victoria, and Margaret D. Jacobs. "Introduction." *Frontiers* 28, 1–2 (2007): ix–xvi.

Haskins, Victoria, and Claire Lowrie, eds. *Colonization and Domestic Service: Historical and Contemporary Perspectives.* New York: Routledge. Forthcoming, 2014.

Hawthorn, H.B., C.S. Belshaw, and S.M. Jamieson. *The Indians of British Columbia: A Study of Contemporary Social Adjustment.* Toronto: University of Toronto Press, 1960.

High, Steven. "Native Wage Labour and Independent Production during the 'Era of Irrelevance.'" *Labour/Le Travail* 37 (Spring 1996): 243–64.

Hill, Richard. *Skywalkers: A History of Indian Ironworkers.* Brantford, ON: Woodland Indian Cultural Education Centre, 1987.

Hine, Darlene Clark. *Black Women in White: Racial Conflict and Co-operation in the Nursing Profession, 1890–1950.* Bloomington: Indiana University Press, 1989.

Hondagneu-Sotelo, Pierrette. *Domestica: Immigrant Workers Cleaning and Caring in the Shadows of Affluence.* Berkeley: University of California Press, 2001.

Howard-Bobiwash, Heather. "Women's Class Strategies as Activism in Native Community Building in Toronto, 1950–1975." *American Indian Quarterly* 27, 3 and 4 (Summer/Fall 2003): 566–82.

Hull, Jeremy. *Native Women and Work.* Winnipeg: Institute of Urban Studies, 1983.

Hurtado, Albert L. "'Hardly a Farm House—A Kitchen without Them': Indian and White Households on the California Borderland Frontier in 1860." *Western Historical Quarterly* (July 1982): 245–70.

Iacovetta, Franca. "'Primitive Villagers and Uneducated Girls': Canada Recruits Domestics from Italy, 1951–52." *Canadian Woman Studies* 7, 4 (Winter 1986): 14–8.

____. "Towards a More Human Academy? Some Observations from a Canadian Feminist Historian." *Journal of Women's History* 18, 1 (2006): 141–6.

____. "Gendering Trans/National histories: Feminists Rewriting Canadian History." *Journal of Women's History* 19, 1 (2007): 206-213.

Iacovetta, Franca, and Wendy Mitchinson, "Social History and Case Files Research." In *On the Case: Explorations in Social History,* edited by Franca Iacovetta and Wendy Mitchinson, 3–21. Toronto: University of Toronto Press, 1998.

Ingraham, Chrys. *White Weddings: Romancing Heterosexuality in Popular Culture.* New York: Routledge, 1999.

Innes, Robert Alexander. "'On Home Ground Now. I'm Safe': Saskatchewan Aboriginal Veterans in the Immediate Postwar Years, 1945–1946." *American Indian Quarterly* 28, 3&4 (2004): 685–718.

Innes, Rob, Brenda Macdougall and Frank Tough. "Band Economies 1897-1915." In *Atlas of Saskatchewan: Celebrating the Millennium,* edited by Ka-iu Fung, 60. Saskatoon: University of Saskatchewan, 1999.

Innis, Harold A. *The Fur Trade in Canada: An Introduction to Canadian Economic History.* With an introduction by Arthur J. Ray. Toronto: University of Toronto Press, 1999.

Jacobs, Margaret D. "Diverted Mothering among American Indian Domestic Servants, 1920–1940." In *Indigenous Women and Work: From Labour to Activism,* edited by Carol Williams, 179–192. Urbana: University of Illinois Press, 2012.

____. "Working on the Domestic Frontier: American Indian Domestic Servants in White Women's Households in the San Francisco Bay Area, 1920–1940." *Frontiers* 28, 1–2 (2007): 165–99.

____. *Engendered Encounters: Feminism and Pueblo Cultures,* 1879–1934. Lincoln: University of Nebraska Press, 1999.

Janovicek, Nancy. "'Assisting our own': Urban Migration, Self-Governance, and Native Women's Organizing in Thunder Bay, Ontario, 1972–1989." *American Indian Quarterly* 27, 3 and 4 (Summer/Fall 2003): 548–65.

Jasen, Patricia. "Race, Culture, and the Colonization of Childbirth in Northern Canada." In *Rethinking Canada: The Promise of Women's History,* edited by Veronica Strong-Boag, Mona Gleason and Adele Perry, 355–66. Don Mills, ON: Oxford University Press, 2002.

Kaufert, Joseph M., Robert W. Putsch, and Margaret Lavallee. "Experience of Aboriginal Health Interpreters in Mediation of Conflicting Values in End-of-Life Decision Making." In *Circumpolar Health 96: Proceedings of the 10th International Congress on Circumpolar Health,* edited by R. Fortuine et al., 44–5. American Society for Circumpolar Health, 1998.

Kaufert, Joseph M., and William W. Koolage. "Role Conflict among 'Culture Brokers': The Experience of Native Canadian Medical Interpreters." *Social Science and Medicine* 18, 3 (2005): 283–6.

Kelm, Mary-Ellen. *Colonizing Bodies: Aboriginal Health and Healing in British Columbia, 1990–1950.* Vancouver: University of British Columbia Press, 1998.

Kelm, Mary-Ellen, and Aboriginal Nurses Association of Canada. *30 Years of Community: Aboriginal Nurses Association of Canada.* Ottawa: Aboriginal Nurses Association of Canada, 2005.

Kinnear, J. "The Professionalization of Canadian Nursing, 1924–1932: Views in the CN and CMAJ." *Canadian Bulletin of Medical History* 11, 1 (1994): 3–22.

Kinnear, Mary. *A Female Economy: Women's Work in a Prairie Province 1870–1970.* Montreal: McGill-Queen's University Press, 1998.

____. *First Days, Fighting Days: Women in Manitoba History.* Regina: Canadian Plains Research Centre, University of Regina, 1987.

____. *In-subordination: Professional Women, 1870–1970.* Montreal: McGill-Queen's University Press, 1995.

Kirkwood, Rondalyn A. "Discipline Discrimination and Gender Discrimination: The Case of Nursing in Canadian Universities, 1920–1950." *Atlantis* 16, 2 (2002): 52–63.

Klein, Laura and Lillian Ackerman, eds. *Women and Power in Native North America.* Norman: University of Oklahoma Press, 1995.

Knight, Rolf. *Indians At Work: An Informal History of Native Indian Labour in British Columbia, 1853–1930.* Vancouver: University of British Columbia Press, 1978.

Knockwood, Isabelle. *Out of the Depths: The Experiences of Mi'kmaw Children at the Indian Residential School of Schubenacadie, Nova Scotia.* Lockeport, NS: Roseway Publishing, 1992.

Knowles, Valerie. *First Person: A Biography of Cairine Wilson, Canada's First Woman Senator.* Toronto: Dundurn Press, 1988.

Konkle, Maureen. *Writing Indian Nations: Native Intellectuals and the Politics of Historiography, 1827–1863.* Chapel Hill: University of North Carolina Press, 2004.

Kozol, Wendy. "Miss Indian America: Regulatory Gazes and the Politics of Affiliation." *Feminist Studies* 31, 1 (Spring 2005): 64–94.

Kulig, J., and S. Grypma. "Breaking Down Racial Barriers: Honouring Pioneer Aboriginal Nurses from the Blood Reserve." *Alberta RN* 62, 8 (October 2006): 14–6.

Lackenbauer, P. Whitney. *Battlegrounds: The Canadian Military and Aboriginal Lands.* Vancouver: University of British Columbia Press, 2007.

Lackenbauer, P. Whitney, and Craig Leslie Mantle, eds. *Aboriginal Peoples and the Canadian Military: Historical Perspectives.* Winnipeg: Canadian Defence Academy Press, 2007.

LaGrand, James B. *Indian Metropolis: Native Americans in Chicago 1945–1975.* Urbana: University of Chicago Press, 2002.

Laliberte, Ron. "The 'Grab-a-Hoe' Indians: The Canadian State and the Procurement of Aboriginal Labour for the Southern Alberta Sugar Beet Industry." *Prairie Forum* 31, 2 (Fall 2006): 305–24.

Laliberte, Ron, and Vic Satzewich. "Native Migrant Labour in the Southern Alberta Sugar-Beet Industry: Coercion and Paternalism in the Recruitment of Labour." *Canadian Review of Sociology and Anthropology* 36 (1999).

Lanceley, Darlene. "The Post-Secondary Assistance Program for Indian Education: The Vehicle for Change and the Voice of Opposition." In *Hitting the Books: The Politics of Educational Retrenchment,* edited by Terry Wotherspoon. Toronto: Garamond Press, 1991.

LaRocque, Emma. "The Colonization of a Native Woman Scholar." In *Women of the First Nations: Power, Wisdom, and Strength,* edited by Christine Miller and Patricia Chuchryk with Marie Smallface Marule, Brenda Manyfingers and Cheryl Deering. Winnipeg: University of Manitoba Press, 1996.

Lawrence, Bonita. *"Real" Indians and Others: Mixed Blood Urban Native Peoples and Indigenous Nationhood.* Vancouver: University of British Columbia Press, 2004.

Lawrence, Jane. "The Indian Health Service and the Sterilization of Native American Women." *American Indian Quarterly* 24, 3 (Summer 2000): 400–20.

Leow, Patty. "The Back of the Homefront: Black and American Indian Women in Wisconsin during World War II." *Wisconsin Magazine of History* 82, 2 (Winter 1998–1999): 82–103.

Leslie, Genevieve. "Domestic Service in Canada, 1880–1920." In *Women at Work: Ontario, 1850–1930,* edited by Janice Acton, Penny Goldsmith and Bonnie Shepard, 71–125. Toronto: Canadian Women's Educational Press, 1974.

Little, Margaret. *No Car, No Radio, No Liquor Permit: The Moral Regulation of Single Mothers in Ontario 1920–1997.* Toronto: Oxford University Press, 1998.

Long, David, and Olive Dickason. *Visions of the Heart: An Introduction to Canadian Aboriginal Issues.* 2nd ed. Toronto: Harcourt Brace, 2000.

Lutz, John. *Makuk: A New History of Aboriginal-White Relations.* Vancouver: University of British Columbia Press, 2008.

Lux, Maureen K. *Medicine That Walks: Disease, Medicine, and Canadian Plains Native People, 1880–1940.* Toronto: University of Toronto Press, 2001.

Lyons, Scott Richard. "The Termination and Removal of Ward Churchill." *The Indian Country Today,* February 23, 2005. Reprinted as "Why Indians Should Defend Churchill: Ward Churchill and the Identity Police." *Counterpunch* February 19/20, 2005.

MacKinnon, Melanie. "A First Nations Voice in the Present Creates Healing in the Future." *Canadian Journal of Public Health* (January – February 2005): 513–516.

Mansell, Diana J. *Forging the Future: A History of Nursing in Canada.* Ann Arbor, MI: Thomas Press, 2003.

Maracle, Lee. *Bobbi Lee: Indian Rebel.* Toronto: Women's Press, 1990.

Marks, Lynne. *Revivals and Roller Rinks: Religion, Leisure, and Identity in Late-Nineteenth-Century Small-Town Ontario.* Toronto: University of Toronto Press, 1996.

Marks, Shula. *Divided Sisterhood: Race, Class and Gender in the South African Nursing Profession.* London: Macmillan Press Ltd., 1994.

Martens, Ethel G. "Culture and Communications—Training Indians and Eskimos as Community Health Workers." *Canadian Journal of Public Health* 57, 11 (November 1966): 495–503.

Marubbio, M. Elise. *Killing the Indian Maiden: Images of Native American Women in Film.* Lexington: University Press of Kentucky, 2006.

May, Elaine Tyler. *Homeward Bound: American Families in the Cold War Era.* New York: Basic Books, 1988.

McBride, Wendy, and David Gregory. "Aboriginal Health Human Resources Initiatives: Towards the Development of a Strategic Framework." *Canadian Journal of Nursing Research* 37, 4 (December 2005): 89–94.

McCallum, Mary Jane. "This Last Frontier: Isolation and Aboriginal Health." *Canadian Bulletin of Medical History* 22, 1 (2005): 103–20.

____. "'I Would Like The Girls At Home': Domestic Labor and the Age of Discharge at Canadian Indian Residential Schools. *Colonization and Domestic Service: Historical and Contemporary Perspectives,* edited by Victoria Haskins and Claire Lowrie. New York: Routledge. Forthcoming, 2014.

McClintock, Anne. *Imperial Leather: Race, Gender and Sexuality in the Colonial Context.* New York: Routledge, 1995.

McCormick Stewart, Pat. "Helping People to Help Themselves—A Community Development Approach to Nursing Education." *The Canadian Nurse* 80, 1 (January 1984): 36.

McIntyre, Marjorie, Elizabeth Thomlinson, and Carol McDonald. *Realities of Canadian Nursing: Professional, Practice, and Power Issues.* 2nd ed. Philadelphia: Lippincott, Williams and Wilkins, 2006.

M'Closkey, Kathy. *Swept Under the Rug: A Hidden History of Navajo Weaving.* Albuquerque: University of New Mexico Press, 2002.

McNicoll, Paule, Frank Tester and Peter Kulchyski, "Arctic Abstersion: The Book of Wisdom for Eskimo, Modernism and Inuit Assimilation." *Etudes/Inuit/Studies* 23, 1–2 (1999): 199–220.

McPherson, Kathryn. *Bedside Matters: The Transformation of Canadian Nursing 1900–1990.* Don Mills, ON: Oxford University Press, 1996.

____. "Nurses, Archives, and the History of Canadian Health Care." *Archivaria* 41, (Spring 1996): 108–20.

____. "Nursing and Colonization: The Work of Indian Health Services Nurses in Manitoba, 1945–1970." In *Women, Health and Nation: Canada and the United States since 1945,* edited by Georgina Feldberg, Molly Ladd-Taylor, Alison Li and Kathryn McPherson, 223–46. Montreal: McGill-Queen's University Press, 2003.

McPherson, Kathryn, and Meryn Stuart. "Writing Nursing History in Canada: Issues and Approaches." *Canadian Bulletin of Medical History* 11 (1994): 3–22.

Medicine, Beatrice. *Learning to Be an Anthropologist and Remaining "Native."* Urbana: University of Illinois Press, 2001.

Meijer Drees, Laurie. "Training Aboriginal Nurses: The Indian Health Services in Northwestern Canada, 1939–1975." In *Caregiving on the Periphery: Historical Perspectives on Nursing and Midwifery in Canada,* edited by Myra Rutherdale, 181-209. Montreal and Kingston: McGill-Queen's University Press, 2010.

____."Indian Hospitals and Aboriginal Nurses: Canada and Alaska." *Canadian Bulletin of Medical History* 27, 1 (2010): 139–161.

____. "Native Studies and Ethical Guidelines for Research: Dilemmas and Solutions." *Native Studies Review* 14, 1 (2001): 83–114.

Meijer Drees, Laurie, and Lesley McBain. "Nursing and Native People in Northern Saskatchewan, 1930s–1950s." *Canadian Bulletin of Medical History* 18, 1 (2001): 43–65.

Midgley, Clare ed. *Gender and Imperialism.* Manchester: Manchester University Press, 1998.

Mihesuah, Devon A. *Cultivating the Rosebuds: The Education of Women at the Cherokee Female Seminary, 1851–1909.* Urbana: University of Illinois Press, 1993.

____. *Natives and Academics: Researching and Writing about American Indians.* Lincoln: University of Nebraska Press, 1998.

Mihesuah, Devon A., and Angela C. Wilson, eds. *Indigenizing the Academy: Transforming Scholarship and Empowering Communities.* Lincoln: University of Nebraska Press, 2004.

Miller, J.R. *Reflections on Native-Newcomer Relations: Selected Essays.* Toronto: University of Toronto Press, 2004.

____. *Shingwauk's Vision: A History of Native Residential Schools.* Toronto: University of Toronto Press, 1997.

____.*Skyscrapers Hide the Heavens: A History of Indian-White Relations in Canada.* Toronto: University of Toronto Press, 1989.

____.*Sweet Promises: A Reader on Indian-White Relations in Canada.* Toronto: University of Toronto Press, 1991.

Miller, J.R., and Myra Rutherdale. "'It's Our Country': First Nations' Participation in the Indian Pavilion at Expo '67." *Journal of the Canadian Historical Association* 17, 2 (2006): 148–173.

Milloy, John. *A National Crime: The Canadian Government and the Residential School System, 1879–1986.* Winnipeg: University of Manitoba Press, 1999.

Mitchinson, Wendy, Paula Bourne, Alison Prentice, Gail Cuthbert Brant, Beth Light, and Naomi Black, eds. *Canadian Women: A Reader.* Toronto: Harcourt Brace, 1996.

Monture-Agnus, Patricia. *Thunder in My Soul: A Mohawk Woman Speaks.* Halifax: Fernwood Press, 1995.

Newhouse, David R., Cora J. Voyageur, and Dan Beavon. *Hidden in Plain Sight: Contributions of Aboriginal Peoples to Canadian Identity and Culture.* Toronto: University of Toronto Press, 2005.

O'Brien, Stacey. "Jennie Nielsen." *Lethbridge Herald.* 5 June 2006, A3.

O'Neill, Colleen. "Rethinking Modernity and the Discourse of Development in American Indian History, an Introduction." In *Native Pathways: American Indian Culture and Economic Development in the Twentieth Century,* edited by Brian Hosmer and Colleen O'Neill, 1–24. Boulder: University Press of Colorado, 2004.

———. "The 'Making' of the Navajo Worker: Navajo Households, the Bureau of Indian Affairs, and Off-Reservation Wage Work, 1948–1960." *New Mexico Historical Review* 74, 4 (October 1999): 375–405.

———. *Working the Navajo Way: Labour and Culture in the Twentieth Century.* Lawrence: University Press of Kansas, 2005.

Palmer, Bryan. *Working Class Experience: The Rise and Reconstitution of Canadian Labour.* Toronto: Butterworths, 1983.

Parnaby, Andy. "'The best men that ever worked the lumber': Aboriginal Longshoremen on Burrard Inlet, BC, 1863–1939." *Canadian Historical Review* 87, 1 (March 2006): 53–78.

Parr, Joy. *The Gender of Breadwinners: Women, Men, and Change in Two Industrial Towns, 1880–1950.* Toronto: University of Toronto Press, 1990.

Paton, Cheryl. "Jean Goodwill: Health care worker encouraged youth." *Windspeaker Footprints.* http://www.ammsa.com/content/jean-goodwill-footprints. Accessed 12 April 2014.

Peers, Laura. *Playing Ourselves: Interpreting Native Histories at Historic Reconstructions.* Lanham, MD: Altamira Press, 2007.

Peiss, Kathy. *Cheap Amusements: Working Women and Leisure in Turn-of-the-Century New York.* Philadelphia, Temple University Press, 1986.

———. *Hope in a Jar: The Making of America's Beauty Culture.* New York: Metropolitan Books, 1998.

Perdue, Theda. *Cherokee Women: Gender and Culture Change, 1700–1835.* Lincoln: University of Nebraska Press, 1998.

Perry, Adele. "'Fair Ones of a Purer Caste': White Women and Colonialism in Nineteenth-Century British Columbia." *Feminist Studies* 23, 3 (Fall 1997): 50–24.

———. *On the Edge of Empire: Gender, Race, and the Making of British Columbia 1849–1871.* Toronto: University of Toronto Press, 2001.

Pettipas, Katherine. *Severing the Ties That Bind: Government Repression of Indigenous Religious Ceremonies on the Prairies.* Winnipeg: University of Manitoba Press, 1994.

Peyer, Bernd C., ed. *American Indian Nonfiction: An Anthology of Writings, 1760s–1930s.* Norman: University of Oklahoma Press, 2007.

Pickles, Katie, and Myra Rutherdale, eds. *Contact Zones: Aboriginal and Settler Women in Canada's Colonial Past.* Vancouver: University of British Columbia Press, 2005.

Pierson, Ruth Roach. *"They're Still Women After All": The Second World War and Canadian Womanhood.* Toronto: McClelland and Stewart, 1986.

Pierson, Ruth Roach, and Nupur Chaudhuri, eds. *Nation, Empire, Colony: Historicizing Gender and Race.* Bloomington: Indiana University Press, 1998.

Podruchny, Carolyn. "Unfair Masters and Rascally Servants? Labour Relations among Bourgeois, Clerks, and Voyageurs in the Montreal Fur Trade, 1770–1821." In *Labouring Canada: Class, Gender, and Race in Canadian Working-Class History,* edited by Bryan D. Palmer and Joan Sangster, 4–16. Don Mills, ON: Oxford University Press, 2008.

Poulin, Grace. *Invisible Women: WWII Aboriginal Servicewomen in Canada.* Thunder Bay, ON: D.G. Poulin/Ontario Native Women's Association, 2007.

Pratt, Mary Louise. *Imperial Eyes: Travel Writing and Transculturation.* London: Routledge, 1992.

Prentice, Alison, et al, eds. *Canadian Women: A History.* Toronto: Harcourt Brace, 1988.

Raibmon, Paige. *Authentic Indians: Episodes of Encounter from the Late-Nineteenth-Century Northwest Coast.* Durham: Duke University Press, 2005.

Ray, Arthur J. *Indians in the Fur Trade, 1660–1870.* Toronto: University of Toronto Press, 1974.

Razack, Sherene H. "Gendered Racial Violence and Spatialized Justice: The Murder of Pamela George." In *Race, Space and the Law: Unmapping A White Settler Society,* edited by Sherene H. Razack, 121–56. Toronto: Between the Lines, 2002.

Razack, Sherene H., ed., *Race, Space and the Law: Unmapping a White Settler Society.* Toronto: Between the Lines, 2002.

Reifel, Nancy. "American Indian Views of Public Health Nursing, 1930–1950." *American Indian Culture and Research Journal* 23, 3 (1999): 143–54.

Roediger, David. *The Wages of Whiteness: Race and the Making of the American Working Class.* New York: Verso, 1996.

Roome, Patricia A. "'From One Whose Home Is Among the Indians': Henrietta Muir Edwards and Aboriginal Peoples." In *Unsettled Pasts: Reconceiving the West through Women's History,* edited by Sarah Carter, Lesley Erickson, Patricia Roome and Char Smith, 47–78. Calgary: University of Calgary Press, 2005.

Roth, Lorna. *Something New in the Air: The Story of First Peoples Television Broadcasting in Canada.* Montreal: McGill-Queen's University Press, 2005.

Rutherdale, Myra. *Women and the White Man's God: Gender, Race and the Canadian Mission Field.* Vancouver: University of British Columbia Press, 2002.

St. Denis, Verna. "Feminism is for Everybody: Aboriginal Women, Feminism and Diversity." In *Making Space for Indigenous Feminism,* edited by Joyce Green, 33–51. Winnipeg: Fernwood Publishing, 2007.

Sangster, Joan. "Constructing the "Eskimo" Wife: White Women's Travel Writing, Colonialism and the Canadian North, 1940–60." In *Creating PostWar Canada: Community, Diversity and Dissent 1945–1975,* edited by Magda Fahrni and Robert Rutherdale, 23–44. Vancouver: University of British Columbia Press, 2007.

———. *Regulating Girls and Women: Sexuality, Family and the Law in Ontario, 1920–1960.* Toronto: Oxford University Press, 2001.

Scott, Joanne, and Raymond Evans. "The Moulding of Menials: The Making of the Aboriginal Female Domestic Servant in Early Twentieth-Century Queensland." *Hecate* 22:1 (1996): 139–57.

Sealey, D. B., and V.K. Kirkness, eds. *Indians Without Tipis.* Vancouver: William Clare, 1973.

Sealey, D. B., and A.S. Lussier. *The Métis, Canada's Forgotten People.* Winnipeg: Manitoba Métis Federation Press, 1975.

Sharma, Nandita. *Home Economics: Nationalism and the Making of "Migrant Workers" in Canada.* Toronto: University of Toronto Press, 2006.

Sheffe, Norman. *Issues for the Seventies: Canada's Indians.* Toronto: McGraw-Hill, 1970.

Shewell, Hugh. *"Enough to Keep Them Alive": Indian Social Welfare in Canada 1873–1965.* Toronto: University of Toronto Press, 2004.

———. "'What Makes the Indian Tick?' The Influence of Social Sciences on Canada's Indian Policy, 1947–1964." *Histoire Social/Social History* 34, 67 (2001): 133–67.

Shoemaker, Nancy, ed. *Negotiators of Change: Historical Perspectives on Native American Women.* New York: Routledge, 1995.

Silman, Janet (recorder). *Enough is Enough: Aboriginal Women Speak Out.* Toronto: Women's Press, 1987.

Simonsen, Jane E. *Making Home Work: Domesticity and Native American Assimilation in the American West, 1860–1919.* Chapel Hill: University of North Carolina Press, 2006.

———. "'Object Lessons': Domesticity and Display in Native American Assimilation." *American Studies* 43 (Spring 2002): 75–99.

Simpson, Audra. "On Ethnographic Refusal: Indigeneity, 'Voice' and Colonial Citizenship." *Junctures,* December 9, 2007, 67–80.

Smith, Andrea. *Conquest: Sexual Violence and American Indian Genocide.* Cambridge, MA: South End Press, 2005.

———. "Native American Feminism, Sovereignty and Social Change." In *Making Space for Indigenous Feminism,* edited by Joyce Green, 93–107. Halifax: Fernwood Publishing, 2007.

Smith, Bonnie. *The Gender of History: Men, Women, and the Historical Practice.* Cambridge and London: Harvard University Press, 1998

Smith, Donald B. "Aboriginal Ontario: An Overview of 10,000 Years of History." In *Aboriginal Ontario: Historical Perspectives on the First Nations,* edited by Edward S. Rogers and Donald B. Smith, 418–23. Toronto: Dundurn Press, 1994.

Smith, Ken. *Mental Hygiene: Better Living Through Classroom Films 1945–1970.* New York: Blast Books, 1999.

Smith, Linda Tuhiwai. *Decolonizing Methodologies: Research and Indigenous Peoples.* London: Zed Books, 1999.

Stasiulis, Daiva K., and Abigail B. Bakan. *Negotiating Citizenship: Migrant Women in Canada and the Global System.* New York: Palgrave MacMillan, 2003.

Steiman, Pauline. "Caring for Indian Outpatients." *The Canadian Nurse* 74, 9 (October 1978): 40.

Stephen, Jennifer A. *Pick One Intelligent Girl: Employability, Domesticity, and the Gendering of Canada's Welfare State, 1939–1947*. Toronto: University of Toronto Press, 2007.

Stevenson, Winona L. "Prairie Indians and Higher Education: An Historical Overview, 1876 to 1977." In *Hitting the Books: The Politics of Educational Retrenchment*, edited by Terry Wotherspoon, 215–34. Toronto: Garamond Press, 1991.

Stonechild, Blair. *The New Buffalo: The Struggle for Aboriginal Post-Secondary Education in Canada*. Winnipeg: University of Manitoba Press, 2006.

Strange, Carolyn. *Toronto's Girl Problem: The Perils and Pleasures of the City 1880–1930*. Toronto: University of Toronto Press, 1995.

Strong-Boag, Veronica. *The New Day Recalled: Lives of Girls and Women in English Canada, 1919–1939*. Toronto: Copp Clark Pitman Ltd., 1993.

Strong-Boag, Veronica, Mona Gleason, and Adele Perry, eds. *Rethinking Canada: The Promise of Women's History*. 4th ed. Don Mills, ON: Oxford University Press, 2002.

Thomlinson, E., D. Gregory, and J. Larsen. "Northern Bachelor of Nursing Program: Issues in the Implementation of a Curriculum to Meet Community and Nursing Needs." In *Redressing the Imbalance: Health Human Resources in Rural and Northern Communities: Proceedings from a Conference Hosted by the Northern Health Human Resources Research Unit, Thunder Bay, Ontario, October 21–24, 1993*, 489–95. Thunder Bay, ON: Lakehead University Centre for Northern Studies, 1995.

____. "The Northern Bachelor of Nursing Program: One Solution to Problems in Health Care Provision." In *Circumpolar Health 90: Proceedings of the 8th International Congress on Circumpolar Health*, edited by B. Postl et al., 145–48. Winnipeg: University of Manitoba Press, 1991.

Thompson, E.P. *The Making of the English Working Class*. London: Gollancz, 1963.

Titley, Brian. "Indian Industrial Schools in Western Canada." In *Schools in the West—Essays in Canadian Educational History*, edited by Nancy M. Sheehan, J. Donald Wilson and David C. Jones, 133–53. Calgary: Detselig Enterprises Limited, 1986.

Turner, Dale. *This Is Not a Peace Pipe: Towards a Critical Indigenous Philosophy*. Toronto: University of Toronto Press, 2006.

Twohig, Peter L. "Recent Writing on Health Care History in Canada." *Scientia Canadensis* 26 (2002): 7–28.

Van Kirk, Sylvia. *Many Tender Ties: Women in Fur Trade Society 1670–1870*. Winnipeg: Watson and Dwyer, 1980.

____. "From 'Marrying-In' to 'Marrying-Out': Changing Patterns of Aboriginal/Non-Aboriginal Marriage in Colonial Canada." *Frontiers: A Journal of Women Studies* 23, 3 (2002): 1–11.

Verge, Patricia. *Angus: From the Heart: The Life of Counsellor Angus Cowan*. Cochrane, AB: Springtide Publishing, 1999.

Vibert, Elizabeth. *Traders' Tales: Narratives of Cultural Encounters in the Columbia Plateau 1807–1846*. Norman: University of Oklahoma Press, 1997.

Voyageur, Cora. "The Community Owns You: Experiences of Female Chiefs in Canada." In *Out of the Ivory Tower: Feminist Research for Social Change*, edited by Andrea Martinez and Meryn Stuart, 228–47. Toronto: Sumach Press, 2003.

Waldram, James B., D. Ann Herring and T. Kue Young. *Aboriginal Health in Canada: Historical, Cultural, and Epidemiological Perspectives.* Toronto: University of Toronto Press, 1995.

Walker, James W. St. G. "The Indian In Canadian Historical Writing." *Canadian Historical Association Historical Papers* (1971): 21–51.

____. "The Indian in Canadian Historical Writing, 1972–1982." In *As Long as the Sun Shines and Water Flows: A Reader in Canadian Native Studies,* edited by Ian A.L. Getty and Antoine S. Lussier, 340–57. Vancouver: University of British Columbia Press, 1983.

Walkowitz, Judith. *City of Dreadful Delight: Narratives of Sexual Danger in Late-Victorian London.* Chicago: University of Chicago Press, 1992.

Watson, Elwood, and Darcy Martin. *"There She Is, Miss America": The Politics of Sex, Beauty and Race in America's Most Famous Pageant.* New York: Palgrave MacMillan, 2004.

White, Richard. *The Middle Ground: Indians, Empires, and Republics in the Great Lakes Region, 1650–1815.* Cambridge: Cambridge University Press, 1991.

Whitehead, Margaret. "'A Useful Christian Woman': First Nations' Women and Protestant Missionary Work in British Columbia." *Atlantis* 18 (1994): 142–66.

Wickwire, Wendy. "'They Wanted … Me to Help Them': James A. Teit and the Challenge of Ethnography in the Boasian Era." In *With Good Intentions: Euro-Canadian and Aboriginal Relations in Colonial Canada,* edited by Celia Haig-Brown and David A. Nock, 297–320 Vancouver: University of British Columbia Press, 2006.

Willet, Julie A. "'Hands Across the Table': A Short History of the Manicurist in the Twentieth Century." *Journal of Women's History* 17, 3 (2005): 59–80.

____. *Permanent Waves: The Making of the American Beauty Shop.* New York: New York University Press, 2000.

Williams, Carol, ed. *Indigenous Women and Work: From Labour to Activism.* Urbana: University of Illinois Press, 2012.

____. *Framing the West: Race, Gender and the Photographic Frontier in the Pacific Northwest.* Don Mills, ON: Oxford University Press, 2003.

____. "'She Was the Means of Leading into the Light': Photographic Portraits of Tsimshian Methodist Converts." In *In the Days of Our Grandmothers: A Reader in Aboriginal Women's History in Canada,* edited by Mary-Ellen Kelm and Lorna Townsend, 117–45. Toronto: University of Toronto Press, 2006.

____. "Between Doorstep Barter Economy and Industrial Wages: Mobility and Adaptability of Coast Salish Female Labourers in Coastal British Columbia 1858–1890." In *Native Being, Being Native: Identity and Difference, Proceedings of the 5th North American Symposium,* edited by Mark B. Spencer and Lucretia Scoufos. Durant: Southeastern Oklahoma State University, 2005.

Willis, Jane. *Geniesh: An Indian Girlhood.* Toronto: New Press, 1973.

Woodsworth, J.F. "Problems of Indian Education in Canada." In *The North American Indian Today: University of Toronto—Yale University Seminar Conference Toronto, September 4–16, 1939,* edited by C.T. Loram and T.F. McIlwraith, 270–1. Toronto: University of Toronto Press, 1943.

Wotherspoon, Terry, and Vic Satzewich. *First Nations: Race, Class and Gender Relations.* Regina: Canadian Plains Research Center, 2000.

Wright, Donald. "Gender and the Professionalization of History in English Canada before 1960." *Canadian Historical Review* 81, 1 (March 2000): 29–66.

____. *The Professionalization of History in English Canada.* Toronto: University of Toronto Press, 2005.

Index